Real Research

Second Edition

Real Research

Research Methods Sociology Students Can Use

Second Edition

Liahna E. Gordon
California State University, Chico

Los Angeles | London | New Delhi
Singapore | Washington DC | Melbourne

FOR INFORMATION:

SAGE Publications, Inc.
2455 Teller Road
Thousand Oaks, California 91320
E-mail: order@sagepub.com

SAGE Publications Ltd.
1 Oliver's Yard
55 City Road
London EC1Y 1SP
United Kingdom

SAGE Publications India Pvt. Ltd.
B 1/I 1 Mohan Cooperative
Industrial Area
Mathura Road, New Delhi 110 044
India

SAGE Publications Asia-Pacific Pte. Ltd.
18 Cross Street #10-10/11/12
China Square Central
Singapore 048423

Printed in the United States of America

Library of Congress Cataloging-in-Publication Data

Names: Gordon, Liahna E., author.

Title: Real research : research methods sociology students can use / Liahna E. Gordon, California State University, Chico.

Description: Second edition. | Los Angeles : SAGE, [2020] | Includes bibliographical references and index.

Identifiers: LCCN 2018044593 | ISBN 9781544339689 (pbk. : alk. paper)

Subjects: LCSH: Social sciences—Research. | Social sciences—Research—Methodology.

Classification: LCC H62 .G6397 2020 | DDC 301.072—dc23 LC record available at https://lccn.loc.gov/2018044593

This book is printed on acid-free paper.

Acquisitions Editor: Jeff Lasser
Editorial Assistant: Tiara Beatty
Production Editor: Jane Martinez
Copy Editor: Diana Breti
Typesetter: Hurix Digital
Proofreader: Rae-Ann Goodwin
Indexer: Judy Hunt
Cover Designer: Anupama Krishnan
Marketing Manager: Will Walters

19 20 21 22 23 10 9 8 7 6 5 4 3 2 1

• Brief Contents •

• Detailed Contents •

• Acknowledgments •

I am indebted to the former students and total strangers who were willing to let me profile them in this book. I greatly appreciate their generosity. I cannot adequately express my appreciation to my invaluable student assistant, Gina White, for designing graphics and providing feedback on the chapters. I am also grateful to Dean Eddie Vela; my department chair, Nandi Crosby-Jordan; and my sociology colleagues for both institutional and personal support during this process.

Thank you to those at SAGE who worked on the book: Jeff Lasser, Tiara Beatty, Jane Martinez, and Diana Breti.

I am appreciative for having had wonderful teachers at Indiana University, especially Drs. Martin Weinberg and Donna Eder. Twenty years out, I still use things you taught me every single day. And I'm so fortunate to have my students at Chico State, whose deep engagement with all things sociological makes teaching a pleasure. Thank you for continuing to make me a better teacher and a better person.

And last but certainly not least, a very deep and special thanks to my family and dear friends: Dad, Mom, Allan, Diego, Jiajia, Cole, Lindsay, and Nandi, all of whom provide me continuous love, even when I'm on the other side of the world. Thank you for supporting me in following my heart. You all mean the world to me.

SAGE and the author are grateful for the input from the following reviewers:

Tawnya Adkins Covert, *Western Illinois University*

Aya Kimura Ida, *California State University, Sacramento*

Amber Nelson, *Marian University*

Jennifer Strangfeld, *California State University, Stanislaus*

Introduction

What Is Empirical Social Research?

Most research methods textbooks start their discussion of research by describing the scientific method, with its focus on total objectivity, replicability, and highly structured procedures. There is, however, great debate among sociologists as to whether sociology is a science and even whether it is desirable to be so. Critical theorists, conflict theorists, feminist scholars, symbolic interactionists, ethnomethodologists, and postmodernists have all heavily criticized scientific approaches to studying society. Additionally, a good deal of sociological research is not, and does not aim to be, scientific. So if not all sociological research is scientific, then what differentiates it from common sense or mere opinion? There are three important characteristics that set research apart. First, social research is **systematic**; that is, the researcher develops a plan of action before beginning the research. Second, social research involves **data**, which are the pieces of information gathered from primary sources. This is what makes it **empirical**—based not on ideas or theory but on evidence from the real world. Third, social research involves **analysis**, meaning the researcher interprets the data and draws conclusions from them. Thus, writing what is typically called a "research paper" does not fit our definition of empirical research because doing so typically involves summarizing the analyses of other authors, not forming a new analysis based on collected data.

Why Is Research Important?

Sociologists consider research essential work, and most professional sociologists spend at least some of their time conducting it. Because it is empirical, systematic, involves the collection of data, and requires an analysis based on those data, many sociologists view research as the most valid form of knowledge on which to base social policy. Additionally, it can be used to test the accuracy of social theory, to document social trends, to make comparisons over time or across geographical regions, to inform people, to gain new insights about social phenomena, and to support arguments in debate.

But why should you, the sociology student, care about social research? After all, relatively few sociology majors become professional sociologists. In my experience, there are three main reasons why you should care about social research. First, research is powerful. By that I mean that to conduct research is to create new knowledge, and to engage in the production of knowledge is to exercise a form of power. In producing knowledge, you have the opportunity to influence what others know and think as well as the actions they may take. Research can also be a powerful tool for helping others to hear the voices and experiences of those who are often ignored or disregarded, for challenging stereotypes, and for correcting social myths. Until recently, this form of power has been exercised by relatively few people. Knowledge production has been (and continues to be) dominated by an upper-middle-class, mostly male, mostly white Anglo elite. Having a wider diversity of people contributing to the creation of new knowledge helps to democratize this form of power.

Second, research skills are in high demand. Virtually every organization, whether it is in the not-for-profit, business, government, or education sector, needs to evaluate and assess its performance, as well as to determine what unmet needs its clients have and how it can meet those needs. That means it needs people who are skilled in collecting the appropriate data, analyzing them, and presenting them in a way that can be understood by those who are not necessarily well schooled in research methods. In other words, in learning how to conduct social research, you are learning very valuable job skills. Even if you do not want to become a "researcher" per se, having research skills not only increases your value in the job market, it can help you do your job better. Say, for example, you are the assistant director of a homeless shelter. In order to apply for federal funding and private grants to expand the services your shelter provides, you need to document the following:

- The number of people using each of the services your shelter currently provides, and how often they use each service

- The demographic characteristics of your population, such as the number of women and children that you serve, or the number of people with mental illnesses

- The number of people helped by your organization who, after 1 year, have regular lodging and employment

- What services your clients need that are unavailable in your area

- The impact on your clients of the federal budget cuts to family planning centers

All of these data require that research be conducted. If you don't have the skills to do the work, you will have to pay someone else to do it, which will further reduce the amount of money that goes directly toward the services that your clients so desperately need. In short, research skills are not only important for those who want to be sociology professors or researchers, but for anyone wanting a leg up in a highly competitive job market. Obviously, one course cannot make you an expert researcher. Certainly, to truly learn the skills of research you will need to take additional courses, read on your own, and/or learn the ropes through hands-on experience under the guidance of an experienced researcher. Nonetheless, even if you do not continue your studies in research methods, by the end of this course you will have learned the basics of research, which means you will have more knowledge than most people about conducting good research—and this can make you more marketable.

Third, knowing about social research, even if you never conduct any yourself, will make you a better *consumer* of social research. Research is used to do everything from endorse the newest weight-loss product to provide the basis for a political candidate's crime reduction plan. Some of this research is very sound, but there is also a lot of *bad,* even meaningless, research being conducted. By understanding how research should be conducted, and how it should not, you will be empowered to critically examine claims made by researchers and to determine for yourself whether the results are worth relying upon.

Methods of Data Collection

There are several different **research methods**—that is, ways to collect data. Here, I briefly describe each of the methods to give you a quick introduction, as a springboard to a more detailed discussion of these methods in subsequent chapters.

Surveys

Surveys involve asking people predesigned questions and, usually, asking them to choose from among the answer choices that you, the researcher, have provided. Their answers are turned into numeric codes so that statistics can be calculated from them. Surveys are designed to gather very specific yet standardized information from a lot of people and to get the same information from everyone surveyed. They are best used for studying social or demographic trends, cause and effect, attitudes, and simple behaviors.

Interviews

Interviews involve asking people questions that are open ended; that is, you haven't predetermined possible answer choices for them. Instead, they freely express themselves in answering your questions. The answers are not analyzed with statistics; instead, they are analyzed for their meaning and themes. The purpose of interviews is to better understand some aspect of the social world from the perspective of the research participants, to see the world as they see it, and to understand that perspective in great depth. Interviews yield very detailed information about the perspectives of only a small group of people. They are best used for studying what goes on in people's heads: their perceptions, interpretations, meanings, and experiences of the social world, as well as their motivations and feelings.

Focus Groups

Focus group research consists of gathering 5 to 12 people together for usually about two hours and asking them some questions on a particular topic in order to get their thoughts, reactions, feelings, and opinions. They are not just individual interviews done all at once; the unique feature of focus groups is that the group discussion creates a type of synergy among the group members, allowing the conversation to go in new directions and for participants to respond to one another in a way that enables them to think of and say things they wouldn't have thought of on their own. Focus groups are very good for generating new ideas, for finding out reactions to different versions of something (a plan, policy, etc.), for investigating topics on which there is very little information, and for understanding the perspectives of different groups of people in some depth.

Observation

Observation involves watching people to document their behavior. It is used to understand how people interact with one another and to find patterns in their behavior. It is particularly good for understanding behavior that the actors are unaware of or that they won't admit to. For example, observation could be used to document whether salespeople treat black and white customers differently. If we were to ask these salespeople in a survey or interview about their behavior, they may likely answer that they treat everyone the same. Observation is the only way to determine, however, whether their behavior actually matches up to this claim.

Ethnography

Sociologists borrowed the method of **ethnography** from anthropologists. It is a method that involves deeply immersing yourself in a culture or subculture to understand it (or some aspect of it). Ethnographers combine formal and informal interviewing, observation, and sometimes content analysis of documents (see below). Its purpose is to understand some aspect of a culture in great depth. It is good for studying the norms, values, and meanings of a culture or subculture.

Secondary Data Analysis

You conduct **secondary data analysis** when you use data that someone else has gathered, usually (though not always) through a survey, and then compute new statistics from the data, producing a new analysis. There are many sets of secondary data that are collected specifically for this purpose, and they generally have gathered a lot of information from a large, often representative, group of people. Secondary data analysis is popular because it allows you to investigate research interests that would have been too expensive or time-consuming had you needed to collect the data on your own.

Existing Statistics

Existing statistics are also based on the data that someone else has collected. Unlike secondary data analysis, however, in which you get the **raw data** (uncalculated) and compute the statistics yourself, with existing statistics you are working with statistics produced by someone else (rather than the raw data). Existing statistics are less likely to come from surveys and more likely to come from the data collection of government agencies. The Department of Education, for example, does not have to survey people in order to determine how many students are enrolled in California schools; these data are part of the department's bureaucratic record keeping. Sometimes you might use those statistics to produce new statistics. For instance, you might gather existing statistics on high school exit exam scores and school spending to determine how much money a state needs to spend on education in order for most students to reach a particular level of achievement on the exams. Other times, you might conduct a new analysis by bringing together statistics that have not previously been analyzed in relation to one another. For example, you might take the existing statistics on the number of violent offenses and property crimes, county unemployment rates, median home prices, school enrollment rates, and income statistics to investigate the relationship between socioeconomic conditions in an area and its crime rate. In order for the use of existing statistics to be considered research by our definition, however, you must do more than simply report the already existing statistics; you must produce a new analysis, even if you did not gather the data yourself.

Content Analysis

Content analysis involves gathering existing texts, images, songs, or other audiovisual products, such as videos or commercials, to analyze them for themes in their content, style, and form. Content analysis is often used to study pop culture, but it can also be used to study, for example, the values imparted in sex education curricula or the capitalist logic in the speeches of American presidents. Researchers conducting content analysis often strive to reveal both the obvious and the more subtle messages or ideas contained within the text or image.

Experiments

Experiments are what immediately come to mind for many people when they think of research methods. It is the method used in the natural sciences and one that gets a lot of visibility in the media. When you conduct an experiment, you take two or more groups and alter the conditions of all but one of those groups in a controlled way in order to understand the effect that each condition has on the group. The analysis is usually statistical. In sociology, it is typically used to understand behavior. Although popular among sociologists in the first two thirds of the 20th century, it is the least frequently used method in sociology today. Box 1.1 is a summary of the research methods described.

BOX 1.1
SUMMARY OF RESEARCH METHODS AND THEIR PURPOSES

Research Method	Description	Purpose
Surveys	Questions with predesigned answer choices	Gather standardized information from many people
Interviews	Open-ended questions answered with free expression	Understand participants' perspectives in great depth
Focus groups	Open-ended questions asked to small groups of people to stimulate discussion	Compare perspectives of different groups of people in some depth
Observation	Watching others' behavior	Document patterns of behavior and interaction
Ethnography	Deep immersion in a culture using interviewing, observation, and content analysis	Understand aspects of a culture
Content analysis	Analyzing existing texts or audiovisual artifacts	Reveal subtle messages contained within text
Secondary data analysis	Using data gathered by someone else and computing new statistics from them	Gather standardized information from many people; save time and money
Existing statistics	Using statistics calculated by someone else and combining them or computing new statistics from them to yield a new analysis	Use (usually) institutional data to understand social trends
Experiments	Altering conditions of two or more groups in a controlled way	Understand the effects of various conditions

CHECK YOUR UNDERSTANDING

Which research method would you choose to:
- Understand men's experiences of divorce?
- Compare differences in interaction patterns between male diners and female diners at restaurants?
- Gauge voters' reactions to a proposed new immigration law?
- Explain the relationship between the rate of unemployment and teen birth rates?
- Evaluate the effects of increases in student fees on students at your college or university?
- Understand a variety of perspectives on three different proposals for decreasing bullying in schools?

Quantitative and Qualitative Research

Some of the research methods above, like surveys and experiments, produce data that are analyzed using statistics. This research is called **quantitative** research. Other methods, like interviews and ethnography, avoid distilling the results down to numbers. Instead, they try to understand such things as

 Tip: You can easily remember the difference between *quantit*ative and qualitative because statistics are *quanti*ties.

meaning, norms, and lived experience in all their complexity, and their analysis remains word based. This research is called **qualitative** research. These two different types of research yield very different information, which also gets used in different ways. Each has its own logic, process, and aim. Each also has its own strengths and weaknesses. Quantitative research has long been popular because it seems more "scientific." Beginning in the 1960s, when computers began to enable researchers to analyze very large amounts of data quickly (rather than calculating it by hand) and to develop more sophisticated statistical techniques, quantitative research came to dominate the field. Even today, the most prestigious journals in sociology (including *American Sociological Review*, *American Journal of Sociology*, and *Social Psychology Quarterly*) still publish predominantly quantitative research. Many faculty at research universities prefer quantitative research because it can be conducted more quickly, which enables them to publish a larger number of articles (a primary criterion by which their performance and prestige are judged). Many research methods textbooks reflect the dominance of quantitative research methods by focusing on them, limiting their discussion of qualitative research to one or two chapters. Qualitative research has always been an important part of sociology, however, and its popularity has tended to ebb and flow. Currently, qualitative research is again gaining favor, and more qualitative research is being accepted into the most prestigious sociology journals. Additionally, a large number of books have recently been published about gathering and analyzing qualitative data, which not only reflects its rise in popularity but also encourages others to try conducting qualitative research. Sometimes people conduct both qualitative and quantitative work to answer a research question, in order to get both kinds of information; in fact, this is called using **mixed methods**, and is increasingly discussed as an ideal. To do this, however, you need to have both the time and resources to do each very well; otherwise, the information you gain may be less helpful than if you had concentrated on doing only one type alone. Box 1.2 summarizes which methods yield quantitative data and which qualitative data. It is important to learn the differences so that you can better understand the logic and process of each method.

BOX 1.2
QUANTITATIVE AND QUALITATIVE RESEARCH METHODS

Research Method	Quantitative	Qualitative	Notes
Survey	✓		
Secondary data analysis	✓		
Existing statistics	✓		
Experiments	✓		
Observation	✓	✓	*Usually qualitative but can be quantitative*
Content analysis	✓	✓	*Can be either, often combines both*
Interview		✓	
Ethnography		✓	
Focus groups		✓	

Basic and Applied Research

Research can also be classified as either basic or applied. **Basic research** (sometimes called "pure" research) is done to learn something new or to satisfy the researcher's curiosity, but does not have immediate practical uses. This is the type of research that most faculty conduct. The goal is to better understand some phenomenon, and perhaps somewhere down the road that understanding may have some implications for policy; the research itself, however, is not meant to change or propose policy. Unless you become a professor or professional researcher, however, you are more likely to conduct applied than basic research in your future careers. **Applied research** is used for immediate practical purposes, such as to identify unmet needs in a population, to find solutions to a problem, or to evaluate solutions. Usually applied research is not meant to be generalized to a large population but is kept local and specific. For example, if you are doing applied research for your school district, you will not be concerned with determining the effectiveness of tutorial centers generally, only about measuring the effectiveness of those in your specific district. In applied research (as opposed to basic), the goal is not just to understand a phenomenon, but to find and/or evaluate solutions to it. See Box 1.3 for examples of applied and basic research. Note that in each case, the applied research is being conducted as the basis for *making decisions* based on the research findings, as opposed to the basic research, which gives us knowledge but isn't meant to be used for decision-making purposes. Intention is important here—just because a researcher has some hope that someday in some small way their research may have an effect doesn't make it applied research; applied research is conducted *for the purpose of* gathering data to be used in decision making, while basic research may inform

BOX 1.3
EXAMPLES OF BASIC AND APPLIED RESEARCH TOPICS

Basic Research	Applied Research
Reasons for differences in choice of college major among various ethnicities	Evaluation of how time spent at the school's new tutorial center affects students' grades
Dating norms among college students	Ways to increase user satisfaction with your company's dating app
The effects of a college education on health in later life	Differences in test scores when using one teaching method versus another
Mental health issues caused or exacerbated by periods of homelessness	Reasons why some homeless youth in Green County are not using either of the two county assistance programs for which they are eligible
Likelihood of voters voting in favor of a particular ballot proposition	Effect of a proposed ad campaign on voters' opinions towards a particular ballot proposition

those decisions, but that is not their primary goal. Applied and basic research use the same research methods to collect their data, but there are some special considerations and issues that arise; therefore, throughout the chapters I discuss some of the issues you might face in using those research methods in an applied way.

The Components of Research

This book is organized so that each chapter covers one particular research method in its entirety, from the logic behind the method to collecting and analyzing the data. Every method has basic components in common, however. Regardless of the particular method you are using, for example, you will have to select who or what to include in your research (this is called *sampling*). Sometimes research methods books discuss these as stages in the research process. Because the order of the stages varies according to which method is being used, however, I conceive of these not as stages (which presumes a set order) but as components of research. Each research method draws on the same basic components, but how you approach these components (and the reasons behind these approaches) varies for each method. Thus, I will address each of these components *as it specifically pertains to that method*. First, however, I need to introduce you to each of these components so that you can then understand them in the context of each method.

Methodology

Many students, and even some professional sociologists, confuse *method* with *methodology*. A research method, as we have already learned, is a method of data collection, such as a survey, experiment, or interview. A **methodology** is a whole philosophical perspective about how research should be conducted, the reasons it should be conducted, and how it should be used. Methodology is closely tied to theory, with different theoretical perspectives endorsing particular methodologies. Science is typically grounded in the **positivist** methodology, which is based on the principles of logic, objectivity, replicability, and highly structured processes. There are other methodologies, however, that are also commonly used in sociology, such as interpretivist methodology, feminist methodology, and critical methodology (sometimes called critical social science). Researchers are generally oriented toward a particular methodology because they agree with its philosophical views on research. They will tend to gravitate toward particular research topics and research methods based on their preferred methodology. Some methodologies are better at answering particular types of questions, however, and so sometimes researchers will vary the methodology they use, depending upon the particular research they are conducting and its purpose. For example, though my own research tends to be interpretivist, when I am conducting research for a nonprofit organization, I often use positivist methodology because having more scientific data will improve the nonprofit's chances of getting much-needed federal funding. The methodology you choose to use will ultimately affect every aspect of your research, from your research question to the way in which you collect your data and how you analyze them.

Theory

By **theory**, I mean ideas about some aspect of life that have been articulated as a clear set of propositions about the way that this aspect of life works or is structured. Symbolic interactionism, structural functionalism, conflict theory, social constructionism, postmodern theory, and feminist theory are all examples of broad theoretical frameworks that describe how things are, why, and what effect it has. Each examines different aspects of social life, with symbolic interactionism, for example, focusing on interaction and meaning, while conflict theory focuses on struggles for power and resources. Other theories are more narrow in scope and only try to explain a specific phenomenon. Social control theory, differential association theory, labeling theory, structural strain theory, and status frustration theory are all examples of theories that try to explain why people engage in deviant behavior. Both levels of theory—broad theoretical frameworks and phenomena-specific theories—are used in research, though often they are used in different ways.

Research is often used to test phenomena-specific theories to see how well the theories hold up in real life. For example, differential association theory basically argues that people are affected by the people around them, and those who spend time with other people who engage in deviant behavior are more likely to do so themselves. If you wanted to test this theory, you may conduct research that asks people on probation about the deviance engaged in by their friends, family, coworkers, and acquaintances. You might track them over the course of their probation, asking at regular intervals about how they spend their time and with whom, and any types of deviance those people may engage in. At the end of the study, you could test to see whether there is a difference in recidivism for those parolees who spend more time with people who engage in certain types of deviant behavior compared to those who spend less or no time with people who engage in deviant behavior. If you found that, in fact, such differences exist, it would provide support for the theory. Although one study alone can't prove a theory true, multiple studies over time and across different populations can provide evidence that support the theory or that negate it, shedding light on its veracity and its potential limitations. Researchers who use research to test theories are more likely to do so using quantitative methods.

Researchers can also use broader theoretical frameworks as a lens through which to view and interpret data. If you were a symbolic interactionist, for example, you might specifically collect data on the meaning of political identities for people's sense of self. In conducting your analysis and interpreting the results, you may look for ways in which those meanings fluctuate depending on context. Although you are not setting out to test the symbolic interactionist idea that meaning is produced interactionally (and thus is fluid and changeable), you may nonetheless pay attention to any variation in meaning those political identities seem to have when the person is with family, in the workplace, or watching the news. You may want to use ideas in the theory to help you understand how and why these variations occur and what that might mean for a person's sense of self. Researchers who use theory to help interpret data are more likely to be doing so using qualitative methods.

Finally, we can use research to build theory. That is, we can collect data and start to find patterns in it. As we find the patterns and the connections between patterns, we may start to develop ideas about what is going on and why. We may even conduct additional studies to gather more data and see how the patterns are similar or different. The more data we collect, the more they can help us to develop and hone our ideas. These ideas may eventually become a theory. This type of research, in which we build theory out of the data, is almost always qualitative in nature, and the process is called conducting **grounded theory**, because the theory that is being constructed is grounded in the data.

Not all research uses theory. With applied research, for example, we aim to use the data to solve a problem or make a decision. Those problems and decisions are very practical and local, and most of the time applied researchers do not use theory to address those problems. With basic research, however, we are much more likely to use theory in one of the three ways mentioned above. Indeed, many researchers are highly critical of basic research that does *not* use theory in one of these ways. Using theory with basic research tends to make the research richer, more interesting, and more useful, in the opinion of many sociologists. Thus while theory is not *always* a component of research, I have included it here because using theory can help guide and improve your research, while also increasing its appeal and relevance to other sociologists. Theory can also direct you in *what* to research and why it's important.

Research Question

Most researchers begin with a research topic about which they are interested in learning more. You might become intrigued by a topic because of some experience

BOX 1.4
EXAMPLES OF RESEARCH TOPICS

- The effect of divorce on children
- Identity formation in transgender people
- Experiences of workplace discrimination among Chicanas
- Portrayal of male sexuality in popular music
- Attitudes about immigration
- Access to affordable health care
- Friendship among gang members

- Changes in marital satisfaction after the birth of children
- Experiences of the grieving process after losing a loved one
- The use of truths and lies in online dating
- The effects of restorative justice programs on victims
- Educational outcomes for DREAMERS

you have had or someone you know has had. You might want to know more about a topic because you believe it is a politically important one. Perhaps you learned about other research that interested you in the topic, so you are keen on learning more. Perhaps you have seen a movie or read a book that got you hooked. Maybe a current event makes you curious. Many sociologists choose their research topic based on how it might help them test a theory or because a theory has suggested that the topic is an important one to understand. There are many sources for inspiration, and the number of possible topics is infinite. Box 1.4 provides examples of research topics.

Tip: Regardless of which research method you use, you should never ask the people in your study your research question directly. This also means that you should never use the word "you" in a research question.

In order to turn your topic into a research project, you need to develop a research question about the topic. Your **research question** is the overall guiding question to which you are seeking an answer. It is intimately linked to your research method: Each research question can best be answered with a particular research method, and, conversely, each research method can only answer particular types of research questions. It is absolutely imperative that you use the appropriate research method to answer your research question, or your research will have little or no value (see Box 1.1).

The most important rule for writing research questions is that your question must be **answerable**. That is, it must be a question that can be answered with data, not a philosophical question whose answer is unknowable or based on personal values ("Is there a heaven?"; "Is capital punishment immoral?"; "Why do bad things happen to good people?"). Additionally, the question must be **feasible**: You must have adequate resources to conduct the research. The three most important feasibility considerations are time, money, and access. Research can be very time-consuming, and some research questions will require more of your time to answer than others. Research can also vary in how expensive it is: Large-scale surveys are very expensive, while content analysis can be quite cheap. You should write a question that you can afford to research. And finally, some groups of people or information are very hard to access. People without an institutional connection (such as people who don't vote), people who guard their privacy (such as the Amish or celebrities), and people who are difficult to contact (such as those without telephones) are among the many groups that are difficult to access. In writing your research question, you need to be sure that you can gain access to the group that will help you answer your research question.

Your research question should be broad enough to cover all the various aspects of the topic that you want to investigate. A good research question is one that can't be answered with a yes/no response and is not answerable with one or two words. Finding out the answer to the question *Does gender affect voters' candidate choice for president?* is not nearly as interesting as learning in what ways it does or does not have an effect. Hence, better versions of this question include *How does gender affect voters' choice of candidate for president?* and *What is the relationship between gender and candidate choice for president?*

Additionally, research questions should include the unit of analysis in the question. A **unit of analysis** is the "who" or "what" that you are studying. In many cases, some kind of individual will be your unit of analysis. *Students, working mothers, restaurant servers,* and *people using the local homeless shelter* are all examples of individuals as the unit of analysis. With some research methods, your unit of analysis will be some type of group, a culture, or even a type of object rather than individuals. For example, in ethnography, the unit of analysis is often the subculture you immerse yourself in. When using existing statistics, your unit of analysis is likely to be cities, states, or nations. And in content analysis, your unit of analysis is going to be the audio, visual, or textual materials you want to analyze: letters, speeches, tweets, advertisements, or movies, for instance. You don't have to include every criteria required for participation in the study, but your reader should have a pretty good idea of who or what you will be gathering your information about from reading your research question. Additionally, the unit of analysis should always be phrased in the plural because you will never study just one participant.

Writing good research questions takes a lot of practice and patience. A research question should be written so that every word is clear, accurate, and says exactly what you mean. You should never have to include examples, explanations, or parentheses in a research question in order to make the question clear. The question should be concise and grammatically correct (remember that questions end in question marks!). It should represent the sum total of what you want to study: Unless you are conducting a large-scale research project, it's generally better to stay away from multiple research questions or subparts of research questions. Instead, broaden or reword your research question so that one single question covers all that you are researching.

 Tip: Words like "can" and "could" don't belong in research questions because they turn the question into a hypothetical that can't be answered. For example, the research question "How could the problem of racism in the workplace be solved?" is unanswerable because it is asking something that hasn't happened yet and so can't be known. We can research people's opinions on what they think might work to solve this problem, but that's different from being able to find the actual solution to it.

Rarely does even an experienced researcher write a usable research question off the top of their head. You should spend time editing your research question so that it truly reflects what you want to know because your research question will be the guide for everything else you do in your research. Typically, a research question is not finalized until after a review of the literature has been conducted.

Hypothetically, your research question will be guided by the research method that you use. In other words, you would use whatever method is most appropriate for answering your particular research question. In reality, however, many sociologists tend to specialize in or prefer particular research methods, and so their research question is shaped by their method: They only write research questions that they know can be answered using their favorite method.

CHECK YOUR UNDERSTANDING

Practice writing and revising a research question on the topic of homelessness. Make sure it meets these criteria:

- It is answerable and feasible.
- It isn't answerable with a yes/no or one- or two-word answer.
- It covers all aspects of the topic you want to investigate without using subparts or multiple questions.
- It says exactly what you mean and doesn't need explanation.
- It is grammatically correct and ends in a question mark.

Then look at Box 1.1 and decide which would be the best research method to use to answer your research question.

Literature Review

To conduct a **literature review** means to search for and read prior studies that have been conducted on your topic. There are several important reasons for doing this. First, it helps you write your research question. If you conduct a review of the literature and find that 10 other people have already answered your research question very well, there is not much point to spending the time and money to do so again. Instead, you might focus your attention on a different aspect of the topic that hasn't been considered by other researchers or on new questions that arose from their research. Most research articles conclude by suggesting future directions for research, and these suggestions can be very helpful in writing your research question. Alternatively, you might decide to apply the same research question to a different group of people. For example, if you find that a lot of research has been conducted on how much and what type of housework married heterosexual men and women do, you might instead focus on how much and what type of housework each person in a gay or lesbian couple does and how that is negotiated. Then, comparing your research with the studies of heterosexual couples, you will learn more about the relationship between gender roles and the division of household labor in general.

You will also conduct a literature review in order to get background information for your topic and to build off others' research. In reviewing others' work on the same topic, you can learn, for example, what problems developed in their research and what the criticisms have been of that research so that you can try to avoid those traps yourself. You can also learn what issues were most important, which have been ignored or excluded from study, and what you might expect to find in your analysis. You would then use this information to write the best research question possible, as well as to design your research so that it's as good as it can be, given your resources.

Literature review also has another meaning. I've already described it as the process of searching for and reading existing research on the topic, and this is the typical way in which I will use the term in this text. But it's important that you be aware of the second meaning as well: A literature review is also the section of a written research report in which the author describes (and sometimes criticizes) this existing research. It is usually the first section of the report, but it is sometimes preceded by a more general introduction. It's usually quite easy to spot because it is full of citations. To write a literature review, then, means to write about prior research on the topic. This is considered an essential part of any academic publication of research because it not only puts your research in the context of the previous research for the reader, it gives credit to those whose ideas and research have informed your own. (See Appendix A for more details on how to search the literature and write a literature review.)

Ethics

We have already discussed the way in which conducting research is an exercise of power because it involves the creation of new knowledge. But it is powerful in another way as well: When you conduct research on a group of people, they surrender information about themselves to you, and you get to decide how that information will be used. That gives you a sort of power over them. Sometimes the information is quite personal; other times, it could be damaging to their jobs or their reputations. In all cases, you have a responsibility to conduct your research and analysis with the utmost attention to ethics.

There are many, many ethical issues that arise in the course of research, and we will address some of those in the following chapters. But for now I will just present you with the general guidelines and issues.

All research on human beings conducted by researchers at a university or a government organization, and sometimes research conducted through a private organization, must get approval from the institution's **Institutional Review Board (IRB)**, which has been charged with ensuring that researchers respect the rights of their research subjects/participants (and therefore is also sometimes called the **Human Subjects Committee**). Federal law dictates many of these requirements, though there are some differences in how each IRB has interpreted these laws. In all cases, however, if you are at such an organization, before you begin doing research on people, you must submit an application describing the research you will be undertaking, the people who will participate in the study, how these people will be recruited to the study, the information that will be collected from them, the manner in which it will be collected, how it will be used, and the steps you are taking to protect the participants from any potential harm that might be caused by their participation in the study.

The federal laws that the IRBs are charged with enforcing cover several basic principles. First, the participants should be **fully informed** about the research, including any processes that they will undergo, and how the research will be used. Second, not only must they be fully informed, but after having received this information, they must give their **consent** to participate. They also have the right to withdraw their consent (stop participating) at any time. Third, they must be **protected from harm** due to their participation in the study. This means protecting their information so that it cannot be used against them and keeping their identities secret. It also means not causing undue stress or danger, either physical or emotional, during their participation in the research. Note that not all organizations have an IRB; for example, not-for-profit organizations and businesses that only occasionally conduct research usually will not have an IRB. If you are conducting research without the oversight or requirements of an IRB, it is still your responsibility to provide your participants with the same protections and to treat your participants and their information ethically at all times.

Sampling

To **sample** is to decide from whom (or from what) you will get your data and how you will choose those sources. It is called sampling because you are only getting information from a subset, *a sample*, of the whole population about which you are asking your research question. If your research question is about first-time parents of newborns, for example, you will only get information from some (not all) parents of newborns. Remember that your **sampling unit** (or unit of analysis) is the people or thing about which you will collect your data—in this case, the parents. Units of analysis are usually individuals, but they can also be organizations, regions, and countries—and, in the case of content analysis, they can be texts or images such as letters of correspondence, illustrations, or even graffiti in bathroom stalls. In each of these cases, in order to sample you would decide on the criteria each person (or country or organization or piece of graffiti) has to meet in order to have the possibility of being included in your study. Using the previous example, you may decide that you only want to include mothers or fathers (but not stepparents) over the age of 18 who have only one child 6 months of age or younger. Next, you would choose one of many **sampling methods**, which is the method by which you decide (in this case) which parents out of all those who meet those criteria will actually participate in the study. (Be sure to note that a *sampling method* is not the same as a *research method*.) You will also decide on a **sample size**—that is, how many people will ultimately be included. Sampling is of extreme importance because all of your data, and therefore your results, will be affected by which people are included and which are excluded from your study.

CHECK YOUR UNDERSTANDING

For the research question you wrote on homelessness, what is your sampling unit?

Conceptualizing and Operationalizing

When we collect data, we are necessarily investigating abstract concepts. Social class, self-esteem, stigma, immigration, and even race and gender can be defined differently, depending on who is doing the defining and for what purpose. The process of **conceptualizing** means developing a precise definition of the concept you are studying. This is closely linked to **operationalizing**, which means then figuring out how to capture the information that will help you tap into (or measure) that definition. For example, say you wanted to do a study of the amount of sexually explicit material that is shown on television. You would first need to define (conceptualize) the concept "sexually explicit." Will you include kissing? Hand holding? What about the image of two people in bed but just talking? Once you have decided exactly what your definition of "sexually explicit" will include, you need to operationalize it by deciding *how* you will measure the *amount* of sexually explicit material. Perhaps you will count the number of different times particular words are said or particular behaviors shown or discussed. But you might also want to include how long each discussion or behavior lasts. Operationalizing is often discussed as a purely quantitative phenomenon; however, qualitative researchers also conceptualize and operationalize, although they do so quite differently than do quantitative researchers. In both cases, however, you clarify the important concepts you are studying and turn them from abstractions to concrete definitions that are captured in some way.

Tip: Operationalizing is sometimes called measurement, especially in quantitative research.

Preparing for Data Collection

In defining the term *research*, I said that research is planned and systematic. The preparation for data collection involves designing the research plan and taking the necessary steps to be ready and able to collect your data in a systematic way. This usually involves deciding on the procedures you will take, pretesting to make sure those procedures will work the way you want them to, and making the necessary logistical arrangements to carry out your research.

Data Collection

These are the steps and procedures to gathering the information you want from your sample, following your research plan. If you are doing a survey, for example, it is the delivery of the survey to the participants, the instructions you give them, the administration of the survey, and the follow-up you do with them. It also includes solving problems that arise during data collection.

Data Analysis

Data analysis is your interpretation of the information you get from your sample. The analytic procedures that you use will depend on your research question and the research method you have chosen. In all cases, however, you are looking for a variety of patterns in the data. Analysis means not only identifying these patterns, but also interpreting what they mean and their implications. As already mentioned, *quantitative* data analysis means computing statistics and then determining what those statistics mean and whether they are significant. This text will not teach you how to do actual statistical analyses, which are typically taught in a separate course. I will briefly discuss, however, some of the easiest types of statistical analysis, as it is hard to understand how best to design a research project if you don't know how you are going to analyze it. *Qualitative* data analysis generally involves looking for patterns in *what* information was provided and/or *how* that information was conveyed. Qualitative analysts look for the obvious patterns and more subtle patterns as well.

Steps for both quantitative and qualitative data analysis also include the steps you take to prepare the data for analysis. For example, if you record an interview, everything that is said on the recording is usually typed into a transcript, so that the researcher can analyze exactly what the participant has said.

Evaluating the Quality of Data and Analysis

Because research methods are grounded in different methodologies, involve different procedures, and provide different kinds of information, we must use different criteria for evaluating the quality of the research. It would make no sense to judge a fictional novel and a travel guide by the same criteria, as they are intended for entirely different purposes. The same is true with qualitative and quantitative research broadly and with each research method in particular. Each is good for providing particular types of information in particular ways, and no method can do everything. Thus, any single research project needs to be evaluated in that context and not criticized for failing to produce something the method itself is not designed to produce. That said, all research should be held to high standards appropriate to the method used.

Conducting research with useful and meaningful results requires planning and extreme attention to detail. Sure, it may be quicker just to slap a research project together, but if the quality is poor, the information you glean from it will be of little use and you will have wasted not only your time but also valuable resources. You will take many steps to ensure the quality of your data. No data are perfect, however, because perfect data aren't feasible; you will have to make many choices that balance the resources you have available with the level of quality that you are willing to accept.

Presenting the Results

People generally don't go through all the work of conducting research only to do nothing with it. Researchers usually present their work to an audience in some

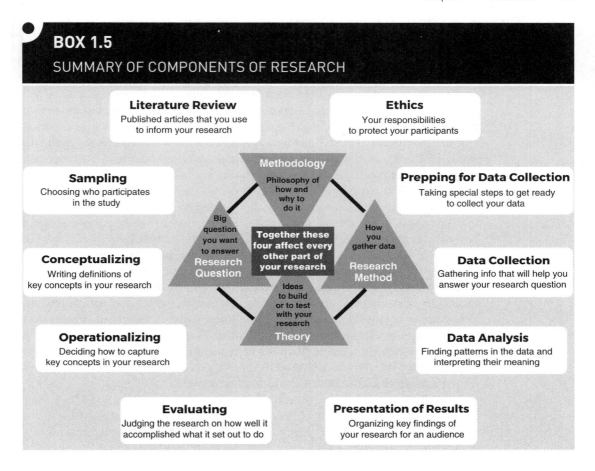

BOX 1.5
SUMMARY OF COMPONENTS OF RESEARCH

Literature Review
Published articles that you use
to inform your research

Ethics
Your responsibilities
to protect your participants

Sampling
Choosing who participates
in the study

Prepping for Data Collection
Taking special steps to get ready
to collect your data

Conceptualizing
Writing definitions of
key concepts in your research

Data Collection
Gathering info that will help you
answer your research question

Operationalizing
Deciding how to capture
key concepts in your research

Data Analysis
Finding patterns in the data and
interpreting their meaning

Evaluating
Judging the research on how well it
accomplished what it set out to do

Presentation of Results
Organizing key findings of
your research for an audience

Methodology
Philosophy of how and why to do it

Big question you want to answer
Research Question

Together these four affect every other part of your research

How you gather data
Research Method

Ideas to build or to test with your research
Theory

form. Sociology professors and some other social researchers present their research orally at conferences, in articles written for scholarly journals, or in the form of books. If you are conducting research for that homeless shelter you manage, you will present the research in written form to the organizations providing the funding for the shelter and possibly to the public in oral or visual form. If you are conducting research for your employer, you will present the research in oral, written, or visual form to your boss or a committee. Research results can be used to add knowledge, to assess and evaluate, to decide social policy, and to gain funding. None of that can happen, however, if you don't share what you have learned in your research.

Box 1.5 presents a summary of the components of research. Notice that the four components in the center (theory, methodology, research method, and research question) affect one another, but taken together, they also set the stage for the rest of your research project. They will affect every other component of the research, including how you carry out those tasks. These components thus start each of the following chapters. Make sure you pay attention to them because if you understand these foundations well, the rest will make logical sense and follow more easily.

Reading This Text

Learning about conducting research can be a difficult process. For many students, it's like learning an entirely new language; after all, you've already learned 41 new terms! My experience is that one of the ways that learning research methods can be less daunting for students is by teaching them to read and study for this class differently than they do their topical classes, like Sociology of Gender or Introduction to Sociology. In order to learn research methods, you need to both learn the new vocabulary words, of which there will be plenty more, and also understand how they fit together. Additionally, conducting research means making lots of decisions. There rarely is one right answer, and research is always a trade-off between feasibility and quality. You will be presented in this text with many of those decisions, along with the options for fulfilling them. In some cases, I have provided decision paths to help you determine how to make these decisions. Your job is to understand how each decision you make will impact your research, as well as how it will affect the other decisions you will subsequently have to make. Making flash cards, therefore, is not generally the most efficient way to study for this class because they tend to help you learn individual vocabulary words but do very little to help you understand the concepts in relation to one another. Instead, I recommend you either outline or diagram the chapters (depending on whether you are a verbal or visual learner) so that you have a holistic view of the research process. Additionally, after reading about each new concept introduced, you should stop and ask yourself, How would I use this in my research? Why? Is it optional or required? How will it impact my study?

I also can't impress upon you enough the importance of doing the Check Your Understanding exercises, even if they aren't assigned to you for class. If you want to save time studying, doing these exercises is one of the keys—it may take a few minutes to do each, but in the long run, it will cut down on study time because you will remember the information better. Reading is a somewhat passive task, and thus you will quickly forget much of the information you read. But the Check Your Understanding exercises require you to immediately apply what you have just read. In fact, I have placed them throughout the reading instead of at the end of each chapter because using the information *immediately* after reading it is the most efficient way for your brain to process the information and store it. Practicing what you have just read converts the information from being passively (and temporarily) stored in your memory to being used, an active task that creates new neural pathways that change the way that your brain stores the information, making it easier to recall and for longer periods of time. Additionally, it is a perfect way for you to identify where you are getting confused. I have tried to write this text in a clear, straightforward, somewhat casual manner so that it is easy to understand. Thus students often read a chapter and think, "Yep, I understood all that!" But understanding what someone is saying about doing something is different than actually *doing* the task yourself, and by doing, you will be able to pinpoint where exactly things become less clear for you, providing you an opportunity to ask questions and get clarity. And, perhaps not surprisingly, asking questions is also an active task that helps you to store and retain the information. All in all, it is worth the effort. I strongly recommend you give it a try.

Summary Points

In addition to all the new vocabulary you learned in this chapter, remember the following points as we begin a more in-depth look at each of the research methods:

- Research is different from common sense or opinion, but it is not necessarily "scientific."

- Each research method has a different purpose, and your research question must be matched with the appropriate research method.

- Quantitative and qualitative research differ in their approaches to collecting and analyzing the data. They yield very different information and for different purposes. Be sure you are clear on which research methods are quantitative and which are qualitative. Each can only be judged by its own standards.

- Research questions are essential to producing good research. Take your time with them, word them carefully, and make sure they can be answered with the research method you choose.

- Maintaining strong ethical standards in your research should be among your highest priorities in conducting research. Not to do so is not only unethical; it can also lead to sanctions from the university or the federal government.

- To best learn the information in these chapters, outline or diagram them. When reading the following chapters, make sure you understand the choices you will have to make in conducting your research, what your options are, and how each option will affect your study.

Key Terms

analysis 1	focus group 4	qualitative 7
answerable 12	fully informed 16	quantitative 7
applied research 8	grounded theory 11	raw data 5
basic research 8	Human Subjects Committee 15	research methods 3
conceptualizing 17	Institutional Review Board	research question 12
consent 16	(IRB) 15	sample 16
content analysis 5	interviews 3	sample size 16
data 1	literature review 14	sampling methods 16
data analysis 18	methodology 9	sampling unit 16
empirical 1	mixed methods 7	secondary data analysis 4
ethnography 4	observation 4	surveys 3
existing statistics 5	operationalizing 17	systematic 1
experiments 5	positivist 10	theory 10
feasible 12	protected from harm 16	unit of analysis 13

Interviewing

Interviews are a form of *qualitative* research in which you ask questions with the goal of eliciting as much rich, detailed information as possible from your participants. It is important to note that sometimes people refer to conducting face-to-face surveys as "interviewing" because it's done in person. This is a misnomer, however, as it bears little resemblance to interviewing. Face-to-face survey "interviewing" is really nothing more than reading a survey aloud to participants and recording their answers for them. **Interviewing** (sometimes called *qualitative interviewing* for clarity), however, involves asking questions about complex topics that cannot be reduced to a predetermined set of multiple-choice answers. Interviewing is aimed at eliciting lengthy responses and explanations that include extensive detail. Additionally, in interviews, the vast majority of the talking is done by the *participant*, not the researcher, because it is impossible to get into someone else's head and understand what they are thinking if you are doing most of the talking! The opposite is true of face-to-face surveys, in which the interviewer does most of the talking. By the term *interviews*, then, I always mean qualitative interviews.

Qualitative research in general is somewhat less likely to be used in applied ways than is quantitative research, but it can be a helpful tool. When interviewing is used for applied research, it is most typically used for **evaluation research**, whose purpose is to evaluate a program or policy. Interviewing is particularly appropriate when the program or policy being evaluated has clearly failed to have the desired effects, or when there has suddenly been a drastic or unexpected change in the program's outcomes and you want to gain a deep and thorough understanding of why this is so. Interviewing is also used to conduct **needs assessments**—investigations of what services or programs a particular client base most needs. By conducting interviews about clients' experiences, you can find out which needs are not being met for your clients and what remedies might best improve their situations. For example, if the students on academic probation whom you are interviewing talk more about battling depression and anxiety than about difficulty learning the material, then perhaps it's more important for the university to expand its

Laura Gale

Laura works as a service facilitator for a county in Wisconsin to provide youth who have diagnosed mental illness with voluntary community and mental health services. Her first interview usually takes place with the youth and their family in their home. She works hard in this interview to build rapport with the new clients so that they will honestly discuss the challenges they face and will trust her in the delivery of services. Her focus in the first interview is on understanding the family's needs and the issues that are causing them to seek support at this time, and on figuring out whether there are any urgent issues needing referral to a crisis agency. She also tries to gain an understanding of the family's strengths and challenges to best figure out how to help them confront the issues they are facing. Laura uses the information from the first interview to ask more targeted questions in a second interview. These questions are designed to elicit from the youth (of whatever age) in their own words the behaviors they want to change. During the interview, Laura works with the youth to turn these desired changes into goals, and together they determine how they will know when the youth has achieved their goals. From there, Laura and her team focus on interventions and providing a wrap-around team to support the youth and their family in achieving their goals.

Feven Seyoum

Feven Seyoum graduated with a BA in sociology and soon thereafter began working as a case manager for an international care program in the state of Washington. She works with children, mainly between the ages of 7 and 12, who have been detained by border patrol when crossing into the country alone without documentation. When the children are transferred to her program (within 72 hours after detainment), Feven conducts semi-structured interviews with them (usually in Spanish) about their voyage, the conditions in their home country, and their family in the United States. Of particular importance is creating good rapport with the children, who may have had a terrifying journey and are often afraid to get family members in trouble with Immigration. She takes notes during the interviews and enters them into a computer system that stores them as part of the case notes. Once family members are located, she also interviews them about their ability to care for the child.

counseling services or outreach, rather than its tutoring program. Interviewing is also sometimes used in conjunction with survey research: the interviews are used to help understand the complexities behind the most important, unexpected, or disquieting findings from the quantitative analysis. Additionally, interview research is sometimes used to put a "face" to survey findings, so that the audience is reminded that the statistics are not just abstract numbers but are based on real people.

There are two predominant types of interviews: semi-structured and loosely structured. In **semi-structured interviews**, you develop a list of questions in advance that you will ask of all the participants. You may not word the question exactly the same way for each participant, but the questions will basically be the same for all the interviews, although not necessarily in the same order. You will augment these questions during the interview with many other spontaneous follow-up questions that elicit more information about the participant's responses (see Box 2.1). New interviewers often choose this form of interviewing because they feel more comfortable having predetermined questions in front of them. It is also the form of interviewing that researchers who primarily engage in or were trained in quantitative research prefer because it allows them to collect generally the same information from all the participants, making it more standardized and therefore—to the quantitative mind—more useful.

Although semi-structured interviewing is a legitimate form of qualitative research, experienced interviewers with a background in qualitative research are more likely to prefer **loosely structured interviews**. In a loosely structured interview, you do not develop a list of interview questions in advance. Rather, you begin the interview by introducing the general topic and asking a starting question. Most all of your other questions will then develop directly from what the participant says (see Box 2.2). It often sounds frightening to the novice researcher to go into an interview without a list of questions on which to rely. Yet remember, it's what you do in regular conversation all the time: You listen, and then you ask a question based on what the other person has told you. Thus, it feels much more "natural" than a semi-structured interview. Unlike natural conversations, however, in loosely structured interviews you usually have a list of general topics that you want to cover in the interview; therefore, you will occasionally introduce new topics from the list into the conversation. At the end of the interview, you may also consult your list to make sure that all the topics were covered in some way, whether the participant spontaneously discussed the topic or you introduced it. If so, you simply end the interview; if not, you may introduce the remaining topics. Many qualitative researchers prefer this form of interviewing because it is based more on what is important to the participant than what the researcher guesses is important, and this can help the researcher better see the world through the participant's eyes. Because that is the goal of this research method, many qualitative researchers view loosely structured interviews as more effective.

For applied research, the loosely structured interview is more beneficial than the semi-structured interview because it best helps you reach the goals of deeply understanding the participants' perspectives. If students are failing despite the new tutoring and mentoring that your afterschool program has put into place, and you want to understand why, you will more completely understand if you let the participants lead you to what is important. Their failing grades may have little or nothing to do with what goes on in the classroom or in the afterschool program and, instead, may be related to domestic violence, cultural norms and expectations, lack of proper nutrition, or something else you never even considered. But if you assumed that the failing grades were necessarily a by-product of something going on in the classroom, and you conducted a semi-structured interview focused on this premise, you would entirely

BOX 2.1
QUESTIONS IN A SEMI-STRUCTURED INTERVIEW

What follows is an excerpt from a student's interview with a professional working in the juvenile justice system. I have omitted the participant's responses, but notice that the questions here tend not to depend upon the participant's answers. In other words, the questions are generally determined in advance, though they may not be worded in the same way or in the same order for each participant, and some follow-up questions are necessary.

Interviewer: Over your career working with juveniles, what have been some of the biggest challenges, specifically working within the system?	Predetermined question
Interviewer: Yeah, definitely. And then what were some of the challenges you faced working with the juveniles' parents? I don't know how much you do of that.	Predetermined question
Interviewer: What different types of emotions have you experienced with your job?	Predetermined question
Interviewer: Did you ever find yourself getting callous and numb to what you saw?	Predetermined question
Interviewer: What aspects of the system do you think are failing to reduce recidivism?	Predetermined question
Interviewer: Do you have any specific cases that stuck with you where it was really like, "I guess all the odds were against the kid, and they just failed horribly"?	Predetermined question
Interviewer: Do you have any other vivid examples?	Follow-up question
Interviewer: I know you already mentioned some of the successes with the system. Do you have any others?	Follow-up question
Interviewer: Focusing now on substance abuse, do you think we are succeeding in treating substance abuse?	Predetermined question
Interviewer: Can you tell me about the problems that you encounter with some adolescent substance abuse?	Predetermined question
Interviewer: How do you personally establish a bond with the kids in your caseload?	Predetermined question
Interviewer: The issue of gangs hasn't really come up yet, but I'd be interested to hear a little bit more about your experiences with it.	Predetermined question put in context
Interviewer: What differences do you see between the kids that are associated with gangs and the kids that aren't? Like . . . do you think there are differences between the two?	Predetermined question
Interviewer: So what are your feelings on trying to sentence juveniles as adults?	Predetermined question

BOX 2.2
QUESTIONS IN A LOOSELY STRUCTURED INTERVIEW

What follows is an excerpt from a student's interview with a middle-aged Chicana woman about the cultural messages she received about sexuality. I have omitted the participant's responses. Contrasting these questions with those of the semi-structured interview in Box 2.1, without even knowing what the participant has said, we can see that the vast majority of the interviewer's questions were not predetermined but stem directly from the participant's responses.

Interviewer: Can you describe to me the earliest memory you have where your family began to openly discuss the topic of sex with you?	Predetermined question
Interviewer: So while they gave you specific books to look at, they didn't really engage you in a conversation or try [participant interrupts] . . .	Question from listening
Interviewer: Okay, so it may have happened?	Clarifying question
Interviewer: You mentioned that you're the youngest of four. Do you think that being the youngest, they did things differently to kind of let you know what was OK and not OK for a girl to do in terms of her sexuality?	Predetermined question put in context
Interviewer: How did that make you feel?	Question from listening
Interviewer: Well, yeah, that's what I was going to say. It sounded like a celebration of becoming a woman and it sounds like you felt very special, that it meant a lot for you.	Affirmation of what participant said
Interviewer: And the way that your mother handled it, you know the celebration and making it very, very comfortable for you, do you think that sort of reflected what other families were doing? Or do you think she was a little different?	Question from listening
Interviewer: OK, and how much do you think that's been an influence on how you feel about sex today?	Question from listening
Interviewer: Can you describe what you're feeling? Because it sounds pretty intense when the conversation comes up.	Question from listening
Interviewer: And how strongly do you think that reflects the way you were brought up, in that they didn't openly discuss it with you?	Question from listening

miss the important information you were seeking. Because in applied research decisions are made based on the data you gather, it is of utmost importance that the data truly reflect the totality of the participants' perspectives and experiences, not just your presuppositions about what is important.

Methodology

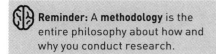

Reminder: A **methodology** is the entire philosophy about how and why you conduct research.

Qualitative interviewing is most commonly grounded in **interpretivist methodology**. The interpretivists aim, first and foremost, to understand, as deeply and fully as possible, the world through someone else's eyes—to know what it feels like to walk in their shoes, and to see and understand the world as they do. You can begin to accomplish this goal by allowing your participants to try to explain to you in as much depth and detail as possible what they have experienced and how they have thought and felt about it. It is nearly impossible, however, to do so through the use of the "scientific method," which is cold, detached, and highly structured. If you want your participants to open up and share their innermost thoughts and feelings with you, you have to create a warm and genuine relationship with them, one based on trust. They have to feel that you will not judge them for what they reveal and that you will try hard to understand things from their perspective, even if you do not share their experiences. Everything about interviewing research, from finding participants to analyzing the data, is grounded in this logic and these fundamental goals. To this end, interviewers usually approach the interview as a collaborative effort. The researcher and the participant work together to produce the information: the researcher by asking the relevant and important questions and the participant by providing honest responses to them. This teamwork approach to research leads interpretivists to usually refer to the people who take part in their research as **research participants** rather than as "respondents" or "subjects," neither of which connote the trust, genuineness, or collaborative aspects of the interview relationship.

You may have heard that research should always be objective or unbiased. Interpretivists have a different perspective on this. They maintain that *all* research is biased in some way: Even the topics that the most scientific of researchers deem worthy of investigating come out of a sort of bias. In this context, **bias** is any characteristic, experience, knowledge, or attitude that might affect the research you do. For interpretivists, trying to eliminate all bias from their research is a waste of time because bias is impossible to avoid. Instead, interpretivists believe that you should be up front about your biases and disclose them in your report. For example, if you are a white female researcher investigating the unique issues that face Asian American women as they pursue college degrees, you might reveal this information in your research report because being white and female will have affected how you interpret the data they have provided you. Bias, according to interpretivists, is unavoidable. Objectivity, on the other hand, means something entirely different. To an interpretivist, to be **objective** is to put your own views and experiences aside and to accurately report the views and experiences of the people you are studying, even if you don't like their views. It is to be open to anything the participant shares and to remain nonjudgmental about it.

When interpretivist methodology is used, it will, like all methodologies, affect every aspect of the research process. Because among the central aims of interpretivists is understanding the world as others experience it, they ask research questions that seek this sort of understanding. They choose samples in a way that will help them understand very well the experiences of a few people in certain contexts but that don't aim to generalize that understanding to other people. They don't worry about bias in sampling or data collection but always try to remain objective (by their definition). They focus all their efforts in data collection in getting as much in-depth, rich data as they can, rather than on getting the same information from every respondent. Additionally, even if two interpretivist researchers analyze the same data, they will come up with different analyses because each will focus on different aspects of the data; in other words, analysis is not cut and dried but allows many interpretations to be made (although each of those will be strongly supported by the data). Finally, interpretivists will judge the quality of research on its depth, honesty, and the richness of the data rather than on how scientifically the research was conducted. In short, every aspect of the research project will be affected by the methodology used because the philosophy you use (methodology) about how to do your research will affect everything about how you actually do it.

Theory

Interpretivist methodology originally came out of symbolic interactionism, and hence much interview research has been grounded in symbolic interactionist theory. Today, researchers working from many theoretical perspectives, including social constructionism, feminist theory, conflict theory, critical theory, and discourse analysis (which comes from the work of Foucault), use interviews in their work. Rarely are these researchers trying to test their theories because interpretivist methodology is not based on testing hypotheses but on understanding different perspectives and worldviews. Hence, researchers often use a given theory to guide them in choosing their research question, designing their research, collecting their data, and interpreting it. For example, if the topic were online dating, a symbolic interactionist might focus on how people lie, exaggerate, omit, and minimize to create a specific self-presentation for potential matches; a feminist theorist might look at the ways in which women overtly and subtly pressure potential male matches to produce specific forms of masculinity; a conflict theorist might investigate competition in the erotic marketplace; and critical theorists may look at the ways in which dating app users use hookups, dating, and romance to fill the nagging void in themselves created by the alienation inherent in the capitalist system. Each of these researchers will also use the chosen theory as a lens through which to view the data and interpret the results. A symbolic interactionist, for example, might be particularly tuned into presentations of self and how meaning gets negotiated in interaction. A feminist theorist, on the other hand, may pay more attention to the use of gendered language, to subtle issues of power, and to how gender is performed by the respondents both in their lives and in the interview context itself.

Other researchers may start without the guiding lens of a theoretical perspective but have the goal of building theory from their data. If a researcher is looking to increase our understanding of intersecting identities, for example, they may interview people about different experiences in their lives and attempt to understand how the intersections of their identities came into play during these experiences. Based on the data that is elicited during the interviews, the researcher may try to expand our theoretical understanding of intersectionality by looking for patterns in the ways in which intersecting identities are experienced, managed, hidden, and/or used in interaction. Loosely structured interview research lends itself particularly well to building theory because it allows participants maximum freedom to talk about what's most important in their own experiences, thus enabling the researcher to identify patterns during analysis that accurately represent the participants' experiences, rather than the researcher's ideas about those experiences. Additionally, the various procedures and steps taken in the analysis of interview research is well-suited to building theory.

Research Questions

Interviewing is the best method for understanding meaning, lived experience, and complex emotions and perspectives. It is also particularly good for developing detailed descriptions and for understanding decision-making processes. It almost always has individuals as the unit of analysis, and this should be reflected in your research question. Examples of research questions that are appropriately answered through the use of interviews are provided in Box 2.3.

Tip: Notice that research questions for interviews very often start with the phrases *In what ways* and *How do*. Be careful about starting with the word *What*, as those questions are more likely to be answerable with just a few words.

Interviews are *not* appropriate for studying demographic or social trends, attitudes, opinions about issues, or concepts that are best measured with numbers or amounts, such as likelihood of voting a particular way, level of self-esteem, or frequency of sexual intercourse.

It is important to note that it is also very difficult to study cause and effect using interviews because the participant's *perceptions* of the cause (or effect) of a particular behavior may not *actually be* the real cause (or effect). For example, we are likely to attribute our success or failure in school to the amount of studying we do, to our personal motivation, or to our level of skill or intelligence. Statistical tests, however, have long revealed that our race and social class are perhaps more important determinants in our success or failure than are any of these other factors (Bowles & Gintis, 1976, 2002; Bowles, Gintis, & Osborne, 2002; Jencks & Phillips, 1998). Thus, we don't always accurately assess cause and effect, even in our own lives. Nonetheless, sometimes as researchers we want to understand how people *interpret* the causes of their own behavior or that of other people because it helps us understand their subsequent decisions. For example, your friend may have left her boyfriend because he is an alcoholic, but if *he* thinks

BOX 2.3
RESEARCH QUESTIONS APPROPRIATE FOR QUALITATIVE INTERVIEWS

Research Question	Appropriate for Interviews Because It Examines ...
How do college students decide whether to experiment with drugs?	decision-making processes
How do people cope with suicidal thoughts?	lived experience
How do young feminists understand gender roles in their romantic heterosexual relationships?	meaning
How do middle school teachers describe the changes in their classroom experiences since the passage of the No Child Left Behind Act?	detailed description
What do recovering alcoholics perceive as the causes of their addiction?	perceived causes
In what ways do siblings of people with cancer perceive family dynamics to have changed after the cancer diagnosis?	perceptions, complex emotions
How do patients at the Central State Free Health Clinic perceive barriers they face to being healthy?	perceptions
How do butch lesbians come to conceptualize their identities?	process
In what ways do students perceive their learning experiences in college to have changed after participating in Northern State University's *A's for Everyone* tutoring program?	perceptions, perceived effects, evaluation research
How do male college students perceive power to manifest within their sexual relationships?	complex issues
How do mothers on welfare explain their own need for assistance as compared to that of other mothers on welfare?	perceived causes

it's because she didn't love him enough, he is unlikely to seek help for his drinking problem. His assessment of the cause of the breakup may be inaccurate; however, his perception of it still has real consequences. Research questions investigating participants' perceptions of cause and effect must be carefully worded to clarify that the research investigates the participants' *perceptions* or *understandings* of causes or effects, *not the actual* causes or effects.

Finally, interview research is not appropriate for comparing groups of people. Comparisons are actually cause-and-effect type questions—if you are comparing men's experiences to women's experiences of a particular phenomenon, for example, what you are really trying to do is look at the causal effect of gender, and interview research is not an appropriate method for studying causal relationships. Additionally, the sample sizes are too small in interview research and the types of phenomena

Reminder: The **unit of analysis** is the "who" or "what" you're collecting data about. Units of analysis should always be stated in the plural in research questions because you will never study just one person for interview research.

too complex to be able to isolate specific differences or to attribute their causes. Instead, in interview research we look for the *commonalities* in experiences among participants, even if those participants seem very different from one another. This enables us to look for patterns in the commonly experienced aspects of a phenomenon, which enriches our understanding of its complexity.

I have included examples of common mistakes in writing research questions for interviews in Box 2.4. Use them to double-check the questions you write.

BOX 2.4
AVOID THESE COMMON ERRORS IN WRITING RESEARCH QUESTIONS FOR INTERVIEW RESEARCH

Research Question	Explanation of Error
How do managers view their employees' productivity?	Productivity is measured quantitatively, so it isn't appropriate for interview research.
What do college freshmen men think about college women who've had abortions?	This is a question about attitudes or opinions about someone else, which is not appropriate for interview research. Research questions should focus on the participant's *own* experiences.
How do high school teens describe how fellow classmates are bullied?	This asks people to describe other people's experiences. Interviewing is meant to allow people to explain their *own* experiences, not experiences of others.
How do college seniors describe their living arrangements?	Participants will not be able to talk for at least one hour about this topic. Research questions appropriate for interviewing should be investigating something with enough depth that a participant can talk for at least one hour about it.
How have students' study habits changed after receiving free tutoring help?	This is a cause and effect question, which cannot be answered through interviewing. We could only ask about their *perceptions* of the changes.
What do companies notice about employee workplace morale?	In interviewing research, the unit of analysis is the individual. "Companies" needs to be changed to an individual as the unit of analysis, such as employees or managers.
What strategies are used to get back together with an ex?	The unit of analysis is missing: Who is using these strategies?
How does a person living abroad for the first time explain their process of adapting to the new culture?	The question is written in the singular ("a person"). You will never interview only one person in a research project, so research questions should always be written in the plural.

CHECK YOUR UNDERSTANDING

Write two research questions about poverty that are appropriate for interviewing research. One of your questions should be appropriate for basic research and one for applied research. Make sure both follow these criteria:

- They are answerable and feasible.
- They aren't answerable with a yes/no answer or just a few words.
- They cover all aspects of the topic you want to investigate without using sub-parts or multiple questions.
- They say exactly what you mean and don't need explanation.
- They are grammatically correct and end in a question mark.

Now write an explanation of why each of these research questions is appropriate for interviewing.

Literature Review

The process of reviewing the literature for interviews is done in the same way, and for all the same reasons, as when using other research methods. Even though you are conducting qualitative research, in your review it is important to include both qualitative and quantitative research. You should use this research to help you develop and refine your research question. If you will be using a loosely structured format, you will also use the literature to help you generate a list of possible topics to be covered in the interviews. If you will be using a semi-structured format, you will use the literature to help you develop your list of interview questions. These can be inspired by the findings of other researchers, by questions asked by other qualitative researchers (you may borrow good questions that they used during the interview, for example), and by your critiques of the existing research. You may also find research that has produced results the researchers were unable to explain because the method they were using was not able to do so. For example, let's say you are interested in how doctors make decisions about how to treat patients based on nonmedical information, such as appearance, apparent intelligence, social class, race, gender, and so on. In your review of the literature, there is a study that finds that doctors are less likely to prescribe pain-relieving narcotics to black patients than to white patients (Associated Press, 2008). The authors imply that this is so because of stereotypes that black patients are more likely to be drug users. This, however, is just a guess because the researchers used existing statistics (the hospitals' records) as their method. This enabled them to see racial differences that doctors may have been unlikely to admit to, or even realize, but it doesn't help them know what the doctors were actually thinking when they made the prescription decisions. After reading the article, you might decide to ask the doctors in your sample what factors they take into consideration when prescribing pain medication; specific negative experiences they have had with unknowingly prescribing pain medication when it would have been better not to; how they think race might affect their own prescription decisions; and whether they think the racial disparity occurs at their hospital, and why. In addition to helping you generate topics and interview questions, the literature review should be used to help you generate a list of codes that you will use in your analysis (see the Data Analysis section later in this chapter).

Ethics

The steps that interview researchers must take to protect their participants are quite extensive. First and foremost, you must get full written informed consent from the participant. To do this, you provide the participant with an **informed consent statement** that details the research process and all of the steps taken to protect the participant's identity. This statement is fairly formulaic, with standardized phrases and structure; it is definitely not a place to exercise your creativity. Usually informed consent for interview research includes the following:

- Start with a short, one- or two-sentence description of the research topic as well as the general areas that will be covered in the interview.

- Provide a description of who may participate in the research, including all of the qualifications for participation (for example, "single mothers over the age of 18 who have never been married").

- State who is conducting the research and describe how the research will be used (for publication, for presentation to an employer, etc.).

- Provide an estimate of the amount of time the interview will take and the number of interview sessions to which the interviewee is agreeing.

- If the interview will be audio or video recorded, this must be stated in the informed consent statement.
    - Additionally, the participant must be advised that they have the right to have the recording device turned off at any point during the interview and that you will only recommence recording with the participant's permission.
    - You must state who, other than yourself, will see or have access to the recordings (such as an advisor, research assistant, or paid transcriptionist) or read the completed transcripts.
    - You must also disclose what you will do with the recordings and transcripts after the completion of your research. (Usually, though not always, the recordings are destroyed.)

- Assure the participant that the research will be completely **confidential**, which means that no one other than you will know their identity. Steps taken to protect the participant's identity include the following:
    - replacing the participant's name with a **pseudonym** (fake name) in the transcripts and in labelling recordings

o deleting identifying information (such as hometown, name of high school, name of place of employment, etc.) from the transcripts

o if the recordings are kept or backed up on a physical device, such as on a thumb drive, keeping them in a locked room or cabinet

o password-protecting the electronic recording and transcript files

o keeping no record that links the participant's name with their pseudonym

- State that participation in this research is completely voluntary and that the participant may withdraw from the research at any time without penalty or repercussion. This means that if the participant wants to withdraw their information even after the interview has been analyzed, you must not include it in the final analysis or report.

- Advise the participant of their right not to answer any questions they do not wish to answer.

- State that the participant has a right to ask additional questions about the research and that these questions will be answered.

- Fully disclose any potential risks of participating in the research. With interview research, there usually is little to no risk, but sometimes participants may be warned that they may feel some emotional discomfort if the interview is likely to include questions about emotional or traumatic events, such as a death in the family, a battle with anorexia, or an act of violence that they have experienced.

- Disclose any immediate benefits to the participants for their participation in the research. Again, in interview research, there usually are none, but occasionally a researcher may provide a small monetary token for participation or conduct a raffle in which one of the participants in the sample wins a prize.

- Provide your contact information.

- Provide the contact information for the chair of the governing Institutional Review Board (IRB). The participant needs to be advised that they may contact this person if they feel that any of their rights as a research participant have been violated.

- Finally, the informed consent statement should have a statement indicating that the participant has read the entire document, that all their questions about the research have been answered, and that they have given their consent to participate in the research. This should be followed by a place for the signature and the date. In all but rare cases, the participant should sign their real name, not the pseudonym, on the informed consent statement.

You should keep the signed consent form in a private and secure location. Additionally, you should give an unsigned copy of the document to the participant so that they not only have a record of their rights, but also the contact information for yourself and the chair of the IRB, should they have further questions. Box 2.5 is a sample of an informed consent statement. Of course, it goes without saying that you must not only inform the participant of all of these steps taken to protect them from harm, but also carry through with them. Not doing so is not merely unethical; it also runs the risk of sanctions from the IRB or supporting organization, or a lawsuit from one of the participants.

BOX 2.5

SAMPLE INFORMED CONSENT STATEMENT FOR INTERVIEWING

You are invited to participate in a study on the classroom experiences of African American men at Big River State University. The purpose of this study is to understand the ways in which African American men perceive their race to affect their experiences as students. You are eligible to participate if you identify as an African American male, are at least 18 years of age, and have been enrolled as a full- or part-time student at BRSU for at least one entire semester. This research is being conducted by Dr. Rita Book, a professor in the Department of Sociology at BRSU. The results of this research will be used for campus and professional presentation, as well as for publication.

If you decide to participate in this study, you will take part in one face-to-face interview lasting between 2 and 3 hours. Approximately 20 participants in all will be interviewed. These interviews will be recorded and later transcribed. I will turn off the recorder at any time if you ask me to do so, and I will not resume recording without your permission.

Your participation in this research is entirely confidential. Your name will not appear on any of the recordings, files, or transcripts. You will choose a fake name, which will be used on the recordings, transcripts, and final report. Any identifying information will be changed or deleted. The only people who will hear your recordings will be myself and a paid transcriber. Transcripts and digital recordings will be stored on a password-protected computer, and they will be destroyed at the end of the research project.

Your participation in this research is entirely voluntary. You have the right to ask questions about this study and to have your questions answered. There are no anticipated risks or benefits to you from your participation in this research. You do not have to answer any questions that you do not want to answer. If you decide to participate in this study, you have the right to withdraw your participation at any time without penalty.

If you have questions or concerns about this study, you may contact me, Dr. Book, at (987) 555-1234, or via e-mail at rbook@brsu.edu. If you feel your rights as a research participant have been violated, you should contact the chair of the Human Subjects in Research Committee at BRSU, Dr. Strict, at (987) 555-5678.

I have read the above and have had all my questions about participation in this study answered to my satisfaction. I understand that my participation in this study is completely voluntary and that I can withdraw from this study at any time without penalty.

Signature _____

Date _____

Special Considerations

If a participant is under the age of 18, you must receive informed consent from their parents. Depending on the child's age, you may also be required to get their consent to participate. If you are going to conduct research with minors through an organization (such as their school), you will also need to get permission from the head of the organization (in this case, the principal and the school board).

Regardless of the participant's age, if you ask questions that are likely to yield any information about illegal behavior, you must use extra caution and employ additional steps to protect them, including full disclosure in the informed consent statement about how that information will be used and what the possible consequences are to the participant for providing you with that information. In rare cases, the recordings, notes, and transcripts of researchers have been subpoenaed in legal cases when the judge had reason to believe that the researcher had information relevant to the case (Rosich, 2005). The bottom line is that the participant should never suffer any harm or negative repercussions from their participation in your research.

Sometimes it becomes clear during the course of an interview that a participant needs some sort of help with issues in their life. For example, a participant may admit to having a physically abusive partner or to struggling with an addiction that is out of control. These cases are ethically tricky, as you are a researcher, not a trained therapist, and therefore should refrain from acting as such. Nonetheless, it is generally appropriate to offer the person resources that may be able to provide them help, such as information about the local domestic violence shelter or addiction treatment programs. The ethics are more vague, however, about how far to involve yourself in getting the participant help. If they don't have transportation to the shelter, for example, should you offer to drive them? Should you call them to check in on how they are doing or whether they received the help you recommended? The answers to these questions are unclear, and it is up to you, the researcher, to decide what you think is the most ethical response while maintaining both personal and professional boundaries. When in doubt, I recommend consulting with colleagues or researchers you respect, while of course being careful to maintain your participants' confidentiality.

Other Ethical Issues

In addition to protecting the participant from harm, other ethical considerations can arise in interview research. For example, you may find yourself interviewing people you do not like, either because you don't find their personalities agreeable or because they have engaged in behavior of which you disapprove or that you consider immoral. Scully and Marolla (1985), for example, interviewed convicted rapists in prison about their motivations for raping women. Pryor (1996) interviewed men who had a history of molesting children. These researchers were appalled by the participants' behavior, but for their interviews to be successful, they had to maintain a nonjudgmental and respectful demeanor, regardless of how abhorrent they found the behaviors they were asking about. Some people may consider it unethical *not* to raise objections in these kinds of situations, but a researcher's focus is on the ethical treatment *of the participant*, which takes priority. After all, not only is the participant sharing with you their perspective on the world, but if your goal is to understand the world through their eyes in order to better understand their actions, then you have to be willing to accept that they see things differently than you do. To pass judgment or to treat the participant disrespectfully is not only an ethical issue; it will also jeopardize the quality of your data. Would *you*, after all, continue to reveal your true thoughts to a person you felt was judging you for your beliefs? Michael Kimmel (2017), himself Jewish, interviewed neo-Nazis, Klansmen, and other white supremacists for his book *Angry White Men*. He did not hide his Jewishness from his participants, and he often told them before the interview that he would not agree with them, but neither would he try to convince them. Instead, he listened respectfully, as he told them he would:

> In this book, I try to look into the hearts and minds of the American men with whom I most disagree politically. I try to understand where their anger comes from and where they think it's going. I do so not with contempt or pity, but with empathy and compassion. (p. 11)

As an interviewer, this is the way in which you must treat all of your participants.

A related issue is your portrayal of the participant in your analysis. Some researchers feel that portraying participants in unflattering or even disparaging ways is unethical. Although you may have learned many things about your participant during the course of the interviews that you find unsavory or even distressing, the participant would likely not have agreed to take part in the research if they had known that it would be used to make them (or people like them) look bad. Additionally, unflattering portrayals can negatively affect the people you have studied or groups like them. If your actual participants read the study, it may hurt their feelings or affect their sense of self-esteem. At the very least, it will likely lower others' opinions of the population you are studying, which can have both intangible and concrete effects on that group. More important, once you present your results, you have no control over how others will use that information, so a mildly negative portrayal of your participants could get blown into something much more severe. All of that being said, it is at the same time considered unethical to withhold important findings from your research simply because it may be unflattering to your participants. Like many ethical dilemmas, there is no easy solution to this problem, but generally interview researchers try to be honest with their findings, while also avoiding negatively portraying their participants. Sometimes you can do this by focusing not on the behaviors or characteristics that make you uncomfortable, but on the situations, contexts, reactions, or other forces beyond their control that play a role in these behaviors, or by balancing the negatives with other positives that you have learned through the interview as well. Other times you can successfully and ethically negotiate this simply by writing your analysis in a way that shows your respondents as human (and thus as feeling, thinking, and vulnerable), rather than as simple stereotypes or caricatures. Kimmel (2017), for example, talks in his book about the ways in which the anger felt by his white supremacist participants was justified, although misdirected, in his view. He specifically states that many of them are not "bad men" but "true believers in the American Dream," and that though he finds their discourse dangerous and hate filled, he also balances that by validating their underlying disappointment, anger, fear, and disillusionment brought on by an economic shift that has taken away what they had been promised.

CHECK YOUR UNDERSTANDING

If you were carrying out research based on one of your research questions about poverty, what are all the things you would need to do to protect your participants? Remember to apply the principles of ethics to each particular case, so that if you are interviewing adolescents, for example, you will do some things differently than if you are interviewing adults.

Sampling

Because interviews are usually based on interpretivist methodology, your goal as an interviewer is to understand the perspectives of your participants as fully and deeply as possible. In order to do so, you need to use a sampling strategy that will provide you with participants who are willing to share detailed and thorough informa-

 Reminder: Sampling is how you go about choosing the people who will participate in your research.

tion with you about what might be fairly private issues. Additionally, this method of research is time intensive, so you need participants who are willing to spend the time to give you the information you need and will not just try to get through it as quickly as possible. For these reasons, it is inappropriate to try to randomly choose people to participate in your research. Instead, you need to target people who are interested in, and maybe even excited about, your research. Interview researchers therefore generally use **nonprobability sampling**, which means that not everyone in the population shares the same chance of being chosen to participate in the research. This will certainly bias your research—those who are interested in or excited about your research are people who may have had particular types of experiences regarding your topic or who want their perspective to be heard. Although such bias can be a serious problem in quantitative research, it is *not* considered problematic in interpretivist research because with interviews you will avoid **generalizing** your findings beyond your sample to a larger population. That is, you must *avoid* making any claims about anyone outside of your sample. For example, even though you found that the teachers in your study expressed great frustration with having to design their curricula to the standardized tests their students take, you cannot then conclude that this frustration is typical or even that any teachers outside your study share it. The limitation of this, of course, is that the information you learn is confined to a very small group of people. The benefit is that by not trying to generalize, your sample can be biased without having any negative effects on your study because you are not claiming that these participants are in any way representative of other people in the population. Even if you draw a very unusual sample of highly disgruntled teachers, you will understand the experiences, frustrations, and perspectives of those disgruntled teachers very well. It does not mean that you can say anything about any other teachers, but you have the opportunity to learn a lot about why those particular teachers in your sample are so terribly unhappy. To the interpretivist researcher, *this* is in fact the goal of research. It is not to try to learn something that applies to everyone in some sort of unbiased, scientific way.

The logic, therefore, that underlies interview sampling is based neither on representativeness nor on randomness, as it is for most quantitative research. Instead, it is based on selecting the people who can *best* help you answer your research question (see Box 2.6). *Best* always includes the requirement that the participant is interested in the project and is willing to spend the necessary time with you on it. The more interested and willing the participant is, the better the data you are likely to get, so these characteristics are of utmost importance. A majority of interview research, therefore, uses the strategy of calling for volunteers by posting fliers, placing ads in local newspapers, putting announcements on websites like Craigslist or on a website with substantive content related to your project, sending out e-mails to related distribution lists, or making announcements to relevant groups and organizations. This is called **convenience sampling** because you are not strategically selecting the individuals in your sample but instead are alerting people of the opportunity to participate and allowing them to choose you, which is ostensibly a more convenient and expedient way of sampling. (Most interview researchers have, however, learned that convenience sampling is actually not very convenient—finding enough volunteers who fit the minimum requirements for participation can require a lot of time and work, as well as a willingness to be creative in advertising for participants.)

Snowball sampling is the other most common sampling method for interview research. **Snowball sampling** involves recruiting people who participate in the research and who then recruit other people to participate in the research as well (and who, in turn, might recruit more participants for you). This method is particularly suitable when the groups of people you want to participate are difficult to find or identify, are likely to know others like themselves, and are unlikely to participate in official organizations through which you might contact them.

Sometimes it is important to your research question to be selective in your sampling, in which case you would choose a different, usually somewhat more difficult, sampling method. This is known as **purposive sampling** because the participants are *purposely* chosen for a particular reason. For applied interview research, especially evaluation research, it is very important to avoid interviewing only those people who will tell you what you want to hear. For this reason, in applied research you should use purposive sampling, rather than convenience sampling, whenever possible. Although there are more than a dozen different purposive sampling methods, most don't get used very often; by far the most common is **maximum variation sampling**, in which you try to recruit a sample with as much diversity of experience and opinion as possible. Although interview research is never representative, seeking maximum diversity in your sample ensures that you take into account the wide variety of experiences likely to be found among this population when making decisions that may have serious consequences to their lives. It is important to note, however, that this is a special case for applied research only (especially evaluation research or needs assessment). Basic research rarely requires purposive sampling such as maximum variation sampling. Additionally, it is much harder in basic research to employ purposive sampling than in applied research because in applied research most often the population is very limited, already known to staff within the organization for which you are conducting the research, and thus easy to identify and locate. It is much harder to find such diversity when the population is wide open, unknown, and difficult to locate. Thus the overwhelming majority of sampling for basic interview research uses convenience sampling.

BOX 2.6
DECISION PATH FOR QUALITATIVE INTERVIEW SAMPLING

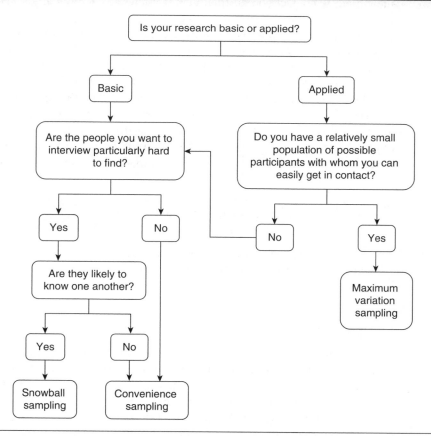

Note: While this is the typical path for decision making, there may be unusual circumstances that require different decisions.

Gatekeepers

Sometimes, in order to gain access to the people in a population to let them know about your study, you need to use a **gatekeeper**. This is a person who is in a position to grant you the access you need to some group of people. It may be the owner of a website related to your research, the head of an organization that deals with issues pertaining to your research, or an influential member of the group to which you need access. Gatekeepers are not always the most obvious people—often an executive assistant, for example, may be a more important gatekeeper than the CEO of an organization. Appropriate gatekeepers can greatly reduce the amount of time and energy needed to find all the participants for your sample. It can increase, however, the ethical issues you may face, as well as the number of steps you must take to protect the rights of your participants. For example, gatekeepers cannot give you contact information for people they think might be willing to participate in your research unless they have permission from those people to do so. Instead, the gatekeeper must either get the permission of the individual to give you the contact information, or the gatekeeper must give the information about the study to the potential participants and allow them to contact you on their own if interested. Additionally, when all is said and done, you cannot reveal to any gatekeeper which individuals have actually participated (or agreed to participate) in your study; nor can the gatekeeper offer incentives to participate that would require you to reveal the names of the participants, such as a teacher offering extra credit for students who do an interview with you, or a boss offering comp time for participation. In fact, if the gatekeeper has a position of power over the possible participants, then they *must* make it clear that any person's decision to participate or not in your research will have no bearing on their status, either positive or negative, at the organization, and that the decision to participate is completely voluntary. As the researcher, it is your responsibility to make sure that all persons recruited through that gatekeeper understand this before consenting to participate.

CHECK YOUR UNDERSTANDING

If you were sampling for your two interview research questions on poverty, which sampling method would you choose for each? Why?

Sample Size

Because interviewing is aimed at understanding the participants' experiences and perspectives in great depth and detail, and also because you will not try to generalize your findings, the sample size for interviewing is usually relatively small. The exact size depends on how large the research team conducting the interviews will be and on how long the interviews run. A lone researcher interviewing participants for approximately 1 hour each will use a larger sample size than the researcher whose interviews take several sessions each for a total of 5, 10, or even 15 hours. Also, the larger the number of interviewers working on the project, the larger the sample size will likely be. Given these tremendous variations, there is no "right" sample size. Typically, interview research uses sample sizes of 15 to 30 participants, though as many as 50 may participate if the researcher schedules shorter interviews by multiple interviewers. Sample size doesn't frequently exceed 50 for this research method. Similarly, sample sizes smaller than 15 are somewhat rare in published sociological research, unless the researcher is taking a **case study** approach, meaning the researcher concentrates very heavily on only a handful (sometimes as few as three or four) participants but interviews them for many hours (sometimes 100 or more) over the course of months or even years. Case studies, however, are much more common in psychology than in sociology, where they are rare.

Before you can apply for IRB approval, you must decide exactly who is eligible to participate in your project (such as single mothers over the age of 18 who have never been married), your sampling strategy, and your approximate sample size. This information is part of the IRB application. After receiving IRB approval, you may then begin the process of recruiting your sample. Note that it is forbidden to begin recruitment *prior to* receiving approval from your IRB.

CHECK YOUR UNDERSTANDING

Again thinking about your two research questions on poverty, how large of a sample would you use for each? Why?

Preparing for Data Collection

In interview research, preparation for data collection can begin while you are awaiting approval from the IRB (sometimes even before) and often continues into the early stages of participant recruitment. Preparing for interviews primarily involves practicing interviews on the topic, securing the necessary equipment, and making logistical arrangements.

If you have never conducted interviews before, you should spend several weeks working on developing your interviewing skills. Ask friends, family, and acquaintances if you may practice interviewing them. It doesn't have to be on your research topic—just get some practice asking questions, listening, and eliciting as much detail as possible. Many new interviewers are surprised at how much skill it actually takes to conduct a good interview, and these skills are only developed through practice. You may also be surprised to find that the less you know about an individual personally, the easier it is to interview them, so don't be afraid to ask people you don't know or barely know, such as the friends of friends or the neighbor you say hello to but don't really know. After all, you won't know your actual research participants either, and it is good to practice interviewing strangers. As you begin to feel more comfortable with the process, you may ask your practice interviewees to role-play different difficult interviewing scenarios, such as being terse in their answers, getting angry or crying, or straying far from the topic in their answers. Practice dealing with these situations. Although they are not the norm in interviews, they do occasionally come up, and feeling confident that you can deal with them will make you much less nervous going into your real interviews. You should also practice the moments that new interviewers often find somewhat awkward: explaining the informed consent statement, transitioning from informed consent to beginning the interview, and ending the interview. All researchers, even experienced interviewers, should practice at least one or two interviews on their topic with people who fit the same criteria as the people in the sample. These are called **pilot interviews** and will not be counted in the actual sample or used in the final analysis. The purpose of these pilot interviews is to make sure that the topics you intend to cover in the interview are appropriate and relevant and that your questions are answerable. Additionally, they will help to improve the quality of your data by alerting you to possible difficulties or problems before they have a chance to compromise the data you are collecting.

I also recommend that interview researchers reverse roles during a practice interview. Ask someone to interview you on the same topics and use some of the same or similar questions that you might use in collecting your data. The interview will be less smooth, of course, because your "interviewer" will not know which ideas to pursue with follow-up questions or which details to elicit, nor will they likely have excellent interviewing skills. Nonetheless, if you write down a list of interview questions and then have someone ask you the questions and try answering them yourself, you will learn a lot that will improve the quality of the data you gather. If you are very different than your participants will be, you may need to revise the topics or questions for this kind of practice interview. For example, if you are interviewing teen mothers about how they cope with stigma, and yet you have not been a teen mother and perhaps haven't even been pregnant, you can instead answer similar questions about some other characteristic or behavior that has caused you to be stigmatized. Although not ideal, it still affords you the opportunity to better understand how your participants will feel being interviewed. You should use this exercise to reflect on why some questions were easier to answer than others; how vulnerable you felt answering the most sensitive questions, and how that affected your responses; and what the interviewer did that put you at ease, or helped you to provide more detailed information. This experience can then be used to improve the interviews you conduct.

In addition to practicing interviewing, you will need to secure the necessary equipment. Most interviewers record their interviews, which is highly recommended. You will therefore need charged batteries and a reliable recorder that can produce high-quality recordings. If you use a digital recorder, you will probably use a computer program that facilitates the transcription of digital recording. It is never a good idea to record the interview on your cell phone—it is too easy for it to get accidentally erased, and it doesn't provide enough protection for confidentiality. For transcription, you may want to purchase a foot pedal that connects to your computer. Newer versions are adapted from older pre-digital recording transcription machines, but they greatly increase the control you have over playback, allowing you to easily pause or rewind while continuing to type, thus decreasing transcription time. In addition, if you will be using a computer program to help you manage your data, you should obtain and learn to use the software.

Logistical arrangements primarily focus on finding a comfortable, private, safe place to conduct the interviews. You can interview participants in their own homes, but be aware that if there are other people present in the home at the time of the interview, or if there are interruptions from children, pets, phone calls, or other general distractions, it will negatively affect the quality of your data. In some circumstances, you may be able to interview the participant in your own home, but again, the presence of other people or distractions will reduce the quality of your data. In addition, safety can be an issue. Some participants, especially women, may not feel safe going to a stranger's home; likewise, there may be cases in which researchers feel anxious having strangers coming to their home or knowing where they live. Neutral locations always work well but are particularly advisable for evaluation research as long as they are away from the actual organization, as they may encourage more honest answers. If you are choosing such a location, it needs to be a quiet, comfortable, and private place that is readily accessible to the participants and that, preferably, can be reserved in advance. Some community centers, city buildings, public libraries, university campuses, or places of worship have appropriate rooms that can be used, although sometimes they charge a fee. Another logistical issue to handle is arranging your schedule, as much as possible, so that you will be available to conduct interviews at times that are convenient for your participants. You should also make sure that interested potential participants can contact you via phone and that any message they leave will not be heard by others, which would compromise their confidentiality. Also, you should prepare a drawer in a locking file cabinet or other secured place to store transcripts and completed consent forms.

Data Collection

Once you have received approval from the IRB, have completed preparations for your interviews, and have scheduled an interview time with your first participant, you are ready to begin collecting your data. For both types of interviews (loosely or semi-structured), the primary determinant in the quality of your data will be how well you establish rapport with each of your participants. **Rapport** (pronounced ra-POR) is the relationship of trust, cooperation, mutual respect, and sense of ease you have with one another. Any interview in which you fail to establish at least a decent amount of rapport with the participant will be arduous and of poor quality. Because rapport is so vital to producing good research, you will take a number of steps to establish rapport with each participant.

Establishing Rapport

1. In early communication with the participants about the research, be polite, pleasant, and enthusiastic about the project.

- You should also take great care to make sure that they fit the criteria you set for participation, that they understand what the research is generally about, that they know how long you expect the interview to take, and that their decision to participate is entirely voluntary and they do not feel in any way pressured to participate.

- No matter how desperate you are for participants, you do not want to interview someone who has consented out of a sense of obligation, guilt, or pressure. Not only is this ethically questionable, it likely won't be a pleasant experience for either one of you, and the data that it yields will most certainly be of poor quality.

2. Dress appropriately for the interview.

   - What you wear depends on whom you are interviewing—you should dress differently to interview the CEO of a Fortune 500 company than you would to interview a college student, a prison inmate, or a mother living in subsidized housing.

   - Although you need not dress in exactly the same way as your participant, you should, nonetheless, make sure that your appearance is neither intimidating nor likely to undermine your credibility.

3. When you and the participant first arrive at the meeting place, engage in easy, casual conversation.

   - It doesn't have to be lengthy or personal, but even asking whether the participant had any trouble finding the place or talking about the weather can help to break the ice and make both of you feel more comfortable when the interview actually begins.

4. After the interview has begun, give the participant your full and concentrated attention.

   - Show your interest in the participant's answers by asking follow-up questions and by demonstrating attentive listening.

   - Give both verbal cues and nonverbal cues that let them know that you are listening and want them to continue.

5. Express genuine empathy.

   - If they are relaying an experience that made them angry, you might say, for example, "How frustrating for you!" If they discuss a difficult time in their life, you could respond, "I can only imagine how hard that must have been."

   - Your responses should feel genuine, not forced, and your facial expressions should match your responses. That is, if you say something to express empathy but have a bored look on your face, it will seem fake and likely damage, rather than encourage, rapport.

6. If you personally disagree with the participant's interpretations or perspectives, or if they are describing behaviors that you find troublesome (or even horrifying), you should take care not to convey this to them.

   - Both verbal and nonverbal cues should be nonjudgmental on your part.

   - Remember, your goal is to understand what they think or what they have experienced, not to condemn or change them.

7. Believe what the participant says, and convey this to them through your verbal and nonverbal cues.

   - Rarely do participants lie outright. The more rapport you establish, and the more they feel they can trust you with information without being judged, the less likely this will occur.

   - If you try to trick your participant or trip them up in what you think is a lie, you will most certainly destroy the trust necessary for the interview to continue.

   - Relatedly, never badger a participant. Sometimes we are so wedded to what we believe must be true, we have a hard time accepting an answer that doesn't match up with our expectations.

     o For example, one of my students conducted a research project on how people decided to convert to Catholicism amid all the allegations of sexual abuse and the Church's position on controversial issues. The student became interested in the topic because she herself was considering becoming a Catholic. During one interview, she asked a participant about the doubts he had about converting. The participant said very plainly that he had no doubts. Because she had her own doubts, however, and because other participants had expressed doubts in previous interviews, the researcher did not believe her participant. She continued to ask the question several times, at which point it became badgering, and the participant got frustrated.

     o A better way of handling this situation would be to try to rephrase the question once, but no more. Then switch to finding out more about the person's answer. For example, you might say, "That's really interesting. Some of the other people I have interviewed have expressed quite a few doubts. Why do you think your experience has been so different from theirs?" This not only provides you with more information on the issue, but also preserves the trust and respect you have built with the participant.

8. Become comfortable with silence.

   - Some participants need to think about your question before they answer, rather than just rattling something off the tops of their heads. Don't assume that just because there are a few seconds of silence the participant doesn't want to answer the question or is unable to.

- Sometimes if you remain silent after a participant answers a question, that silence will encourage them to add more information to their response. My students are regularly amazed at how well this strategy works.

If you are conducting evaluation research, you will need to pay special attention to fostering as much rapport with the participants as possible in order to get honest answers. Although honesty is important to the validity of any interviewing research, in evaluation research the respondents are perhaps more likely to feel that you, the interviewer, have an agenda or want to hear particular answers. For this reason, it is sometimes best for an outsider (someone not related in any way to the program being evaluated) to conduct the interviews, so that participants feel the researcher is objective. If you cannot have an outsider do it, then you must convince your participants with your verbal and nonverbal cues that you truly are interested what they have to say and not just in validating the program. You must make sure they understand that you are willing to listen to all their experiences with the program, no matter how negative or positive.

Additional Steps to Improve Data Quality

For all interviewing research, besides establishing rapport, you will need to do a number of additional things to ensure the quality of your data:

1. Audio record the interview!
   - It is very difficult to take accurate and complete notes during an interview without slowing the participant down while you are trying to keep up, which can compromise the quality of your data (if they are busy repeating things for you to write down, or are waiting for you to catch up, they will say less).
   - Additionally, for most people it is difficult to listen intently, write down everything the participant says, and still come up with spontaneous questions that elicit rich information. Recording allows you to concentrate on what's most important—listening to your participant.
   - Finally, the accuracy of your data will be much greater if you record the interview because in doing so you will capture exactly what the participant said and how they said it.
   - Even so, participants in applied research may be particularly hesitant to have their interviews recorded, especially if they do not trust the confidentiality of the interviews, or if they believe there is a possibility of being sanctioned for negative evaluations. Although recording significantly increases the quality of your data and analysis, if either of these seems to be a concern to the participant, it is better to put the respondent at ease and not record than to have them watch every word they say because you have insisted on recording them.

- Make sure that you test your equipment with the participant before beginning. It is a huge waste of your time and theirs if you conduct a 2-hour interview, only to realize that your recorder didn't capture any of it. If your recorder does fail, use the jotted-notes technique described below during the interview.

2. If you cannot record the interview, do not try to write down everything that the participant says—you will never succeed, and you will miss much of the important information that the participant gives you. Instead, take quick, jotted notes, only writing down words and phrases that will trigger in your mind more complete details of the interview later.

   - Keep the note-taking as unobtrusive as possible, and avoid slowing the respondent down or asking them to repeat themselves.

   - Learn shorthand or develop your own style of shorthand so that you can write quickly yet still read your notes later.

   - Immediately after the interview, write down, as fully as possible, everything you remember the participant having said, as closely to verbatim as your memory allows. Use your jotted notes to trigger your memory.

3. Questions should be **wide open**, meaning they should not be answerable with yes/no responses or with a couple of words or a short phrase.

   - Your goal in interviewing is always to elicit as much detailed information as possible. Avoid questions that sound like a multiple-choice response on a survey. For example, "How have your perspectives on this issue changed since that first meeting?" will elicit better data than "Now, do you agree with him more or less than you did before?"

   - Yes/no questions should only be used to check your understanding, or for clarification purposes ("So, do you mean that you think it was unfair of her to do that?").

4. In order to elicit as much rich detail as possible (called **thick description**), ask questions about specific instances and examples instead of asking for generalizations.

   - For example, "Can you walk me through your morning today, step by step, from the time you woke up until you left the house?" will likely yield a more in-depth answer than "What do you do to get ready in the morning?"

   - Box 2.7 shows several examples of the types of questions that elicit details about specific examples.

   - Novice interviewers often fear that getting many details about one particular experience won't give them the information they need, and so they try to go for generalizations—what usually or typically happens instead of what occurred in one particular instance. In fact, the opposite is true because generalizations don't allow for the level of detail that really provides insight and that allows you to conduct a strong analysis.

5. Never start an interview with questions requesting demographic information.

   - Interviews are not an appropriate method for collecting large amounts of demographic data, but sometimes you want to ask a few such questions, such as the participant's age or occupation.

   - Do not, however, begin an interview with these questions. The first questions you ask will set the tone for the interview and will signal to the participant what kind and how much information you want them to supply. If you begin an interview with demographic questions, you signal to the participant that all their answers should be short and unreflective.

   - Instead, your first question should ask for a lot of detail in order to set the proper tone for the interview.

   - Be patient about demographic information—often this information will be mentioned in the course of the interview without your even needing to request it. If not, wait until the end of the interview to ask these questions.

6. Try to avoid putting words in the participant's mouth.

   - Instead of asking, "Did that make you feel relieved, or was it kind of scary?" ask, "How did that make you feel?"

   - This will help to ensure that you are getting a direct view through the participant's own eyes, rather than their reactions to your assumptions.

7. Try to be clear about whether you are asking about their behavior, thoughts, or feelings (Weiss, 1994).

   - You can ask about all three, but not all at once.

   - You might begin, for example, with "How did you break the news to her?" (behavior), and then follow that with "What were you thinking while you were trying to broach the subject?" (thoughts). You might finally ask, "How did you feel after you told her?" (feelings). This will provide you with more detailed information and help the participant to stay focused.

8. End the interview by asking two questions: "Is there anything else you would like to add?" and "Is there anything I didn't ask about that I should have?"

   - This gives the participant the opportunity to clarify or stress the importance of previous statements, to revise a statement that they have been reconsidering during the rest of the interview, or to bring up issues that you hadn't considered but that they feel are important to your topic.

   - Sometimes these questions can produce another 30 minutes or more of useful data.

BOX 2.7

KEY WORDS ELICITING INFORMATION ABOUT SPECIFIC EXAMPLES

- How did you tell him for *the first time* that you love him?

- Tell me a little bit about *the last argument* you two had.

- Can you describe for me a *particularly memorable* evening you two shared together?

- What was *the best* present he ever gave you?

- Can you remember *a time when things* in your relationship *were particularly* stressful?

- Perhaps you could recount for me the conversation you had *last night.*

- Can you give me a *recent example* of how you two have come to a compromise on that issue?

9. Immediately after you leave the interview, take a few minutes to write down what you think were the most important issues and themes that arose during the interview, anything that struck you as surprising or unexpected, and new questions or topics that you would like to add to future interviews. This is helpful both for analysis and for improving your subsequent interviews.

Semi-Structured Interviews

If you are conducting semi-structured interviews, in addition to the above you will want to follow these guidelines as well:

1. Memorize your questions, and only occasionally glance at a cheat sheet. This will make the interviewee feel more comfortable.

2. Word the questions in a relaxed, casual way, so that they sound more natural. Avoid asking formally worded questions that sound stiff and may be off-putting.

3. Remember that this is not a survey—you do not need to ask each question with exactly the same wording to each participant; in fact, to do so can make the question seem awkward and clumsy.

   - When possible, link the question to what the participant has just said. This can make the participant feel like their answers are useful and interesting to you. It also allows for smoother transitions and a more natural flow to the interview.

4. Avoid asking questions that they have already addressed just because you haven't formally asked the question yet.

   - "You may have already answered this one, but . . ." usually yields little new information and causes awkwardness because the participant may not know how much to repeat of what they have already told you.

- Instead, ask specific questions that prompt the participant to elaborate on particular points they have already made in order to fill out the information you are looking for on that topic.

- For example, instead of asking, "You may have already answered this, but how was it to go back and forth between your mom and dad's house?" ask, "You've already brought up how the rules differed between your mom's house and your dad's house, and you said your mom was much stricter. I'm curious about how it felt, then, to go back to your mom's on Sunday evenings after spending the weekend with your dad, who you said pretty much let you do anything."

5. Be flexible about the order in which you ask your questions, so that they seem to flow more naturally from the participant's answers, thus allowing you to avoid awkward transitions.

Loosely Structured Interviews

Here are some guidelines for best practice if you are conducting loosely structured interviews:

1. Go into the interview knowing what topics you want to cover, but remember to let the participant's experiences and responses direct the interview.

   - *Eighty percent or more of your questions should flow directly from what the respondent is saying.*

   - In responding to questions, participants drop **markers**: passing references to information that they think might be relevant.

     o By mentioning the information, the participant is signaling to you that they have this information and that they are willing to tell you more about it, if you are interested.

     o A main task for all interviewers, but especially for those conducting loosely structured interviews, is to identify markers and decide which to let drop and which to ask more about (you can never follow up on every marker).

     o It is as if the participant is giving you a driving tour of a city, pointing out various landmarks and points of interest, and then says to you, "Let me know if you want to stop and get out to look at any of these places." In the loosely structured interview, the participant is the tour guide of their experiences, giving you markers to consider, and it is up to you to say, "I think I'd like to spend some time here, at this one."

   - Refer again to Box 2.2 to see a list of questions that a student researcher asked during an interview about the messages she received from her family about sexuality. I omitted the participant's answers to these questions to highlight how you can tell just from her questions that she is picking up on markers, so that her questions flow directly from what the participant had just told her.

BOX 2.8

INTERVIEWING DO'S AND DON'TS

START WELL

- Keep early communication pleasant, polite, and enthusiastic
- Make sure they are consenting
- Warm up with chit-chat
- Dress appropriately

DON'T ASSUME

- Don't assume you know what they think or feel
- Don't put words in their mouth
- Instead, ask for clarification or more information

PAY ATTENTION

- Give your full attention
- Use verbal and nonverbal cues to convey your interest
- Follow up on markers

DON'T BADGER

- Don't push your participants to say what you want to hear
- Instead, ask them why they see things differently

SHOW EMPATHY

- When participants express emotion, show that you understand
- Validate their feelings

DON'T JUDGE

- Your role is to listen and try to understand, not judge
- Your face and nonverbals remain neutral if you don't like what you hear

BE SPECIFIC

- Ask for specific instances
- Ask for details
- Specify whether you are asking about behaviors, thoughts, or feelings

DON'T JUMP THE GUN

- Don't start with demographic questions—let them come up or save them until the end
- Don't end your interview before asking whether they have more to say

BE QUIET

- Get comfortable with silence
- Give them time to think about their answers
- Let the participant do 80–90% or more of the talking

DON'T STRESS

- Don't think about your next question while they are talking—just listen
- Don't keep looking at your list of topics/questions
- Don't try to take copious notes while they talk—record instead

2. Listen fully to the participant rather than thinking about what your next question is going to be.

   - If you focus on your next question, not only will it distract you, causing you to miss potentially important markers, but the participant will often be able to sense your lack of attention and will begin to provide shorter and shorter answers; this, of course, will reduce the quality of your data.

   - *You don't need to think of new questions; if you just listen, you will find markers that will give you your next question.*

3. Keep a list of general topics to cover, but put it out of sight.

   - When you don't have any new markers on which you want to follow up, and no burning questions come to mind, pull out the list, saying, "Let me see what we haven't covered yet"; or, if it's toward the end of the interview, state "Let me see if I've missed anything."

   - Using this technique helps keep you from feeling like you have to think of a next question instead of really listening; it also helps you focus on what is important to the participant, rather than on the topics you presuppose to be important.

   - In addition, it eases the transition for a significant change in topics, making the process less awkward.

Box 2.8 provides a summary of the do's and don'ts of interviewing research.

Data Analysis

Transcription

Unlike with most quantitative research, qualitative analysis happens *concurrently with* data collection. Ideally, as soon as you finish your first interview, you should transcribe it and begin analysis on it, even while you conduct more interviews. The first step is to **transcribe** the interview, which means to type out, word for word, what was said during the interview. Transcription is a very time-consuming and tedious process, although the amount of time required varies greatly, depending on the transcriptionist's typing ability and the quality of the recording. It takes a reasonably good typist about 2 to 3 hours to transcribe 1 hour of interview, provided the recording is of high quality. It can take the same typist 6 to 8 hours to transcribe 1 hour of recording with poor sound quality. This happens when the microphone was too far away to clearly pick up the voices, when the speakers dropped the volume of their voices while speaking (as they often do when discussing more private or emotional matters), or when there was a lot of background noise. Transcription is time-consuming enough that it must be taken into account when making decisions about the feasibility of an interview project and when choosing a sample size. Some researchers have the resources to hire paid transcriptionists to do this step for them, while others prefer to do the transcription themselves. Some researchers argue that they learn much more about the interview by transcribing it themselves (including what they can improve upon in their interviewing skills) because their attention is focused differently than during the actual interview. Transcribing your own recordings may also make the transcriptions more accurate because you have the benefit of memory to help when something is inaudible on the recording.

Although you may hope to skip the transcription process by using voice recognition software, at the time of this writing, most of the technology is not quite advanced enough to do this well in an interview situation. Two or three programs that are newly on the market claim that they convert interview recordings directly into text transcripts, but most reviews say that they just aren't very accurate, and they require so many corrections that they save little time. Sound conditions during interviews are very different than when one person speaks directly to a voice recognition program like we are used to doing on our phones: In interview situations, recordings vary in quality, there may be background noise, speakers often drop their voices to low levels, there are large volumes of talk, you and the participant may have very different accents or inflections, and dialog always has some overlap in speaking. These conditions make speech recognition much more difficult for interviews than the short commands generally communicated by one person to Siri or Alexa. If you do try to use voice recognition software, you will need to listen to the recording as you correct the errors, which can sometimes occur every few words, and you will need to indicate who is speaking at each speech turn. You will also need to indicate such things as pauses, laughter, and instances when both people talk at once. Additionally, you should be careful about using any speech-recognition software that requires you to upload the interviews to a cloud: this may be considered a breach of confidentiality by your IRB (or may make you more vulnerable to a breach of confidentiality). Meanwhile, qualitative interviewers everywhere eagerly await the day that speech-recognition technology is advanced enough to produce an accurate transcript with few errors, significantly decreasing both the time and cost of interview research.

Steps in Data Analysis

The process of qualitative analysis is an **inductive** one, which means that rather than testing existing theories and hunches to see whether the data support or contradict them, you instead start from the data and, as you analyze it, you develop hunches and theories. In other words, the theories and hunches *come out of* the data that you have gathered, rather than the other way around. This is one of the reasons that interview research is particularly good for helping to develop new theories.

The analysis process usually begins with **coding**. Coding is the process of identifying important themes in what the participant said or in how it was said. **Codes** are usually one to four words long and are shorthand for abstract concepts or themes that characterize pieces of the data. To code, the researcher identifies a section of the transcript (sometimes a phrase, a sentence, or a whole paragraph) and writes the code name next to it. For example, next to the description of a spouse's extramarital affair, you might put *betrayal, dishonesty, infidelity,* and/or *breaking wedding vows*. It is common to have several codes for any section of a transcript. There are no right or wrong codes, and different researchers can come up with different codes for the same interview, though they should all be guided by the research question. There are several different types of codes. **A priori codes** are codes that you brainstorm before you begin analysis—and perhaps even before you conduct your first interview. They are the themes and issues that you expect to arise, given your knowledge of the topic. A priori codes are often inspired by the literature review. **Open codes** are codes that you develop while reading through the transcript. They are the themes and issues you see emerging in the data. Most of the time these open codes are **analyst-constructed codes**—that is, you have come up with them yourself. Sometimes, however, open codes are **indigenous codes**, which means they are concepts that the participants themselves use. For example, if you are interviewing people about femininity and several of your participants distinguish between "girly-girls" and women who are, in their words, "normal girls," you might adopt both as indigenous codes. All these types of codes are used to mark up the entire transcript, identifying each section with the desired codes. A list of codes is kept, and each code should be given a definition, so that you remain consistent in your coding over time. With each new transcript, you will add new codes. Again, to maintain consistency, you must keep a record of these so that if you create a new code while reading transcript #5, you can go back to transcripts #1 through #4 to look to see if the code should be applied, now that you know to look for it. The process of coding each transcript (using all the types of codes, including a priori codes) and assigning definitions to each code is sometimes called **open coding** to distinguish it from subsequent steps of analysis that also include "coding" in their names.

Tip: *A priori* (pronounced: ay pry OR ee) is a Latin term that means "conceived beforehand." So *a priori* codes are codes that you develop *prior* to starting your analysis. Indeed, most a priori codes are developed near the beginning of the research process, while reviewing the literature.

The second stage of analysis is usually to make sense out of all this coding. Sometimes called **axial coding**, it involves using the codes to look for patterns. Lofland and Lofland (1995) describe several common patterns that researchers look for, including frequencies, magnitudes, types, processes, and structures. To aid our discussion of these patterns, let's suppose you are researching feminist identities. Although **frequencies** might sound quantitative, it just means looking for the themes or patterns that were most frequently found in the data. What were some of the most common experiences or perspectives that people had related to their feminist identities? Looking for **magnitudes**, on the other hand, recognizes that sometimes something really big or important only happens occasionally, or to only a few individuals in your sample. Even though it wasn't among the most common patterns, it nonetheless had a huge impact when it did happen and therefore is important information. Having a parent who refuses to conform to gender stereotypes may not be a common phenomenon, but it may have a huge impact on the development of a feminist identity. Sometimes researchers look at whether some of the concepts or experiences they are studying fall into different **types**. This means that not all the participants had the same experiences with the phenomena, but some of the experiences were similar to one another and could be grouped accordingly. For example, you may discover that your participants described experiences of discrimination at work that could be grouped into four different types of discrimination, or there were three different ways in which your participants interpreted the meaning of "being feminist." Looking for **processes** means searching for a series of steps or stages that are common for all or many of the participants in their journeys from point A to point B, such as the stages each went through from knowing little or nothing about feminism to self-identifying as feminists. Finally, to analyze the **structure** of a phenomenon you're studying means to break it down and identify its essential parts. Note that this is different than types: Although the participants may have described several different types of discrimination they have experienced, every act of discrimination has specific components that make it count or qualify as discrimination. In analyzing for structure, you try to identify those components. Axial coding usually begins when all, or most, of your interviews have been completed. Sometimes researchers look for all these types of patterns; more often, they search for those patterns most closely suggested by their research question and their data. In applied research, you are probably more likely to focus on patterns of frequency and magnitude (and perhaps process, depending on your research question) than on structure or type. These patterns are summarized in Box 2.9.

The patterns that you identify during axial coding become your hunches about what is going on in the data. The final, but absolutely essential, step of analysis is sometimes called **selective coding**. It involves testing to see whether your hunches are, indeed, backed up by the data. In this step, you comb through the transcripts again to find everything in them that supports your patterns. This helps to verify that there is, indeed, a good amount of evidence for your hunch. Next, you comb again through the data to look for any and all negative cases. **Negative cases** consist of evidence that contradicts, does not support, or is an exception to the pattern. This step is *vital*—it is what makes qualitative analysis systematic and keeps it from being "just opinion." In other words, by searching for and identifying all the negative cases, you are searching for all the evidence that would suggest your hunch is incorrect. If you find more than

BOX 2.9
AXIAL CODING: FIVE TYPES OF PATTERNS

Frequency	• The frequency with which an experience is shared across participants
Magnitude	• An experience that may not happen often or to many participants, but has a huge impact when it does
Type	• Different variations of an experience may sort into categories or kinds
Process	• The steps or stages of an experience
Structure	• The compontents or parts that make up an experience

a few negative cases, then you either have to decide that you were mistaken and focus on other patterns, or you must revise your description of the pattern so that it applies to the negative cases as well—which then turns them into supporting evidence. If this happens, you will then need to repeat the entire process of selective coding until you have few or no negative cases and a preponderance of evidence supporting your pattern.

Throughout all the stages of analysis, you will also write **memos**, which are notes to yourself about ideas that you have, new questions or hunches that arise, new leads that you would like to pursue later, or issues that you find puzzling. Memos can also be written to document where you are in the analysis process, which is especially important if it will be even a few days before you resume analyzing. It's amazing how many great ideas you forget and how much work you end up needlessly repeating if you don't write memos. Box 2.10 summarizes the different stages of qualitative data analysis, including memo writing.

BOX 2.10
DIAGRAM OF STEPS IN QUALITATIVE DATA ANALYSIS

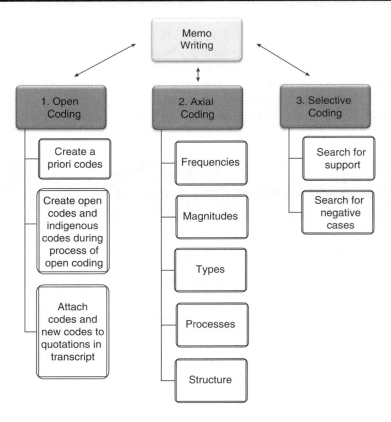

It is important to point out that there are several different types of qualitative analysis that are appropriate for interviewing. I have described one of the most common, but there are others. Narrative analysis and discourse analysis, for example, focus less on *what* is said than on *how* it is said. Life-course analysis and life-history analysis focus more attention on the sequencing of events and the impact of the particular historical moment on these events. The various types of analyses tend to differ primarily on what they are looking for, but there can also be some differences in how the analyses are carried out. In all these cases, however, you search for patterns and must also check yourself to make sure that there is ample evidence of the patterns that you identify.

CHECK YOUR UNDERSTANDING

Try coming up with a list of 10 a priori codes that you could use in analyzing your interviews for one of your research questions on poverty.

Timing of Data Analysis

I have already mentioned that qualitative data analysis should happen concurrently with data collection. This is for two main reasons. First, in interpretivist research, the aim is to understand the phenomena you are studying as fully as possible. As you analyze the data, new questions may arise, and you might want to know new or different information. Thus, your analysis should inform your subsequent interviews. During the course of the data collection, the interviews should continually change to reflect the new issues, ideas, and themes that you need to understand. Second, interpretivist methodology posits that the people you are studying know and understand more about their world and their experiences than you, the researcher, ever can, so interpretivists often enlist their participants to help with the analysis during the interview process. For example, you think you are beginning to see a pattern in the data. In your next interview, you might say, "I've already conducted several interviews, and it seems to me that people tend to use three different strategies for dealing with that situation: avoidance, confrontation, and distancing. What strategy do you use? Have you ever used any strategies besides these three? Can you think of any examples when you've seen someone else using a different strategy?" Alternatively, you might seek the participant's interpretation of the data by asking, for example, "Several people I've interviewed have told me that they have had difficulty making friends in this community. Why do you think this is?" Both of these tactics allow you to elicit new and relevant data and also to check whether your hunches hold up or the participants can give you new insights.

Using Software in Data Analysis

Traditionally, qualitative data analysis was done by hand—researchers coded by writing directly on the transcripts, sorting the data into piles based on the codes assigned, and then sifting through those piles again and again to conduct the axial and selective coding. Today, most qualitative researchers use a software program to help them organize the data and to make each step of the analysis easier. Although these software packages are typically referred to as "qualitative analysis programs," they don't in fact analyze the data for you. Much like word-processing programs, which don't write your papers for you, they simply make the mechanics of the process simpler. There are several well-known packages that have been on the market for years, continually improving as the technology advances, including ATLAS.ti, NVivo, and MAXQDA. There are also several newer, cloud-based programs, though these need to be used with caution—when you store data on a cloud, you do not have total control over it, and potentially confidentiality could be breached. For this reason, downloadable software packages remain more popular among professional researchers than cloud-based applications, but some cloud-based sites are now offering extra firewalls and enhanced security. Although each program operates a little differently, they all aim to simplify the process of coding and to allow you to more easily sift through the data. For example, with just a couple clicks of the mouse you can view everything you coded in all your interviews as, say, *dishonesty*, so that you can then look to see whether there are patterns that you can identify, such as different types of dishonesty. Most of the software also allows you to make diagrams to depict the relationships between codes (which is especially helpful for those who are visual thinkers) and to write memos and cross-reference them with particular codes or sections of the transcripts. Some of the software also enables you to code images and audio files, as well as text.

Conceptualizing and Operationalizing

 Reminder: **Conceptualization** is the process of developing precise definitions for the abstract concepts you are studying, and **operationalization** is the process of deciding how to capture the information in order to measure those concepts.

In interview research, the processes of conceptualizing and operationalizing do not exist as separate stages and occur throughout the research process (a) before data collection, (b) during data collection, and (c) during analysis.

Before data collection, you may conceptualize while working on your literature review by writing definitions of concepts you want to ask about in your interviews. Then, you operationalize these concepts by deciding how you are going to elicit the information you want about them from your participants. For loosely structured interviews, this happens when you decide on the list of interview topics; for semi-structured interviews, it happens when you decide on the questions you will ask.

During the actual interviews, conceptualization sometimes becomes an explicit part of the interview itself: It is not unusual to ask a participant what a concept or term means to them. For example, during your interviews with African Americans about the supports and challenges they face to their intersecting identities within the black community, you may ask them to define what they mean when they use the term "black community." In this case, you are using the participants' definitions in order to better understand, and ask questions about, their experiences, as well as to inform the way you yourself conceptualize the term in your research. Similarly, operationalizing also happens during the interview process when you decide which markers to follow up on and which to let go of. In doing so, you are deciding how best to elicit the information you need.

Finally, during data analysis, the entire process of open coding involves moving back and forth between conceptualizing and operationalizing. When you create new codes, you write definitions of them (which is to conceptualize them) so that you can maintain consistency in your coding. You then operationalize by deciding which codes to apply to which sections of the transcript. This is considered operationalizing because in attaching codes you are deciding which statements in the interview are providing information about particular concepts (codes); it can be thought of as measuring the concepts.

Thus, conceptualization and operationalization are integrated throughout the research process in interview research and do not constitute separate stages of the process. Note that because data collection and analysis are usually done concurrently, that also means that the conceptualizing and operationalizing you do during analysis can affect the operationalizing you do during subsequent interviews. In other words, as you develop and define your codes and use them in analysis, they will likely start to affect which markers you follow up on during the interviews. This is a strength, as it can help you elicit increasingly detailed and precise information that can help you identify patterns in the data.

Evaluating the Quality of Data and Analysis

We have already discussed many steps that need to be taken at each stage of the research process to ensure the high quality of your data and your analysis. In interview research, the quality of data and analysis is evaluated on their **validity**. The more the data accurately represent the experiences and perspectives of the participant, the more valid they are. It is important to note that interviewers realize that no report or description that a participant gives can ever be 100% complete—it is simply impossible to capture every aspect of an experience in words and convey it to another person. Nonetheless, the aim is for data that are as valid as possible. One sign of **data validity** is detailed answers with concrete examples. Additionally, the transcripts of good interviews show that the amount of time the interviewer spent talking is minimal and that most questions posed were followed by long and detailed answers from the participants. This is because in order to fully and accurately understand another person's perspective or experience, you have to have as much detailed information about it as possible. Obviously, rapport plays a role here because participants will be willing to give you more information when you have established good rapport with them.

To ensure the validity of applied research, the participants must be made to trust that there are no rewards or penalties for anything they say. In other words, for data to be valid, they must be absolutely confident that nothing they say will be used against them in any way or earn them any favors or positive regard in relation to the program or policy. Additionally, because the participants will be informed of the uses of the data, they will understand that what they say may have an effect on decisions that are made and, therefore, on their own lives or the lives of others. This can be a real incentive to participate in the research, but it can also tempt some participants to hide, misrepresent, or overemphasize certain aspects of their experiences in order to influence the decisions in a particular way. Although you can never completely eliminate this possibility, good interviewing skills can help to minimize it.

The validity of the analysis for interviews is based primarily on how well it represents the data. In other words, a **valid analysis** is one that identifies patterns that are well supported in the data. This is why selective coding is so crucial—it helps to ensure the validity of your analysis. The validity of the analysis is also based on how accurately you depict the ways in which the participants experience or view the phenomena. That is not to say that the analyst can't ever make interpretations that differ from those of the participants. For example, in interviews with men who have been in unhealthy relationships, several participants may express that the main reason they didn't leave those relationships was that they knew their partner really loved them, and they thought their partner could change. As an analyst, you may come to the conclusion that these men exhibit signs of codependency, though none of the men indicated that they thought of or recognized this as a possibility. It is legitimate for you to draw that conclusion—provided, of course, that there is good evidence that supports it and that there are few or no negative cases. You must, however, differentiate for the audience of your research between what the participants said and what you, the outsider, believe is going on. To confuse the two or neglect to draw the distinction is to compromise the validity of your analysis.

Qualitative research is too often unfairly evaluated as deficient simply because the critic has judged it based on the criteria by which we judge quantitative research. This is not only unjust; it shows a fundamental lack of understanding of the logic, goals, and strengths of interpretivist research. Qualitative research should never be found deficient based on its lack of generalizability, its unrepresentative sample, or its departure from the scientific method. Remember, interpretivist research neither claims nor aims to be generalizable or representative, and it would be virtually impossible to gather good interview data using cool, detached, bias-free, highly structured scientific procedures. Additionally, qualitative research does not set out to predict behavior or to determine cause-and-effect relationships. It also is **not replicable**; that is, if someone else conducted the same research, even with the same participants, they would produce neither the same data nor the same analysis as you did. This is because participants tell different aspects of their stories in different ways to different people. Think about someone asking you on a Monday morning, "So, how was your weekend?" Your response would probably differ depending on who was doing the asking, how well you know them, and what their relationship is to you, as well as the location, time, and context in which they are asking. You may give three different answers to your boss, your best friend, and your grandmother. That is not to say that you would lie to any of them; rather, you would give more or less detail about particular experiences and would choose to include or exclude information based on who asked the question. The same is true with interviewing research: Participants will give different information to different interviewers, based on the amount of rapport they have, the skill of the interviewer, the level of detail requested, and the particular markers on which the interviewer decides to follow up. Therefore, interview research should not be judged negatively for its lack of replicability. Instead, it is essential to evaluate interview research based on its own merits and on how well it reaches its goals of understanding as thoroughly as possible the experiences and perspectives of the research participants.

Interview research *should* be judged on the following:

- The degree to which the interviewer accurately and vividly conveys the participants' meanings, understandings, and experiences

- The degree of rapport with the participants that the interviewer can demonstrate

- The degree to which the data support the patterns identified by the researcher

- Evidence of a search for negative cases and a discussion of those negative cases and what they mean for the patterns identified

- A clear distinction between the researcher's analysis and the participants' perceptions if the analyst sees patterns the participants don't see

- The degree to which the researcher recognizes the limits of the research and stays within those limits (for example, doesn't try to generalize findings to a larger population)

Presenting the Results

Whether you are presenting your results in writing or orally, interview analyses are generally presented in the same way. Start with an introduction that includes the theoretical perspective you are using (if any). After briefly discussing your research question, the methods you used to collect your data, some information about your sample, and the basic procedures you used to analyze the data, you begin to discuss the patterns you found in your analysis. For each pattern (or each main point you wish to make), you should explain that pattern and then provide at least one, and sometimes up to several, quotations from the participants' interviews that both exemplify and support your point. The quotations should be verbatim (or nearly), though the grammar or punctuation may be cleaned up so that it is easier for your audience to follow (because natural speech is often confusing and awkward when written down). Each quotation should be identified with the pseudonym of the participant who said it, and you will be more likely to convince your audience of the validity of your analysis if you use quotations from as many different people in your sample as possible, rather than drawing many quotations from just a few participants. In addition, you should discuss any negative cases you found for each pattern. This will further help give your audience confidence in the validity of your analysis. You should end your presentation with a discussion of the implications of the research. This includes theoretical implications (Does viewing this topic through this theoretical lens shed new light on the topic? Does it suggest that the theory is missing an important aspect of the participants' experiences that it should take into account? Where does your data suggest the theory needs more clarity or depth?). It also includes implications for future research (What new issues does your analysis suggests need further research? What's the next group or population that should be studied? What other methods could be used to build upon your newfound results regarding this phenomenon?). Additionally, the implications should make it clear what this research means for real people's lives (What types of social action might be suggested by your research?

How would this action affect your participants?). If the research is applied, you should make clear recommendations about what decisions or solutions you determine the data best supports.

Summary Points

- Qualitative interviews are the best method for investigating the complexity of social life and for truly understanding others' experience as they perceive it.

- Interviewing is based not on the principles of the scientific method, but on techniques for fostering rapport with the participant in order to yield rich data that are high on validity.

- Although the results are not generalizable, the interviewer will understand the experiences of a small group of people extremely well.

- Interviews allow the participant to direct the researcher toward important areas of relevance that the researcher may have never considered had a more structured research method been used.

- Conducting high-quality interviews is a skill that requires time and practice.

- Analysis occurs simultaneously with data collection, and it is made systematic by the search for evidence and negative cases.

Key Terms

a priori codes 56
analyst-constructed codes 56
axial coding 56
bias 28
case study 43
codes 55
coding 55
conceptualization 60
confidential 34
convenience sampling 40
data validity 61
evaluation research 23
frequencies 56
gatekeeper 42
generalizing 39
indigenous codes 56
inductive 55

informed consent statement 34
interpretivist methodology 28
interviewing 23
loosely structured interviews 25
magnitudes 56
markers 52
maximum variation sampling 40
memos 58
methodology 28
needs assessments 23
negative cases 57
nonprobability sampling 39
not replicable 62
objective 28
open codes 56
open coding 56

operationalization 60
pilot interviews 44
processes 57
pseudonym 34
purposive sampling 40
rapport 45
research participants 28
selective coding 57
semi-structured interview 24
snowball sampling 40
structure 57
thick description 49
transcribe 54
types 56
valid analysis 62
validity 61
wide open 49

Observation and Ethnography

Observation is a research method in which you carefully watch people, usually in a natural setting (that is, not one you have created or manipulated), over a period of time in order to learn about their patterns of interaction and behavior. Most of the time, researchers use observation to collect qualitative data, but occasionally it is used quantitatively. If you count the number of people who are talking on their cell phones as they pass by your university's student union building, for example, you could collect quantitative data on the gender of the talkers, how many of them are walking alone, and how many are with groups, as well as the percentage of those talking on their cell phones out of the total number of people passing. This is quantitative because you are simply counting people who are and are not talking on their cell phones. Most often, however, observation is conducted qualitatively, focusing on a small group of people to understand the nuances of their interactional and behavioral patterns. Qualitative observation involves watching people carefully and in detail, often over long periods of time. For example, you might set out to observe how workers go about establishing friendships and coalitions at a brand-new work site, such as the opening of a new retail store. You would watch employees at the store over a period of many weeks or months. Rather than counting the number of employees engaged in particular behaviors, you would take detailed notes (called **field notes**) on the minute details of what you observe them doing and saying. Because this type of observation—qualitative observation—is much more commonly used than quantitative observation, that will be our focus throughout this chapter.

Ethnography is a research method related to observation. As with observation, watching people and taking detailed field notes about their behavior are primary tasks of the ethnographer. Three key features distinguish it from "pure" observation, however. First, in doing ethnography you immerse yourself as deeply into the culture or subculture as possible in order to understand it as well as you can. Although observers may (though not necessarily) remain somewhat detached or removed from the people they are observing, ethnographers *must* become deeply immersed. For example, in observation research, if you observe homeless people in a park three times per week, the people you are observing may not even be aware that you are observing

REAL PEOPLE, REAL RESEARCH

Paige O'Connell

While Paige was a senior sociology major, she was hired by a consulting firm whose objective was to help the California Energy Commission to understand social and cultural issues in energy use. They hired student researchers across the state, and each researcher conducted mini-ethnographies with a different subculture or population. Paige focused on people who live in tiny houses. She attended meetings of the Tiny House Club on campus and participated in their efforts to build a tiny house. She also conducted formal and informal interviews with people who were living in tiny houses or who were actively working toward that goal. Her observations and interviews focused on the ways in which people in tiny homes interact with technology such as cell phones and laptops, as well as how they approached energy usage. As part of her data collection, she took field notes and transcribed her interviews.

Jessica Moore

Jessica is a clinical case manager at Easter Seals. She currently works on analyses of problem behavior for teens with autism. She and her team have set up four conditions that may influence the teens' behavior. They first conduct a preference assessment to determine what conditions the participant prefers (such as food or sensory items) prior to creating each condition, in order to determine what to give access to or withhold. They then run the conditions in a predetermined order for brief periods of time. They conduct detailed observations to determine which conditions elicit the highest rate of problem behavior. Different observers are trained to be consistent with one another in their observations and notetaking. Jessica then analyzes the observers' notes from across the different conditions to develop effective interventions to reduce the problem behavior.

them; in this case, though you are watching them, you certainly are not immersed in their culture. Anything that happens to them outside the park remains outside of your knowledge, and the only behavior you can witness is that which occurs in the park during the three times per week that you sit down to do your observations. As an ethnographer, however, you would not just watch this group of homeless people from afar. You would hang out with them, not only observing them in the park, but going with them wherever they go during the day, eating with them, perhaps even sleeping where they sleep. And, most typically, you would not do this just three times a week, but as much as you possibly can every day for a period of several months or even a year or two. In this way, you would observe not only what goes on at the park, but everything that this group does, in order to better help you understand its subculture. I should be careful to emphasize here that not all observation researchers do their research from afar—many do integrate themselves into the group; ethnographers, however, *always* do.

Second, though observation research is based on watching and listening to naturally occurring behaviors and conversations, ethnography combines them with other ways of collecting information that is used as data. Ethnographers do not only watch; they often conduct qualitative interviews, use available documents, and ask people who are knowledgeable about the setting informal questions that provide them with more information. Ethnographers use all available resources to get information that will help them better understand the culture or subculture they are studying, while observation researchers rely primarily on their own powers of observation for data.

Third, ethnography takes significantly longer. Ethnography requires at least several months, and sometimes years, of cultural immersion in order to answer the research question. Observation, on the other hand, usually lasts a few weeks to a few months. This difference is significant, and the depth and complexity of your research questions should reflect these different time investments; that is, research questions for observation usually tap into phenomena that are less complex than those of ethnography.

Now that I've made these distinctions, it is important to note that sometimes the boundaries between observation and ethnography can become somewhat blurred, and the descriptions above are in some ways ideal types, with the distinctions being less clear in actual practice. In many ways the two methods have more commonalities than differences—hence their treatment together in this chapter. Throughout this chapter, when the differences are important, I will be careful to differentiate observation from ethnography, but keep in mind that when I do, I am referring to them as ideal types.

Ethnography is rarely used in applied research because it requires too much time—if there is a problem to solve or decision to be made, it just isn't feasible to wait a year or two to address it while you immerse yourself in the subculture. Observation, however, sometimes is used in applied research. When observation is used this way, it may typically be in a classroom or workplace setting for evaluation of some policy, curriculum, or organizational change that has been made. (See Chapter 8, on experimental evaluation research.) Applied observation research is particularly useful when studying children: observation of their behavior is sometimes more telling than interviews would be because children can have a hard time articulating their thoughts or even thinking about how a policy or curricular change has affected them. Sometimes observation is used to recommend rather than evaluate policy changes by assessing what is not working in a particular context and identifying the changes needed.

CHECK YOUR UNDERSTANDING

You have been hired by a major department store chain to study managers' interactions with employees in the workplace in order to help the company better understand how to motivate and retain employees. Would you choose observation or ethnography for this research project? Why?

Methodology

Like interviews, both qualitative observation and ethnography are based on interpretivist methodology. With ethnography, your viewpoint is expanded beyond the perspective of individuals to a particular cultural or subcultural perspective. That is, you try to develop a cultural understanding of the phenomenon you are studying. With observation, on the other hand, instead of trying to understand how people *see* the world, which is internal and not observable, your primary aim is to try to really understand their patterns of behavior and interaction. Despite the different focus, observation still fits within interpretivist methodology because you are trying to understand the interactions as a native within that group would understand them; that is, you try to understand them as thoroughly as the people whom you are studying and to interpret their behaviors as they would. With both observation and ethnographic research, then, understanding a few people or one context in great depth is your aim, not generalizing your findings beyond those you study.

 Reminder: Interpretivist methodology is a research philosophy that generally aims to understand the world through someone else's eyes.

As with all methodology, because it is the underlying philosophy guiding the research, interpretivist methodology affects all aspects of observation and ethnographic research: the research question, the sampling strategy, the way in which the data are collected, the method of analysis, and the criteria by which we can evaluate the research. Thus interpretivist research done with these two research methods shares many characteristics with interview research. For example, the relationship between the researcher and participant (presuming they know you are observing them) must be based on trust. Allowing someone to watch and document their every move makes a participant every bit as vulnerable as does revealing their innermost thoughts and feelings, so the participant must feel comfortable enough with you that they are willing to behave in their usual ways while you are observing. If you don't achieve sufficient rapport with your participant, they may change, disguise, or temporarily cease behavior about which they don't trust you to know. The participant must feel confident that in conducting your observations you will remain nonjudgmental regarding any behavior in which they engage. Additionally, they must trust that you will not use the information in ways that will hurt them personally, or that will disrupt the intragroup dynamics already in play. In exchange, the participant will allow you to watch them go about their daily activities, sometimes in very personal contexts. In this way, the research is a collaborative project between the researcher and participant in producing the data.

The data collection is done concurrently with analysis, with the analytic process affecting the emergent design of the data collection. That is, as you begin to notice patterns, you may alter your focus, or the behaviors/interactions you choose to observe. You may also observe for new or different facets of those behaviors (for example, perhaps you initially were focused on verbal exchanges, but as your analysis proceeds, you begin to think that the nonverbal cues are more important than you originally recognized, so you begin to pay more attention to them).

As with interviews, the goal of the observer or the ethnographer is not to be "scientific" or "unbiased"; rather, it is to get as accurate a picture of behavioral and interactional patterns as possible. Replicability is impossible: I have had 30 students watching the same preschool classroom for the same 30-minute period, and they have all seen different things. Different researchers will focus on and perceive different aspects of behavior based on their interests, backgrounds, and personalities. The physical vantage point from which they make the observations also makes a difference. Is this biased? Yes. But remember that interpretivists believe that *all* research (even the most "scientific") is biased. Rather than trying to avoid bias or sweep it under the rug, interpretivists would say that you should acknowledge those biases outright and discuss in your research report the ways in which your biases might have affected the data you collected. This allows your readers to judge for themselves the accuracy of your data.

 Reminder: For interpretivists, **bias** is any characteristic, experience, knowledge, or attitude you have that might affect the research you do.

Theory

Early symbolic interactionists engaged in ethnographic and observation research. Today, researchers coming from a wide range of theoretical perspectives engage in both observation and ethnographic research, including feminist theorists, ethnomethodologists, conflict theorists and neo-Marxists. Ethnography and observation research have particularly been used to study school environments and teen culture, homelessness, and criminal activity, and so sometimes use the smaller-scale theories that get used with those specific topics.

Theory often is used to help determine the research question, which concepts might be important to the research, the behaviors to observe, and, for ethnographic research especially, the field site in which to do it. As with interview research, you might view the data through the lens of a particular theory to help you identify and interpret the patterns. Or, you might inductively build theory from the observational and ethnographic data that you gather.

 Reminder: To work **inductively** means you let the hunches and theories develop out of the data itself, as opposed to collecting data in order to test pre-existing theories and hypotheses.

Research Questions

Observation

Observation is excellent for understanding patterns of behavior and interaction. It is particularly useful for studying behavior to which people might be unlikely to admit, or about which they might be totally unaware. Observation research can only answer questions about things you can see and hear, however, and is unable to answer questions about motivations, feelings, perspectives, or anything else that goes on in people's heads.

Additionally, although it is an excellent method for documenting sequences of events, observation research is not a good method for determining causes or effects of behavior because it is difficult to determine causes visually; just because one behavior precedes another does not mean that the first *caused* the second. The exception to this rule is if you are using observation to conduct a type of applied research called **evaluation research**—that is, in order to evaluate the effectiveness of some policy or program changes that have been made. In this case, you could only ask research questions about cause and effect if you plan on conducting your observations at the same site(s) both before and after the changes have been made, in order to make comparisons between the behaviors before and after the change. For example, if you want to see how your school's anti-bullying campaign is working, you would need to observe the kids on the playground, in the halls, in the lunchroom, and coming and going from school *before* the campaign begins; that way, after the children have been exposed to the campaign, you can look to see if it has made any changes in their behavior. Thus, questions about effectiveness (a form of cause and effect) can be asked using observation, but only with a highly structured research design, and when you can compare the behaviors both before and after the program/policy is instituted (Chapter 8 is devoted exclusively to this type of program evaluation research). We will learn more about cause and effect in the next chapter, but for now, it should be underscored that this is a special use of observation research—one that must be done very carefully and methodically, in a more structured way than is most basic observation research.

In sum, research questions suitable for observation research focus on describing observable behavior and interaction. Examples of good research questions that can appropriately be answered with observation are shown in Box 3.1. In all of these cases,

BOX 3.1
RESEARCH QUESTIONS APPROPRIATE FOR OBSERVATION RESEARCH

Research Question	Appropriate for Observation Research Because It Examines . . .
How do parents initiate conversations with strangers at children's parties?	interactional patterns
What nonverbal behaviors do college students engage in while flirting?	nonverbal behaviors
How do cashiers and customers interact while the purchases are being rung up?	behavior that is so routine that the participant doesn't reflect on it
How do restaurant servers treat thin customers similarly or differently than they do overweight customers?	behavior to which the participant is unlikely to admit
How is white privilege reinforced by white professors in the classroom?	behavior about which the participant may be unaware
How does the implementation of the "Customer Service Extraordinaire" training program affect employees' interactions with customers?	evaluation of a program through identifying changes in behavior

BOX 3.2
AVOID THESE ERRORS IN WRITING RESEARCH QUESTIONS FOR OBSERVATION

Research Question	Explanation of Error
How do bartenders emotionally endure hearing customers' sad stories night after night?	Not appropriate for observation because it asks about how bartenders feel and cope with a certain circumstance. Observation research cannot determine what goes on inside people's minds.
How does the treatment of white children differ from the treatment of Native American children in a middle school setting?	Treatment by whom (other students, the teacher, etc.)? The unit of analysis, such as teachers, needs to be included in the question.
How well do teachers' methods of teaching keep students paying attention?	This is a quantitative question; most observation research is qualitative.

the behaviors and interactions tell us not only about the particular individuals being studied, but also about the norms and values of the culture or subculture to which they belong. Note that despite this, your unit of analysis in observation research is individuals, not the culture or

 Reminder: Your **unit of analysis** is the "who" or "what" you are collecting information about.

subculture. Also note that, as the question about wait staff in Box 3.1 demonstrates, observation research may effectively be used to study comparisons across different groups. Use Box 3.2 to make sure you avoid common errors in writing research questions for observation research.

CHECK YOUR UNDERSTANDING

Write a research question about education that is appropriate for observation research. Explain why this research question is appropriate for observation research.

Ethnography

Research questions appropriate for ethnography also focus on observable behavior and interaction, though because other sources of data such as interviews may be used as part of the research, ethnographers are not as strictly limited to research questions that focus exclusively on behavior. Often (though not always), ethnographic research questions focus on the level of culture, subculture, or group and use one of these as the unit of analysis rather than the individual. Ethnographic research cannot answer research questions about cause and effect. Additionally, ethnography is not an appropriate method for studying comparisons between groups or field sites because the goal of ethnographic research is to immerse yourself as deeply as possible in a particular culture, so it is impossible to fully do so in more than one culture at the same time.

Box 3.3 lists some research questions appropriate for ethnographic research. Notice that all of these require in-depth knowledge of the culture or subculture to answer the research question. Because data collection in ethnography takes a long time, you can help differentiate for yourself whether a research question is appropriate for

BOX 3.3
RESEARCH QUESTIONS APPROPRIATE FOR ETHNOGRAPHY

Research Question	Appropriate for Ethnography Because It Examines . . .
How do gang members establish and reinforce hierarchies within the gang?	behavior within a subculture
What are the norms that govern friendships among elementary-school-age girls?	norms of a subculture
How do Amish communities shield their children from the influences of modern American culture?	group behavior within a subculture

BOX 3.4
AVOID THESE COMMON ERRORS IN WRITING RESEARCH QUESTIONS FOR ETHNOGRAPHY

Research Question	Explanation of Error
How do teachers handle tardy policies with students who come to class late?	This question would not require extensive research. Ethnography requires immersion in a setting for at least 6 months. This question is more appropriate for observation research, which requires much less time for observing.
What is the social norm for rural town high school students in regard to school clothing choices compared to larger city high schools?	A comparison between two groups is not possible in one ethnographic research study because in ethnography you immerse yourself as deeply as possible in one group, which doesn't allow you to be simultaneously immersed in a second group.
How do newly hired employees at Google navigate the social environment at a new workplace?	This is not appropriate for ethnographic research because Google is a huge company, and new employees will be spread out across many different departments rather than constituting a single social group. Thus you could not immerse yourself in a single group of these employees. Also note that the focus here is on the individual, but in ethnography the unit of analysis is usually the subculture; in this case, it should be the subculture of Google.

ethnographic research by asking yourself if it is something complex enough that it could be studied for months or years. If not, it may be a more appropriate topic for observation research. Also note that although observation would be an important part of the data collection, research questions for ethnography also leave room for other methods of data collection, such as interviewing. Refer to Box 3.4 for examples of common errors to avoid in ethnographic research.

CHECK YOUR UNDERSTANDING

Write a research question about a school-related subculture that is appropriate for ethnographic research. Explain why this research question is appropriate for ethnographic research.

Literature Review

The literature review is done in the same way and for the same reasons as the other methods. For the observer or ethnographer, the literature review is especially helpful in providing important guidance and information in choosing a location or group for observing (**field site**). If you are interested in observing classroom interactions, for example, you would review the literature on classroom interaction to try to determine what we know about patterns of interaction across different contexts (different types of schools, grade levels, student-body or faculty demographic characteristics, etc.). You may choose a site significantly different from the others that have been studied to see whether the patterns found by other researchers hold up even when the sites of observation are quite different. Or you may try to choose a site that is very similar to that in another study to see whether the findings represent a larger social pattern. A third strategy would be to try to match the field site you choose very closely to one used in previous research with the exception of one key characteristic, such as the racial or social class composition of the school.

You will also use the literature review to help you identify what you want to focus your observations on and how to operationalize what you observe. In reviewing the literature, you may become interested in learning more about a particular behavior reported by another researcher, or about the absence of any mention of a behavior that you expect exists. Additionally, your literature review can sensitize you to behaviors that you might have otherwise overlooked or deemed insignificant.

Finally, by reading research reports written by other observers and ethnographers, you can learn something about how to write up your research. Unlike statistical research, there are many different styles of presenting observation and ethnography, and each of them is less formulaic than the write-ups of research using some of the other research methods. Thus, in doing your literature review, you can also look for a style of research presentation that will best fit with your topic, your data, and your objectives.

Ethics

The ethical precautions that you must take for observation and ethnography depend, in part, on whom you are observing and where you are observing them. Observations that are done in **public places** in which there are few or no restrictions on who may be there, such as a city park, shopping mall, subway car, or airport, generally do not require informed consent. **Semi-private places** are those that are not totally restricted, yet are not open to just anyone—there are some criteria or typical characteristics for being there. Additionally, the people are usually assumed to be there for a common purpose, and if there are ongoing gatherings there, it is generally the same people who gather each time, such as a classroom, a Weight Watchers meeting, or a Bible study group. **Private places** are those that are not open without invitation. Offices, homes or apartments, baby showers, medical appointments, weddings, and RVs are all examples of places or events that are considered private. For observation research, informed consent is generally required for observations in semi-private or private places, but not for those in public places. Ethnography often spans all of these types of locales and therefore requires informed consent. Informed consent statements for observation and ethnography usually include the following:

- Start with a short, one- or two-sentence description of the research topic.

- Provide a description of who is eligible to participate.

- Describe how the research will be used (for example, for publication or for presentation to an employer).

- State who will be observed and in what contexts and locations.

- Provide an estimate of how often and for how long participants will be observed (for example, twice a week during lunch break) and how long the research will continue (for example, 6 months).

- Assure the participant that the research will be completely confidential, which means that no one other than the researcher will know the identity of the participants.
  o Steps taken to protect the participants' identities include giving each participant a pseudonym to be used in field notes and on video recording labels and hiding the location of the observations. For example, if you observed at Chico High School, you might end up giving the school the pseudonym Cal High, and then be somewhat vague about the location of the school so that it can't be identified, such as that it is located in a small city in northern California.

- o Identifying information about any of the participants must be deleted from the field notes.

- Outline the steps that will be taken to ensure that the field notes (and video recordings, if there are any) are kept secure and confidential.
  - o Both should be kept in a locked room or cabinet.
  - o Electronic files should be password-protected.

- If the interview will be audio or video recorded, this must be stated in the informed consent statement.
  - o Additionally, the participant must be advised that they have the right to have the recording device turned off at any point during the interview and that you will only recommence recording with the participant's permission.
  - o You must state who, other than yourself, will see or have access to the video recordings.
  - o You must also disclose what will be done with the video recordings after the completion of the research. (Usually, though not always, the recordings are erased.)

- State that participation in this research is completely voluntary and that the participant may withdraw from the research at any time without penalty or repercussion.

- Fully disclose any potential risks of participating in the research.
  - o Often there are none, but because field sites can sometimes be difficult to disguise, there may be the risk that someone will identify individuals in your study by identifying the field site, which could cause embarrassment or affect their reputation.

- Full disclosure of any immediate benefits to the participants for their participation in the research. (There usually are none.)

- Provide your contact information.

- Provide the contact information for the chair of the governing Institutional Review Board (IRB). The participant needs to be advised that they may contact this person if they feel that any of their rights as a research participant have been violated.

- State that the participant has a right to ask additional questions about the research and that these questions will be answered.

- Finally, the informed consent statement should have a statement indicating that the participant has read the entire document, that all their questions about the research have been answered, and that they have given their consent to participate in the research. This should be followed by a place for the signature and the date. In all but rare cases, the participant should sign their real name, not the pseudonym, on the informed consent statement.

BOX 3.5
SAMPLE INFORMED CONSENT STATEMENT FOR OBSERVATION AND ETHNOGRAPHY

You are invited to participate in a study on the interactions between nurses and patients in medical settings. The purpose of this study is to understand the role these interactions play in your overall treatment at the hospital. You are eligible to participate if you are currently being treated by a physician at Seaside Hospital for nonemergency care, are at least 18 years of age, and have the capability of making your own medical decisions (that is, you do not need a family member to make medical decisions for you). This research is being conducted by Dr. Robyn Banks, a professor in the Department of Sociology at Seaside University. The results of this research will be used for campus and professional presentation, as well as for publication.

If you decide to participate in this study, I will be observing the conversations you have with the nurses during your stay at the hospital. I may take notes about these conversations during and after the conversation. Participating in the study does not grant me permission to see your medical files, to which I have no access.

Your participation in this research is entirely confidential. Your name will not appear in any of my notes. You will be given a fake name, which will be used in my notes and in my final research report. The name and location of the hospital, as well as the identities of the nursing staff, will also be changed in the final report. Any information that could be used to identify you as an individual will be changed or deleted. That being said, if you have a very unusual medical condition, your identity may be harder to hide, and someone reading the report may be able to discern your identity.

No one aside from myself will have access to my notes. My notes will be written in a notebook that will remain on my body at all times while I'm on hospital grounds. Immediately after leaving the hospital, I will transfer my notes to a computer, which will be password-protected. The original handwritten notes will be stored in a locked filing cabinet, and will be destroyed at the end of the research project.

Your participation in this research is entirely voluntary. Your participation in this study will have no impact on the medical care you receive. You have the right to ask questions about this study and to have your questions answered. You may experience some emotional discomfort from having conversations about your medical condition observed. There are no other risks to your participation in this research; nor are there any anticipated benefits to you. If you decide to participate in this study, you may ask me to leave the room or to stop taking notes at any time. You have the right to withdraw your participation at any time without penalty.

If you have questions or concerns about this study, you may contact me, Dr. Banks, at (987) 555-1234, or via e-mail at rbanks@seaside.edu. If you feel your rights as a research participant have been violated, you should contact the chair of the Human Subjects in Research Committee at SU, Dr. Strict, at (987) 555-5678.

I have read the above and have had all my questions about participation in this study answered to my satisfaction. I understand that my participation in this study is completely voluntary and that I can withdraw from this study at any time without penalty.

Signature _____

Date _____

Special Considerations

As with interviewing, if you plan to observe anyone under the age of 18 in a private or semi-private venue, you will need the consent of the parents; the consent of those responsible for the location; and, in some cases (check with your IRB), the consent of the minors being observed. Additionally, if your observations will likely include illegal behavior, you will need to take extra precautions to protect your participants. This may include keeping field notes with a type of shorthand or code that makes them difficult for anyone but you to decipher, keeping details of illegal behaviors out of your field notes, destroying field notes upon completion of the research, and being willing to spend time in jail for contempt of court rather than releasing field notes that would incriminate one of your respondents in illegal activity. Although you may be intrigued by learning about criminal activity, observation research that includes illegal behavior is fraught with ethical issues and dilemmas. If you know in advance that your participants are planning to commit a crime, you could be charged in relation to the crime if you do nothing to stop it. Additionally, you may feel an extreme sense of guilt, shame, or regret if anyone gets hurt during the commission of that crime. For these reasons, in addition to the dangers to yourself and others, such research projects should not be undertaken by anyone but the most experienced researchers.

Other Ethical Issues

It typically is very important to protect not only the identities of individuals you observe, but also the location of your observations. The reason is simple: If your audience can pinpoint the location of the observations (or the group being observed), the confidentiality of many of the individuals in your research may be compromised. Let's take again our example of observation research at Chico High School. Although it is a large school, there may be only one African American teacher on campus or one middle-aged male teacher in the Spanish department. Additionally, because there are so few of them, all of the administrators will be easily identifiable, as will some of the students: The captain of the football team, the student with the blue mohawk, the victim of regular harassment or bullying, or the exceptionally gifted art student may all be readily identifiable to those who know people at or are affiliated with the institution. It is important, therefore, not only to keep the location of observation as unidentifiable as possible, but also to change or omit information that may make a participant vulnerable to identification.

Another common ethical issue that arises in observation research and ethnography is that of the researcher's self-presentation and the use of deception. Some researchers feel that they will get better data if their real identities and purposes are not revealed. A researcher investigating Alcoholics Anonymous, for example, may believe that they will get a truer sense of the group if they represent themselves as both a researcher and a recovering alcoholic, thus putting others at ease and creating a sense of shared experience (hence rapport) with those they are observing. Additionally, they may believe that the people they are observing will behave more naturally (thus producing more valid data) if they think the researcher is "one of them." In general, however, it is best to *avoid* whenever possible the use of deception in your research. Although such deceit might have the advantage of easing initial acceptance of the research by the group, if you are caught lying or misrepresenting yourself, the risk is great that it will destroy your credibility with the group and thus jeopardize members' willingness to continue cooperating in the research. Using deception in your research means that you will have to lie—probably repeatedly—to maintain your deception. And though the risks are great (indeed, your entire research project is at risk should you get caught), the reward is minimal: It may take you longer to build rapport or acceptance from group members who know you are unlike (or maybe even skeptical of) them, but eventually displays of honesty, trust, and respect will build a deeper degree of rapport than will deception. Although group members may initially modify their behavior somewhat in order to make certain impressions on the researcher, this rarely lasts for long (Berg, 2007), and as the observer becomes a regular fixture in the setting, members resume their natural behavior. Deception should be used only when there is no other alternative for gathering the data.

A very real issue for observers, and especially ethnographers, is what to do if not everyone in the group agrees to participate in the research. This is a thorny issue, and your local IRB will have specific requirements in this case (see also Box 3.6). The lack

BOX 3.6
DECISION PATH FOR CONSENT IN OBSERVATION AND ETHNOGRAPHY

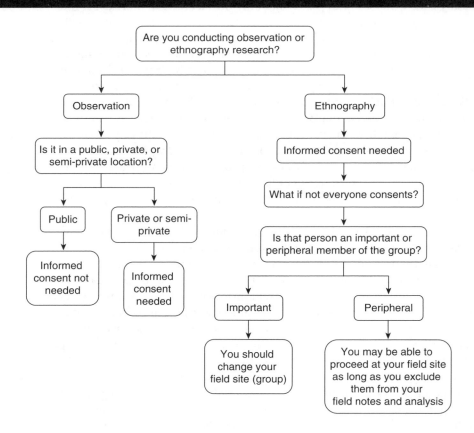

of consent for participation by one person in the group may be manageable if that person is somewhat peripheral to the group. Your IRB may allow you, for example, to proceed with the research as long as you take no field notes about behaviors involving this individual and they do not appear anywhere in your analysis. This becomes more difficult, however, if they are a central figure or leader in the group. Not only would that mean excluding a higher percentage of behaviors and interactions that you observe, but that person is likely to exert greater influence on others in the group, and their lack of participation may make it difficult for you to establish the sort of trust and rapport needed to gather highly valid data. In this case, or if several members of the group decline to participate, you will be better off finding a new site for your research—one where you will find more willing participants.

CHECK YOUR UNDERSTANDING

If you were carrying out an observation research project based on your research question about education, what are all the things you would need to do to protect your participants? Remember to apply the principles of ethics to this particular case, so that if you are observing minors, for example, you will do some things differently than if you are observing adults.

Sampling

Observation

In observation research, sampling requires decisions about who will be observed and which behaviors and interactions will be observed. This means you will be sampling many different times at many different levels: location, people, behaviors on which to focus, and times and dates. Each of these requires different decisions, making sampling a multilayered, ongoing, and somewhat complex process.

The first, and perhaps biggest, decision you will make about sampling is the location or group for your observations. Most often, you will only choose one location (though, occasionally, observation researchers with large budgets and a lot of time will choose multiple locations for comparison purposes). This is a very big decision because *everything* about your research will be affected by where you choose to observe. There are several factors that typically go into this decision. One is *access*: You must choose a location where you will be allowed to observe, and where both the participants and the gatekeepers will be willing to cooperate. A second is *theoretical appropriateness*: Not only should your research site be one to which you will have access, but it should be one of the best choices for helping you answer your research question. This site should offer opportunities, characteristics, or other features that interest you substantively and theoretically, so that it is a good and logical choice for learning about the phenomenon you are setting out to research. A third is *feasibility*: Your location should be someplace that you will have both the time and money to observe. If observing here involves travel, you need to be sure that both your budget and time schedule take this into account, with extra money left over in case you need to spend more time observing than you had originally planned.

Once you have chosen a location, you will also need to sample days and times for your observations. If you are researching the ways in which teachers interact differently with boys and girls in preschool, you would not just observe the lunch hour every Friday simply because you have that time free. There may be very special things about the lunch hour that produce different types of gendered interactions with the children than you would find at other times of the day. Additionally, Fridays may be systematically different in some way than other days. Perhaps on Mondays the boys take care of setting the table and getting the room ready for lunch, while on Fridays it is the girls who take on these tasks. If you only observe on Fridays, you might conclude that traditional gender roles are more heavily reinforced than they actually are. Hence, unless your research question specifically directs you to observe during a particular time, you must draw a sample of the times at which to observe. Sometimes researchers choose days and times with some sort of **random sampling**—that is, those chosen purely by chance, such as being drawn out of a hat. Often, however, the sampling strategy you will use will be *strategic* (purposive). Knowing the preschool's schedule, you may choose to observe at different time periods in order to be representative or inclusive (during lunch time, at parental drop-off, during group play, during storybook time, during independent play, and during nap time). Alternatively, you may choose times that you have reason to believe (based on your own experiences, the literature review, or your own prior knowledge) will be most and/or least likely to yield gendered interactions between the teachers and children. Perhaps you know that when celebrating birthdays with their classmates, the teachers sit the girls at one table and the boys at another, which is not the way the children usually sit when they eat their lunches and snacks together. Because your research question is about gendered interactions, you might decide that observing during this sort of sex-segregated activity is important. This is called **theoretical sampling** because you are choosing situations to observe that are of theoretical interest to you. In practice, of course, a variety of considerations get taken into account when choosing times: the school's schedule, your own schedule, your theoretical interests, and a concern with being representative or at least inclusive in your observations. Note that your sampling methods for dates and times of observations do not need to be determined prior to the start of the research. Indeed, it is often important to make these sampling decisions *after* having spent some time observing in the field, and even to continually reevaluate and readjust your sampling as you gather more data and learn more through the observations you have already completed. The exception to this is if you were conducting evaluation research and observing both prior to and after the implementation of some program or policy, in which case you would want to use the same sampling methods for dates and times of observations across the two tests.

Another feature for which you must sample when doing observation research is the interactions or behaviors that you will observe. If you are observing in a classroom of even 10 preschoolers, it will be absolutely impossible to observe everything that they all say and do at one time. You must therefore decide on what and whom you will focus. This will change often and is highly flexible. Sometimes you might choose those behaviors or interactions that are occurring nearest to you or are easiest to observe (**convenience sampling**). Other times you will use theoretical sampling to decide where you want to position yourself and upon what you will focus. You might purposely choose situations that you think are most likely to be different from the ones you've already observed, or that involve children who don't usually interact with one another, because you think these will provide you with more or new information. Sampling the people and behaviors on which you decide to focus may be flexible and ever-changing. You will make countless and continual decisions about the focus of your attention as participants move about the location, engage in new or different behaviors, and take part in new interactions. It is generally best, especially in the earlier stages of data collection, not to be rigid about this stage of your sampling or to adhere strictly to your preconceived notions about what you *should* be paying attention to. Instead, be open to all the possibilities of what is happening around you, and use your research question to guide you in making your decisions. That being said, having some general ideas of how you might sample can help give you some focus during your observation and make the process of observation less overwhelming. In other words, in the early stages of data collection, it's a balancing act: It can be helpful to have some ideas of how you will sample, but you should still be open to new possibilities. The further you get into your data collection, the more specific and precise your sampling of behaviors and interactions will likely become.

BOX 3.7
SAMPLING FOR OBSERVATION

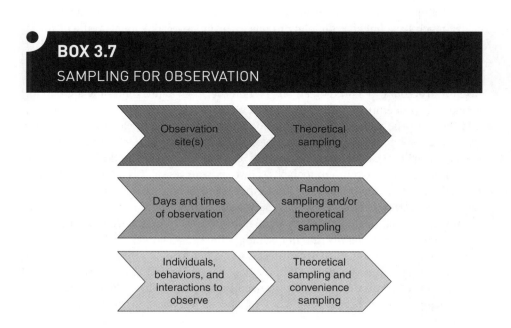

Observation site(s) → Theoretical sampling

Days and times of observation → Random sampling and/or theoretical sampling

Individuals, behaviors, and interactions to observe → Theoretical sampling and convenience sampling

As you can see, sampling for observation is complex and ongoing. Though you will choose the site early in your research project, you will continue to make sampling decisions *every single time you observe*, as you choose the people, behaviors, and interactions on which to focus your attention (see Box 3.7). Thus, in observation research, sampling is not a discrete stage of the research process; it is an ongoing activity about which you must continually think. It is very important that you also document all of your various sampling decisions in your field notes, so that in analyzing and reporting on the data you can reflect on how your sampling choices affected the data you collected.

CHECK YOUR UNDERSTANDING

Describe how you would sample for your observation research on education. In so doing, be sure to answer each of the following questions:

- Where would you conduct your observations? How would you choose the site(s)?
- When (days and times) would you conduct your observations? How would you choose these days and times?
- How would you sample the behaviors and interactions that you will observe? How would you decide what to sample?
- When would you make all of these sampling decisions?

Ethnography

Sampling for ethnography is simpler than it is for observation. In ethnography, you pretty much have only *one* sampling to make: the group of individuals you will study. In ethnography, this one group is your **case**—it will yield the sum total of all your data and what you learn. Thus, although the procedure is simple, the decision is a serious and weighty one into which you should not enter lightly. The same sorts of considerations taken into account for choosing an observation site apply here to choosing a group for conducting your ethnography: The people must be willing to cooperate in your research, and they must be a theoretically interesting group that can best help you answer your research question. In interviews, if you have one interviewee who was not a very good choice, you will have many other participants (cases) to compensate for this. If you choose a bad research site for your ethnography, however, your research is in trouble. Because of the intensity of the immersion, most ethnographers only choose one site for each research project. If it ends up not being such a good choice, your entire project is compromised. Thus, ethnographers often spend a great deal of time choosing their field site.

Ethnographers generally do not sample times, behaviors, or interactions as observers do because it is usually unnecessary. When you do ethnography, in order to be as immersed in the culture as possible, you will spend as much time as possible with the group. Hence, you don't need to sample for times during the day or days during the week because you will be spending just about every day with them.

Similarly, in all of this time you will be spending with the group, you will witness a huge range of behaviors, so it is not necessary to sample them—you will observe and write about *as much as you possibly can*, rather than focusing on particular behaviors or interactions.

> ### CHECK YOUR UNDERSTANDING
>
> Going back to your ethnographic research question on an educational subculture, describe how you would choose your case. Then describe how sampling for ethnography is different than sampling for observation.

Conceptualizing and Operationalizing

Conceptualization and operationalization do not constitute separate steps in the research process for either observation or ethnography. They occur repeatedly *before, during,* and *after* data collection. When you decide what concepts are important to answering your research question and you define them, you are conceptualizing. For example, if your research question is about the pressures placed on team members of student athletes, you will need to come up with a working definition of *pressure*. Let's say your definition of the word is "explicit or implied expectations expressed verbally or nonverbally that teammates will exhibit particular behaviors, characteristics, or achievements." This is **conceptualization**: writing the definitions of the abstract concepts that are important to your research. The next step, then, is **operationalization**: deciding which behaviors you will observe for. In other words, you are deciding which behaviors, of the many you will see, are relevant to your study and will capture the information you need. In our example, you will need to decide which specific behaviors are likely to reveal or constitute *pressure*. Yelling at, teasing, complimenting, and putting guilt on someone might all constitute, in some situations, *pressure*, as might giving steep rewards for achievement and negative sanctions for lack of achievement. Now that you have operationalized *pressure*, you will then try to look for examples of these behaviors in your observations. You will also keep your eye out for other behaviors that might constitute pressure that you hadn't previously thought of or observed, and if you see one, add it to the list of things that you continue to look for. This is also operationalizing, because it is the process of determining which behaviors capture the abstract concept (*pressure*) that you are trying to observe. In other words, in observation and ethnography, operationalizing is an ongoing activity that occurs through the process of data collection, not just a mental exercise that occurs in advance. Conceptualization and operationalization also occur during the analytic process of coding of field notes, in the same way that they do for the coding of interview transcripts. That is, developing codes and giving them definitions is conceptualizing, while the process of open coding the field notes using those codes is operationalizing.

CHECK YOUR UNDERSTANDING

Thinking about your research on education, take one concept that you think would be important to your research and conceptualize it by writing a working definition of it. Then operationalize the definition by coming up with a list of behaviors that might fit. Once you are involved in collecting the data, what else would you do that would count as operationalizing?

Preparing for Data Collection

 Reminder: The **IRB** is the Institutional Review Board that is charged with protecting the rights and well-being of people who participate in research.

The preparation for data collection must be carefully timed with your application to the IRB. In order to apply for IRB approval, you will need to know the site that you want to observe, about how often you will observe, and over what period of time. Thus, if you will be observing in a private or semi-private space, you will need some confidence that those at the site will, indeed, permit you to conduct your research there. At the same time, you can't ask for informed consent until after your research has been approved by the IRB. Thus, you may have informal or tentative conversations with someone at the site to determine the feasibility and access you will have so that you may apply for IRB approval; however, you cannot directly ask for participation until after you have received that approval.

 Reminder: A **gatekeeper** is someone affiliated with the group, site, or organization who introduces you to the right people and helps you to overcome any stumbling blocks in getting permission/cooperation for your research.

Much of the preparation for observation research is focused on finding a good site for your observations. Gaining access to such a site might require the help of a gatekeeper who can help you get permission and cooperation from those responsible for the site and from the participants. Gatekeepers must be chosen carefully—they should be well respected by the people whose cooperation or permission you need. They should also have some influence, even if it isn't formal influence, over those people. They should be reliable and trustworthy, and seen by others as such. In addition, they should understand the group well, so that they know to whom to go for what purpose, how to make your research appeal to different people within the group, and to whom you will need a formal or informal introduction.

Once you've chosen your site, you can begin thinking about how you want to collect your data. Just as with interviews, if you haven't done this type of research before, it is a good idea to practice some observation before you begin your actual project. Observation can be particularly overwhelming to the novice researcher, so getting comfortable observing in a variety of different locations will help enormously when you begin observing at your actual site. Practice observing in places where you just go to watch, as well as in situations or groups in which you are an active participant.

Notice how different it is to observe in these two different contexts. This can help you decide upon the role you will take in your research. You may prefer to be a **nonparticipant observer**. That is, you will not participate in the activities that you observe— you sit on the periphery and focus all of your attention on watching. The advantage of this is that your attention is highly focused, and you can choose to observe a wide range of behaviors and interactions, not just those that involve you. The disadvantage is that participant behavior might be more likely (especially at first) to be altered from its natural occurrence because the participants are highly aware that you are watching them. Additionally, though you have a good vantage point for observing behavior, there is a difference between watching and doing. Think about watching a team sport. Sitting in the stands allows you a bird's-eye view of everything that goes on, but actually playing on the team gives you a close-up, detailed view of some parts of the game, while also giving you knowledge of the emotional, physical, and intellectual processes that occur for players during the game. Thus, you may prefer not to watch from the periphery, but to be involved in the group as a **participant observer**—that is, someone who is a full participant in the group and is also observing the group from the inside. Some researchers distinguish a third possible role: the **observer participant**. This is a sort of middle ground between nonparticipant observer and participant observer, in which you engage in some of the activities in which you observe, but it is clear to you as well as to the participants in your research that your primary objective is observation, not participation. Your decision about which of these three possible roles you wish to take should be based on your research question, your participants, what's feasible (it may not be feasible as a 45-year-old researcher to be a participant observer in adolescent social groups, for example), and your own preferences.

Another aspect of preparing for data collection is the detail work of getting prepared with all the supplies you will need for conducting your observation or ethnographic research. This will include notebooks or computers for note taking, and possibly audio or visual recording devices if you will be recording any of your observations. You must be absolutely certain that you have a secure location in which to store field notes and any audio or video recordings, as confidentiality would quickly be compromised if someone else were to happen upon them.

Data Collection

Once you have gotten both IRB approval and consent from participants, you may begin your data collection. The data collection processes for observation and ethnography are generally both rather lengthy; thus, don't feel that as you start your data collection you must begin answering your research question immediately. Usually observers and ethnographers begin by getting a lay of the land: meeting participants and beginning to learn their names—and, if applicable, their positions; learning about the physical layout of the environment;

 Reminder: All universities and governmental organizations have IRBs, as do many organizations that provide research funding, but other entities may not. Even if your organization doesn't have an IRB, it is your responsibility to take all the same steps that an IRB would require in order to protect your participants.

learning the routine (formal or informal) that participants typically follow; beginning to learn the slang or jargon used by the participants; and generally getting a feel for the place, the people, and their behaviors. Taking field notes is a primary task of data collection in observation research—and continues throughout the study—but it is an especially important part of this first stage, when everything is new to you. We often become acclimated to new contexts and surroundings, so that they seem "natural" to us, but before that happens, the strangeness and newness of it can give us insights into the setting and its happenings. Think about your first few days on your campus or your workplace—some things might have seemed odd to you or different than they do now. You may have been confused, amused, infuriated, or surprised by some of what you saw or experienced those first few days. Ethnographers and observers use these "moments of strangeness" as points of inquiry and insight for their research.

If you are conducting observation research or ethnography, you will need to determine how openly you are able to take notes about the behaviors you are observing. This will depend both on the context and the role (nonparticipant observer, participant observer, or observer participant) that you have chosen to take. If you are able to take notes openly, you must be careful not to spend so much time with your head in your notebook that you miss what you should be observing. If you take notes clandestinely, you need to find appropriate ways to excuse yourself periodically so that you may go somewhere private and get down important information before you forget it. In both cases, the notes you take should be **jotted notes**—that is, limited notes that include only important key words or phrases that will trigger your memory later that same day. Then, when you have the luxury of being out of the observational setting and can focus your attention solely on writing notes, you will use those jotted notes to help you construct more detailed field notes.

Field notes should include **thick description**, which means using very specific details, so that when you read them again in 6 months or a year, you can picture *exactly* what was going on at the time of observation. In some ways, reading field notes can be like reading a novel—the description should be so detailed that you are practically transported to that place in time when you read them. In addition, you should be careful in your field notes to separate your observations from your interpretations, guesses, and hunches. Although there is no one right way to take field notes, it can be helpful to structure your notes so that you separate your interpretations from your observations.

There are many ways to do this. I was taught to divide field notes into descriptive notes, personal notes, theoretical notes, and methodological notes (Corsaro, 1985). Over the years, I have found it helpful for students to also include a fifth category: interpretive notes. **Descriptive notes** are observations—that is, things you can perceive directly with your senses. These are differentiated from interpretations, which are your meanings, understandings, or conclusions. Noting that a person is smiling, for example, is an observation, while describing that person as being happy or pleased is an interpretation: You can see the smile, but you conclude that the smile means the person is happy or pleased.

In the format of field notes I'm offering here, observations belong under descriptive notes, but your interpretations of those observations should be labeled as **interpretive notes**. This helps to differentiate what you see from what you interpret, which keeps the differences clear in both your mind and in your analysis. **Personal notes** include your own reactions to and feelings about your experiences in the situation. **Theoretical notes** are those that record your hunches, guesses, and the connections you make to sociological concepts, existing literature, and/or sociological theories. **Methodological notes** are those that document your sampling choices, especially what you focused your attention upon and why, any difficulties in collecting your data, and anything that might have affected the data you were able to record that day. In general, descriptive notes should be the most prevalent in your notes, with interpretive notes the next most common. In comparison, methodological and theoretical notes will generally be shorter and less frequent entries in your field notes. The proportions will change some, however, the longer you have been conducting your research. Early in the observations, you will primarily be writing descriptive, interpretive, and personal notes. Trying to avoid too much focus on theoretical notes will help you to remain open to what you see, rather than fixated on preconceived notions you had before coming into the field or that you develop before you really understand the setting. As your research progresses, however, you will have increasingly more theoretical notes, as your observations over time lead you to make hunches and to connect your data to sociological concepts and theories. If you choose to use this style, you should write all five types of notes so that they are interspersed throughout your field notes. In other words, you will *not* write all your descriptive notes and then all your interpretive notes, followed by all your theoretical notes, etc. Rather, you will begin writing your descriptive and interpretive notes, and as you describe observations and interpret them, you will develop hunches, thus adding theoretical notes. Methodological notes are often found at the beginning and end of a day's fieldnotes, as you remind yourself of the sampling and other decisions you made. Time, date, and location of observation should *always* appear in your field notes.

Whether or not you use this particular style of note taking (there are others) for your field notes, you *must* record your field notes as soon as possible, and *absolutely on the same day.* You will lose an amazing amount of your memory of what you observed when you go to sleep. Because analysis of observational data is heavily dependent on field notes, the completeness and accuracy of your field notes are of highest importance. I know one ethnographer who had a 1.5-hour commute to her field site, and then, after a 12-hour day in the field, was hungry for dinner upon returning. Because the drive and meal would cause a delay in writing her field notes, she recorded herself talking through her observations of the day on the commute home, and she then used the recordings later in the evening as the basis for her field notes, adding organization and details as she wrote.

Regarding applied research, if you are conducting observation research as part of a needs assessment (rather than to evaluate policies), the research can be done much like basic observation research. If you are conducting evaluation research, however, your research must be much more structured and planned because evaluation research is essentially trying to determine the effect of a program or policy, which requires more structure and precision than generally trying to understand what goes on in a natural setting. Because observation research for evaluation research has some very important differences from what has been described here, I will address it separately in ample detail in Chapter 8.

Ethnography

The process of observing and writing field notes is basically the same for both observation and ethnography. If you are conducting ethnographic research, however, there are additional aspects of data collection to which you will need to pay attention. As you begin to immerse yourself in your field site, you should try to find a **guide** who is a member of the group you are studying and who can help you get along in their culture, answer your questions, and generally help you with your research. (This may also be useful in observation research, depending on the site, group, and research question.)

In addition to observation, if you are conducting ethnography, you will probably want to interview, both formally and informally, a variety of people in the group you are studying. **Formal interviews** typically follow a loosely structured format, and often seek participants' interpretations of and feelings about the things you have observed (note that "formal" here indicates that the interview is prearranged and is identified to the participant as an interview—not that you will be more structured or sterile in your interviewing style). You might also use what you have observed to ask about the history of particular behaviors prior to your arrival and about changes or recurrent patterns in these behaviors. For example, if you are observing in a classroom, and you find that two children seem to go out of their way to avoid a third one, you might ask the teacher about the history of the relationship among these three students. Interviews should always be focused on specific instances or behaviors so as to elicit as much rich information as possible.

As opposed to formal interviews, **informal interviews** consist of the inquiries you might make during casual conversations with members of the group. For example, after observing a tense moment between two participants, you later might find yourself waiting for a bus with a third participant. You could casually bring up the incident ("Wow, that got pretty tense in there!") and gauge the participant's reaction. If they respond, you might ask questions such as "Does that happen between them a lot?" Whatever useful or interesting information arises in your conversation should appear in your field notes, even though it's not a formal, recorded interview. The basic ethics of observation and interviewing still apply here: You should never pressure or coerce participants into talking about something they don't wish to discuss with you, even if you are not in a formal interview setting.

In conducting ethnography, you are not limited to observation and interviewing, though these will probably be your most frequently used sources of data. You can also collect documents and artifacts. If you are studying pressures on athletes, for instance, and you are conducting your ethnography with the university men's basketball team, you might also clip newspaper articles about the team or record news segments from the local television station. You might save some of the advertisements for the games, the e-mails the coach sends to the team, or the photos shared with you by a fan. You might look for more historical sources of information about a player, such as old newspaper articles from before he joined the team or his high school yearbooks, to learn more about him. All of these can become sources of data when conducting ethnography that are used to augment the information you get from your observations and interviews.

Data Analysis

In conducting both observation and ethnography, you engage in data collection and data analysis concurrently. Indeed, as you write field notes, you will be making hunches and guesses, and putting pieces of the puzzle together. One part of the analysis is a formal analysis of the field notes. This can be done with one of the same qualitative data analysis programs that are used to analyze interview transcripts, or it can be done by hand. This analysis involves reading and rereading the many field notes that you've taken, and coding them in the same fashion that you would code interview transcripts. Because so much of the analysis occurs concurrently with data collection, however, and patterns begin to be identified in the field notes, observ-

 Reminder: This stage of analysis is called **open coding** and involves attaching key phrases to parts of your field notes.

ers and ethnographers sometimes skip the open-coding step and instead proceed directly to searching for patterns (**axial coding**) and selective coding.

In the format for field notes that we discussed earlier, you included your hunches and guesses in your theoretical notes. As you get further into the data collection, these hunches and guesses begin to become more complex, and essentially are about patterns you see in the data. As you make connections and hunches that begin to look like patterns, you will want to "test" these by looking (both in previous field notes and in subsequent observations) for instances that support the patterns you think you're seeing, *as well as for those that don't*. This is selective coding, adapted to the observation/ethnography context. Remember that **selective coding** is the search for evidence to support the patterns that you identify, combined with the search for **negative cases** (evidence that contradicts the pattern). So if I am observing the men's university basketball team, and as I observe I begin to think that maybe the biggest pressure is not from coaches but from other players, I would specifically start observing for ways that players put pressure on one another, but I would also observe for ways that the coach, family, friends, significant others, and even the players themselves apply pressure to the members of the team. I would further look for ways that all of these various people help to *diffuse* that pressure. In other words, I would specifically look *not only for support for my hunch, but also specifically for things that would contradict my hunch*.

As with interviewing, the further you get into your data collection, the more focused your observations will become. Your theoretical notes should direct your data collection so that you are following up on all the leads you have identified in your field notes, testing them, searching for negative cases, revising those leads when they don't pan out, and then testing them again.

Evaluating the Quality of Data and Analysis

Observation and ethnographic research are both evaluated on their validity, much like interviewing research. In the cases of observation and ethnography, **data validity** means that the data accurately reflect what has transpired. Obviously, it is not possible to describe every single move or utterance that happens in the field, but the data should as accurately as possible describe what the researcher has seen (and, in the case of ethnography, also the perspectives of those participants who have been interviewed). One sign of data validity is that the field notes are specific and detailed and filled with thick description. Your write-up should include a level of detail that allows your audience to picture the setting and actions in their minds as if they were there. A second sign of data validity is that the researcher's interpretations remain separate from their observations and are clearly identified as such. To confuse the two or neglect to draw the distinction is to compromise the validity of your analysis. Third, you will also need to demonstrate to your audience the degree of rapport you had with your participants, as participants are more likely to behave naturally when they trust you, and this is key to gathering valid data.

Analytical validity for observation and ethnography is based on how well the patterns you identify are supported by the data. This is why it is important to conduct your data collection and analysis simultaneously—a valid analysis comes from paying careful attention during the observation to both supporting *and* negative cases. Further axial and selective coding of the field notes after the completion of data collection also helps to bolster the validity of the analysis.

Presenting the Results

There are many different ways to write up ethnography and observation research, and the best way to familiarize yourself with the range of presentations is to read some ethnographic research. Sometimes ethnography is written almost as a story, proceeding chronologically through the course of the research. Other times it may be presented analytically—that is, organized by analytical themes. Sometimes it is character based: each section delves more deeply into a participant or subgroup of participants in the research. Ethnography, perhaps more than any other form of social research, is most likely to be written in the form of a book, both because the write-up has such thick description that it can feel almost like reading a novel, and because the research often takes place over such a long period of time that it is difficult to convey the information in a short amount of space.

Regardless of the particular format used to present the results of ethnographic or observation research, much of the same basic information will be included in your oral or written presentation. You will provide a brief overview of the existing literature, including any theoretical perspective you have been working from. Next you will include your research question, perhaps with information on how and why this question changed during the course of data collection (if it did). You will spend a considerable amount of time discussing your method of data collection, including how you chose your site(s), the role of any gatekeepers in helping you get access to it, the role you took (participant observer, nonparticipant observer, observer participant), how you got permission from participants, and how you developed rapport with the participants. In addition, you will discuss how you took your notes (openly or clandestinely) and, most likely, the process of writing your field notes. If you conducted observation, you will discuss the sampling you did (including of times/days, as well as how you chose behaviors/interactions upon which to focus) and why. In both observation and ethnography you will also discuss **reactivity**: the effect of the research on the participants. In other words, you will talk about how being observed affected the behavior of the people you observed and any changes in that behavior over the course of your research.

Once you cover all the important information about collecting your data, you will present your analysis. For observation research, the results are often demonstrated much like those of interview research, in which you present each theme or pattern from your analysis, using quotations or summarized examples from your field notes (or interview transcripts) to lend support to the pattern. Often you will provide several supporting examples for each pattern. You will discuss negative cases, again using quotations and examples from your field notes. Although there are a wider variety of ways to present ethnographic research, the analysis will also use quotations and examples from field notes, from formal and informal interviews, and from collected documents or artifacts (if applicable) to support the analysis, as well as to present specific negative cases. The more detailed the presentation of examples and quotations are, the more confident your audience will be in the validity of your analysis.

Summary Points

- Observation is the best method for investigating behaviors of which people are unaware, to which they aren't likely to admit, or on which they don't reflect much. It is also the best method for studying naturally occurring interactional patterns.

- Ethnography is a more time-intensive method that requires deep immersion within a culture or subculture. For this reason it is generally not used for applied research. It is best used for understanding cultural patterns and norms.

- Because interpretivism is the methodology underlying both interviews and observation/ethnography, there are many similarities. One important difference is that the sampling process for observation is complex, multilayered, and ongoing.

- The primary task during data collection for both observation researchers and ethnographers is the writing of field notes.

- The process of analysis for both observation and ethnography is similar to that of interviewing, and it requires not only looking for evidence to support your conclusions, but a thorough search for negative cases as well.

Key Terms

analytical validity 90
axial coding 89
case 89
conceptualization 83
convenience sampling 81
data validity 90
descriptive notes 86
ethnography 65
evaluation research 70
field notes 65
field site 73
formal interviews 88

gatekeeper 84
guide 88
informal interviews 88
interpretive notes 87
jotted notes 86
methodological notes 87
negative cases 89
nonparticipant observer 85
observation 69
observer participant 85
operationalization 83
participant observer 85

personal notes 87
private places 74
public places 74
random sampling 80
reactivity 91
selective coding 89
semi-private places 74
theoretical notes 87
theoretical sampling 80
thick description 86

Surveys

Today, surveys are the most commonly used method of research in sociology. They are a form of *quantitative* research, and thus the results are analyzed statistically. In order to do this, surveys pose **closed-ended questions**: questions with answers provided and from which the respondents choose. Thus, the respondents rarely put their answers in their own words, and instead their answers are standardized so they are easily compared with those of other respondents. This is much like the difference between a multiple-choice test and an essay test, with surveys using multiple-choice-type questions and answers.

There are five main modes of survey delivery: mail, online, phone, face to face, and take-home. **Mail surveys** are usually sent to the respondent's home, but they may also be sent to a place of work. Mail surveys are **self-administered**—that is, the respondent fills the survey out on their own, and thus the respondents must be relied upon to accurately follow the directions and carefully read the questions and answers. Mail surveys are somewhat expensive to conduct, due to copying and postal costs, but less expensive than some other types of surveys, and they are good for asking sensitive questions that a respondent might not want to answer in a phone or face-to-face survey. Mail surveys have low **response rates** (lots of people selected for the sample never complete the survey), however, and they require a lot of time-intensive follow-up that increases the cost of conducting the survey. In addition, because they are self-administered, directions and **skip patterns** (directing respondents to skip particular questions on the survey based on their answer to an earlier question) must remain simple and easy to follow.

Online surveys are also self-administered, except that the participant fills the survey out over the Internet, rather than with paper and pencil. Although online surveys can be expensive if you purchase software to conduct the survey, many researchers now use inexpensive survey hosts available online. There are many, including LimeSurvey, Survey Gizmo, and Typeform, as well as commercial sites such as SurveyMonkey, Qualtrics, Survey Analytics, and Polldaddy, among others; capabilities vary by program, and costs are typically low (at the time of this writing they average about $35 a month for access to some, but not all, of their advanced features). Online survey data

REAL PEOPLE, REAL RESEARCH

Max Smith

As a probation officer, part of Max Smith's job is writing presence reports. He meets with the defendant and uses survey instruments to determine whether there are any circumstances that should be taken into consideration by the judge when deciding the defendant's sentence. He uses different assessment instruments for domestic violence, sex offenses, and other criminal offenses. The instruments are provided by the state and ask a variety of questions about the defendant's life and their offense. Max follows survey research protocol, asking questions exactly as written and recording the answers. He also asks some open-ended questions to further inform his recommendations. His report provides his perceptions of the defendant and his assessment of the level of honesty with which they answered the questions. Max takes all of this into account when preparing his sentencing recommendations for the judge.

Carrie Jo Diamond

As the board chair at the NorCal OUTreach Project, Carrie Jo Diamond created a needs assessment of the LGBTQ+ population in their rural area. Specifically, they wanted to get a better understanding of who made up that LGBTQ+ community, of how safe people feel, and how comfortable they feel accessing resources. The respondents came from the four nearest counties. Rather than create all 60 questions themself, Carrie Jo used measures that they borrowed from needs assessment examples from other LBGTQ+ centers. Because the population was small and there was no way to gather a sampling frame, they used an Internet survey and convenience sampling; they kept the survey open on their webpage for nearly a year. Their hope was to get as close to a census of the population as possible.

are also quick: Many studies report that more than half the people who responded to their survey did so within the first 3 days of data collection. Additionally, because online surveys are self-administered, they are good for asking personal questions. Furthermore, because skip patterns can be programmed so that the appropriate questions appear based on each respondent's answers, online surveys are good for complex surveys and questions. The biggest drawback of online surveys, however, is that they still are affected by a sampling bias based on age and social class: although 93% of U.S. households have computers, 20% of Americans over 65 do not have a computer in the home, and 25% of adults who do not have a high school degree don't have a computer in the home. Additionally, there is racial bias as well, with American Indians and Alaskan Natives being least likely to have a computer (almost 15%), followed by African Americans (10%) (American Community Survey, 2016). Thus, depending upon your population, many people (especially the elderly, the poor, and people from some ethnic groups) are likely to be excluded from your survey if you conduct an online survey. In addition, if the survey is too long, respondents are likely to stop halfway through, leaving you with incomplete surveys. It is also generally very difficult to collect a random sample using online surveys, making it impossible to generalize the data. This is a major drawback because generalizing to a larger population is usually one of the primary objectives of survey research. Finally, online survey response rates tend to be the lowest among all survey types.

Phone surveys are administered by a member of the research team: the instructions and questions are read to the respondent over the phone, and the caller records the respondent's answers. Phone surveys are very expensive to conduct, usually requiring a staff of well-trained callers. In addition, phone surveys must be short (generally no more than 20–25 minutes), or else respondents may opt out or hang up in the middle of the survey. Although phone surveys used to have relatively good response rates, they have steadily declined over the last two decades: from typically about 35% in 1997 to only 9% in 2016 (Pew Research Center, 2017). With caller ID and a migration to mobile phones rather than landlines, respondents can be very difficult to reach. That said, extensive research on phone surveys shows that in most ways, the nonresponse does not seem to present much bias. That is, as long as *both landlines and cell phones* are contacted, those who respond are not significantly different from those who do not, except on measures of political and community engagement (that is, those who participate are more likely to be involved in their communities and in politics), and hence phone surveys remain a viable mode of delivery (Pew Research Center, 2017). Additionally, because they are researcher administered, complicated survey designs and skip patterns are possible.

Face-to-face surveys are researcher administered, with a member of the research team asking the respondent each question aloud, and then recording the respondent's answers. Face-to-face surveys are the most expensive of all the survey types, requires highly trained people to administer, and are very time intensive. Because people are most likely to acquiesce to a real person in front of them, however, it has the highest response rate of all the survey types; and because it is researcher administered, it can utilize a complex survey design. It also allows access to the widest group of people because the respondent does not need a phone, computer, or sometimes even a permanent address to participate in the survey. Additionally, it makes it possible for those who have difficulty reading or who have a language barrier to participate in the research.

Finally, **take-home surveys** are those that are left at a particular location or given out to a group, with directions that the respondent take the survey, fill it out on their own (self-administer it), and send or turn it back in to a specified location at their convenience. This mode of delivery requires copying but not postal costs and so is one of the cheaper and least time intensive of the delivery modes; however, it generally yields very low response rates and is unlikely to produce a representative sample of the population, making it impossible to generalize the data.

Clearly, each of these modes of delivery has strengths and weaknesses, and the mode you choose should be based upon your research question, your sample, and the resources (time, money, and access to respondents) that you have available to you. A summary of these strengths and weaknesses is provided in Box 4.1.

BOX 4.1
COMPARISON OF SURVEY MODES OF DELIVERY

	Mail	Internet	Phone	Face-to-Face	Take-Home
Administered by	self	self	researcher	researcher	self
Expensive compared to other surveys	medium	low	high	high	medium-low
Good for sensitive questions	yes	yes	no	no	yes
Complicated questions and skip patterns OK	no	yes	yes	yes	no
Response rate	low	low	low	high	low
Quick turnaround time	no	yes	no	no	no
Sampling bias likely	no	yes	no	no	yes
Long surveys OK	no	no	no	yes	no
Can likely generalize results	yes	no	yes	yes	no

If you are conducting applied research, especially if it is for a local not-for-profit organization, you are probably somewhat less likely to use phone or Web surveys, and somewhat more likely to use self-administered or face-to-face surveys because phone surveys require a great deal of resources to conduct, which is often not feasible for nonprofits; also, many not-for-profit agencies serve people who may not have telephones or regular access to the Internet. If you conduct face-to-face surveys, you are also somewhat less likely to use special software for recording the respondents' answers and are more likely to record participants' answers using pencil and paper because resources are often more limited for applied research. This means, of course, that time and people will be needed to enter the data and clean them, and survey administrators will need to be well trained on using the survey instrument.

Methodology

Survey research is based on **positivist methodology**, which means it is conducted as scientifically as possible. This is very different from the interpretivist methodology used with interviews and observations. Positivist research is characterized by an adherence to highly structured and predetermined processes for sampling, data collection, and data analysis. The guidelines and rules to follow in data collection and analysis are very specific and meant to be followed as precisely as possible. The steps in each process should be done in the same order each time and carried out in

Reminder: Methodology is the philosophy about how and why to do your research, and it affects every aspect of the project.

the same way each time, regardless of who is conducting the research. This helps to make the research **replicable** (repeatable). Unlike in qualitative interviewing, where so much depends upon the rapport between the participant and the researcher, in positivist research *who* conducts the research should make no difference in the results. In other words, if you and I both use positivist methodology, and employ the same procedures for sampling, data collection, and analysis, we should come up with the same results.

Fundamental to positivism is the attempt to be completely objective and eliminate all bias from a study. Positivists believe that research should be unaffected by a researcher's personal beliefs, values, or identity, and the researcher's role should be that of a disinterested scientist. To this end, survey researchers take many steps to avoid bias and ensure objectivity. To remain **objective**, to positivists,

 Tip: Note that the definitions of objectivity and bias are very different for positivists than for interpretivists; be sure not to confuse them.

means to remain neutral about the results of your study, and not to try to influence them in any direction. Objectivity also means not getting emotionally involved in the research (which could introduce bias). **Bias** is any sort of influence that can skew your results by encouraging the research to come out differently than it otherwise would. In survey research, signs of bias include questions that are worded so that people are encouraged to answer in one way rather than another, or ordering of questions so that earlier questions influence their answers on later questions. In survey research, the sampling methods, data collection methods, wording on a survey, and even the order of the survey questions are all very carefully crafted to minimize any type of bias. For example, sampling should be done completely randomly so the sample won't be biased.

Survey researchers' relationships with research participants are also quite different from those of interviewers and ethnographers. What an interviewer or ethnographer sees as developing rapport, a survey researcher views as a potential source of bias that must be minimized as much as possible. Hence, survey researchers, like all positivists, try to keep their relationships with participants minimal, formal, and distant. For example, they are less likely to call those who participate in their research "participants" and, instead, usually refer to them as "respondents," or sometimes even "research subjects," to convey a more formal relationship. Survey researchers try to treat all respondents in exactly the same way, which is formally yet politely, and to reveal little or nothing about themselves to the respondents because it is possible that such information might potentially bias the respondents' answers. In face-to-face and phone surveys, most interactions the administrator is likely to have with the respondents are scripted and carefully worded so that no bias might be introduced by them.

Finally, because they have the goal of testing theory, positivists want their research to be **generalizable** to large populations (the results can be applied to people who did not participate in the survey directly). Getting in-depth information about a few people makes it difficult to test theories that pertain to large groups of people; therefore, positivists have as a primary aim collecting information that can be generalized from their sample to a larger population. In order to do this, you must collect the same data from each person, and the sample must be representative of the population to which it will be generalized. The sampling methods used are, therefore, quite different from those used by interpretivists.

Theory

The primary aim of positivists is to test theories by breaking them down into smaller units called **hypotheses** (hunches about the correct answers to your research question) and then testing them to see whether the data support the hypotheses, and thus the theory. In the physical sciences, positivists ultimately are working toward discovering universal laws that apply to everyone or everything, such as the law of gravity. In the social sciences, few positivists aim to discover universal laws, but survey research nonetheless remains **deductive**—that is, you start with ideas (in the form of theories and hypotheses) and gather data to test them, rather than the other way round (getting the ideas and hunches directly from the data and then finding the patterns that emerge, which is **inductive** research and is used with qualitative methods).

The kinds of theories that positivists test are less likely to be grand overarching theoretical frameworks—such as feminist theory, conflict theory, or postmodern theory—and more likely to be smaller-scale theories that attempt to explain a particular phenomenon. For example, surveys have been used to test assimilation theory (immigration), social integration theory (acceptance into friendship groups), cultural spillover theory (violence), ethnic competition theory (racism among the political right), and affect control theory (the relationship between emotions, definition of the situation, and behavior). Note that these theories generally are not major theoretical perspectives, but what sociologist Robert Merton (1968) would have called "theories of middle range," that is, theories of some smaller measurable phenomenon, as noted in the parentheses. Researchers write hypotheses based on basic propositions of the theory applied to a particular context. These hypotheses are then tested by conducting surveys and seeing whether the data support the hypotheses. If not, this suggests that there may be contextual limitations or mistaken assumptions within the theory. If the data do support the theory, the findings are often combined with other data to help clarify and strengthen the theory.

Not all survey research tests theory, although sociologists generally favor survey research that does. That said, sometimes survey researchers simply try to document social attitudes or trends without testing theory, or they try to replicate a previous study to see whether the results remain consistent over time. Applied survey research is also unlikely to test theory, especially if it is a needs assessment or evaluation research. The exception to this is when evaluating a program or policy that was based on theory. Some educational theories, for example, have yielded particular curricular methods or programs that might be evaluated with survey research, and evaluating them may indirectly test the theory upon which they are based.

Research Questions

Survey research is an excellent method for studying many of those things that interviews, observation, and ethnography can't: demographic characteristics, social trends, attitudes, self-reports of simple behaviors, levels of knowledge, and to some extent, cause and effect. It is also a good method for predicting future behavior and for understanding how demographic characteristics can affect attitudes or behaviors even when the individual respondents don't perceive such an effect. It is not able, however, to provide detailed descriptions, unique information about individuals or events, or accurate understandings of the ways in which people experience or interpret the world. Nor can it answer questions about complex emotions, perspectives, or meanings. Examples of research questions that are appropriately answered through the use of surveys are provided in Box 4.2; common errors to avoid are found in Box 4.3.

Although some survey research questions are **descriptive**, meaning that they seek to describe the characteristics of something (What methods of punishment are parents over the age of 40 most likely to use on their young children? How do students spend their time on spring break?), this is more likely to be the case for applied research. Most basic research questions are **explanatory**, meaning that they seek to understand the relationship between two or more factors or phenomena, or to understand how one affects another (How does parents' age affect their styles of child discipline? How do race, gender, and social class affect the likelihood that students will

BOX 4.2
EXAMPLES OF RESEARCH QUESTIONS APPROPRIATE FOR SURVEY RESEARCH

Research Question	Appropriate for Surveys Because It Examines . . .
How does religious belief affect attitudes about gender equality?	attitudes
Among homeless people, who uses services provided by the city and how?	demographic characteristics
What is the relationship between social class and religiosity?	social trends
How does age affect television viewing behaviors?	simple behaviors
What knowledge do the uninsured have about low-cost health care options in Chicago?	knowledge
How does employment affect the likelihood that students will finish their college education in 4 years?	cause and effect

BOX 4.3
AVOID THESE COMMON ERRORS IN WRITING RESEARCH QUESTIONS FOR SURVEY RESEARCH

Research Question	Explanation of Error
How do college students choose whether to experiment with drugs?	Survey research cannot provide detailed information about decision-making processes.
What do women think about while giving birth?	Not appropriate for surveys. Survey research cannot answer questions about complex experiences.
How do people with disabilities experience the world around them?	Survey research cannot provide accurate understandings of the ways in which people experience the world.
How does race affect the likelihood that college students will choose to major in sociology?	Question is too narrow. You would have too few questions on the survey.
What could companies do to decrease sexual harassment?	"Could" makes this question a hypothetical, and therefore not answerable with research.

engage in casual sex over spring break?). These factors or phenomena are called variables. **Variables** are the characteristics you measure that will differ from one person in your sample to another. *Age at last birthday, college major,* and *belief that "big-box stores" hurt the local economy* are all examples of variables.

The overwhelming majority of times, individuals will be the **unit of analysis** (the who or what you are studying) in survey research questions. Occasionally, however, the unit of analysis may be an organization or department. For example, if you want information about all of the nonprofit organizations in your town, *not-for-profit organizations* would be what you collect data about, though obviously an individual at each organization would need to fill out the survey. *Organizations* is the unit of analysis because the organizations are what you would be asking questions about. Much of the time the unit of analysis will appear in your research question, but sometimes, when the unit of analysis is the general U.S. population, the question will be phrased simply as asking about the relationship between two variables. If you do not state the unit of analysis in the question, it will thus be assumed that you will be doing a large nationally representative sample of adults in the United States.

Once you have written your research question, you should generate a list of hypotheses that you will test (though some researchers prefer to start with their hypotheses and then write the research question). Each hypothesis will state your guess about the relationship between two (and no more than two) variables. In other words, the purpose of each hypothesis is to predict how respondents' answers on one question (or set of questions) affects their answers on another. Each hypothesis, therefore, will state the effect you think the independent variable has on the dependent variable. The **independent variable** is the variable that you think is having an effect on another. The **dependent variable** is the one that is being affected. For example, if you suspect that gender will affect how much a respondent reports studying, your independent variable will be *gender* and your dependent variable, *number of hours spent studying last week*. In this particular case, it is very clear which variable is the independent variable: it wouldn't make any sense to say that *the number of hours spent studying last week* affected respondents' *gender*. Note that in other cases it may not be so clear. If the two variables were, instead, *GPA* and *number of hours studied last week*, at first glance it may seem logical to say that *the number of hours studied* must be the independent variable because it affects *GPA*. But many students with a high GPA also talk about how important it is to them to keep their GPA up and not let it fall. Similarly, some students with lower GPAs talk about needing to raise their GPA to stay off of academic probation or to get into graduate school. Thus, someone's current GPA may affect how many hours they choose to study. Ultimately in such cases, it is up to the researcher to decide which is the independent and which is the dependent variable, based upon their research question, their hypotheses, the literature review, and basic logic.

Because hypotheses predict how responses to the independent variable affect responses on the dependent variable, hypotheses always compare **categories** (possible answer responses) of the independent variable. That means if your independent variable is *gender* and your dependent variable is *number of hours studied last week*, you would compare the differences in how respondents who are male answered the question about number of hours studied compared to how females answered it. In this case, both male and female are categories of the independent variable *gender*. Note that if your independent variable has more than two possible answer choices, your hypothesis may address all of these categories of the variable (*Seniors are more likely to report studying at least 20 hours last week than are students of any other class standing*), or just some of them (*Seniors are more likely to report studying more than 20 hours last week than are frosh*).

Each hypothesis, like your research question, should be clear, precise, and specific. It not only should indicate that there is a relationship between two variables, it should also describe what effect the independent variable is expected to have on the dependent. Note that this is generally much easier to do if you are working from an explanatory (rather than descriptive) research question. Examples of a research question and its corresponding hypotheses are provided in Box 4.4.

Notice that there are many hypotheses given for just one research question, and each hypothesis examines the relationship between *exactly two* variables. Also notice that the hypotheses are very specific in their wording. Writing hypotheses is important because not only will it guide your analysis, but it will also help you identify the variables you need to include in your survey, as well as give you clues about how you will want to operationalize them.

Students sometimes struggle with writing hypotheses at first, so I am including some examples of common errors to avoid in writing them in Box 4.5. Use these examples to help you avoid committing these errors.

.4

PLE OF RESEARCH QUESTION AND CORRESPONDING HYPOTHESES

Research Question:

What demographic characteristics affect condom use among unmarried men?

Population: unmarried men

Independent variable: demographic characteristics

Dependent variable: condom use

H1: Men in monogamous heterosexual relationships are less likely to have used a condom the last time they had sex than are men not in monogamous heterosexual relationships.

Independent variable: relationship status

Categories of independent variable being compared: in and not in heterosexual monogamous relationship

Dependent variable: likelihood of having used a condom during last sexual encounter

H2: Men between the ages of 30 and 50 are more likely to have used a condom the last time they had sex than are men under 30 or over 50.

Independent variable: age

Categories of independent variable being compared: under 30, between 30 and 50, and over 50

Dependent variable: likelihood of having used a condom during last sexual encounter

H3: Men under the age of 30 are more likely to have used condoms the last time they had sex than are men over 50.

Independent variable: age

Categories of independent variable being compared: under 30 and over 50

Dependent variable: likelihood of having used a condom during last sexual encounter

H4: Men who have sex exclusively with men are more likely to have used a condom the last time they had sex than are men who have sex exclusively with women.

Independent variable: gender of sexual partners

Categories of independent variable being compared: exclusively men and exclusively women

Dependent variable: likelihood of having used a condom during last sexual encounter

H5: Men who had more than two sexual partners in the last year are more likely to carry condoms than are men who had fewer than two sexual partners in the last year.

Independent variable: number of sexual partners in last year

Categories of independent variable being compared: less than two and more than two

Dependent variable: likelihood of carrying condoms

H6: African American men are more likely than Latino men to report that they used a condom every time they had sex in the past month.

Independent variable: ethnicity

Categories of independent variable being compared: African American and Latino

Dependent variable: likelihood of using a condom for every sexual encounter in past month

H7: Latino men are more likely than men of other ethnicities to report having never worn a condom during sex.

Independent variable: ethnicity

Categories of independent variable being compared: Latino and other ethnicities

Dependent variable: likelihood of never having worn a condom during sex

H8: There is a positive relationship between income and likelihood of reporting having used a condom for every incidence of sex.

Independent variable: income

Categories of independent variable being compared: not specified

Dependent variable: likelihood of using a condom for every sexual encounter

H9: Men who identify themselves as "very religious" are less likely to ever use a condom than are men who identify themselves as "somewhat" or "not at all" religious.

Independent variable: religiosity

Categories of independent variable being compared: very religious, somewhat religious, and not at all religious

Dependent variable: likelihood of having ever used a condom

BOX 4.5

AVOID THESE COMMON ERRORS IN WRITING HYPOTHESES

Hypothesis	Explanation of Error
Online students have an easier time staying on schedule with assignments because they have the option of logging into class at any time as compared to on-campus students because they must show up to regularly scheduled classes.	Hypotheses should not include explanations. Simply state the comparison: *Online students have an easier time staying on schedule with assignments as compared to on-campus students.*

(Continued)

(Continued)

Hypothesis	Explanation of Error
Democrats will support laws to limit the purchase of semi-automatic guns.	*Democrats* is the population. The independent variable is missing, which means a comparison is missing. If the independent variable is *political party affiliation*, then two possible categories of the independent variable you could compare are *democrats* and *republicans*, with one being more likely than the other to support the laws.
Male students who work more than 40 hours per week are less likely to have student loan debt than female students who work less than 20 hours per week.	There are two independent variables here: *sex* and *number of hours worked*. A hypothesis can only have one independent variable. You can compare by *sex* or by *number of hours worked*, but cannot compare by both in one hypothesis.
Sociology majors are more likely to be of ethnic descent than are those majoring in business.	Hypotheses need to be very clear in their wording. In this example, it is not clear what is meant by *ethnic descent*.
People with bachelor's degrees are more likely to regret their career choice.	The independent variable is missing, which means a comparison is missing. If the independent variable is *highest degree attained*, then two possible categories of the independent variable you could compare are people with *bachelor's degrees* and people with *master's degrees*, with one group being more likely than the other to regret their career choice.
People who are not religious are more likely to have divorced parents than parents who are still married.	This hypothesis has only one category of the independent variable (*people who are not religious* is a category of the variable *religiosity*), but two categories of the dependent variable (*parents' marital status*). Hypotheses should always compare categories of the independent variable because you are saying that as their answer changes on the question about religion, their answers will also change on the question about parents' marital status. Without stating the possible change (comparison) of the independent variable, you are not examining the relationship between the variables.
Skills developed in the study of sociology help with a career in social work.	This is simply a statement, not a hypothesis. A hypothesis makes a prediction that people with different answers on one question (the independent variable) will also answer another question (dependent variable) differently. Here, there is no prediction about answers on either question.

Applied survey research typically starts a bit differently: The researcher often begins with a list of **research objectives**—a list of the specific things that the researcher and the various stakeholders want to learn from the research. You can find examples of objectives used for an applied study of sociology alumni in Box 4.6. The objectives are then used to write the research question, to conduct the literature review, and to develop a list of variables to include in the research. Hypotheses can be utilized in applied research, but the research objectives often replace hypotheses because applied researchers are generally more interested in finding out particular information than in testing theory.

BOX 4.6
EXAMPLE OF OBJECTIVES FOR AN APPLIED STUDY OF SOCIOLOGY ALUMNI

Research Question:

How have sociology majors at Wildflower State University fared in their careers since graduating?

O1: To investigate initial and eventual job placements for sociology majors after graduation.

O2: To determine how difficult it was for sociology alumni to find a career placement after college.

O3: To assess level of preparedness of sociology alumni for the job market.

O4: To determine whether alumni have needed additional education in order to become adequately prepared for the job market.

O5: To determine the frequency with which sociology alumni pursue graduate-level studies.

O6: To assess level of preparedness of sociology alumni for graduate-level studies.

O7: To identify the job skills sociology alumni wish they had acquired or acquired more of.

O8: To determine which skills learned in their sociology majors alumni currently use most in their jobs.

O9: To assess current job satisfaction among sociology alumni.

O10: To determine alumni's satisfaction with work-life balance.

CHECK YOUR UNDERSTANDING

Write an *explanatory* research question about childrearing that is appropriate for survey research. Write at least five hypotheses that correspond to your question. Which mode of delivery would you choose for this survey? Why?

Literature Review

The process of reviewing the literature for survey research is the same as it is for other research methods. In addition to helping you focus and refine your research question, you should also use it to help you write your hypotheses and to identify variables that should be included in your survey. You will use the existing literature to help you identify important variables that you want to include because others have fruitfully studied them, as well as important variables that seem to be missing from prior studies. Furthermore, not only can reviewing the literature help you identify potential variables for inclusion in your study, but it should also help you decide how to operationalize your variables. In quantitative research, to **operationalize** is to decide how you will measure the variable. For example, if you are going to use the variable *social class* in your study, you can look to see how others have measured social class, how their chosen measurement affected their results, and which of those ways you think will be most appropriate and beneficial to your particular study.

During your review of the literature, you will likely also consult reference books that contain existing measures of variables. That is, they are books that have collections of measures that other people have used in research on a particular topic. You may choose to borrow one or more of these measures, which can simplify the process of operationalizing your variables, and because many of these measurements have been tested for reliability and validity, using them may yield higher-quality data than coming up with your own, untested measurement. Alternatively, you can use one or more existing measures as a starting place for thinking about how you might operationalize your variables differently.

Finally, the existing literature may be used in comparison with your own statistical results. Finding similar results as another researcher can improve the support you have for a hypothesis. Finding very different results than another researcher can indicate that more research must be conducted before strong conclusions can be drawn, or it may be used to demonstrate why particular variables (or measures of those variables) previously used have been misleading or yielded incomplete information.

Conceptualizing and Operationalizing

Unlike in interview and observation research, the process of conceptualizing and operationalizing for survey research is a separate and distinct stage of the research process. It is the stage at which you move from having ideas about what you want to measure to having a completed **instrument** or **questionnaire** (the survey itself). Conceptualizing and operationalizing usually begin with the literature review, when you critically examine the ways in which other researchers have conceptualized and operationalized the variables you will be using.

To **conceptualize** means to determine the definition you will use for an abstract concept, such as *social class*, *academic success*, or *support for abortion*. All of these are abstract concepts that can be turned into variables. To conceptualize them, you must first decide what, for example, *academic success* means in the context of your research. In other words, the definition you choose should be carefully guided by your research question and hypotheses, and you should not include aspects of the concept that are not directly relevant to your hypotheses and research question. Thus, different researchers sometimes conceptualize the same variable in different ways not only because they think of it differently, but because their research question may dictate differences in the way in which it is conceptualized. So, for example, if you are surveying employees at large corporations about their job satisfaction, you may conceptualize *job satisfaction* differently than if you are surveying the general public about its overall levels of life happiness and including job satisfaction as one small variable in the study.

Let's start from the beginning: your research question. Suppose your research question is *What is the relationship between civic engagement and job satisfaction?* First, you need to define what you mean by both *civic engagement* and *job satisfaction*, but here we'll focus just on the latter for brevity. So let's say you define *job satisfaction* as "the degree to which one feels content with and rewarded by the tasks, responsibilities, compensation, and work environment of a job." You will then operationalize that definition by (1) determining which aspects can best capture or measure this concept and (2) writing hypotheses and survey items that will measure the variables. So, based on your definition, you may decide that *level of enjoyment of daily tasks, amount of satisfaction with degree of responsibility, amount of satisfaction with recognition received, amount of satisfaction with salary, amount of satisfaction with benefits packages, perceived quality of relationships with coworkers, perceived quality of relationship with boss,* and *level of stress in the workplace* are the particular aspects of job satisfaction that you want to measure. Each of these then becomes a variable in your research. Notice that your variables are based on your conceptualization, and in the survey you must measure *every* aspect of the conceptual definition we use. Sometimes you may use only one variable to measure an aspect of the definition (such as measuring responsibility by the variable *satisfaction with level of responsibility*), and other times you may need to use multiple variables to measure a single aspect of the conceptual definition (*relationships with coworkers, relationship with boss,* and *level of stress in the workplace* all measure *work environment*).

Let's go on to say that you learn from your literature review that people like helping others in their job and feeling like they are making a difference in their community, but that doing work directly with marginalized and underprivileged groups is also difficult and has a high burnout rate. So, perhaps one of your many hypotheses is *Employees who help clients who are financially stable will report higher levels of enjoyment of daily job duties than those who provide direct services to clients who are poor.* In this hypothesis, *financially stable* and *poor* are both categories of a variable we'll call *client's social class,* which is the independent variable. The dependent variable in this example is *level of enjoyment of daily job tasks.* To test this hypothesis with our survey, we of course need to operationalize both variables, but here we'll just focus on the dependent variable. To operationalize *level of enjoyment of daily job tasks,* you will need to decide how many questions you will use to measure this variable. Will it simply be a single statement (such as, *I generally enjoy the primary daily tasks that I do in my work)* with levels of agreement as possible responses (strongly agree, somewhat agree, somewhat disagree, strongly disagree), or will it need to be more complex with, for example, multiple aspects of *level of enjoyment of daily job duties* being measured? Your answer depends on how much detail you want about this particular variable and how important it is to your research. If you decide to use multiple survey items, you will want to further conceptualize this variable. Let's say you choose to define *level of enjoyment of daily job tasks* as *the degree to which an employee reports feeling engaged in and appropriately challenged by the primary tasks performed in their job on a daily basis, without feeling overwhelmed.* You would then need to write at least three different survey items to measure the dependent variable in your hypothesis: one survey item that asks about how engaging they find these primary tasks, one that asks about how challenging they find the tasks, and one that asks about how overwhelmed they feel by the tasks. Used together, these survey items (along with survey items measuring *clients' social class*) will then allow you to test your hypothesis that *Employees of non-profit and governmental organizations who help clients who are financially stable will report higher levels of enjoyment of daily job duties than those who provide direct services to clients who are poor.* I have illustrated this process in Box 4.7 using an example from our earlier hypotheses so that you can see the steps more clearly.

BOX 4.7
EXAMPLE OF CONCEPTUALIZING AND OPERATIONALIZING FOR SURVEY RESEARCH

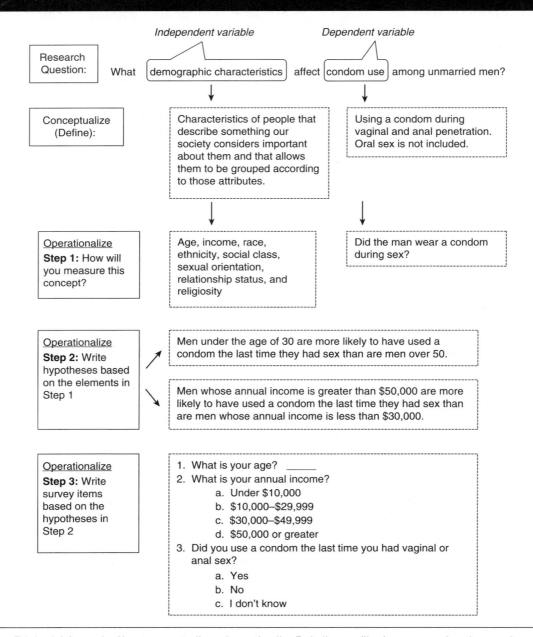

Independent variable

Dependent variable

Research Question: What [demographic characteristics] affect [condom use] among unmarried men?

Conceptualize (Define):

Characteristics of people that describe something our society considers important about them and that allows them to be grouped according to those attributes.

Using a condom during vaginal and anal penetration. Oral sex is not included.

**Operationalize
Step 1: How will you measure this concept?**

Age, income, race, ethnicity, social class, sexual orientation, relationship status, and religiosity

Did the man wear a condom during sex?

**Operationalize
Step 2: Write hypotheses based on the elements in Step 1**

Men under the age of 30 are more likely to have used a condom the last time they had sex than are men over 50.

Men whose annual income is greater than $50,000 are more likely to have used a condom the last time they had sex than are men whose annual income is less than $30,000.

**Operationalize
Step 3: Write survey items based on the hypotheses in Step 2**

1. What is your age? _____
2. What is your annual income?
   a. Under $10,000
   b. $10,000–$29,999
   c. $30,000–$49,999
   d. $50,000 or greater
3. Did you use a condom the last time you had vaginal or anal sex?
   a. Yes
   b. No
   c. I don't know

Note: This is a brief example of how to conceptualize and operationalize. Typically, you will write many more hypotheses and survey items than are listed here.

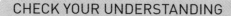

CHECK YOUR UNDERSTANDING

Write a conceptual definition of one concept you would want to measure in your research on childrearing. Which variables will you use to measure this definition?

Levels of Measurement

Once we have identified the variables we want to use, we then begin constructing our survey items. This includes not only writing survey items, but also deciding from which answer choices respondents may choose. In making these decisions, you will need to choose from various levels of measurement. There are four levels: nominal, ordinal, interval, and ratio. It is important to understand each of these levels because they determine what kinds of statistical analyses you can run on the data, and they also affect the reliability of your data.

Nominal measures are those for which respondents can be divided into groups but that can't be ranked in any way. Gender, ethnicity, and religion are all variables that can only be measured at the nominal level. That is, we can divide people into 5, 10, or even 15 different religions, but no matter how many possible choices we give the respondent, it doesn't make sense to say that Buddhism is more or less than Taoism, or that Baptists are higher or lower than Lutherans. Ranking them just doesn't make sense; we can only differentiate between them.

Ordinal measures, on the other hand, are those for which the respondents are divided into groups and can be ranked in a particular order. For example, if we ask respondents how much they agree with a particular statement, we can say that people who responded that they strongly agree with the statement agree with it *more* than people who say they somewhat agree with it, and people who somewhat agree with it agree *more* than people who say they somewhat disagree with it. Thus, the possible responses (called **response categories**) in this case can be ranked by level of agreement. *Highest degree obtained* is another example of a variable being measured at the ordinal level. We know that someone who has a bachelor's degree has more education than someone whose highest degree is a high school degree, and this latter person has more education than someone who did not complete a high school degree, so the responses can be ranked by the level of education.

Interval measures are those that not only can be divided into categories and rank ordered, but also allow you to mathematically determine exactly how much difference there is between one response (or person) and another. For example, if you ask for the respondents' grade-point averages, we not only can rank order them so that we know that the 3.5 student has better grades than the 3.0 student, but we can also mathematically calculate that the difference in the two GPAs is 0.5.

Ratio measures are the highest level of measurement. We cannot only divide them into categories, rank order them, and mathematically calculate the difference between responses, but they also have an absolute zero, so that we can determine not just an absolute amount of difference between them, but also the proportional

BOX 4.8
EXAMPLE OF GROUPINGS AFFECTED BY LEVEL OF MEASUREMENT USED

The following diagram illustrates how different levels of measurement will affect the grouping of your respondents. The variable being measured is *number of hours slept last night*. First, here are our 10 responses:

Alexandra: 8 hours	Kate: 7.75 hours	Vince: 6.5 hours	Suzanne: 7.25 hours	Lucy: 10 hours
Anna: 2.5 hours	Megan: 9.5 hours	James: 5.0 hours	Carlos: 6.25 hours	Antonio: 7.0 hours

Nominal Measurement:

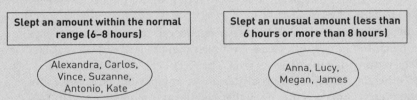

Notice that with this nominal measurement, we know that four people slept an unusual amount of time, but we cannot say whether they slept more or fewer hours than those who slept a normal amount of time.

Ordinal Measurement:

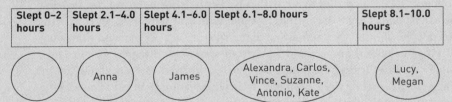

Notice how these measurements can be rank ordered: We know that Lucy got more sleep than Anna did, though we don't know by exactly how much.

Ratio Measurement:

In this case, we cannot only easily see that Lucy got more sleep than James, but also she got *twice* as much sleep as James.

BOX 4.9

QUESTION AND RESPONSE WORDING FOR DIFFERENT LEVELS OF MEASUREMENT

Nominal:

Did you work for pay this week?
a. Yes
b. No

Ordinal:

About how many hours did you work for pay this week?
a. 1–10 hours
b. 11–20 hours
c. 21–30 hours
d. 31–40 hours
e. More than 40 hours
f. I didn't work for pay this week

Ratio:

How many hours did you work for pay this week? _____

amount. So, for instance, if we take a quiz worth 50 points, and you get all 50 correct, and I only get 25 answers correct, we know not only that you got 25 more points than I did but that your score was *twice as high* as mine. Box 4.8 is a diagram of three of these different levels of measurement. You may notice that there is no interval level of measurement shown in this diagram. That's because the variable being measured, *number of hours slept*, has an absolute zero—that is, it is entirely possible that one can get zero sleep in a night, and therefore the level of measurement is ratio, not interval. If the variable were height in inches, however, the measurement could only be interval, not ratio because no one can be 0" tall. Even babies start out with a height greater than 0"! Interval and ratio levels of measurement by definition are mutually exclusive, and thus a variable cannot be measured at both the interval and ratio levels.

When you are writing survey items, the level of measurement you choose will affect the way in which you write the question, as well as the answer choices you give. Nominal responses will only contain words, no numbers. Ordinal responses may contain either words or numbers, but if there are numbers, each answer choice gives a range. Interval and ratio responses must be in numeric form and are usually fill-in-the-blank responses rather than multiple choice. Box 4.9 shows examples of survey questions and their responses for each level of measurement.

Note that even though the ordinal measurement asking about number of hours worked for pay includes a response of 0 hours, it is an *ordinal,* not ratio, level of measurement because if a respondent chose any of the other answers, you could not mathematically calculate how many more or less hours they worked than another respondent.

Generally, survey researchers prefer to gather information at the highest level of measurement possible because the information is more specific. If you know exactly how many hours someone worked for pay this week, you can always reduce that to a lower level of measurement by, say, grouping it into 1–10 hours, 11–19 hours, 20–29 hours, etc., or even into more than 20 hours and less than 20 hours. But if you collect the information at the ordinal level you cannot get the more specific information later: If someone chooses 11–19 hours, you will never be able to determine *exactly* how many hours that person worked. Nonetheless, this desire for more specific information must be balanced with the respondents' patience for fill-in-the-blank answers. Generally, respondents prefer to be given answer choices, both because it helps them with recall and because it takes less work to circle an answer or click a button than to write in a response. So survey researchers must decide when it is worth getting more specific information and when they can sacrifice that level of detail for the respondents' convenience.

When using nominal or ordinal levels of measurement, it is extremely important that your response categories be both exhaustive and mutually exclusive. **Exhaustive** means that *every* respondent will have an answer choice that fits their response, even if that choice is "other." **Mutually exclusive** means that no person should be able to fit their answer into more than one category, unless specifically instructed to choose all responses that apply. In the following example, the categories are *not exhaustive* because there are more than three possible religions, and some people will not belong to any religion at all.

What is your religious affiliation?

a. Jewish
b. Christian
c. Muslim

In the next example, the question is not *mutually exclusive* because Catholics and Baptists are also Christians.

What is your religious affiliation?

a. Christian
b. Catholic
c. Baptist
d. Jewish
e. Muslim
f. Buddhist
g. Other
h. I don't affiliate with any religion

Writing Survey Items

In addition to choosing levels of measurement for each variable, operationalizing also means deciding upon the exact wording of each item. Wording is very important, as it can make all the difference in how someone understands or responds to the question. The following is a list of things to avoid in wording your questions, with an example of each.

- **Avoid biased wording** or leading questions, sometimes also called **loaded questions**, which may influence the respondent to answer in a particular way. Sometimes I see items in which the bias is obvious: *Do you believe that families who are supportive of their loved one's choice of a humane, dignified death should be free from criminal prosecution?* In this example, *supportive, choice, humane, dignified, free,* and *criminal prosecution* are all leading or biased words, any of which on their own could influence a respondent's answer, much less all together. Just as important, however, is realizing that some words, even when not clearly biased, will gain more support or sympathy than others. Researchers have found, for example, that asking about *assistance to the poor,* for example, is more likely to yield support than is *welfare* (Pew Research Center, 2014).

- **Avoid threatening questions,** which people either will not want to answer or will not answer honestly. *Do you physically abuse your children?* is an example of a threatening question.

- **Avoid double-barreled questions,** which ask about two different things at once. For example, *Should the United States create more skilled jobs and discourage American companies from producing their products overseas?* asks two separate questions: one about creating jobs, and the other about discouraging companies from foreign production. If someone answers "no" to this question, you don't know if that person thinks we should create more jobs but not discourage foreign production, or if they believe we should not create more jobs at all.

- **Avoid double negatives,** which get very confusing for the respondent. Using double negatives is especially likely to accidentally happen when you are asking people to agree or disagree with statements that include *not* plus negative words such as "prohibit" and "exclude": *The United States should not prohibit the use of genetically modified seeds in agriculture.* If you disagree that the United States should not prohibit these seeds, you are actually saying that you disagree that we should allow these seeds; or, put another way, you agree that we should not allow them. See why double negatives should be avoided?

In addition to avoiding the above, you should also *do* the following when writing survey items:

- Only ask questions that a respondent can reasonably answer or can reasonably remember. *How many hours did you usually spend watching television per week in high school?* is not something people can accurately answer, especially if it has been several years or more since they have been in high school.

- Try to keep questions as specific as possible. Asking, *In general, do you prefer to watch comedies, sports, news, dramas, or reality television?* is not as specific as asking, *Thinking about your favorite tv shows that you are watching this season, which category is most represented among them: sitcoms, sports shows, television news programs, dramas, or reality tv?* People often think that asking in general will be more accurate, but actually the opposite is true: people's ideas about themselves often do not match their actual behaviors, and behaviors often change more rapidly than one's self-image. Additionally, people may gloss over or not even be aware of behaviors that don't fit with their self-image. Hence it's always more accurate to ask for specifics than generalities.

- Try to keep time frames as narrow as possible. Asking *How many hours of television did you watch last night?* will yield more accurate information than *How many hours of television do you watch per night?* Although it is true that it is possible that yesterday someone watched more or less tv than usual, as long as there is no systematic way in which "yesterday" was different for all or most of your participants, keeping the time frame very concrete and specific will always yield more accurate data because with generalities, people calculate averages that aren't actual mathematical averages and that don't actually represent their behavior. If you ask them how much tv they generally watch, and some nights they binge-watch 8 hours and other nights they watch only 1, one person may calculate this average as 4 or 5 hours, others may say 2 (because they only watched 1 hour of tv more nights than they watched 8 hours), others may say 1. In other words, the way respondents come up with a "general" answer is unreliable because it differs from person to person. If you ask about last night (or last week), yes, they might have watched more than usual last night, but other respondents will have watched less than usual, and it is assumed, with random sampling, that these overages and underages will even out across participants. The exception to this is if last night was different in some way that affects most of your respondents—for example, Super Bowl Sunday, a long weekend, Halloween, the Academy Awards, election night, a Hollywood writer's strike, or a day that terrorist attack occurs on American soil. In other words, if this day is somehow significantly different from most days in a way that is likely to greatly increase or decrease the number of hours that people usually watch television, then the information about last night will be biased information. In this case, you should keep your time frame specific, but avoid collecting your data on days or in weeks (during Thanksgiving week, for example) that are likely to yield such biased information.

- Keep questions as short as possible while maintaining specificity. This is especially important if you are conducting phone surveys, in which you should assume your respondents will only be half-listening as they answer your questions while cooking dinner, channel surfing, or texting.

- Only ask questions that are relevant to most of your respondents. Otherwise, use a skip pattern. A skip pattern directs some respondents to skip a number of questions, usually based on their answer to a previous question called a **filter question**. For example, if your filter question is *Have you smoked a cigarette, pipe, or cigar in the last year?*, you may use a skip pattern, in which those who answer "no" to the filter question skip the next five questions, which are about smoking habits. If, however, you only had one question to ask about smoking for those who answered "yes" to the filter question, you would follow it up with a single question, which would then be called a **contingency question**. For example, using the same filter question, you may follow that with the contingency question, *How many times have you smoked a cigarette, pipe, or cigar in the last week?*

- When giving people a scale of responses, provide opposites (see Box 4.10). If you want to know how difficult they find something, giving them the response categories *very difficult, somewhat difficult, somewhat easy, very easy* will yield better data than providing them *very difficult, somewhat difficult, not very difficult, not at all difficult*. With the latter, respondents are much more likely to choose the middle two response categories than the end categories. This is because *not at all difficult* implies an absolute—they have never had even a moment of difficulty with it; therefore, if someone has had any difficulty at all, even if it's minimal, they are unlikely to choose *not at all*. On the other hand, *very easy* is not as absolute, so more people will choose it even though it is on the same end of the response choices.

BOX 4.10
COMMON OPPOSITES TO USE FOR RESPONSE CATEGORIES

easy	difficult
likely	unlikely
agree	disagree
satisfied	dissatisfied
responsive	unresponsive
helpful	unhelpful
supportive	unsupportive
like	dislike
important	unimportant
interested	uninterested
relevant	irrelevant

- Avoid absolutes. I often see *always*, *almost always, sometimes, rarely, never* as answer choices, for example. But these absolutes in your extreme categories bias your data. *Always* signifies that it happens every single time—not missing even once; *never* means that out of 1,000 times it hasn't happened even once. This encourages people to choose the middle categories somewhat falsely. Imagine you are asking how often someone cooks dinner. Even the most devoted cook has missed a meal because of illness or a family celebration or has had a family member make dinner for a birthday or anniversary. The person in this position is more likely to choose *almost always* than *always*, so the number of people who choose *always* will be extremely small. You will get more usable data, meaning spread out across all of the response categories, if you instead use end categories that are less absolute, such as combining an absolute with something a little less absolute, such as *always or almost always* and *rarely or never*. Now someone who cooks 29 out of 30 days in a month can still choose that category without exaggerating.

- Vary question types to avoid response sets. **Response sets** occur when you have so many questions of a similar type that respondents stop thinking about their answers and start giving the same response to every question. This is especially likely to happen with **Likert-scale items**, which present a statement and then ask respondents how much they agree or disagree with it. Although Likert-scale items are useful, you can avoid response sets by varying the type of item, such as grouping 8 or 10 Likert-scale items together, but then going to other question types, such as asking about frequency of behavior, before returning to another grouping of Likert-scale items. Additionally, you should vary whether the item is posed as a positive or negative, so that respondents must think about what their answer means. For example, if you are studying satisfaction with jobs, you may ask them how much they agree with two positive items *(My supervisor appreciates the work I do* and *I enjoy the majority of the tasks that are part of my job description)* and then follow it with a negative item *(I think I deserve more respect at work than I typically get).* Here, note that "positive" and "negative" refers to the overall meaning—in this example, whether they feel positively or negatively about their job. Using "negative" words in the sentence, however, like *don't, isn't,* and *never* are likely to cause a double negative. If the example above was instead worded as *I don't get the respect I feel I deserve at work* and the respondent then disagrees, it in effect becomes *I disagree that I don't get the respect I feel I deserve at work.* It is less confusing when we use "positive" words even to connote a negative overall meaning, as in *I think I deserve more respect at work than I typically get.* The variation in wording allows us to avoid response sets while still avoiding double negatives.

- Think carefully about whether you wish to include a **neutral category** (such as "neither agree nor disagree," or "neither positively nor negatively") in Likert-scale and similar items. There are different modes of thought on this: Some researchers argue that some people really do feel on the fence about issues and that if we force them to choose one side or the other by omitting a neutral response category, we are distorting their views. On the other hand, we know that regardless of their actual opinion, respondents are likely to choose a neutral category when provided because it is an easy (and more socially acceptable) response; this is especially true if the issue is one the respondent hasn't pondered much. Thus, by providing a neutral option, you may get more people claiming they are neutral than actually are. Hence, whether you decide to provide neutral categories is a strategic decision based on the information that will be most helpful to your particular project. Whichever you choose, however, you should be consistent throughout the entire survey: If a neutral category is provided for one answer, it should be provided for all similar question types.

- Carefully consider the decision of whether to include *don't know* or *does not apply* responses. *Don't know* means that the respondent either can't decide on an answer or doesn't have enough information to provide an answer. This is different from being neutral on an issue, which means that the person has an opinion, and it is a middle-of-the-road opinion. Thus, deciding whether to include *don't know* responses is a separate decision from that of neutral categories. Again, there isn't one right answer, and it should be a strategic decision based on what information will be most helpful to you. You should consider, however, that if a neutral category is provided but no *don't know* category is available, the people who really don't know will most likely choose the neutral category. Providing a *don't know* category allows you to separate out the truly neutral responses; but again, some people will choose *don't know* simply as an easy answer choice that requires little thought.

- Avoid asking respondents to agree with a question. If you use a Likert scale, your items must be in the form of *sentences*, not questions. *Do you believe that your salary is a fair one, given the work you do?* should have "yes" and "no" responses, not levels of agreement. Similarly, *How fair do you think your salary is, given the work you do?* should have responses ranging from "very fair" to "very fair." But because they are phrased as questions, neither of these items should ever be responded to with levels of agreement; it simply doesn't make sense. If you want response categories to be levels of agreement, use an item phrased as a sentence: *I believe my salary is fair, given the work I do.*

CHECK YOUR UNDERSTANDING

Choose one of the variables you have decided is necessary to measure for your research on childrearing. Write the question and response choices you would use to measure that variable, being sure to keep the response choices mutually exclusive and exhaustive. After you've written them, take a look at the question and its response categories. Which level of measurement did you use? Explain. Is it possible to write this question at another level of measurement? If so, write it again at each level of measurement at which it could possibly be measured.

Sampling

Probability Sampling

Like all positivist research, survey research aims to be as scientific as possible in its sampling so as to eliminate **sampling bias** (bias introduced by using a sample that does not represent the population). Thus, you should strive for a sample that is **representative** of the population being studied, which will allow you to generalize your findings from the sample to the larger population. Remember, this is of utmost importance in most survey research because one of the primary goals of survey research is to generalize the results to a larger population. Conducting a survey that can't be generalized often defeats the very purpose of the survey. To accomplish the goal, survey researchers generally use some form of **probability sampling**, meaning that every person in the population has an equal chance of being selected to participate in the research.

Although you must design your sampling strategy prior to applying for IRB approval, you may not begin contacting anyone in your sample until after you have received this approval. In order to begin drawing a sample, you must first identify your **population**—that is, the group to which you wish to generalize your findings. Then you must also secure or develop a **sampling frame**, which is an actual list of as many of the people within that population as possible. For example, if you wanted to survey all full-time, currently enrolled students at your university (the population for your study), you would need to get a list of all students who fit those criteria (the sampling frame). Note that sampling frames are rarely perfect representations of the population. If, for example, the Office of the Registrar gave you a list of all currently enrolled students carrying at least 12 units at your university as of the first day of classes this semester, some students would have dropped out between the first day of the semester and today, so some names on that list would be invalid. Likewise, some students who had delays in their financial aid checks may not have been allowed to register until they paid their fees, which may not have been until a few days after the semester started; so again, some names may be missing from the sampling frame and thus can't be sampled. Sampling frames are rarely perfect, but you should strive to get the best, most complete sampling frame available to you.

After securing your sampling frame, you will choose one of several probability sampling methods to draw your sample. All of these methods share two characteristics: The process of sample selection is truly random, and each person has an equal chance of being selected. Probability sampling is very important to survey research: without it, survey results cannot be generalized to a larger population. Because this is usually a primary aim of survey research, it is important to use probability sampling in survey research whenever possible. Note that it is much more difficult, however, to conduct probability sampling with certain modes of delivery: Take-home surveys very rarely use probability sampling, and it can be difficult to do so with Internet surveys as well. Posting an announcement on a website or using social media to recruit participants is not probability sampling. The only way to do probability sampling with Internet research is to have a sampling frame that includes personal contact information for each person in the population, to draw your sample from the sampling frame using one of the four probability sampling methods, and then to contact the selected people directly, asking them to log in to your survey and take it online. This is the only way to ensure that it is truly random and that everyone has an equal chance of being selected. Any other way of conducting Internet surveys, such as posting an announcement on a website or making announcements in person to particular groups of people and asking them to fill out your survey online, are neither random nor representative and do not count as nonprobability sampling.

There are four ways to draw a random sample. A **simple random sample** is one in which each name on the list is randomly assigned a number. To select the individuals who will be part of your sample, you use a **random numbers table** (a list of numbers in total random order and numerical combinations) or a **random numbers generator** (a software program that is available for free on the Internet, which generates a list of random numbers).

Tip: Note that when describing the kind of sampling you use, you should never just say "probability sampling"; you should always specify which of the four types of probability sampling you specifically used.

In **systematic random sampling**, a single number is calculated, based on the size of the population and the desired sample. If, for example, you have a population of 16,432 students and you want a sample of 800 students, you would divide 16,432 by 800 to come up with 20.54. This tells you that you would need to choose every 20th student on the list. To do this, you would use a random numbers table, choosing one number for your starting place. Say it is 284. You would count down the list to the 284th person, and then starting with that person as #1, you would count off every 20th person, who would then become part of your sample. Note that because in systematic random sampling you will never choose two names right next to each other on the list, the sampling frame itself must be randomized before drawing the first number, otherwise you will likely introduce bias into the sample. For example, if your list were ordered alphabetically by last name, you would likely introduce ethnic bias because some ethnicities are more likely to have last names that begin with particular letters. G, H, R, N and S, for example, account for a large number of last names in Spanish. But using the above example, if you were only choosing every 20th name, and they were in alphabetical order, you may only choose one or two G's. This would lead to fewer Latinos being chosen for your sample than other ethnicities, therefore biasing your study and making it less generalizable. Thus in systematic random sampling, randomizing the list before drawing your sample is extremely important.

Both simple random sampling and systematic random sampling are entirely random. This does not necessarily ensure, however, that your sample will end up exactly like your population. For example, you may randomly choose 20% more Asian Americans than Latinos, when your population is actually evenly split. If ethnicity will be an important variable in your research, then it may be important for you to have a sample that is more similar to your population in this regard. In **stratified sampling,** before randomizing you divide the possible respondents into particular groups, such as into ethnicities. Once the sampling frame is divided into the appropriate groups, you *then* randomly choose the respondents *within* each group, usually using the same steps as simple random sampling. One important caution here: We only stratify if it's important to get a substantial number of respondents from *underrepresented groups* in a population. In other words, in many possible populations, Asian Americans are underrepresented compared to white Anglos, and so you might need to stratify in order to ensure that enough Asian Americans are selected to participate in your study if that is an important group in your research and in several of your hypotheses. You would not, however, probably stratify for gender even if you have several hypotheses on gender because in most populations there is a fairly even gender split. Thus the likelihood is that by using simple or systematic sampling, you would *randomly* choose enough males and females to participate even if you don't get exactly equal numbers of each sex. If Asian Americans are only 15% of your population, however, it would be less likely that randomly enough Asians may be chosen; consequently, you would stratify. That said, note that this depends entirely on your population—if the population is stay-at-home parents and gender is an important variable in the research, and the number of stay-at-home dads is tiny compared to the number of stay-at-home moms, then it would be important to stratify by gender. In a population of voters, on the other hand, the numbers of males and females registered to vote are close enough that stratifying isn't needed. It's also extremely important to note that you can only sample based on information you have in your sampling frame. That is, if you simply have a list of names, without race or ethnicity identified, you can't stratify by race or ethnicity because you can't always tell what someone's ethnicity is by looking at their name. The name "Laura Springer" may sound white, but she may be a Korean woman who was adopted by a white family. "Rosa Hernandez" may be a black woman married to a Latino man. Thus in order to stratify, you can't just guess—your sampling frame must contain the information about the categories into which you want to stratify.

Sometimes you do not have adequate information about individuals for your sampling frame to contact them, but you do have information about groups or organizations with which they are affiliated. In this case, you might choose **cluster sampling**. In cluster sampling, the groups are naturally occurring; that is, the participants are already in some way divided into groups before you sample them. For cluster sampling, you randomly choose naturally occurring groups from the sampling frame and then sample *all* of the individuals within that group. For example, say that the university won't release to you the contact information of all the enrolled students. You can, however, get a list of all the courses taught on campus and who teaches those courses, through the schedule of classes. The classes are considered naturally occurring groups because students were already grouped together into classes without you having grouped them. You could use cluster sampling by taking all the courses on the list and then randomly select classes, using the same steps as simple random sampling or systematic sampling. Once you have identified the classes that are in your sample, you will then try to survey *every* person in each of those selected classes by, for example, asking each of those teachers if you can come in and conduct the survey during class time. In cluster sampling, the larger the number of naturally occurring groups you have the more generalizable your results will be. If you only had 10 groups and chose three, the likelihood of bias is strong because people who are naturally grouped together tend to be similar in at least some ways, and they would be overrepresented in your sample. If you have thousands of groups (such as classes) and randomly choose hundreds of them, however, the chance of bias is minimized.

It is important to note that for phone surveys, random samples are usually drawn differently. Typically, they employ **random digit dialing**, in which a computer program randomly generates phone numbers within a specific geographical region. This facilitates the sampling process, especially if you are drawing a large sample over a wide geographical area, such as a national sample, because you don't have to have a physical list of every person and their telephone number. The sampling frame is considered to be all legitimate phone numbers. This is deemed essentially the same as simple random sampling because the computer is randomly generating the phone numbers, just as a random numbers generator would produce a list of random numbers. Box 4.11 contains a summary of the different types of sampling, with examples.

BOX 4.11
PROBABILITY SAMPLING TECHNIQUES AS APPLIED TO SURVEY RESEARCH

Sampling Method	Description	Example for Survey Research
Simple random sample	Each person is given a number, and people are chosen using a random numbers generator.	Every student listed by the Registrar's office as currently enrolled is given a number, which has been randomly chosen using a random numbers generator.
Systematic random sample	Sampling frame is randomized, then each person is given a number. First number is randomly chosen, then count down the list to every nth item to select it. N represents the number in the sampling frame divided by the total number desired in the sample.	Every enrolled student is listed in randomized order. To sample 1,000 out of 16,458 listed, start at a random place on the list, and then choose every 16th person listed (16,458/1000 = 16.45).
Stratified random sample	Sampling frame is divided into groups and then simple random or systematic sampling is used to select a given number of items from each group. Only used when one or more groups is highly underrepresented in the population.	Students are divided into on-campus and online-only students. Simple or systematic random sampling used to choose 500 students from each list, for a total of 1,000 students.
Cluster sample	Groups are randomly chosen, and every person from the chosen groups is included in the sample.	Students are already naturally divided into different majors. Majors are listed in random order. Simple random sampling is used to choose 20 majors. All students declared in each chosen major are asked to participate.

Nonprobability Sampling

Survey researchers *always* choose probability sampling when they can because they want to generalize the findings, and probability sampling is required in order to do this. Sometimes, however, a probability sample is not possible. This can be because there is no way to develop a sampling frame for the population, such as when the population is relatively small but there are no clear identifying characteristics or organizations available to contact these people. Examples include college students who have a parent who has spent time in prison, or college students who are caring for a sick or aging family member. Although there certainly are students on your campus who fit this population, there is no clear way of identifying who they are. Sometimes the population can be large, but again, there is no clear way of finding who is part of it, such as people who have had a spouse who cheated on them, or people who have stopped practicing the religion in which they were raised. In these cases, it would be impossible to use probability sampling, and you would instead need to use nonprobability sampling. As you may recall from interviews, one of the caveats of nonprobability sampling is that *you cannot generalize from your sample to the population*, because the sample will be neither random nor representative. This was not an issue in interviewing research because as interpretivist research, the goal of interviewing is to understand a small group in a lot of depth. Survey research is positivist, however, and designed to gather information from larger groups of people and to generalize that information to the entire population you are studying. Using nonprobability sampling for survey research, therefore, is a very serious limitation; it is considered a significant weakness of the study, as not only can you *not* generalize, but most certainly your sample will be biased. Nonetheless, when probability sampling is not possible, nonprobability sampling is your only choice.

The nonprobability sampling method most likely to be used by survey researchers is **convenience sampling**. As in interview research, this generally involves advertising for participants through social media, pop-up announcements on a website, fliers, newspaper advertisements, ads on Craigslist, announcements at related group meetings and clubs, and the like. Remember that Internet surveys often draw on convenience samples and therefore are not generalizable. When a store gives you your receipt and then asks you to log in and participate in their online survey, this is convenience sampling. Because those people who decide to log in are people who are either generally very pleased or very displeased with their shopping experience, or want the promised discount that is sometimes offered as an incentive, the sample will be biased, and thus the data they gather is not very useful (though often their main purpose is to collect your personal information to target you with more advertising, not actually to understand customers' opinions about their store).

Sometimes researchers will attempt to draw a sample that is similar to their perceptions of the actual population by drawing a quota sample. In **quota sampling**, the respondents are still volunteers reached through many of the same means as convenience sampling, but you set a specific number of people that you wish to have in your sample with specific characteristics. You may decide that 100 of the 300 people in your sample will not be white. In this example, after you have 200 white people who have agreed to participate, you turn away all other white volunteers, even if you have not yet gotten 300 volunteers. I must reiterate here that even if quota sampling gives you a sample that you think may resemble your larger population, because it is nonprobability sampling *you cannot generalize your findings to the larger population.* Although these nonprobability sampling methods are important tools when it is impossible to draw a probability sample, whenever possible you should use a probability sample when doing survey research.

In applied research you may be somewhat more likely to conduct a census than to sample your population, depending on the overall population size. A **census** is an attempt to collect data from *every single person* in the population. This is obviously more feasible if the population size is small or if you have an opportunity for face-to-face contact with every member of the population. If, for example, you are trying to assess the satisfaction level of patients at a health clinic, you may ask every patient to participate in the survey as they check out of the clinic.

Box 4.12 provides a decision path for sampling for survey research.

CHECK YOUR UNDERSTANDING

For your research project on childrearing, what is your population? What is your sampling frame? Which sampling method would you choose for this project? Why? Describe in detail the steps you would take to implement this sampling strategy.

Sample Size

Your sample size will depend on the size of your population, on your mode of survey delivery, and on the resources available to you. Although there are a variety of complex mathematical formulas that survey researchers sometimes use to determine their ideal sample size, they are beyond the scope of this book. Here, I simply give you a few general guidelines. First, larger samples do not necessarily mean better samples. In fact, drawing a sample that is too large can be a waste of time and money because if you have used probability sampling, you can fairly accurately generalize with even a relatively small sample. For example, if you are conducting a national random sample of all likely voters, you would be no more accurate in generalizing from a sample of 50,000 than you would from a sample of 3,000; yet the sample of 50,000 would cost you many more thousands of dollars to collect. On the other hand, even with a small population, rarely are sample sizes smaller than 100 because once those 100 people get divided up by variables, the numbers become too small to conduct meaningful statistical analyses. For example, if you have a sample size of 80 company employees and you want to compare the responses about job satisfaction given by male employees and female employees, you might only end up with a group of 25 female employees. Additionally, if you want to see how those female employees responded differently depending on whether they held management positions, you may end up with a group of only 5 or 6 female managers. This makes it very difficult

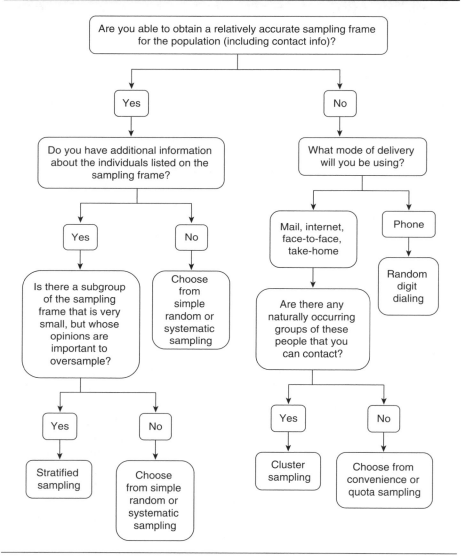

BOX 4.12

DECISION PATH FOR SAMPLING FOR SURVEY RESEARCH

Note: While this is the typical path for decision making, there may be unusual circumstances that require different decisions.

to calculate statistics, not to mention generalizing to the larger population. The goal, of course, is to get a sample size that is large enough to analyze productively, but still small enough to conserve resources.

That being said, the larger your population, generally the smaller the percentage you need to take for a good sample. Sample sizes for national samples usually fall somewhere between 1,000 and 3,500 respondents and are often on the lower end of that range. If there are 200 million adults over the age of 18 in the United States, a sample size of 2,000 is only 0.00001% of the estimated population. If you are conducting a study on a small population, however, such as the number of workers at a company, and your population is 5,645, you may take a sample of about 565 people, which would be approximately 10% of the population. With an even smaller population, such as 1,000, we might take a sample size of 300 people, which is 30% of the total population. One of the primary reasons we use a larger proportion of a small population is that we need enough people to participate in order to be able to calculate reliable statistics. If we took only 3% of a population of 1,000, that would be only 30 people, and when we divide people up by answer categories, that may have us trying to compare 12 people who answered *strongly agree* with 10 people who answered *somewhat agree*, 3 *somewhat disagree*s, and 5 *strongly disagree*s. Trying to find a pattern in why these participants gave different answers is impossible with such small numbers. Additionally, a small proportion of a small population increases the risk that, even if drawn randomly, the sample won't accurately represent the population. On the other hand, using a 3% sample size for a national study would mean having to survey almost 10 million people. That is not only time and cost prohibitive, it is unnecessary: We can represent the population nearly as accurately with 2,000 adults as we can with 10 million using a probability sample, and the small difference in accuracy isn't enough to offset the tremendous cost and time difference. In all, survey researchers generally try to avoid sample sizes of less than 100, even with small populations, and infrequently choose sample sizes of more than 3,500, even with national samples.

Response Rate

It is important to **oversample** your population (draw more people for your sample than you actually want or need) in order to take into account your final response rate. In calculating the number of people you will contact about participating in your research, you should keep in mind that inevitably some of the information in your sampling frame will be out of date, and you will need to drop those people from your sample. Additionally, you will be unable to make contact with some people, perhaps because they have caller ID and don't answer the phone for unknown phone numbers, or because their e-mail account identifies your e-mail about your research as junk mail and automatically discards it. Again, you will need to drop these people from your final sample size. Additionally, some (possibly many) people you succeed in contacting will nevertheless choose not to participate in your research. They may directly decline to participate, neglect to ever fill out the survey, or fill it out but never get around to returning it to you. These people also need to be taken into account when drawing your sample. Because survey researchers generally expect a response rate of 50%–60% (though the response rate for online surveys is as low as 25%–30%, and the response rate for some face-to-face surveys is as high as 100%), you may need to draw a sample of up to about twice the size of what you hope your final sample size will actually be, depending on the mode of delivery you are using. It is also important to note that research concerning very private issues or deviant behaviors may have even lower response rates.

Low response rates introduce bias into research. That is, when there is a low response rate, it may be assumed that there are some ways in which the people who participated in the research are different from the people who declined to participate. Additionally, the higher your response rate (assuming a probability sample), the more confidence you can have in generalizing to the larger population. For these reasons, it is essential to try to increase your response rate as much as possible; and, as you will see later in the chapter, you will take many steps during the process of data collection in order to maximize response.

CHECK YOUR UNDERSTANDING

For your research on childrearing, how large do you think your population is? How large of a sample do you want to end up with? Taking into account response rates, how large of a sample will you need to draw?

Ethics

The particular steps you need to take to protect your participants in survey research will depend on which mode of delivery you choose and the survey questions you ask, as well as on the particular requirements of your local IRB.

Regardless of mode of delivery, for all survey research you must do the following:

- Give each survey a case number. Record only the case number, and no identifying information, on the survey. Keep the records matching the case numbers to any names or contact information locked away, and keep them separate from the completed surveys so that no one but you can match the specific survey responses with a particular respondent.

- Only report in the **aggregate**, which means you will never report on the answers of any one respondent individually, but only as part of a larger group.

- If the population is a very small, mostly homogenous one, avoid asking too many questions about identifying characteristics. For example, if your sample consists of teachers in the local school district and you include race, gender, age, marital status, subject area taught, and grade level taught, even though there may be several hundred faculty in the district overall, there may only be one unmarried Latina high school math teacher in her 30s in the entire district. Should anyone other than you accidentally see her survey or the data file, it may be possible to easily identify the respondent, thus breaching her confidentiality.

Informed consent for different modes of delivery can vary substantially, partly in terms of what you need to include, and partly in terms of how much explanation you need to provide for the different points. Here I will first describe the general parts of informed consent for surveys and then discuss specific variations for each mode of delivery. Informed consent for surveys may contain the following:

- A description of the research topic

- A statement of who may participate in the research

- A statement of who is conducting the research and how it will be used

- An estimate of how long it will take the respondent to complete the survey

- A statement that participation in this research is completely voluntary (the statement that is used in interviewing about withdrawing at any time is usually omitted)

- Notification that the research will be completely confidential *or* anonymous, as appropriate (remember, it can't be both). Additionally, provide a statement that no individual information about the respondent will be released— only information about the group will be reported (that is, reported in the aggregate).

- Full disclosure of any potential risks for participating in the research (with survey research, there usually are none unless you are asking about violence done to them or other potentially traumatic experiences, in which case you must state that they may experience emotional distress in answering some of the questions)

- Full disclosure of any immediate benefits to the participants for their participation in the research. Again, in survey research, there usually are none, but occasionally a researcher may provide a small monetary token for participation or conduct a drawing in which one of the participants in the sample wins a prize.

- Your contact information. Additionally, contact information for the chair of the governing IRB may be provided, and the participants can be advised that they may contact this person should they feel that any of their rights as research participants have been violated.

Mail Surveys

Most mail surveys are **confidential**, meaning you, the researcher, know who participated in the research, but you keep that information entirely secret. It is important to differentiate confidentiality here from anonymity. When research is **anonymous**, even the researcher does not know the identities of the respondents. Because with mail surveys you have the names and addresses of the people to whom you send the survey, and because you will most likely keep track of who has sent in their survey so

BOX 4.13

SAMPLE INFORMED CONSENT STATEMENT FOR MAIL OR TAKE-HOME SURVEY

The Department of Sociology at Greenfield State University is conducting this survey of alumni experiences. You may participate if you graduated with a sociology degree from Greenfield State between 2000 and 2018. The information will be used to help sociology students learn about the careers sociology students can go into, as well as to help the Department of Sociology assess its curriculum. The survey will take 10–15 minutes to complete. Your responses will be kept entirely confidential. If you have questions about this survey, you should contact Dr. Justin Case at jcase@gsu.edu. Thank you for your participation!

you can remind those who haven't to please do so, most mail surveys are confidential but not anonymous.

In addition to assuring respondents of confidentiality, researchers using mail surveys must be sure to inform respondents about the research. Typically, this is done with a brief statement at the top of the survey, rather than with a full informed consent statement; however, some IRBs may require fuller statements. Usually for mail surveys the statement does not need to be signed; by filling out the survey, the respondents are giving their **implied consent**. In other words, if they didn't consent, they simply wouldn't fill out the survey or return it to you. Therefore, the fact that they completed the survey signals their consent. Box 4.13 is an example of such a consent.

Online Surveys

Although online surveys are self-administered like mail surveys, researchers typically need to take extra precautions to protect confidentiality and to get informed consent from respondents. Potential respondents know that there are security risks and a high number of scams on the Internet, so you need to assure them that not only is your survey bona fide, but their information will, indeed, be protected.

Sometimes researchers using online surveys send announcements about the survey to particular e-mail addresses; other times information about the survey is simply posted on particular websites, and people visiting the website decide whether to follow the link. If you are e-mailing individuals, your survey can be anonymous only if you choose not to keep track of who has responded, which means that you cannot send reminders about filling out the survey. In addition, you must protect the confidentiality of those addresses, just as you would information obtained through snail mail. If, on the other hand, you recruit by posting a link about the study on a website, then responses will typically be anonymous because there is no need for follow-up reminders for nonresponders. In addition, you must protect the IP address of the computer from which the respondent replied to the survey. This is trackable and therefore needs to be kept protected.

At times the informed consent for online surveys is similar to that of mail surveys, with a short paragraph preceding the survey. More often, however, it

BOX 4.14
SAMPLE INFORMED CONSENT STATEMENT FOR ONLINE SURVEY

We invite you to take part in an online survey being conducted by the Department of Sociology at Greenfield State University. You are eligible to participate in this survey if you graduated from GSU between 2000 and 2018 with a major in sociology. The purpose of this survey is to evaluate the sociology program at Greenfield State and to explore the various careers of our sociology alumni. The results of the survey will be used to refine the sociology curriculum and to provide beneficial career information to current and future sociology majors.

This survey will take 10–15 minutes of your time. All of your information will be kept entirely confidential. All of your answers will be encrypted before they are sent to a password-protected data file. In addition, your name will never be linked to your answers, and your answers will never be discussed individually but only in combination with those of other alumni.

Your participation is completely voluntary. There are no projected risks involved in your participation, but there may be rewards. In order to thank you for your participation, at the end of the survey all participants will have the opportunity to enter their name in a drawing for one of two $125 gift certificates to the A.S. Bookstore, which are redeemable online. When you complete the survey, you will be automatically redirected to a page on the Department of Sociology's website. If you wish to enter the drawing, simply enter your name when prompted. Entering the drawing will not in any way compromise your confidentiality: Because the website and survey are on different computer servers, your survey responses can in no way be linked to your name.

If you have any questions or concerns about this survey, please contact Justin Case at jcase@gsu.edu. If you believe your rights as a research participant have been violated, please contact the chair of the Institutional Review Board, Dr. Strict, at (987) 555-5678.

If you agree to participate, please click on the button below to proceed to the survey.

Thank you for your participation!

resembles the full informed consent statements of interview and ethnographic research because researchers (and IRBs) want to make certain that respondents to online surveys (a) know that the research is bona fide and is neither a scam nor a marketing gimmick and (b) understand the steps that will be taken to protect their information (see Box 4.14). The informed consent statement will be followed by either a "next" button or an "I agree to participate" button that must be clicked in order to begin the survey. Although it's not a signature, it acts as such, and connotes active agreement to participate.

Phone Surveys

The steps generally taken to protect respondents' contact information in phone surveys are the same as that of mail surveys, except that everything is said much more briefly, in part because it is understood that taking too long to cover a full informed consent statement will try the patience of the potential respondents, reducing the overall number of people who are willing to participate. Additionally, it is phone numbers that need to be protected rather than addresses. The status of your survey as confidential or anonymous depends on whether you are using random digit dialing

BOX 4.15
SAMPLE INFORMED CONSENT FOR PHONE SURVEYS

Hi, Bree, I'm calling today from the Department of Sociology at Greenfield State University. We're talking to our alumni about their jobs and work experience. Let me just confirm that you graduated with a sociology major from GSU between 2000 and 2018. Yes? I promise I'm not selling anything and won't ask you for money. We just want to survey our alumni so that we can realistically help current students understand the careers they can go into, and so that we can adapt our curriculum to best prepare them for these careers. The survey will take 10–15 minutes and everything you say will be kept entirely confidential. Your participation is vital to help us understand the kinds of work our alumni have ended up doing, but your participation is completely voluntary. Is it okay if we go ahead and begin?

or whether you are working from a list (sampling frame) of specific individuals. If you are doing the former, you may be able to offer anonymity to your respondents; if it's the latter, your survey will be confidential. For phone surveys, the informed consent is obtained orally. In addition to the usual informed consent components, you should also make a statement that this is not a marketing gimmick and that you are not trying to sell anything. We also usually add to the statement that their participation is voluntary something that encourages them to participate, such as "Your participation is extremely important to the research but is voluntary."

Despite the brevity of the informed consent, unlike online and mail surveys, implied consent is not acceptable; the caller must ask if the respondent agrees to participate (or, alternatively, if it is all right to begin the survey), and the respondent must give an affirmative response to this question in order for the survey to proceed (see Box 4.15).

Face-to-Face Surveys

If the researcher will be administering the survey to the respondent by reading the questions aloud and recording the respondent's answers, the survey must be confidential because the researcher knows the identity of the respondent. Additionally, the informed consent usually follows the same model as the longer version of online informed consent, except that the respondent generally signs their name on the informed consent statement (see Box 4.16). Occasionally, the informed consent for researcher-administered, face-to-face surveys more closely resembles that for phone surveys. Contact your local IRB for its specific requirements and guidelines.

Take-Home Surveys

Take-home surveys are usually anonymous because there is typically no follow up for nonresponse. Informed consent usually follows the same rules of thumb as those of mail surveys.

BOX 4.16
SAMPLE INFORMED CONSENT STATEMENT FOR FACE-TO-FACE SURVEYS

We invite you to take part in an online survey being conducted by the Department of Sociology at Greenfield State University. You are eligible to participate in this survey if you graduated from GSU between 2000 and 2018 with a major in sociology. The purpose of this survey is to evaluate the sociology program at Greenfield State and to explore the various careers of our sociology alumni. The results of the survey will be used to refine the sociology curriculum and to provide beneficial career information to current and future sociology majors.

This survey will take 10–15 minutes of your time. All of your information will be kept entirely confidential. All of your answers will be kept in a password-protected data file. In addition, your name will never be linked to your answers, and your answers will never be discussed individually but only in combination with those of other alumni.

Your participation is completely voluntary. There are no projected risks involved in your participation, but there may be rewards. In order to thank you for your participation, at the end of the survey all participants will have their name entered in a drawing for one of two $125 gift certificates to the A.S. Bookstore. If you win the drawing, you will be notified by email, and you may redeem your prize online.

If you have any questions or concerns about this survey, please contact Justin Case at jcase@gsu.edu. If you believe your rights as a research participant have been violated, please contact the chair of the Institutional Review Board, Dr. Strict, at (987) 555-5678.

Thank you for your participation!

I understand that my participation is entirely voluntary, and all of my questions about the research have been answered.

Signature _____

Date _____

Box 4.17 is a checklist of the informed consent components that must be included in each mode of delivery.

Special Considerations

As with any research, if you intend to research minors, you must get the written consent of their legal guardians. Also as with any research, if you ask questions about illegal behaviors, you must fully inform the respondents of the potential risks of participating in your study. More often, survey researchers ask personal questions about behavior that isn't illegal but may (in some cases) be considered deviant, such as questions about sexual experiences and behaviors, amount of alcohol regularly consumed, or the current state of their marital relationship. In these cases, it is best to offer anonymity and to take extra steps to protect their information, not only because any leak of information could be very damaging to the respondent's reputation, but because your respondents will be more likely to answer these questions honestly if they feel confident that their responses will truly be protected.

One of the issues that may arise in applied survey research, especially evaluation research, is that respondents may need extra assurance that their participation in

BOX 4.17
INFORMED CONSENT BY MODE OF DELIVERY

	Mail	Online	Phone	Face-to-Face	Take-Home
Survey topic	yes	yes	yes	yes	yes
Requirements for participation	yes	yes	yes	yes	yes
Who is conducting	yes	yes	yes	yes	yes
Purpose	yes	yes	yes	yes	yes
Statement not selling anything	no	no	yes	no	no
Length of time	yes	yes	yes	yes	yes
Guarantee of confidentiality OR anonymity	yes	yes	yes	yes	yes
Description of steps taken for maintaining confidentiality OR anonymity	no	yes	no	yes	no
Statement: Participation is voluntary	no	yes	yes	yes	no
Statement of risks	only if there are risks	yes, even if there aren't any risks	only if there are risks	yes, even if there aren't any risks	only if there are risks
Statement of benefits	only if there are benefits	yes, even if there are no benefits	only if there are benefits	yes, even if there are no benefits	only if there are benefits
Your contact Info	yes	yes	no	yes	yes
IRB contact info	no	yes	no	yes	no
Passive consent	yes	no	no	no	yes
Active/affirmative consent	no	yes	yes	yes	no

the survey will in no way affect their status with the organization. For valid data, for example, your respondents must feel that if they express dissatisfaction with the services provided by your homeless shelter, they will not lose their spot at the shelter, be disqualified from future use of the shelter, or be treated differently by shelter staff. Additional measures may be needed to protect anonymity or confidentiality. Respondents may not be willing to give truthful answers to questions about sensitive topics if they already know the people conducting the survey, either because they may be embarrassed, or because they may fear that they will be treated differently. If, for example, the homeless shelter has a rule that no one using drugs is allowed to stay at the shelter, then it would be inappropriate (and generally a waste of time) to have shelter staff members administering a survey that asks a question about current drug use because respondents may be afraid of being made to leave if they answer truthfully. In this case, it would be important to have people not usually identified with the shelter administering the survey, and also to guarantee anonymity of responses.

If you are conducting applied research, you must be particularly sensitive to presenting the survey in a neutral manner. The data from your homeless shelter survey might, for example, be used to apply for funding for the shelter. Although it is OK to mention this to potential respondents in describing the purpose of the survey, you must be careful not to encourage them to change or exaggerate their answers in order to help you gain more funding. Telling respondents that "the more need we can document in the community, the more funding we can get" may be interpreted as a request to indicate that they are experiencing more need than they actually are. Although you might feel that there's no real harm in this because homeless shelters never receive enough funding anyway, this is not the case: Not only is it a breach of ethics, it is also a potential danger for your shelter. People are rarely consistent in their overestimations, so if you do the same survey 2 years from now, hoping to document an increase in need in the community, you may have trouble. If respondents were encouraged to overreport their level of need the first time, you will have difficulty the second time showing the increase in need that they actually have experienced.

CHECK YOUR UNDERSTANDING

Write the informed consent statement you would need for your research project, based on the mode of delivery you chose when you wrote your research question.

Preparing for Data Collection

Applied Research

Applied research is often used to accomplish a wide variety of goals at once. For example, if you are surveying the people who use the local homeless shelter, you may want to collect data that can assess the clients' satisfaction with the services, as well as collect data that can help you determine the most important areas for your next expansion in services, while at the same time gathering information about the shelter's clients that you can use for applying for an increase in government funding of the shelter. All of these different data needs must be weighed and taken into consideration during survey design. If any of the information will be used for official reporting to another agency, or for application for funds, there may be very strict guidelines about the acceptable ways in which that data may be collected or used, and this must also be taken into consideration. The Office of Housing and Urban Development (HUD), for example, has questions already designed that it wants homeless shelters to use when reporting to HUD about homelessness in the local community. Thus, you must carefully anticipate all of the possible uses of the data, and assess the impact these different uses might have on the design and implementation of the study.

Finalizing the Survey Instrument

Most obviously, preparation for data collection involves writing your survey. We have already discussed writing good survey items and response categories, but in addition to operationalizing your variables in this way, survey writing also involves ordering the questions and formatting the survey. Choosing the question order is important because answers to earlier questions can have effects on the way that people interpret or answer later questions, introducing bias into your results. Although there are no concrete rules about how to avoid this, you should always think carefully about how your chosen question order might affect responses. Sometimes researchers use a **split-half design**, in which they randomly split the sample in half, using the same questions but in two different orderings to test for order effects. This is especially helpful during pretesting to let you know in advance whether there is an order bias.

An important rule of thumb in choosing item order is that the first few survey items should be interesting and engaging to the participant, without being difficult to answer. More personal questions should come later in the survey. Survey items should also be grouped by topic and logically flow, otherwise it may lead to confusion, increasing the likelihood that respondents may drop out of the survey. One additional, but very important, rule about ordering is to save demographic questions until the end. Never start a survey with questions about race, marital status, level of education, gender, age, or income unless you are using the item in a skip pattern or to filter people who do not fit into the parameters of your sample from responding to the survey. Demographic questions should be saved until the end for two main reasons: (a) they are boring, and you want to begin your survey with items that will interest your respondents so that they remain willing and motivated to complete the survey; (b) they can also be sensitive, especially questions about age, education, race, and income. If you leave demographic questions until the end of the survey, the respondents have already invested enough time and energy into the survey that they are more likely to provide you with the information. If you place them at the beginning, however, you may lose respondents who feel the information is too personal.

In addition to deciding question order, you must also provide instructions and transitions for your respondents. Survey instructions appear at the beginning of the survey, and when the type of question changes, new instructions should also be given. **Transitions** help to make the survey flow smoothly, by introducing new question topics. Transitions can also be used to inform respondents about your reasons for asking particular questions, which not only puts the questions in context, but also can assure the respondents that questions they may otherwise feel are "none of your business" have a good reason for appearing on the survey.

In preparation of data collection, you must also format the physical appearance of your survey. Although formatting is less important in face-to-face and telephone surveys (though it needs to be clear and user friendly for the survey administrator), it is extremely important in self-administered surveys. Here are some general guidelines for formatting:

- Don't try to fit too much on a page, even if you are attempting to save on printing costs. When items are crowded, it creates visual confusion for the respondent. Single-space items (including response categories), but skip a line between items, and use a large enough font size that people can easily read the text.

- Place response categories under the survey item (rather than next to it), and list categories vertically down the page, rather than from left to right. The exception is if you use a **grid pattern**, which is commonly used when several survey items all share the same beginning of the question or are very closely related, and all have the same response categories. Box 4.18 contains an example of a grid pattern. Grid patterns are recommended when you have four or more survey items that all have the same responses, as they simplify survey completion for the respondent. Using too many items in a grid pattern (more than 10) or too many grid patterns, however, may increase the chance of a response set.

- Never let a page break separate a survey item and its response categories, never let some response categories continue onto another page, and never let a page break interrupt a question.

The last step of completing the survey instrument is to carefully proofread the survey. There should be *absolutely no* typographical, grammatical, or punctuation errors on the survey. Question numbering should be correct and consistent. Formatting of response categories should be consistent (for example, if one response category starts with a capital letter, all of the response categories should start with a capital letter; if one set of response categories is labeled with lowercase letters, all the response categories should be labeled with lowercase letters). Inattention to these details signals to your respondents that you are neither thorough nor careful, casting doubt on how carefully you may handle the confidentiality of their data or present the results.

Training

For phone surveys and face-to-face surveys, training your research team is one of the most important steps in preparing for data collection. Even people experienced in administering surveys need to be trained for your particular survey. Good training focuses on making sure that everyone on the research team understands the purpose

BOX 4.18
EXAMPLE OF A GRID PATTERN

Please indicate how important or unimportant the following skills are to your current job.

	Very Important	Somewhat Important	Somewhat Unimportant	Very Unimportant
Problem-solving	⬭	⬭	⬭	⬭
Written communication	⬭	⬭	⬭	⬭
Public speaking	⬭	⬭	⬭	⬭
Data collection	⬭	⬭	⬭	⬭
Statistical or data analysis	⬭	⬭	⬭	⬭
Computer skills	⬭	⬭	⬭	⬭
Leadership	⬭	⬭	⬭	⬭
Ability to work effectively in a team	⬭	⬭	⬭	⬭
Analytic thinking	⬭	⬭	⬭	⬭
Ability to work independently	⬭	⬭	⬭	⬭

of the survey; that they comprehend the ethical issues involved (particularly confidentiality or anonymity); and, most important, that they become very familiar with your particular survey instrument. Such training involves a lot of decision making on your part: Most of the interaction that the survey administrators have with the respondents will be scripted, and every person involved in administering the survey has to do it exactly the same way as everyone else in order to protect reliability. In a phone survey, for example, you have to script not only the introduction after the respondent has answered the phone, but how the administrator should respond to each anticipated reason that a potential respondent might initially decline to participate. In addition, administrators need to be trained in how to respond when asked for clarification on survey items, when and how to probe for more information, how to follow any skip patterns in the survey, and how to manage their voice speed and tone. In face-to-face interviewing, those administering the surveys should additionally be coached on the use of any visual aids, and if answers are being recorded on a laptop computer, trained to use the computer program for recording the respondent's answers.

Pretesting the Survey

Regardless of the particular mode of delivery, preparation for collecting survey data focuses heavily on pretesting the survey. There are several ways to do this, and it is advisable that you use more than one pretest method. First, you can show your survey to people who are knowledgeable about the topic and/or about the population you will be surveying. This can include colleagues who are experts in the area, as well as community leaders, service providers, and people who take leadership roles within the population you are studying. For example, if you are surveying people about their access to health care, you might ask for input on the survey from colleagues who also study this issue, and from someone at the Medicaid office, from someone working at the local free clinic, from someone at the local hospital, and perhaps from a private-practice physician; you could also try someone who might have insight into special populations you are trying to reach, such as an immigrant community or agricultural workers. After showing them the survey, make changes to the survey based on their insight and recommendations (realizing, of course, that not all of these people will be experts in survey research design, and so their recommendations must be evaluated and sometimes modified in order to fit with best practices in survey construction).

Second, you can conduct cognitive interviews with people who are very similar to those you will recruit for your survey. During a **cognitive interview**, respondents who are members of your research population go through the survey from start to finish orally, not only reading the questions and responses, but also narrating the reasons why they chose to respond the way they did. For example, if the survey item asks the respondents how much they agree with the statement *I am pleased with the quality of service I received*, after the respondents answer the question, an interviewer might then ask, "Why did you choose *somewhat agree*? When you read *quality of service,* what came to your mind? Did you take anything else into account in choosing your answer?" In other words, the cognitive interview is aimed at understanding why and how respondents chose their answers in order to make sure that the survey items are valid and that the answers given to those items mean what the researcher thinks they mean. Additionally, the cognitive interview helps to identify places where the survey may be confusing to some respondents, to identify how appropriate the reading level is for the target population, and to identify instances in which the respondents have experiences or opinions that were not foreseen by the researcher, so that the response categories provided were either not exhaustive or not mutually exclusive. Finally, cognitive interviews help improve the reliability of the survey because they help the researcher determine how uniformly the questions will be understood by respondents. The number of cognitive interviews that you will conduct depends on the size of your population, your resources, and the cost of your survey.

Similar to cognitive interviews is behavior coding, another method of pretesting a survey. Behavior coding is primarily conducted with face-to-face and phone surveys, but could also be adapted for self-administered surveys (perhaps particularly Internet surveys). **Behavior coding** involves using close and careful observation while the survey is being administered to individuals who are similar to those in your target population. The primary goal is to look for any possible errors or problems in the survey. For example, if there is a question that multiple respondents ask to be repeated, it may indicate that the wording of the question is confusing. If respondents ask for clarification ("Does volunteer work count?"), it indicates that the wording needs to be more precise. Every time such an event occurs during the survey, the researcher carefully notes the problem for use in revising the survey. Additionally, behavior coding is used to determine how well directions are followed by the person administering the survey: Do they properly follow the skip pattern? Do they read each survey item exactly as worded? Do they hesitate or get tongue-tied while reading a particular item? Do they read the transitions properly? Each deviation from the protocol is also noted, and used either to improve training for those administering the surveys, or to clarify/change the protocol so that it will be properly followed—something that is important for the reliability of the survey.

Sometimes survey researchers conduct focus groups as part of their pretesting of surveys. Typically, this involves having a small group (5–12 people) that is very similar to your target population fill out the survey individually, and then join in a **focus group** (group interview) that focuses on its reactions to the survey questions that were asked ("Were there any that made you uncomfortable? Any that you didn't understand?"). The focus groups may also be used to get information about what topics or items they think were missing from the survey.

Finally, regardless of which other methods of pretesting the survey that you might choose, it is *highly* advisable that you pilot-test your survey. **Pilot testing** can be thought of as a trial run of the survey: It is administered *exactly* as it will be for the "real thing," with people drawn from the same target population. Additionally, the survey results from the pilot test are analyzed before the survey is actually launched. This way, any errors or problems that arise either in administering the survey or in analyzing the results can be detected before the survey is done "for real." Although the sample for the pilot test is drawn from the target population, these respondents are omitted from the actual sample, and the results of the pilot surveys are not used in the final data analysis.

Data Collection

After you have pretested your survey, made changes to it and finalized it, gotten IRB approval, and drawn your sample, you are ready to start collecting your data. Some of the actual procedures for data collection vary according to which mode of survey delivery you are using, so we'll address each one separately.

Mail Surveys

Because mail surveys typically have low response rates, many steps are taken to improve this rate. First, before sending out the survey, each person in the sample should be sent an introductory letter in which you alert the respondent that the survey is on its way, and you explain a little bit about the survey, how the respondent was chosen to participate, and why their participation is so important to its success. You should also include your contact information in case the respondent never receives the forthcoming survey. Within a week of the introductory letter, you should send out the survey with a cover letter that again describes the survey and explains how very important the respondent's participation is. Two weeks after sending out the survey, send out reminder postcards to all participants, reminding them to complete the survey and mail it back. The postcard should include contact information in case the respondent never received the survey or needs a replacement survey sent. After 2 more weeks, send out a second copy of the survey to all the people in the sample who have not yet responded, again impressing upon them the importance of their participation. Finally, for those who have still not responded, choose an alternate mode of survey delivery: Perhaps you can conduct the survey over the phone or provide them a Web link for completing the survey online. Sometimes at this stage researchers try sending a final copy of the survey so that the respondent must sign for the delivery, or send it via special delivery. By following all of these steps, you can hope to achieve about a 60% response rate (Groves et al., 2011).

Phone Surveys

Most phone surveys utilize a **CATI** (computer-assisted telephone interviewing) **system**. The CATI system contains not only the questions for the administrator to read, but also prompts, directions for the survey administrator, as well as record-keeping for refusals, half-completed surveys, and so on. The survey administrators input the respondents' answers directly into the computer, which is logged directly into a data file, eliminating the need for data entry.

Administrators should be properly trained in using the survey instrument, as well as the CATI system. It is extremely important that each respondent has the survey delivered to them *in exactly the same way* as every other respondent, regardless of who administers it, and so great care is taken to make sure that not only is every question read completely and accurately *exactly as written*, but even the administrators' voice tone, modulation, and speed should be as standardized as possible. In order for respondents to have time to accurately follow and digest the questions and answer choices, for example, most survey researchers have their administrators speak at a speed of about two words per second. Supervisors typically have the capability of listening in (unannounced) on the phone calls made by survey administrators, in order to detect deviations from the protocol and to identify possible sources of error.

Response rates for phone surveys have dropped significantly in the past decade, so many steps are taken to ensure as high a response rate as possible. Phone calls must be made throughout the day and evening, as well as on weekends, so that people can be reached regardless of their schedule. Each attempt at contact is recorded as "busy," "no answer," "voice mail," or "message left." Additionally, there is an attempt to convert each refusal to participate into agreement to complete the survey. The researcher scripts the appropriate responses for each reason for refusal, and these often include reiteration of the importance of the person's participation to the study; assurance that the information will be kept completely anonymous or confidential (as appropriate); promises regarding the actual time required to complete the survey; reiteration of the purpose of the survey; assurance that the survey is being conducted for social research (or a not-for-profit), as opposed to being for sales or marketing purposes; and suggestions that the survey gives the opportunity for the respondent's "voice to be heard" or to "be counted." If a potential respondent replies that they don't have time at the moment, that the designated respondent is not at home, or other delaying techniques, these are treated as potential conversions and are followed up on as many times as necessary to successfully administer the survey. **Hard refusals**, when a potential respondent flatly declines to participate, are also treated as possible conversions. The rule of thumb is that, typically, survey researchers will continue to call the potential respondent until they receive two or three hard refusals—unless the refusal is accompanied by a specific request to be removed from the call list, in which case the researcher is obligated to comply.

Face-to-Face Surveys

Like mail surveys, face-to-face surveys often require an introductory letter and a fair amount of follow-up. Although some face-to-face surveys are conducted on the spot, more often an initial letter is sent and is followed by a follow-up phone call or visit, whose purpose is to arrange a time for the administration of the survey. The day before the survey is to be administered, a second phone call or visit is typically used to confirm the date, time, and location of the meeting. If the respondent cancels the appointment, or does not show up, further letters, phone calls, and/or visits may be required in order to secure the respondent's participation.

Like phone surveys, those conducting face-to-face surveys typically use a computer program (computer-assisted personal interviewing, or CAPI, program) in conjunction with a laptop computer to lead them through the administration of the survey and the recording of respondents' responses. Also like phone surveys, administrators of face-to-face surveys must follow strict protocol, including those regulating voice speed and modulation. This requires significant training for survey administrators, as great care must be taken to make sure that the administration of the survey is **reliable**— that is, that regardless of which administrator conducts the survey, the respondent's answers will remain the same. You should keep in mind that sometimes, even though an administrator has done an excellent job of conducting the survey, their own race, gender, age, or other physical characteristics may bias the responses that the respondent gives. A survey about racism may yield unreliable results if the administrators are racially diverse. For this reason, researchers sometimes purposely match respondents with administrators who share particular characteristics with them, such as their sex, race, or age.

In some ways, face-to-face surveys are like qualitative interviews. Administrators must be concerned about maintaining their appearance, being polite and friendly, and putting the respondent at ease. Unlike qualitative interviews, however, the principles of positivism dictate that survey administrators should minimize chitchat; avoid revealing personal information about themselves or their opinions; and keep the researcher–respondent relationship as brief, superficial, and impersonal (but friendly) as possible.

Face-to-face surveys also often use visual aids to help respondents. For example, when there are many possible answer choices, the administrator might show the respondent a card with all the possible answer choices, so that the respondent not only hears them, but is able to read the responses as well, aiding in recall and reliability.

Online Surveys

Online surveys, like mail surveys, are self-administered, so once the survey has been designed and uploaded, the majority of the work for the researcher involves contacting potential respondents. If the survey is aimed at a population with a known sampling frame (such as all alumni at your university with a sociology major), then you will need to contact the individuals chosen in your sample, either by e-mail, snail mail, or phone to alert them to the availability of the survey and the importance of their participation. Often, you will want to track respondents so that you can follow up with reminders to those who don't respond after the first week or two. The form of the reminder will vary according to the particular contact information you have for the potential respondent. Additionally, after two reminders have been sent, you may increase response rates by offering the survey through another mode of delivery, such as a phone survey or a mail survey.

If the population is one without an identifiable sampling frame (such as people who use websites as a primary source of information about health issues), then you will need to post a link to your survey on relevant websites (which usually requires the permission of the Web host, and sometimes costs money). Although posting announcements about your survey on social media such as Facebook has recently become a popular way to recruit respondents, it is considered a much less desirable way to recruit than by posting your announcement on relevant websites because people who are connected to one another on social media tend to be very similar to one another; this, of course, introduces a very large bias into your study.

Evaluation Research

If you are trying to evaluate a brand-new program or policy, you may actually conduct two surveys, a pretest and a posttest. A **pretest** is the survey you would conduct before the new policy went into effect or before people had participated in the new program. This survey gives you baseline data against which you can compare the **posttest**—the survey that would be conducted after the policy has gone into effect or after people have gone through the new program. In comparing the posttest data to those of the pretest, you can see whether, indeed, the new policy or program has made any differences, and if so, in what ways. In order to make the comparisons effective, the items on each survey instrument *must be the same*. For more information on evaluation research, see Chapter 8.

CHECK YOUR UNDERSTANDING

Describe the steps, based on your chosen mode of delivery and your research questions, that you would take both in preparing for data collection and in actually collecting the data.

Data Analysis

Data analysis for survey research generally begins with the creation of a codebook. A **codebook** is a document that tells the people doing data entry exactly how to code each response. **Coding** in quantitative research is different than it is in qualitative research: it means assigning numerical values to each answer given by a respondent. In qualitative research, each person coding the same transcripts or field notes will code the data differently. In survey research (and all quantitative research), coding should always be consistent within a single project, and coding conventions mean that coding is fairly standardized across projects. Codebooks include the question exactly as it appeared on the survey, the possible answer choices, and the codes assigned to each answer. Additionally, they include information on how to code an answer that was left blank (**missing data**). The creation of the codebook often occurs while waiting for the respondents to return the surveys.

Cleaning the Data

Once the codebook has been created, and survey responses are coming in, you may start to enter the data into a computer file, which you will use to calculate the statistics. Sociologists typically employ statistical software packages such as SPSS or Stata, but a basic spreadsheet program like Excel can also be used if the analysis will involve simple statistics. Data entry is typically required only for mail surveys because phone, face-to-face, and Web survey data are automatically entered into a computer system as part of the data collection process. In these cases, you would need to wait until all the data have been collected; then you can import the data file into the statistical package you will be using.

After all the data are entered or imported, you will need to clean them. **Cleaning the data** means checking them for errors and making decisions about problematic answers. There are several steps to doing this. To check the data for errors, you will **spot-check** the data entry by choosing, for example, every 10th respondent and verifying that their answers have been accurately entered into the data file. A second step is **contingency cleaning**, which means checking to see whether answers to contingency questions match up to how the respondents followed the skip pattern. In other words, if only married people were supposed to answer items 5–10, and the data file shows that case #321 answered that they were *not married*, but there are responses recorded for them for items 5–10, it indicates a possible error in the entry of the marital status information. Finally, you should run a frequency distribution report for each variable. A **frequency distribution** is the tabulation of how many respondents chose each of the possible answer choices for a question. By producing a printout of the frequencies for each variable (also called "running frequencies"), you can check to make sure that there are no odd, highly unexpected, or unacceptable answers. For example, if you conducted a simple, random sample of all the households with telephones in the nearest metropolitan area, and your frequencies tell you that 100% of the respondents were female and 0% male, you know that there is some sort of a problem: It would be nearly impossible with a random sample of a large general population to be exclusively female. As another example, if you were looking at the frequency for the variable *number of children* and one of the responses is 88, you might realize that there was a typing error made during data entry, as it is highly unlikely that someone has 88 children, and more likely that this person has 8 children. These errors are important to spot because they make an enormous amount of difference in the results you get. If you had not caught the 88 error, for example, you might think that the average number of children of respondents in your sample was 45.2, rather than 2.6. In addition to checking for errors, cleaning the data requires that you decide what to do with these and other problematic responses. Do you go ahead and reenter the 88 answer as 8, or do you decide to treat it as missing data—that is, a nonresponse to the question?

There may be other problematic responses you need to deal with during your cleaning of the data. Sometimes people do not fit the criteria you've specified for answering contingency questions, yet they have answered the question anyway. For example, you've directed respondents to skip question #10 if they answer "no" to question #9. One of your respondents answered "no" to question #9, but instead of skipping #10 as they were supposed to, they went ahead and answered it anyway. You need to decide whether you will count either of those answers, or whether you will treat the answer to #9 (and hence #10) as missing data. If you have asked respondents to only check one answer, but someone checks two, you need to decide how you will handle this problem. Also, if a respondent quits the survey five questions before the end, you need to decide whether you will use the responses the person did give or whether you will throw out the entire survey. None of these issues has "right" answers—they are decisions that must be made by every survey researcher. Once you are confident that your data file is free of errors, and you have made decisions about all of the problematic responses, your data file is considered *clean* and hence ready for analysis.

Web-based surveys, phone surveys, and some face-to-face surveys (those administered using a computer program) usually require very little data cleaning because there are fewer data entry errors when responses are entered as part of the administration of the survey itself. Those that do occur are not detectable through data cleaning, as there is no hard copy or other document against which to check the responses. Furthermore, most computer administration programs make it impossible for respondent/administrator errors to be made. The programs can be set up so that, for example, if the respondent is only supposed to answer with one response choice, the computer will not allow more than one to be chosen. Likewise, the software can be programmed to automatically skip contingency questions for people who do not fit the criteria for those questions. If you have collected data from one of these types of surveys, you simply need to import the data into a statistical software package (some all-in-one packages allow you to use the same package as that with which you recorded the data).

Statistical Analysis

There are many types of statistical procedures that you can use for your analysis, and describing them is way beyond the scope of this book. I will simply give you a quick introduction to a few of the most basic ones. First, statistics may be univariate, bivariate, or **multivariate**. **Univariate** statistics are those that look at only one variable at a time, such as the mean, median, or mode of a variable. Frequency distributions are also a type of univariate statistics. These are the statistics you will most likely use for a descriptive research question. **Bivariate** statistics are those that examine the relationship between two variables. Crosstabs are among the most simple, and common, types of bivariate statistics, and we will look at them more in depth. Bivariate statistics are used to test hypotheses for explanatory research questions.

A **crosstab** is so called because it is a tabulation of frequencies across the rows or down the columns of a table. Box 4.19 shows an example of a crosstab. The crosstab is the entire table, which shows us something about the relationship between two variables: in this case, *education levels* and *belief in spanking*. Convention is that the categories of the independent variable are listed down the left side, and the categories of the dependent variable are listed across the top. In this particular case, the independent variable is *level of education* and the dependent variable is *belief in spanking*. The crosstab shown in Box 4.19 demonstrates that 33.5% of those respondents with less than a high school education strongly believe that spanking is necessary, while 28.5% of those with a high school education, and 20.9% of those with a college education, strongly believe this is true. It also shows us that only 4.5% of those with less than a high school education strongly disagreed that spanking is necessary, as compared to 12.3% of those with a graduate degree who strongly disagreed. In addition, the table shows us that overall, 27.3% of the respondents strongly agreed that spanking is sometimes necessary, as compared to only 6.6% that strongly disagreed.

BOX 4.19

EXAMPLE OF A CROSSTAB: PERCENTAGE OF RESPONDENTS AGREEING THAT SPANKING CHILDREN IS NECESSARY, BY HIGHEST DEGREE OBTAINED, 1972–2016

Highest Degree Obtained	Belief That Sometimes Spanking Children Is Necessary (%)				
	Strongly Agree	Somewhat Agree	Somewhat Disagree	Strongly Disagree	Row Totals
Less than high school	32.2	46.0	16.8	5.0	100
High school	28.0	48.4	17.8	5.8	100
Junior college	26.6	47.4	18.7	7.2	100
Bachelor	20.6	46.4	23.6	9.4	100
Graduate	16.3	42.4	27.3	14.0	100
Total	26.5	47.2	19.4	7.0	100

Source: GSS 1972 –2016 Cumulative Data File, accessed through the University of California, Berkeley, Data Archive (http://sda.berkeley.edu/archive.htm).

We can summarize the results presented in this table by saying that there seems to be a negative relationship between *level of education* and *belief in spanking*; that is, the higher the level of education, the less likely the respondent is to report believing that spanking is necessary. This is a **negative relationship** because as the value of the independent variable goes up, the value of the dependent variable goes down. Saying it is a negative relationship also tells us, however, that as the value of the independent variable goes down, the value of the dependent variable also goes up. In other words, what makes it negative is that the dependent variable changes in the *opposite direction* as the independent variable. Conversely, if higher levels of education were associated with increased levels of agreement that spanking is necessary, then we would say there is a **positive relationship** between these two variables because as level of education increases, level of agreement that spanking is necessary also increases. By saying it's a positive relationship, we are simultaneously indicating that as level of education decreases, the level of agreement also decreases. In other words, the relationship is positive because the dependent variable changes in the *same direction* as the independent variable. Box 4.20 provides a visual representation of this.

BOX 4.20
POSITIVE AND NEGATIVE RELATIONSHIPS

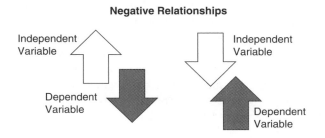

Positive Relationships

Independent Variable

Dependent Variable

Independent Variable

Dependent Variable

Negative Relationships

Independent Variable

Dependent Variable

Independent Variable

Dependent Variable

CHECK YOUR UNDERSTANDING

Describe how you would analyze the data for your research project on childrearing.

Causality

It is important not to infer from a crosstab more than can actually be determined; we cannot, for example, know from a crosstab whether the relationship between *level of education* and *belief in spanking* is a causal one. In other words, we can see that there is an **association** (relationship) between the two variables, but we don't know whether *level of education* is an actual cause of *belief in spanking*. It may be, for example, that the relationship is a **spurious** one, meaning that another variable has affected both level of education and belief in spanking. Those with higher levels of education may come from families with less traditional beliefs about family and children. People coming from families with less traditional beliefs may also be more likely to reject traditional forms of discipline, such as spanking. We also don't know that *level of education* came first. It may be that someone has had beliefs about spanking all the way back to childhood, before ever making any decisions about level of education. With our crosstab, then, we cannot tell which variable came first (*level of education*, or *belief in spanking*); nor can we tell whether there may be another variable exerting influence on both of these variables. There are three rules for determining causality:

- There must be an **association** between the variables (when one changes the other also changes).

- The independent variable happened before the dependent variable (**temporal order**).

- All other **plausible alternative explanations** for the change in the dependent variable have been eliminated.

Tip: Crosstabs *cannot* tell you if there is a correlation. Despite sloppy usage in popular speech, a correlation is actually a specific type of association between variables that is determined using either Spearman's or Pearson's test of correlation. If you do not run one of these tests, you cannot say anything about whether there is a correlation.

Thus, with the crosstab we can only assert that we have evidence that there is an *association*, not a *causal relationship*, between the two variables because we cannot be certain of the temporal order and we have not eliminated the plausible alternatives. In other words, the association might be a spurious one. Also note that to prove that there even is an association we need more stringent statistical tests—with crosstabs, we can merely look for *evidence* that such an association exists. More advanced statistical techniques that are beyond the scope of this book can be performed to test for associations and causal relationships.

In discussing quantitative analysis, it is important to emphasize that although calculating the statistics is often called "analysis," in actuality, the real analysis comes not in the computation of the numbers, but in the interpretations you make of those numbers. In other words, you—the analyst—must tell your audience what those numbers mean, and why they are important. Additionally, because it is impossible to report all of the statistics you will have generated in the course of your analysis, you will need to decide which statistics to report—which, again, means deciding which numbers are important, and why.

Evaluating the Quality of Data and Analysis

The quality of survey data is based in part on an assessment of the reliability and the validity of the data. Survey questions are **reliable** if they are understood in the same way by every respondent. Take, for example, a survey item used in the evaluations of teaching on my campus: *The teacher regularly monitors student learning.* I interpret that item to mean that a teacher regularly asks students to demonstrate what they have learned through assignments, tests, and in-class participation, and that the faculty member assesses that learning to make sure that students are learning what the teacher wanted them to learn. When I have asked my students how they interpret this item, however, some have said that it means that the teacher doesn't move on to the next topic or concept until they are sure that all of the students have understood the material. Other students have said that it means asking for questions in class, to make sure that students understood what was just explained. Still others interpret it as making sure that students know throughout the semester what their grades are in the class. The very fact that this item can be interpreted so differently means that it lacks reliability.

In addition to using reliable measures, in order for survey research to be reliable, every respondent must have been asked the questions in exactly the same way, in the same order (unless you are testing for order effects), and under similar conditions—all of which make the detailed training of administrators crucial. Unlike in qualitative interviewing, survey researchers cannot decide partway through the data collection process to ask new questions based on the information they are getting from early respondents, and they can't decide to change questions after data collection has begun in order to clarify or improve questions. Survey items must be perfect to begin with—thus the importance of pretesting the survey.

Good survey research must be reliable. Reliability, however, does not in and of itself make it good research; it must also be valid. You will recall that **validity** generally means that you are measuring what you think you are measuring. Thus, **measurement validity** means that the indicators you use in a survey are measuring the variable that you think they are measuring. Asking respondents if they had a date for Valentine's Day is probably not a very valid measure of whether they are in love. The major problem with measurement validity for survey research is that it is very difficult to turn complex, abstract concepts into measurable variables. How, for example, would you accurately measure whether someone is "in love" using survey items? The feeling is too complex to capture in survey questions. This is why, although qualitative interviews lack reliability, they are generally more valid than surveys, as they are better able to get at the complexities of issues. Although the problem of validity is never completely eliminated in survey research, you can do a few things to help improve (or at least test) the validity of your items. First, you can make sure that your measures make logical sense. Measuring *being in love* by asking respondents how many newspapers they have read in the last month is not valid. Second, you can see whether there are existing indicators that have been used by other researchers, and then compare the results of your indicators with theirs. If they are similar, this lends some evidence corroborating the validity of your measures. A third way is to use multiple survey items to measure a single aspect of the concept you are measuring, especially if the concept is complex. Fourth, you can run a statistical test (called a factor analysis) that will allow you to see how well the responses to each of these items hang together; that is, if you have used 10 items to measure *being in love*, and if respondents who say they are in love have answered those questions with few or no contradictory responses, then you have some evidence that your items are valid. Finally, you can compare the responses you get to some other independent measure. For example, if the people who, by your measures, are in love are more likely to get married within a year than are the respondents who were not shown to be in love, you again have some evidence that your measures are valid.

Validity can also refer to the analysis. **Analytic validity** for survey research means the proper statistical techniques have been used, and the results have been appropriately analyzed. In other words, you must accurately interpret the statistics and not claim more than a statistic can tell you. Likewise, the validity of your analysis requires both that you choose statistical techniques that are appropriate for what you want to know and that your data fit the minimum requirements for each statistic. Some statistics can only be calculated, for example, on interval or ratio-level data. Your results would be lacking validity if you tried to compute a mean for a variable that was measured at the nominal level. You can't compute the "average" religion, for example, or the "average" city of residency, but you can compute an average age of respondents and an average annual income if both of these variables are measured at the ratio level.

In addition to assessing reliability and validity, the quality of survey data is also based on the sampling procedure. Probability samples yield higher-quality survey data about a population than do nonprobability samples. If nonprobability sampling is used, it must be made very clear that the results are limited to the people sampled and not generalizable. Additionally, having the most complete possible sampling frame, the highest response rates, and the least amount of missing data will yield higher-quality data.

Presenting the Results

Presentation of survey research usually starts with a review of the literature and a discussion of the theoretical perspective that you are using, especially if you are conducting the research to test the theory. Next, usually you introduce your research question, the methods you used to collect your data, some information about your sample, and the basic procedures you used to analyze the data. Then you begin to discuss the statistical patterns you found in your analysis. Whether you are presenting the material for an oral presentation or a written report, the results are usually presented in a very similar way, using tables or charts as well as describing them orally or in writing. You do not need to describe every number in every table; rather, you will usually focus on the strongest, weakest, and most surprising results that you have found. Sometimes you may choose to compare these results with those found in other studies or with your own previous findings. In such cases, if your results differ significantly from those of the other studies, you will probably want to offer at least an educated guess as to why the results differ. You will want to clearly state which of your hypotheses have been supported by the data and which have not. If you are testing theory, you will want to explain the implications this research has for the theory. If you are conducting applied research, you will want to offer concrete suggestions for policy or programming that are supported by the data. Many reports of basic survey research end with suggestions for productive directions for future research on the topic that will go beyond or extend the current study.

Summary Points

- Survey research is best for studying relationships between variables, including causal ones, which respondents may not even be aware of.

- This method is based on positivist principles and must be carried out in a highly standardized, very precise way, with no room for flexibility or changes once data collection has begun.

- The aim of most surveys is to generalize the results from a smaller sample to a larger population. This requires probability sampling. As compared to qualitative research, you will be able to learn less in-depth information, but if properly conducted, you will be able to extend your results to a much larger group of people.

- The stages of survey research are distinct and conducted in a specified order, with research design being completed prior to the start of data collection, and data collection being completed prior to the start of data analysis.

- Both reliability and validity of data and of analysis are necessary for high-quality survey research.

Key Terms

aggregate 126
analytic validity 148
anonymous 127
association 146
behavior coding 137
bias 97
biased wording 113
bivariate 144
categories 101

CATI system 139
census 123
cleaning the data 142
closed-ended questions 93
cluster sampling 120
codebook 142
coding 142
cognitive interview 137
conceptualize 106

confidential 127
contingency cleaning 142
contingency question 115
convenience sampling 122
crosstab 144
deductive 98
dependent variable 101
descriptive 99
double-barreled questions 113

5

Secondary Data Analysis

Although very popular in sociology, surveys can be very expensive to conduct, especially large-scale surveys that are representative of the population. In addition, it doesn't make sense to spend the time and money conducting your own survey if someone else has already done a survey that reasonably measures the variables of interest to you. Hence, many researchers opt to use secondary data rather than conduct surveys themselves. **Secondary data** are data that another researcher (or team of researchers) has collected, but which you analyze. Strictly speaking, any type of data that another researcher has collected using any research method could be secondary data, but when sociologists say they are using secondary data, they almost always mean secondary *survey* data. In other words, the primary researcher has designed the survey, selected the sample, collected the data, prepared a codebook, and input the data into a data file. As a secondary researcher, you request (and sometimes pay for) a copy of the survey instrument, information on the sampling techniques, the codebook, and the data file with all of the **raw data** (unanalyzed data) in the file. Your main job as a secondary researcher is to conduct the statistical tests and interpret the results. Even though you haven't collected the data yourself, secondary data analysis fits our definition of research because (a) both the data collection and analysis are *systematic*; (b) the data have been collected (albeit by other researchers) from primary sources and are therefore *empirical*; and (c) you don't simply report the data, but have to *analyze* and interpret them.

Methodology

Like survey research, the use of secondary data is usually grounded in **positivist methodology**. That is, in using secondary data, you will try to be as scientific as possible, aiming for replicability, objectivity, and an absence of bias. As with survey research, those using secondary data analysis usually aim to generalize their research to

 Reminder: Probability sampling means that the respondents were chosen completely at random and that everyone in the sampling frame had an equal chance of being chosen.

REAL PEOPLE, REAL RESEARCH

Leanna Gonino

As an undergraduate at Central Michigan University, Leanna used secondary data analysis to test symbolic racism theory. The theory generally argues that whites no longer perceive blacks as being disadvantaged, and thus they believe that policies aimed at improving the lives of blacks amount to unfair and unearned advantages. The theory further posits that as blacks gain equality, these beliefs among whites become stronger. Leanna wanted to test the effect that Obama's presidency had on these attitudes. She used General Social Survey (GSS) data to examine changes in attitudes among whites and blacks between the Obama and Bush administrations. Using advanced statistical procedures, she was able to control for age, gender, Hispanic ethnicity, education, and income. This allowed her to isolate the effects of race and of the different presidential administrations. Leanna's results showed some support for symbolic racism theory, in that whites were, indeed, less supportive of the policies than blacks. She did not find, however, that there was any change in whites' support of these policies after Obama's election, providing evidence against the theoretical proposition that whites' attitudes toward such policies become more negative with gains in race equality. Her paper went on to win the undergraduate paper award at the North Central Sociological Association and was published in a professional academic journal.

a population beyond the study's sample, and because many secondary data sets are large or national data sets using probability samples, they are often particularly well-suited to such generalizing.

Theory

As with most survey research, secondary data analysis is particularly well-suited to working deductively and testing hypotheses. Because the sample sizes are large and probability sampling was most likely used, the results of secondary data analysis are usually generalizable, an important feature when testing hypotheses. Just as with survey research, hypotheses are generated from existing theory and are then used to test whether various aspects of the theory hold up empirically in the real world. Also like with survey research, the theories being tested are usually theories of middle range that concern themselves with some particular phenomenon (such as assimilation among immigrants or ways that community characteristics affect levels of crime), rather than large overarching theoretical frameworks that try to explain the totality of social life and process. Note that although secondary data analysis can provide evidence that helps to confirm or refute theoretical principles, because it can't be used to understand people's experiences in a deep way, it is rarely used to provide alternative theoretical explanations if the evidence seems to refute the theory. For these same reasons, secondary research isn't usually used to create theory inductively from scratch.

Research Questions

Because secondary data are usually gathered using surveys, the research questions that are appropriate for research using secondary data are identical to the research questions that are good for survey research: demographic characteristics, social trends, attitudes, self-reports of simple behaviors, levels of knowledge, and, to some extent, causal relationships. Also like survey research, this method is *not* good for answering questions about how individuals see or experience the world or about complex emotions or meaning. And even more than survey research, secondary data analysis is almost always used to answer explanatory research questions. Secondary data also almost always uses individuals as the unit of analysis. A copy of the table showing research questions appropriate for survey research from Chapter 4 is reprinted here (with the descriptive questions removed) to refresh your memory (Box 5.1).

As with survey research, you will write many hypotheses. You should do this *prior to* choosing a data set, because it will help to ensure that you choose a data set with the variables necessary to answer your research question.

 Reminder: Explanatory research looks for relationships between variables. Although surveys can't prove causality, in explanatory research we look for evidence that suggests that some variables affect others, as opposed to descriptive research, which simply tells you who does (or thinks) what, without looking for explanations of those behaviors or thoughts.

Applied Research

Secondary data analysis is not a research method that is commonly used for applied research. In much applied research, the research is aimed at either

BOX 5.1

EXAMPLES OF RESEARCH QUESTIONS APPROPRIATE FOR SURVEY (AND THUS SECONDARY DATA) RESEARCH

Research Question	Appropriate for Surveys Because It Examines . . .
How does religious belief affect attitudes about gender equality?	attitudes
What is the relationship between social class and religiosity?	social trends
How does age affect television viewing behaviors?	simple behaviors
How does employment affect the likelihood that students will finish their college education in 4 years?	cause and effect

evaluating a particular program at a particular location, or it is aimed at figuring out the need within a particular community for some new program or service. In both cases, available secondary data sets are not likely to be applicable. If you are conducting applied research on a very large scale, however, such as trying to evaluate the impact of a state or national law, policy, or program, then perhaps there will be a secondary data set that would be helpful. You should not, however, try to use national-level data either to evaluate a local program or to assess needs related to a local problem.

See Box 5.2 for a list of common errors in writing research questions for secondary data analysis. Study these to help avoid making the same mistakes in writing your own research questions.

BOX 5.2
AVOID THESE COMMON ERRORS IN WRITING RESEARCH QUESTIONS FOR SECONDARY DATA ANALYSIS

Research Question	Explanation of Error
How do LGBTQ people decide if and when to come out to their friends?	Survey research cannot provide detailed information about decision-making processes.
How do people emotionally recover after they are involved in a car accident?	Not appropriate for surveys. Survey research cannot answer questions about complex experiences.
How does age affect the likelihood of having a life insurance policy?	Question is too narrow. You would have too few questions on the survey to make it worthwhile.
How do rates of divorce affect life expectancy?	We don't get rates within a population from surveys. These are taken from government offices that officially record life events, not surveys. This question is appropriate for existing statistics, but not secondary data analysis.
What careers are today's college graduates most interested in?	This is a descriptive question. Secondary data analysis is based on explanatory research questions, not descriptive ones.
What type of graduate school programs are preferred by sociology students?	Answerable with just a few words. Also descriptive rather than explanatory.
How do the families of patients at the Sunshine Memory Care Center rate the care received by their loved ones?	Inappropriate for secondary data analysis because evaluation data of a specific facility won't be found in available data sets.
How is self-esteem related to recovery after a natural disaster?	You may be unlikely to find an existing data set that asks about both of these variables.

> ## CHECK YOUR UNDERSTANDING
>
> Write a research question about a controversial social issue of your choosing. Explain why this research question is appropriate for secondary data analysis. Then write five hypotheses related to your research question.

Literature Review

The literature review is conducted in the same way and for many of the same reasons for research using secondary data as it is for survey research: to help you write and refine your research question, to develop hypotheses, to identify important variables, to inform you about a variety of ways in which a variable has been operationalized, and to act as a comparison for your final results. In addition, you can use the literature review to help you identify potential sources for the secondary data that you may use.

Ethics

You might be surprised to learn that even if you are using secondary data, and therefore not surveying respondents yourself, *you will likely still need to get approval* from the Institutional Review Board (IRB). Though your application will certainly qualify as "exempt," many IRBs will still require you to file an application because, as a researcher who will be in possession of raw data, you may have enough information about the individuals in the study to (at least hypothetically) figure out their identities and violate their confidentiality, and therefore you have ethical responsibilities to protect them.

Because you won't be conducting the survey yourself, you are relieved from worrying about many of the steps that must be taken to protect respondents: Issues of informed consent, separating participants' contact information from survey responses, and any issues related to conducting research with minors will all be taken care of by the primary researchers who collect the data. When you get the data file, you will not receive the names, addresses, phone numbers, e-mail addresses, IP addresses, or other explicitly identifying information of the participants. Each respondent will be identified with a case number, and the only way you would be able to identify a particular participant is by figuring it out from the answers the person has provided. For example, if the data set concerns victims of large fires and there happened to have been only one such fire in your local area, and only three of the survey respondents were over the age of 80 and lived alone when they were evacuated, you may be able to figure out which of the respondents was your friend's 86-year-old grandmother, based on the answers those three people gave to the survey questions. It will only be possible to figure out identities if the sample is small and if you have some knowledge of the individuals who took part in the study (even if this is not the case, however, you will likely still need to get approval from the IRB). If you do manage to determine respondents' identities, you are responsible, of course, for protecting their information so that it remains completely confidential.

> **Reminder:** To report in the **aggregate** means that you never talk about individuals in your report; you only talk about them statistically in groups, such as "85% of respondents over 65 reported . . ."

The primary way you will need to protect participants is to report the results of your analysis only in the aggregate, so that individuals cannot be identifiable to others by their answers. Additionally, you will need to continue to protect the respondents by keeping the raw data locked up when it is in print form and password protected when it is in electronic form.

Preparing for Data Collection

"Data collection" in the section heading above is perhaps a misnomer, since you won't actually be collecting the data yourself. But you will need to prepare for your data analysis, and that will involve several steps, the most important of which is finding an appropriate data set to use. There are literally hundreds, maybe even thousands, of data sets available. Many of these data sets have been gathered explicitly for the purpose of making them available to other researchers as secondary data sets. The **General Social Survey (GSS)**, for example, is conducted every two years by the National Opinion Research Center (NORC) and is a face-to-face survey of demographic, behavioral, and attitudinal questions given to a national representative sample of American households. The GSS is widely used in sociological research. The U.S. Census's American Community Survey is another widely used secondary data set, and it also consists of a nationally representative sample of American households, though the questions are focused on demographics and life circumstances rather than attitudes about social issues. Some data sets, like the GSS and the American Community Survey, concern broad areas of information, but many of the available data sets are narrower in scope, meaning that they have a particular focus: politics, health care, aging, economics, education, and so on. Some data sets are available for free, some cost money, and for some the availability and price depend on whether you are affiliated with a university.

To find an appropriate data set, you should consult the existing literature, but you will also want to search the various **data repositories** (organizations that store secondary data sets for researchers to use) to see what each has available. Box 5.3 has a list of some of the popularly used general social science data repositories—note that there are others not listed here, including repositories with more specialized focus, such as religion in contemporary social life and criminal justice data. In looking for a data set, you are searching for a set that does the following:

- Has the information that will allow you to answer your research question

- Includes as many variables as possible that you will need in order to test your hypotheses

BOX 5.3
POPULAR DATA REPOSITORIES OF SECONDARY DATA SETS

Repository	Web Address
Inter-University Consortium for Political and Social Research (ICPSR) Data Archive	https://www.icpsr.umich.edu
Roper Center for Public Opinion Research	https://ropercenter.cornell.edu
Pew Research Center for the People and the Press	https://people-press.org/dataarchive
University of California, Berkeley, Archive of Social Science Data	https://sda.berkeley.edu/archive.htm
Odum Institute for Research in Social Science	https://odum.unc.edu/
The Dataverse Project: Open Source Data Repository	https://dataverse.org/
UK Data Service	https://www.ukdataservice.ac.uk/get-data

- Operationalizes the variables in ways that are both appropriate and valid for what you want to measure

- Uses a sample that is as close as possible to the population you are trying to understand

- Employs sampling procedures that yield a sample as representative as possible of the population you are studying

Sometimes there will be more than one appropriate data set, and your challenge will be to choose the one that best fits with your research question. Conversely, you may not find any data sets that fit your research question or hypotheses well. In this case, you will have to decide whether you can compromise and choose a data set that may not be ideal but that is good enough, so you won't have to conduct your own survey. And finally, you may find that none of the available data sets really meet your needs, and you will need to conduct your own survey research in order to answer your research question.

CHECK YOUR UNDERSTANDING

Using the Internet, go to at least two of the data repositories in Box 5.3 and look for a data set that would be appropriate to use for answering your research question. Consider topic, population, sample, variables, and when it was conducted. Explain why it is a good one for your research question and hypotheses. In what ways does this data set fall short?

BOX 5.4
DECISION PATH FOR CHOOSING A SECONDARY DATA SET

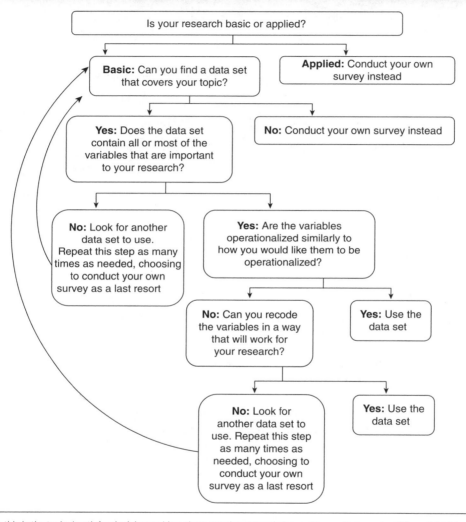

Note: While this is the typical path for decision making, there may be unusual circumstances that require different decisions.

Conceptualizing and Operationalizing

 Reminder: For survey research, to **conceptualize** is to write a definition of the important concepts; to **operationalize** is to write questions that measure the information you want to capture.

Although you are not designing a survey instrument yourself, you will still need to make some decisions about conceptualizing and operationalizing. As already suggested, you will need to decide if the way the variables are measured in the data set works with the way you have conceptualized for your research. In other words, does this way of operationalizing the variable make sense for your research, given your research question and hypotheses? Has it really captured what you want to measure? Is it operationalized at a level of measurement that is useful to you, given the hypotheses you want to test? Note that even though the data have already been collected, you can make small alterations to the way that a variable is measured. Obviously, you can't change the way the questions were asked, but you can change the ways the results are tabulated. It is common practice for researchers using secondary data to recode variables. To **recode a variable** means to change the numerical codes that are assigned to particular responses or to change the response categories themselves (and in the process, also changing the numerical codes assigned to them). For example, the questionnaire may have asked respondents their race and given them six categories from which to choose: *white, black, Latino, Asian/Pacific Islander, Native American,* or *other*. You may find, however, that having six categories is not that useful to you. If your hypotheses don't differentiate between different groups of people of color, you may not want your data split into six categories. If your hypothesis is *People of color are more likely than white respondents to support gun control legislation,* then having only two categories (*whites, people of color*) will help you test your hypothesis better than having six categories. In this case, you might recode the response categories *black, Latino, Asian/Pacific Islander,* and *Native American* into one category that you call *people of color*. This type of recoding is common and is sometimes referred to as **collapsing a variable**, though what you really are doing is collapsing the response categories for a variable. It would not be unusual for you to collapse many variables in the data set so that the variables are most useful to you.

You can also collapse a variable by changing it from a ratio or interval level of measurement to an ordinal level of measurement. For example, if the survey asked respondents to write in the actual number of hours they worked for pay last week (ratio level), you might turn this into an ordinal-level measurement by sorting people into six categories: *0, 1–10, 11–20, 21–30, 31–40,* and *40+*. To collapse variables you can program the statistical software package to recode the variables for you (in other words, you don't have to change each person's answer by hand), but you will need to change the codebook to reflect the changes that you have made.

 Reminder: Interval/ratio levels of measurement ask for an exact number, while **ordinal** levels of measurement ask for a number within a range, so that categories can be ranked but exact differences can't be calculated.

You can recode a variable by reassigning an individual's answer to a different response category. Taking the same example, you may have people who respond to the race question by choosing *other,* but whom you don't consider to truly fit that category. If one respondent chooses *other* but writes in that they are Italian, you may decide that for your purposes Italians are actually white and recode that person's answer so that numerically they are coded as *white* and not as *other*. Similarly, if someone writes in that they are "part of only one race—the human race," you might decide to recode that answer so that it doesn't count as *other* but as **missing data** (that is, you treat it as if the person didn't answer because you still don't know what race the person is). Unlike collapsing variables, reassigning an answer to a different response category cannot be done by a computer program. Rather, as the analyst, you must make a decision about how to code each individual answer, and you would do have to do this type of recoding by hand.

The process of recoding variables can be a lengthy one, especially if the data set is very large. It also requires an extreme level of precision and attention to detail; if you make a mistake in collapsing a variable, your research results will be meaningless, and these errors can be very hard to detect once they have been made. For this reason, a backup of the original raw data file should always be kept in a secure location, and with no changes made to the file, in case you make an error and must go back to retrieve the original information in the data set.

CHECK YOUR UNDERSTANDING

Looking at your hypotheses, choose one of the variables from the data set you selected and, on paper, recode that variable. Explain why this way of operationalizing the variable is better for your uses than the way it was originally operationalized in the survey.

Sampling

The researchers originally conducting the survey have drawn the sample for your data set, so you will not have to worry about sampling. You do need to make sure, however, that the primary researchers drew the sample from the same population to which you want to generalize your analysis. If not, the data set is not a good one for your purposes (or, at the least, you will need to be satisfied generalizing to the population from which they drew, rather than the one from which you wish they drew). You will also need to make sure that the procedures they used were clear and that you understand who has participated in the study and how they were chosen to do so. You also need to make sure that when you analyze the data, the interpretations and conclusions you are drawing are appropriate for your sample. If the sample is not representative, for example, then you can't generalize your analysis beyond the sample. Similarly, if the sample size is small (even if it is representative), you must be careful not to claim that your analysis is definitive.

Data Collection

Once you have identified the data set you will use, you will need to contact the repository to get the actual data. Again, sometimes you will be asked to pay for access to the data set. You will be provided with an electronic version of the raw data. Sometimes it will already be available in a format that is compatible with the statistical software that you plan to use; in other cases, you will have to convert the data to a compatible format. This can be a very exacting and time-consuming process. In addition, you will need to obtain and become very familiar with the codebook, so that you understand very well the variables and how they are measured. You will also need to become familiar with the questionnaire, the sampling procedures, and the data-cleaning processes that were used. In short, you need to become as familiar as possible with your data.

Data Analysis

Once your secondary data are in the proper format, you are familiar with the code-book and questionnaire, and you have recoded or collapsed any variables you want to change, you are ready to begin analyzing your data. You may conduct all the same types of statistical analyses on your secondary data that you can on any other survey data, with frequencies and crosstabs being among the simplest and most common. You will not only calculate but also interpret the results in the same way you would your own survey data. A caution about using data sets that have been collected over many years, such as the GSS: to calculate bivariate statistics such as a crosstab, the *same* participants must have answered the survey items measuring *both* variables that you want to use in your calculations. For example, if you hypothesize that people who meditate more will get less stressed out, you might be pleased to find that the cumulative GSS data file has a variable called *meditate (Within your spiritual or religious tradition, how often do you meditate?)* and another called *stress (How often do you find your work stressful?)*. The problem is that you can't test your hypothesis with these two particular variables because they were each asked in only one year that the survey was given, but not in the same year as each other. This means that the respondents who answered the question about stress were completely different respondents than those who answered the one about meditation. Because a crosstab examines how a person's answer to the survey item measuring the independent variable affects their answer on the item measuring the dependent variable, the crosstab won't work when the questions were answered by different people.

Evaluating the Quality of Data and Analysis

The quality of research using secondary data analysis is judged by the same criteria as is survey research: reliability and validity. Regarding reliability, you have little control, of course, over how the data were originally collected. It is of utmost importance, therefore, that you investigate this thoroughly before choosing the secondary data set that you employ, as using questionable sources could jeopardize the reliability of your research. You must also make sure that the original questionnaire used reliable survey items: The questions must be clear and specific enough that respondents are all likely to have understood them in the same ways. Some secondary data sources that have been collecting data regularly over many years may have actually tested the reliability of some of the survey items that they consistently use. If so, you will want to review and consider the results of this reliability testing when choosing your data set.

 Reminder: Reliability is the consistency of different aspects of the survey: consistency in how the questions were asked, in how they were understood by the respondents, and in how they were recorded.

The validity of secondary data analysis is going to rest primarily on the goodness of fit between the

 Reminder: Validity in survey research means that you are measuring what you think you are measuring.

variables in your hypotheses and the variables actually measured. For example, let's say you are using the GSS data, and you have a hypothesis that whites hold more negative stereotypes of Latinos than they do of Asian Americans. The GSS includes questions that ask *How warm or cool do you feel toward . . .* for both Hispanics and Asian Americans, but to use the answers to these two questions to test your hypothesis would produce an invalid analysis, because feeling cool toward a particular group is not the same as holding negative stereotypes about it. The measurement may be more a reflection of how well respondents know people in that ethnic group: If you grew up as an African American in a largely Latino neighborhood, you might report feeling more warmly toward Latinos than you do toward Asian Americans—not because you hold more negative stereotypes of Asian Americans, but because you have had more close and positive relationships with Latinos. Thus, if you used this measure to test your hypothesis, your analysis would have low validity.

Finally, you must be sure you understand the sampling procedure used by the original researchers in order to know to what extent you may generalize your findings to a larger population. If you generalize a nonprobability sample to a larger population, for example, your analysis will lack validity.

Presenting the Results

After providing a review of the literature and describing the theory you are testing (if any), you will briefly discuss your research question. Then you will want to name the secondary data set that you have chosen, give some information about the methods that were used to collect your data, and offer some information about your sample. If the data set is not a large or well-known one, you should also discuss why you chose this particular data set. In addition, you should discuss the basic procedures you used to analyze the data, including any recoding you did of variables important to your analysis.

Whether you are preparing the material for an oral presentation or a written report, you will usually present the results in a very similar way, using both verbal and visual formats. In other words, you will represent your statistics using tables or charts, as well as describing them orally or in writing. You do not need to describe every number in every table; rather, you will usually focus on the strongest, weakest, and most surprising results that you have found. Sometimes you may choose to compare these results with those found in other studies, or with your own previous findings. In such cases, if your results differ significantly from those of the other studies, you will probably want to offer at least an educated guess as to why this is so. Many reports of secondary data end with suggestions for productive directions for future research on the topic that will go beyond or extend the current study.

Summary Points

- Secondary data analysis is research conducted by another person, to which you add an analysis. This can save you a tremendous amount of time and money over conducting your own survey.

- Because secondary data analysis is usually based on survey research, it answers the same kinds of research questions and uses the same methodology; furthermore, the original researchers will have used the same sampling and data collection techniques as in survey research.

- It is important to find a data set that fits well with your research question and hypotheses. You may have to compromise by changing your hypotheses to match the way the variables were measured in the data set.

- You will likely have to do a fair amount of recoding and collapsing of variables before you begin your analysis.

- Data analysis will be identical to that of survey research. You need to be careful that you understand the sampling procedures, as well as the reliability of the data collection procedures, so that you understand how well you may generalize your findings.

- Validity issues in secondary data analysis will focus on how well the data set you choose measures the variables you use in your hypotheses.

Key Terms

collapsing a variable 159
data repositories 156
General Social Survey
    (GSS) 156

missing data 159
positivist methodology 151
raw data 151

recode a variable 159
secondary data 151

Existing Statistics Research

Using existing statistics can, like secondary data analysis, save time and money. **Existing statistics** are similar to secondary data, but instead of raw data, you use statistics that someone else has already calculated. Most of the time, however, the statistics do not come from surveys that someone else has collected (the *Uniform Crime Report* is one example of an exception to this). Rather, they come from organizations, often government agencies, that gather the information as part of their record keeping. For instance, it wouldn't make much sense for you to survey the students in your university to find out how much ethnic diversity your campus has, or how many students receive financial aid, or how many have a GPA over 3.0. As part of their regular processes, the admissions office at your school keeps track of the first, the financial aid office keeps track of the second, and the registrar keeps track of the last. Getting this information from these offices not only will save you much time and money as compared to conducting a survey, it will give you better information: The information these offices give you will be as complete as possible because it will cover everyone (not just a sample), and you won't have to contend with sampling issues and response rates like you would have to if you surveyed students about these topics.

When using existing statistics, you would not simply report the racial makeup of the school, the number of those receiving financial aid, or the average GPA. Remember that the definition of research requires that you conduct analysis, so even though the statistics have already been computed for you, you will need to do something additional with them to create a new analysis. This typically involves *treating each statistic as a variable in and of itself,* and then combining the different variables (statistics) in ways that they haven't been combined before to compute new statistics. In existing statistics, the **unit of analysis** (the "who" or "what" you are studying) is never individuals; instead, it is an institution (such as schools or universities) or a geographical location (such as cities, counties, states, or nations). So for this kind of research, each unit of analysis is a case, and for each case, you collect a variety of statistics, each one of those statistics acting as a variable. We could, for example, hypothesize that schools with less ethnic diversity (historically black colleges and predominantly white colleges) have higher average GPAs than schools with a greater balance of students from

REAL PEOPLE, REAL RESEARCH

Rachel Kinney

Two years after getting her BA in sociology, Rachel Kinney was hired as a research analyst by a labor union that represents health care workers (SEIU-UHW). She used statistics from county websites and from the US Department of Labor to calculate wage disparities between workers in different counties and states, taking into account various measures of the cost of living. She also used these and other existing statistics to calculate how giving the workers a small raise (such as 25 cents an hour) would economically impact the county as the workers had more income to spend. These analyses were used by the union in bargaining contracts with the counties.

Elizabeth Mower

Elizabeth got her start doing research when interning for an evaluation research company during her senior year as a sociology major. Now she works for a research firm and uses a variety of methods in her job, including surveys, experiments for evaluation research, secondary data analysis, and existing statistics. In one of her current projects, she is evaluating particular anti-drug interventions during a five-year grant period. While she and her coworkers use multiple methods for this, particularly interesting is their use of existing statistics in order to measure community-level outcomes. They use publicly available data at the county level for such measures as motor vehicle accidents, crimes, emergency room visits, and hospitalizations related to alcohol and/or prescription drugs. They also track children born with health problems related to maternal alcohol use. Because some of the counties are so small and rural, and thus sometimes have very few incidents, Elizabeth and her team aggregate the data at the state and regional levels to calculate the statistics. They also standardize the measures by using annual population estimates in each county or region to calculate incident rates per 1,000 or 10,000 residents. Each of the participating anti-drug coalitions receives a report with tables, charts, and maps of the data analysis for their region, which they then use to further adjust and plan their anti-drug programs.

> **Tip**: In this example, the unit of analysis is *universities*, and the variables are *racial makeup*, *number of people receiving financial aid*, and *average GPA* of all students at the university.

different races and ethnicities. We would then collect statistics for each university and college across the country about the racial makeup of the school, the number of people receiving financial aid, and the average GPA. Finally, we would use that information to compute new statistics that test our hypothesis that there is a negative relationship between racial/ethnic diversity and average GPA. This is not just a simple reporting of GPA or race statistics—it requires collecting information for each of the units of analysis in our sample (universities), getting the needed statistics for each school, entering them into a statistical software program, and computing new statistics that allow us to test our hypotheses.

BOX 6.1

EXAMPLE OF A SPREADSHEET USING EXISTING STATISTICS FOR COMMUNITY-LEVEL VARIABLES

| File | Home | Insert | Page Layout | Formulas | Data | Review | View | ACROBAT | Tell me what you want to do... |

From Access · From Web · From Text — Get External Data
From Other Sources · Existing Connections · New Query · Show Queries · From Table · Recent Sources — Get & Transform
Refresh All · Connections · Properties · Edit Links — Connections
Sort · Filter · Clear · Reapply · Advanced — Sort & Filter
Text to Columns · Flas... · Ren... · Dat...

R20

	A	B	D	F	H	J	L	C
1	Community	% white	Median hshld income	% engish not spok	% blw poverty	%BA blw poverty	%Wrkd FT year round	
2	Anaheim, CA	69.9	81,951	61.7	16.2	5.3	42.7	
3	Bloomington, IN	81.5	31,254	15.5	38	12.3	30	
4	Chico, CA	88.6	43,148	15	25.2	7	32.1	
5	Hilo, HI	17.5	55,815	17.3	17.4	8.2	36.6	
6	Houston, TX	58.3	47,010	48	21.9	5.9	47.1	
7	Isla Vista, CA	64.4	22,304	37.4	63.7	17.2	11.3	
8	Norman, OK	79.5	52,484	10.5	17.9	6.5	43.7	
9	Pittsburgh, PA	66.3	42,450	10.7	22.3	8.2	41.9	
10	Roseville, CA	78.1	78,446	17.6	8.6	3.1	41.8	
11	Seattle, WA	69.2	74,458	21.6	13	5.2	48.8	

Source: All data is from the U.S. Census Bureau American Factfinder (2018).

Box 6.1 is an example of a spreadsheet that we would use to conduct analysis for existing statistics research. Notice that each case is a city or town, and for each case there are a number of variables. Each of those variables is made up of an existing statistic that was drawn from a source of existing statistics (in this case, the American Factfinder, which is run by the US Census Bureau).

Methodology

Like all the quantitative research methods we've studied, research using existing statistics is usually based upon positivist methodology. Specifically, in using existing statistics in your research, you will try to be as scientific as possible and will aim for replicability, objectivity, and an absence of bias. In addition, you will work deductively, testing hypotheses to build theories and generalizing your findings from your sample to a larger population. Because in existing statistics you are not collecting data directly from individuals, it is particularly easy to use this scientific approach.

 Reminder: Replicability means anyone else could use the same procedures you did and come up with the same results; **objectivity**, for positivists, means that you remain neutral about the results of your study and do not try to affect them in any direction; to be **free from bias** means that you follow highly controlled steps to rule out or minimize skewing the results by doing things unscientifically.

Theory

Existing statistics are often used to test theories and hypotheses from those theories. They have been used, for example, by world systems theorists to look at changing amounts of power among countries in the world. They have also been used by conflict theorists to show how much the richest 1% of the U.S. (or world) population owns relative to the rest of the population. This helps to test and document conflict theory's propositions that groups in power actively manipulate the social structure to benefit themselves. Another example is research on racial disparities in arrest and incarceration rates. Indeed, conflict theorists have long used existing statistics to document inequalities among groups, as well as to convincingly show that those who have the most privilege often financially benefit directly from the inequality perpetuated against other groups.

Although much of feminist research uses qualitative methods, quantitative feminist researchers have used existing statistics to document gender inequality and to examine the effects of policies that increase or decrease that inequality. For example, every year since 2006 the World Economic Forum has used a wide variety of measures to rank each nation in the world on a gender equality scorecard to determine which countries have the most and least amount of gender equality and the policies that have increased or decreased that equality (in case you are wondering, at the time of this writing, the United States is ranked #49 out of 144 countries; World Economic Forum, 2017).

Existing statistics are a powerful tool for testing theoretical ideas and hypotheses from large theoretical frameworks as well as from theories of middle range because they are usually drawn from the regular daily recordkeeping of government offices, rather than from surveys or qualitative methods. This helps to eliminate sampling bias, making existing statistics seem very objective, a key element for theorists like conflict and feminist theorists who are making claims that some people already perceive as biased or overly political. The use of existing statistics that are drawn from respected sources, such as governmental sources, helps to bring legitimacy to their claims and makes them more difficult to argue against.

Research Questions

Because existing statistics do not usually come from survey research, this method answers different research questions than does secondary data analysis. Rarely can it be used to answer research questions about attitudes toward social issues or levels of knowledge like survey research and secondary data analysis can. It is very good, however, for answering research questions about officially reported behavior, such as arrests, divorce, voting, and getting laid off. It is also useful for answering questions about demographic characteristics (sex, age, race, income) of a group (students attending your university); population trends (births, deaths, marriages, immigration, migration); economic costs (home prices, gas prices); spending (amount shoppers have spent on Internet purchases, amount cities have spent on attracting jobs to the area); consumption of goods and resources (water use, buying of electronic equipment); and use of services (enrollment at schools, use of the Golden Gate Bridge, amount of medical coverage). Additionally, research questions for existing statistics are always explanatory, never just descriptive. Box 6.2 shows examples of research questions that existing statistics research is good at answering.

 Reminder: Explanatory research seeks to explain the relationship between variables; **descriptive research** only describes characteristics.

Existing statistics are more likely to be used for basic than applied research. Because the statistics available do not evaluate programs, assess individuals' needs, or determine the effectiveness of an intervention, existing statistics research often doesn't fit well with applied research, unless the application is for a unit of analysis larger than the individual. When the unit of analysis is an institution or a geographical area, existing statistics *can* provide important information that might help you predict the needs of a large population or the potential success of a program for a geographic region. For large geographic areas (state or nation), sometimes existing statistics are used to evaluate new laws or

 Reminder: The **unit of analysis** is the "who" or "what" about which you're gathering information.

BOX 6.2
EXAMPLES OF RESEARCH QUESTIONS APPROPRIATE FOR EXISTING STATISTICS

Research Question	Appropriate for Existing Statistics Because It Examines ...
How has the economic downturn affected the financial stability of small cities?	economic costs and spending
How have migration patterns among recent college graduates changed over the last 20 years?	population trends
What is the relationship between standardized test scores and state spending on education?	officially reported behavior and spending
How does local farming affect water availability?	consumption of resources
What is the relationship between rates of immigration and use of medical services?	population trends and use of services
How have changes in voter turnout affected campaign spending?	officially reported behavior and spending
How do college admission rates for African Americans vary by region?	institutions' official decisions
How do crime rates affect home prices?	officially reported behavior and economic costs
How has the legalization of the recreational use of marijuana impacted the economic health of the states that have legalized it?	evaluation of a policy at the state level

BOX 6.3
AVOID THESE COMMON ERRORS WHEN WRITING RESEARCH QUESTIONS FOR EXISTING STATISTICS

Research Question	Explanation of Error
How does speaking a foreign language at home affect the likelihood of being in poverty?	Although these variables exist in existing statistics form, the question has the individual as the unit of analysis. It can't be answered because the gathered statistics don't include the exact same people for each variable. Instead, we have to write the question with a school district, city, county, state nation, or other collectivity as the unit of analysis. *(What's the relationship between ethnic makeup and rates of poverty in American state capital cities?)*
What are recovery rates for people in outpatient substance abuse programs?	This is a descriptive question that doesn't include a dependent variable. Existing statistics research is explanatory and should include both independent and dependent variables.
How have sexual practices changed over the last 20 years in California?	Sexual practices are not likely to be officially reported, and therefore they are not available as an existing statistic.

 Tip: Note that officially reported behaviors are often reported as rates. Rates use a unit of analysis larger than an individual, so they make very good variables for existing statistics research.

policies. For example, you could compare the economic health of states that have cut social service programs and those that have maintained funding for those programs to better inform policy makers on how budget cuts to social services relate to the overall economic conditions of the state. Caution must be taken, however, with these sorts of analyses: There may be so many other differences between states that are not related to budget cuts that you cannot make any valid claims about causality. Comparisons across states (in this example) can help to study effects of a program or policy, and we can combine these with comparisons over time, which can help us develop a timeline that can help us to identify what particular variables happened when, to better isolate effects. But there are usually too many other plausible causes to make definitive statements about causality. See Box 6.3 for common errors to avoid in writing research questions for existing statistics.

CHECK YOUR UNDERSTANDING

Write a research question appropriate for existing statistics research that relates to poverty.

Ethics

You will have even less responsibility for protecting people when you use existing statistics than you did with secondary data analysis: You will not have to apply to the Institutional Review Board (IRB) for approval, you do not need to get informed consent, and you will not need to worry about protecting confidentiality. This is because, by definition, statistics are **aggregated**. In other words, you will have no information at all about how individuals responded to any given question (no **raw data**); you will only have information about the group or subsets of the group. This means you will have no way of even accidentally figuring out the identities of the people whose information was collected. Your only ethical responsibilities in research using existing statistics are to procure the statistics in an ethical manner, to cite your sources, and to accurately report your findings.

Preparing for Data Collection

To use existing statistics, you will need to decide from where you will get your statistics, and which ones to use. Unlike secondary data, you will likely get your information from more than one source. Choosing which statistics you will use is of utmost importance because the statistics and sources you pick will directly affect both the results you get and the conclusions you can draw. There are a wide variety of sources of existing statistics, and your research question and hypotheses will guide which ones you will use. One of the best places to start existing statistical research, the *Statistical Abstract of the United States* is an annual publication that was released by the U.S. Census Bureau from 1878 to 2012. The Census Bureau stopped publishing it in 2012 because of budget cuts, but recently a research archives company named ProQuest stepped in and has started publishing it again, renaming it *ProQuest Statistical Abstract of the United States*. This amazing resource is a compilation of statistics gathered by a wide range of government organizations such as the Census Bureau, the Department of Labor, the Department of Homeland Security, the National Science Foundation, the National Endowment for the Arts, the Federal Election Commission, the Department of Education, and the Department of Agriculture. The volume contains statistics gathered by some private organizations as well. It covers more than 200 broad topics, ranging from travel to telecommunications, from poverty to prisons, and from arts to agriculture. Not only is this the single most important source of statistical information about the United States, each table also directs you to an original source that will usually have many other statistics related to the particular topic. Most of the information in the *Statistical Abstract* is taken at the national level, but there are some state-level and city-level statistics as well, in addition to a small amount of statistics from other nations.

Some other good sources of existing statistics are listed in Box 6.4. There are, of course, a plethora of other excellent sources of existing statistics, and you should conduct a thorough search of relevant sources before choosing the ones you will use. I highly recommend consulting with a librarian who specializes in government documents and knows many of the sources available to you.

BOX 6.4
SELECTED SOURCES OF EXISTING STATISTICS

U.S. Census	National-, state-, county-, city-, or block-level demographic and household information https://www.census.gov/
Digest of Educational Statistics	Information about education https://nces.ed.gov/programs/digest/
Uniform Crime Report for the United States	Crime and criminal justice information https://ucr.fbi.gov/ucr
Vital Statistics of the United States	Yearly population and demographic information https://www.cdc.gov/nchs/products/vsus.htm
RAND California	Statistics for all 50 states (despite the name) on a wide range of social issues; also includes county-level data for California https://www.rand.org/research.html
Statista: The Statistics Portal	Statistics on 600 industries, brands, and services internationally including sales, consumption, use and economic forecasts; also includes statistics on social issues https://www.statista.com/

In general, you should keep in mind that you are looking for statistics that do the following:

- They enable you to answer your research question.
- They operationalize the variables in ways that are both appropriate and valid for testing your hypotheses.

In addition, if you use statistics from a variety of sources, you should try to choose statistics that are compatible with one another by deciding on statistics that have the following characteristics:

- They were all collected in the same year.
- They were all collected for the same geographic locations.
- They refer to data collected at the same level (individual, city, county, state, or nation).

If, for example, you want to understand how rates of mental illness relate to rates of homelessness, poverty, and crime, you may need to consult multiple sources of data, but each needs to be compatible with the others and with your research question. If you find poverty rates by *county*, for example, but mental illness rates by *city*, you cannot accurately draw conclusions about the effects of mental illness on poverty rates because the units of analysis are different (in this example, *county* for the poverty rates and *city* for the mental illness rates). Similarly, if you find mental illness rates for 2016 but poverty rates for 2018, you need to be very careful about drawing conclusions about the relationship between these two variables because the poverty rate may have changed dramatically between 2016 and 2018; this might have also affected the mental illness rates for those years, making your conclusions invalid.

CHECK YOUR UNDERSTANDING

Find at least two sources of existing statistics that will help you answer your research question about poverty. Which statistics in particular will you use from each source? Then explain how compatible these statistics are with one another. In other words, what is the unit of analysis of each? When were each of these statistics collected? What other discrepancies between them must you keep in mind?

Conceptualizing and Operationalizing

When using existing statistics, you must choose statistics computed from variables that were measured in a way that is useful to your research question and hypotheses. You will need to make absolutely certain that you understand how each variable was conceptualized and operationalized when the original data were collected. You *cannot* assume that different organizations, regions, or nations use the same measure. For example, jurisdictions across the United States define some crimes differently, so comparing crime rates from one state with another's can be problematic because the rates may not measure the same behaviors. Furthermore, you *cannot* assume that even the same organization has continued to measure a variable in the same way over time. For example, the Centers for Disease Control and Prevention (CDC) has changed the way it has operationalized AIDS (Acquired Immune Deficiency Syndrome) several times since it first operationalized the condition in 1982. Because AIDS is a disease in which the immune system is so suppressed that other opportunistic infections take over, prior to 1993, people were diagnosed as having AIDS if they tested HIV+ *and* had at least one of the opportunistic infections listed by the CDC. In 1985 and 1987, the CDC increased the number of infections on that list, which resulted in more people being diagnosed with AIDS—not because more people had HIV, but because people with a wider range of infections now fit the definition of AIDS. In 1993, the definition changed again, but this time the CDC not only added more infections to that list, it also reconceptualized the disease so that even if someone didn't have an infection on that list, that person would now have AIDS if they had fewer than 200 CD4+ cells. The effect of this was a dramatic increase in the number of people who had AIDS—people who, the day before, were considered to be HIV+ but not have AIDS literally one day later now fit the new operationalized definition of someone with AIDS. If you are doing research on AIDS rates, this is extremely important information because without knowing that the CDC changed the way it operationalized the variable, you would make erroneous conclusions about the rapid increase in the rate of AIDS. Relatedly, one year later the World Health Organization also expanded its definition of AIDS, but its new definition was quite different from the CDC's new definition, including specific symptoms but not CD4+ cell counts, which is very important information if you are comparing AIDS rates internationally. The point here is that it is fairly common for organizations to change the way they conceptualize and operationalize some variables and for different organizations to use different definitions. You must make sure that you are on the lookout for these differences or you will likely draw some very inaccurate conclusions.

Sampling

Much of the time when using existing statistics, you will conduct a **census** (include all possible sampling units in the study) rather than sample. For example, if you were collecting state-level data, you would use all 50 states in your analysis because 50 is already a small sample size, and excluding any would create a bias in your research. You may sometimes, however, need to draw a sample. For example, let's say that you are investigating the relationship between *spending on education* and *community well-being*, as indicated by measures of crime, physical health, mental health, poverty, and employment. Let's further say that you can access data on all of these variables reported at the city level for every city in the nation. Because studying every city would be a very time-consuming process, you might decide that rather than include all of the cities, you will draw a sample of cities that have more than 10,000 residents. You would start by developing a sampling frame of all the cities in the nation with a population of 10,000 or more, and then use one of the same probability sampling techniques you used in survey research, such as simple random sampling, systematic sampling, stratified sampling, or cluster sampling. Ultimately, you would only include those cities chosen through your sampling technique in your data and analysis. It should be clear by now that because existing statistics research is grounded in positivism, it would be important to *only* use probability sampling techniques, so that you can generalize your findings to all the cities in the United States with a population of at least 10,000. Box 6.5 provides a reminder of the different probability sampling techniques, with examples for existing statistics research.

CHECK YOUR UNDERSTANDING

Looking at your data sources, decide whether you would need to sample for your research on poverty or use a census. Why? If you would sample, how would you do so?

BOX 6.5

PROBABILITY SAMPLING TECHNIQUES AS APPLIED TO EXISTING STATISTICS RESEARCH

Sampling Method	Description	Example for Existing Statistics Research
Simple random sample	Each unit is given a number, and units are chosen using a random numbers generator.	Every city or town in the U.S. with a population over 10,000 people is listed and given a number. Random numbers generator used to choose cities.
Systematic random sample	Sampling frame is randomized, then each unit is given a number. First number is randomly chosen, then count down the list to every *n*th unit to select it. *N* represents the number in the sampling frame divided by the total number desired in the sample.	Every city or town in the U.S. with a population over 10,000 people is listed in randomized order. To sample 500 out of 3,035 listed, start at a random place on the list, and then choose every 6th location listed (3035/500 = 6.07, round to 6).
Stratified random sample	Sampling frame is divided into groups and then simple random or systematic sampling is used to select a given number of units from each group.	Listed cities/towns are divided between large and small: those with 10,000–49,999 people (2,281 towns) and those with 50,000 or more (754 cities). Simple or systematic random sampling used to choose 250 from each list, for a total of 500 cities and towns.
Cluster sample	Groups are randomly chosen, and every unit from the chosen groups is included in the sample.	Cities and towns are divided by type of industry that predominates in the state. Industries are chosen using simple random sampling or systematic sampling, and all cities and towns with the chosen predominant industries are used.

Source: All data is from the U.S. Census Bureau American Factfinder (2018).

Data Collection

Compiling your existing statistics is often a more time-consuming and difficult process than is accessing secondary data. Once you have found your sources for the statistics that you will use, you will need to ready them for further analysis. Doing so usually involves creating a new data file in a statistical software program like SPSS. Each one of the elements in your sample becomes a new case, and each of the existing statistics becomes a variable in your data set. To continue our example of research investigating the relationship between education and community well-being, for instance, each *county* in your sample would become a new case. The *crime rates, employment rates, measures of physical and mental health, employment,* and *poverty* would each become a variable. You would then enter in each county's existing statistic for each variable. This will allow you to run new statistics and conduct new analyses. You could run a crosstab, for instance, that would compare poor counties to rich counties to see how they differ in the amount of money they spend on education. By treating previously calculated statistics as new variables, you can investigate all kinds of relationships that weren't explored by the people who originally collected the data.

Data Analysis

You will use many of the same statistical techniques for existing statistics research that you would with survey data. One difference, however, is that the statistics you have collected as your data will most likely be calculated at the interval or ratio level rather than at the ordinal or nominal level, as are most survey data. This will allow you to use additional techniques, such as calculating **means** (averages), and using more robust statistical tests to determine the strength of relationships between variables. In order to compute crosstabs, however, you will need to collapse the variables into nominal- or ordinal-level data, so that you can easily put them into a crosstab. For example, it would be difficult to show the relationship between education and crime rates for counties if you are measuring them at an interval level because each year of education would have its own row in the table and each rate of crime would have its own column, unless some counties happened to share the same rate. This would make the table unreadable because there would be way too many rows and columns. For a crosstab, then, you might collapse crime rates into three categories: counties with high amounts of crime, medium amounts of crime, and low amounts of crime, while you might break education into counties with less than 25% of the population having a college degree, 25%–50% of the population having a college degree, and more than 50% having a college degree (we probably wouldn't create categories of "50–75%" and "more than 75%" because the number of counties with more than 75% of the population would be extremely small). In short, with interval- and ratio-level data you can do almost anything you can do with ordinal-level data as long as you collapse some of your variables. In addition, you can do other statistics that can only be done with interval- and ratio-level data, which helps to make for new and interesting results.

 Reminder: Interval- and **ratio**-level data use exact numerical measurements, while **ordinal**-level data are categories that can be ranked but exact differences between them are unknown; **nominal**-level data are differentiated as separate groups, but they cannot be ranked, nor can the difference between them be calculated.

Reminder: **Collapsing a variable** means changing the level of measurement to a lower level or combining answer categories/groups.

In drawing conclusions from analyses using existing statistics research, you must exercise some caution, however. We have already discussed how the unit of analysis in existing statistics is not the individual—it is usually already aggregated to the city, county, state, or national level. You must therefore be careful that when you interpret your results, you only are drawing conclusions about *the unit of analysis that you used*, not about individuals. Although you may find that counties with higher rates of mental illness also have higher rates of homelessness, you *cannot* make the leap to say that mentally ill people are more likely to be homeless. Your data, in this instance, are measured at the county level, so you can only draw conclusions about the *relationship between these variables at the county level*, not the individual level. Based on the information you have, you have no way of knowing whether the people in a given area who are homeless are the same individuals who are mentally ill. Note that this is different from the crosstabs we did with surveys and secondary data analysis: Because those were done with variables drawn from the same survey, the *same respondents* answered questions about both variables, so we could actually see how their answer on one variable related to their answer on another. That is not the case with existing statistics, where the variables are drawn from different sources, and the same individuals are not necessarily included in the measurement of both variables (even if they were, it would be impossible to know because we do not have access to the raw data). We can't say that a person's answer on one variable in existing statistics research affected their answer on another because it may not be the same people being counted for each, and we have no way of tracking their individual answers to see whether such a relationship exists. Thus we can only draw conclusions about the aggregated group (in this case, counties) and not the individual.

Evaluating the Quality of Data and Analysis

Just like survey research and secondary data analysis, we evaluate existing statistics research on its reliability and validity. Remember that **reliability** is the degree of consistency in the way that the data are collected. Although you will have little control over the reliability of the original data gathered, you are responsible for determining to the best of your ability how reliably they were gathered, and for sharing this information with your audience.

Validity, on the other hand, means how well you are measuring what you think you are measuring. In the case of existing statistics, the validity of your analysis will largely be based upon how well the statistics you chose to use in your research match the variables in your hypotheses. If your hypothesis has a variable for *gender equality,* and the statistic you are using to measure this variable is the gender gap in pay, the validity of your analysis may be compromised because pay equity may not actually be a good stand-alone measure of gender equality. Responsibility for childrearing, education rates by gender, gender representation in government, percentage of women in executive positions, and legal rights may all be important aspects of gender equality that the pay gap would miss. Thus, you must pay careful attention to try to find the *very best* sources of statistics for your research question and the hypotheses you want to test. If you cannot find good measures for your variables, then you should consider changing your hypotheses, or possibly even using a different research method. Another important factor in the validity of your analysis is, as already mentioned, the attention you pay to drawing accurate conclusions. For example, you must be careful not to examine data pertaining to one unit of analysis (nations, for example) and then try to draw conclusions about a different unit of analysis (individuals, or families).

Presenting the Results

After briefly discussing your research question, providing a literature review, and introducing any theory you may be using or testing, you will want to describe your hypotheses. You will need to give details about each of the sources of existing statistics that you used and why you chose them. You should also include a description of any alterations you made to the statistics (such as changing rates per 100,000 into percentages for easier computations) and any recoding you did of variables. And you should also be sure to discuss the unit of analysis you picked, and how it is appropriate to the statistics you chose to use.

Whether you are presenting your research orally or in written form, you will present your results quantitatively, describing the results using tables and graphs for illustration. If you are using geographic locations as your unit of analysis (city, county, state, or nation), it may also be appropriate to use color-coded maps to represent major findings about differences between regions. As with all quantitative data, you will focus your discussion on the most interesting, surprising, or important findings as they relate to your hypotheses. You may compare or contrast your findings with previous studies on the topic, but if different sources of existing statistics were used, you must take into account how different sources of data may have affected the findings (that is, the differences may be more a reflection of different data sources and collection than actual changes or discrepancies between the studies). As with most studies, you will likely end with a discussion of productive areas for future research.

Summary Points

- Existing statistics research is appropriate when you want information that is collected regularly by an agency and made publicly available, and when you want to know information beyond the level of the individual.

- Existing statistics research requires that you not just report the statistics that you find, but that you combine them together in new ways to create a new analysis.

- You will often have to collect data (statistics) from more than one source of existing statistics.

- Each new statistic that you collect will be used as a variable in your analysis.

- The statistics that you collect must be compatible with one another regarding both unit of analysis and time period that the data were collected.

- The validity of your data and analysis will be determined by how well the statistics you use match what you want to know.

Key Terms

aggregated 171
census 174
existing statistics 165

means 176
raw data 171
reliability 177

unit of analysis 165
validity 177

Content Analysis

Content analysis involves the collection and analysis of any type of textual, visual, or audiovisual material: TV shows, movies, commercials, song lyrics, music videos, speeches, letters, e-mails, tweets, books, posters, magazine articles, Web pages, workplace policies, medical or legal records, historical documents, photographs, or any other written or visual material. Like existing statistics, content analysis involves bringing together and analyzing materials that already exist, rather than creating something new (such as a survey) to collect data. Researchers usually conduct content analysis to better understand some aspect of the norms, beliefs, or discourse of a particular culture or subculture, not to gain insight into the thoughts, feelings, motivations, or behaviors of individuals. This is usually true even when we analyze private communications like letters, diaries, or e-mails. The idea underlying content analysis is that we don't always need to ask people questions in order to understand something about the social world in which they operate: We can learn much about a culture or subculture based on the words and images people use in private communication or for public consumption. Additionally, because people produce or consume these artifacts with different goals, they may not even consciously notice the subtle cultural messages embedded in these materials. As a method that does not involve the participation of people as respondents in the research, and because many audiovisual materials are publicly available, content analysis tends to be an inexpensive form of research whose timeline can be easily controlled by you (because you don't have to wait for participants to volunteer or respond).

Content analysis can be conducted either quantitatively or qualitatively (or in some combination of the two). Though the data collection process is similar for both forms of content analysis, the data analysis process for each differs significantly. **Quantitative content analysis** involves counting how many times various patterns appear in the words or images being analyzed. For example, if you are conducting a quantitative analysis of alcohol advertisements, you might count how often the ads depict alcohol consumption as a daytime or nighttime activity; how often sports are included; whether the ad is coed or portrays only one gender; and whether the alcohol is shown in a bottle, can, glass, or in motion, such as shooting out of a bottle.

REAL PEOPLE, REAL RESEARCH

Karen Segar

With a master's in sociology, Karen works as a research coordinator and is currently evaluating how well official protocols are followed in child custody cases in which there has been a history of domestic violence. The team that Karen supervises extracts the information from each case's public court documents. Thus, Karen's team is conducting content analysis, but for the purpose of evaluation research—a fairly unusual but interesting use of this method. After training, the coders use a standardized coding sheet to help them capture the important information in these documents, such as the kinds of visitation allowed during the court case; who was interviewed and how; whether home visits were conducted; what kinds of questions were asked of the children, if any; and what kinds of medical, education, and legal records were consulted. When the coders are unsure about how to code something in the records, they make notes in the margins and Karen reviews them, sometimes going back to the original document to make the final coding decision. Karen's role also includes quantitatively analyzing the data. She and the rest of the research team hope that the results of the study will directly affect how courts carry out parenting evaluations in these kinds of cases.

Pablo Villalpondo

A recent sociology graduate, Pablo works for a San Francisco–based search engine optimization (SEO) firm that has a relatively new applied use for content analysis. As a bilingual analyst, he tracks and tries to understand people's online search engine behavior in both Spanish and English, to understand what people with various demographics search for, how they search, and how satisfied they are with the content presented to them by major search engines like Google. Pablo uses a variety of software packages that help him to track and analyze the keywords used in searches, as well as to study the algorithms used by different search engines and web crawlers. He uses this information to analyze his clients' websites for deficiencies. He then develops a strategy for his business clients to alter their web content. His work thus combines a quantitative approach to content analysis and a qualitative approach to understanding the artificial intelligence used by search engines.

You might count how many times words describing the taste are used, as well as words describing the effect of the alcohol. You might note the clothing items worn by the people in the ads, the position of their bodies (sitting, standing, lying down, in motion), who (if anyone) is touching the alcohol, and whether they are smiling when doing so. You might keep track of how old the people in the ad appear to be, and the activities in which they are shown engaging. You would then use these counts to identify the images and words that recur frequently, which you would use to tell you something about the norms and meaning of alcohol in our culture. Additionally, you could examine the relationships between different variables to understand how cultural ideas are related to one another.

Qualitative content analysis may involve looking at the exact same advertisements, but instead of counting images and words, you would try to identify particular themes: Does the advertisement evoke sexuality, and, if so, how? What images and words are used that make it feel sexual? What is that sexuality like? Is it aggressive or passive? Is it homoerotic or heteroerotic? Is it from a male or female perspective? What obvious or subtle links are made between the alcohol and sex: Is the alcohol shown as part of meeting a potential sex partner? As part of sex itself? As a tool to gain sexual consent? What words and images convey this message? In the case of qualitative content analysis, then, rather than looking for and counting certain predetermined words and images, you instead search for both subtle and overt themes and messages, and identify the words and images the advertising team has chosen to use in order to convey that theme or message to the reader. Qualitative content analysis may be more exploratory—it allows you to investigate a topic and see what themes arise as you look at the data, while quantitative content analysis requires that you begin with a more precise idea of exactly what sorts of words and images you are looking for. This means you must already be fairly familiar with the types of materials you will be analyzing.

It is important to point out here that content analysis is about analyzing the images and words in the materials gathered, *not* the intentions of the person who produced those images or words or the interpretation of them by the people who see or hear them. Likewise, content analysis is also not able to measure the effect that the materials have on people or on the culture. Content analysts can only describe or count what they see and hear in the materials analyzed.

Methodology

Quantitative content analysis, like other forms of quantitative research, is most often guided by positivist methodology. You will often begin with a list of hypotheses to test, which will help to determine what information you will need to collect from each object in the sample. You will most likely use probability sampling so that the results may be generalized, and you will numerically code the data for statistical analysis. Because no people are directly involved in the research, you don't have to worry about objectivity in your relationship with the subjects, but you do have to maintain objectivity in collecting the data. Quantitative content analysis most often involves fairly large amounts of data, in part because it is a comparatively inexpensive research method, and therefore large samples are often feasible.

Qualitative content analysis, on the other hand, is somewhat similar to the use of semi-structured qualitative interviews. The methodology used is generally an interpretivist one, where the researcher tries to understand the more subtle and complex meanings and themes woven throughout the data that underlie the more obvious content that can be counted. In conducting qualitative content analysis, you may still rely on random sampling strategies (though not necessarily so) but will typically use a smaller sample because the analysis is more complex than mere counting. You will use consistent questions to help you gather similar data from the entire sample, but will be open to new themes that arise from the data, and will not be testing hypotheses or using predetermined variables. The goal in this case is to uncover the deeper and more complex cultural ideas and messages that may not be immediately noticed.

Often, researchers use a combination of both qualitative and quantitative content analysis. Because the methodologies are different, they may be conducted in two separate stages, or the qualitative work may be conducted on only a portion of the larger sample. The qualitative work may be used either as an exploratory stage of the research to help develop more precise variables for subsequent quantitative analysis, or it may be used after the quantitative analysis to better explain the deeper meanings and nuances that could not be thoroughly investigated with quantitative methods.

Some content analysts use a third methodology: **critical methodology**. This methodology takes as its main task pointing out to the reader things they have likely not realized: the ways in which words and images are being used to fool, manipulate, or indoctrinate the audience. Critical methodologists seek to reveal the ways in which power operates in mundane ways without the audience even being aware of it. Thus, critical social scientists think of themselves as activists, but also as objective. Although these two terms normally do not go together, for critical methodologists, they are not contradictory. **Objectivity** to the critical social scientist means questioning the taken for granted so that you are seeing things as they really are, rather than as what you have been led to believe. By questioning cultural norms, beliefs, and discourse, the critical methodologist can shed light on the ways that these beliefs and norms are created and maintained in ways that support particular power arrangements. In content analysis, this is through the words and imagery that are used. The critical methodologist hopes that, much like the boy who pronounces that "the Emperor has no clothes," once people see these power dynamics at play, they will be less likely to be duped or manipulated by them. Thus, their goal is not only revealing the truth, but in doing so, creating a social awareness whereby the population becomes more critical of these power arrangements and the status quo. Thus, from their perspective, their research is both objective and activist: In revealing what most people don't see, they hope to create awareness that may lead to social change.

That being said, because critical methodologists seek to change people's consciousness, there are two ways they may go about their research. The first is to try to build a solid case for the social change for which they are advocating by following many of the research protocols used by positivists. They will choose the materials that they sample in a nonbiased way and prefer large samples, so as to be able to generalize their findings and demonstrate that the patterns they are highlighting are pervasive and not merely present in extreme cases or outliers. They will also be precise in their data collection, using standardized questions and taking standardized notes for each item in the sample so that they get the same information for each item. Furthermore, they often will work in teams to show that the patterns they identify are not just the result of personal interpretation, but that the results were replicated among different researchers within the research team.

Other critical methodologists sample by using materials that best illustrate their points, and thus avoid making generalizations to all such materials. This is similar to the style of research used by many documentary filmmakers. In the *Dreamworlds* movies by Sut Jhally, for example, in which Jhally analyzes the images of female sexuality in music videos, he first identified themes in hundreds of hours of music videos that he studied. Then he chose music genres and particular clips from music videos that best supported his analysis. He doesn't ever claim that *all* music videos fit this analysis, but he does effectively show that many videos from different genres fall into these patterns. From his analysis and the examples he uses to support his points, the audience is likely to see the music videos in a different light, now noticing things they never had before, like camera angles, the male–female ratio in the videos, and the disparities in the ways that the men and women are depicted. Although documentary filmmaking is not held to the same standards of peer review as published social research, some critical social scientists approach their research in much the same manner: They seek to change people's perspectives by building a convincing case using carefully chosen data that are typical but that would not fit a positivist's definition of either random or representative.

Although the critical methodologist hopes to create social change, content analysis is not frequently used for applied research (the same is true for positivist and interpretivist content analysis as well). Critical methodologists hope that those who read their research will see things in a new light, but usually their goal is just to create awareness in their readers, not to help provide a solution to a particular problem or decision. Although someone analyzing alcohol advertisements may try to put pressure on beer companies to change their ads in some way, this is not the same as the company, for example, hiring someone to do content analysis in order to improve its own advertising strategy. The former remains basic research, even though there is some hope for change, while the latter is applied research because it uses research to solve a particular problem or make decisions for a particular organization. Regardless of methodology, content analysis is more likely to be basic research than applied.

Theory

Quantitative content analysis is sometimes used to test theories of middle range, especially social psychological theories. Media and pop culture may be used, but more often quantitative content analysts testing theory will use real-life artifacts, such as tweets, Facebook or Instagram posts, letters, newspaper articles or editorials, speeches, and other objects that are intended in some way to represent real life in nonartistic ways. In this case, the hypotheses are derived from the theory and tested statistically, just like in other positivist research.

Qualitative content analysis is most likely to be conducted not to test theories of middle range, but to use large theoretical frameworks as a lens through which to collect and interpret data. Feminist theorists, symbolic interactionists, conflict theorists, critical theorists, theorists working from a Foucauldian perspective, and social constructionists may all conduct content analysis to exemplify or bolster claims made by the theory or to understand some phenomenon through the lens of that theory. A symbolic interactionist could study dating profiles to see how people present themselves to others, for example, while a critical theorist could look at the ways that consumerism is perpetuated by home remodeling shows. Likewise, feminist theorists might investigate the differences in news portrayals of the murders of white women as compared to women of color, while social constructionists may examine how "terrorists" and "mass shooters" have been constructed differently in the last two decades. In all of these cases, the chosen theoretical framework is used to develop the research question, inform the way that the concepts are conceptualized and measured, and make interpretations during analysis. It may also affect the sampling method used and the size of the sample employed.

Research Questions

Content analysis may be used to answer a variety of types of questions, depending on the kind of material being analyzed. When the unit of analysis is part of pop culture or meant to be accessible to large groups of people (such as things posted on the Web), the questions often focus on cultural norms, how groups of people or particular behaviors are portrayed, the obvious and subtle cultural messages that are sent, and the ways that ideas are framed. If the unit of analysis is private in nature (such as diaries, letters, or e-mails), questions may also focus on behavior reported by the author and their subsequent feelings and reactions to those items. If the unit of analysis is historical, dating back to a specific historical time period or event, the questions may focus on the portrayal of that event, how cultural ideas of the time period were expressed, or the effects (as measured through reported behavior) of a particular event or time period. Content analysis is also appropriate for comparisons of the same or similar artifacts across time, such as advice columns in women's magazines in the 1950s through the 2010s. Box 7.1 contains examples of research questions appropriate for content analysis.

   As already mentioned, content analysis is not good for answering questions about how people interpret those media or pop-cultural portrayals, or the effects that they have. Pop-cultural artifacts do not necessarily accurately depict the lives of the people shown. Teenagers, for example, do not necessarily behave in real life the way that they are depicted in television sitcoms—nor do parents. What is interesting for the content analyst, however, is that particular types of depictions of both of these groups are used regularly—which, though not accurate, tell us something about cultural norms, values, and beliefs. This is particularly important to remember when analyzing historical artifacts because we have less personal experience that would help remind us of the disjuncture between real life and portrayals. Additionally, even in the case of diaries and letters, it is important to note that what was written down is only a slice of someone's life or thoughts. Letters are written with an intended recipient, and the writer may radically change, distort, or entirely ignore certain events or feelings, depending on the person for whom they wrote the letter. Likely, they would give a very different account of their prom date to their grandmother than to their best friend. Similarly, in diaries, people are most likely to write when they are struggling with an issue or problem, and to focus heavily on one issue or problem at a time. Just because a diary is filled with frustration and hope about the interest of a potential lover, it doesn't mean that is the only thing the diarist ever thinks about, or that they aren't facing other, perhaps even more serious, problems or issues. Thus, it is important to realize that what gets recorded or preserved in letters and diaries is only a glimpse into someone's life, not an accurate depiction of its entirety.

Examples of common errors made in writing research questions for content analysis are shown in Box 7.2.

BOX 7.1

EXAMPLES OF RESEARCH QUESTIONS APPROPRIATE FOR CONTENT ANALYSIS

Research Question	Appropriate for Content Analysis Because It Examines . . .
How do television game shows reinforce racial stereotypes?	portrayal of a group of people
How is discourse used in presidential candidates' political speeches to promote partisan hostility?	subtle cultural messages
What changes have occurred in the portrayal of men's bodies in sports magazines in the last three decades?	portrayal of a group of people; comparison over time
What do people tweet about their anger and its causes?	public expressions of personal thoughts
In what ways is the use of alcohol and drugs normalized in the Facebook postings of college students under the age of 21?	cultural norms
How do newspaper articles about debates over gay marriage reinforce or challenge heteronormativity?	framing of ideas
How are gender roles portrayed in the diaries of American pioneer women headed West?	expression of cultural ideas; historical evidence
How do popular song lyrics depict love?	framing of ideas
How has discourse in medical textbooks about what constitutes a healthy pregnancy changed over time?	comparison over time
How was the nation's reaction to the assassination of Dr. Martin Luther King, Jr. portrayed in media editorials in southern states as compared to those in northern states?	comparison of different portrayals of an historical event

---

BOX 7.2

AVOID THESE COMMON ERRORS WHEN WRITING RESEARCH QUESTIONS FOR CONTENT ANALYSIS

Research Question	Explanation of Error
How do children learn gender roles through television watching?	This question asks about something that occurs in the children's minds, which can't be studied with content analysis.

(Continued)

(Continued)

Research Question	Explanation of Error
Why do movies contain so much violence?	This question is unanswerable with content analysis because the movies themselves, which should be the unit of analysis for content analysis research, can't answer the question why.
How does violence in video games affect children's behavior?	In this question, the unit of analysis is the children rather than the video games because you would observe children's behavior. In content analysis, however, the unit of analysis should be the media object. This question is also a cause and effect. On both counts, this question would be more appropriate for experimental research.
Where are most of the images of violence in our media today?	This question doesn't specify a unit of analysis, and thus is so broad that it can't be answered using content analysis.
How can reality shows be improved to highlight more positive rather than negative behaviors?	"Can" makes this a hypothetical, and therefore unanswerable with research. Additionally, the reality shows themselves (the unit of analysis) can't suggest improvements, only people can.

CHECK YOUR UNDERSTANDING

Write a research question related to race that is appropriate for content analysis. Explain what materials you would analyze in order to answer this question.

Literature Review

The literature review for content analysis is done the same way and for the same reasons as for the other methods. You will want to familiarize yourself with the research that has already been conducted so that you identify specific themes, images, or wording to look for when you analyze, and how you might measure them. You may try to find articles about a similar topic, but one that has been studied using a different group of materials, such as using the results from a well-known study of the portrayal of girls in children's books to help with your study of the portrayal of girls in children's music. Much of the literature you review may not itself use content analysis; you may wish to use other research in order to get a sense of the norms and beliefs about a particular topic, as well as how those may have changed over time. In studying the portrayal of young girls, you also might look at research that addresses cultural beliefs about childhood, as well as research on adult gender roles. If you are conducting historical content analysis, you will also want to give yourself a good foundation for understanding the events and conditions in that time period, as well as of particular behaviors or beliefs that were then in transition.

Sampling

After writing the research question and conducting the literature review, the next step you will likely take is choosing your sample. Although qualitative and quantitative researchers draw their samples differently from each other when using other research methods, in content analysis the process is often identical, regardless of whether the research will be quantitative or qualitative. It involves not only choosing the general category of materials you will use, such as children's television cartoons, but the exact items as well—in this case, the specific titles and episodes you will use. Because content analysis is usually a relatively inexpensive research method to conduct, you are likely to draw a large sample. Sometimes, if there are a limited number of such materials, your sample will be a **census**, meaning the sample exactly (or almost exactly) matches the population of possible items. In the case of content analysis, that means that you include every available instance of the material in your analysis. If you were analyzing sociology textbooks for a Sociology of the Family course, you might choose, for example, every published textbook for this and similarly titled courses available from every American and British publisher, including out-of-print editions, from the past 10 years.

If your population is larger, such as children's television cartoons, it will be impossible to do a census, and you will need to select which cartoons, which episodes, on what channels, and during what time period. Much like that for observation research, the sampling strategy may be multilayered, with different techniques used for different sampling decisions. You may use **theoretical sampling** to choose the time period from which to sample your cartoons. Knowledge you have about the industry, the broadcasting cycle, relevant legislation, or related cultural/historical events may influence the time period you select. If you know, for example, that two independent animation studios were bought out by a larger corporation within the last 2 years, you may seek to include cartoons from both before and after the buyouts. Similarly, if your research question seeks to make a comparison, the time comparisons you make should be informed by your literature review. Rather than randomly comparing cartoons from 1978 to those from 2018, for example, you would likely have theoretical reasons for choosing the years you did. You also may take accessibility into account: Perhaps 1978 is the first year for which you are able to access a large number of recorded cartoons. Additionally, if you were choosing to study only cartoons currently being broadcast, accessibility may affect the length of time for which you sample. If you are only able to record two shows at once on your DVR, you may end up sampling for a longer period of time (a month) than if you were able to record an unlimited number of shows at once (perhaps a week or two).

Once you have chosen your time period, you will need to pick a sampling method for selecting the specific items to be included in your final sample. Frequently, you will choose some sort of random sample, using one of the four probability sampling techniques: simple random sample, systematic random sample, stratified random sample, or cluster sample. These were discussed in Chapter 4 and are reviewed in Box 7.3. In each case, the selections are made randomly, and each item (in this case,

BOX 7.3
PROBABILITY SAMPLING TECHNIQUES AS APPLIED TO CONTENT ANALYSIS

Sampling Method	Description	Example for Content Analysis
Simple random sample	Each item is given a number, and items are chosen using a random numbers generator.	Every cartoon episode scheduled to air is listed and given a number. Random numbers generator used to choose episodes.
Systematic random sample	Sampling frame is randomized, then each item is given a number. First number is randomly chosen, then count down the list to every nth item to select it. N represents the number in the sampling frame divided by the total number desired in the sample.	Every cartoon episode scheduled to air is listed in randomized order. To sample 300 cartoons out of 1,054 listed, start at a random place on the list, and then choose every 4th cartoon listed (1,054/300 = 3.51, round to 4).
Stratified random sample	Sampling frame is divided into groups and then simple random or systematic sampling is used to select a given number of items from each group. Used when a group you want to study is highly underrepresented.	Listed cartoons are divided between those with girls and with boys as the protagonists. Simple or systematic random sampling used to choose 150 cartoon episodes from each list, for a total of 300 cartoons.
Cluster sample	Groups are randomly chosen, and every item from the chosen groups is included in the sample.	Cartoons are divided by the time that they are broadcast. For 30-minute shows, there are 336 possible time slots in a 7-day period. Time slots are randomly chosen using simple random sampling. All episodes on all channels broadcasting at the randomly selected time periods are included in the sample.

each aired episode) has an equal chance of being selected. Remember that the benefit of probability sampling is that the results are generalizable to the larger population of materials (all aired television cartoons during the selected time period).

Sometimes, however, especially if you are using interpretivist or critical methodology, you may choose a nonprobability sampling technique, such as theoretical sampling, in order to select the cases that are most theoretically interesting. Instead of choosing all of the aired cartoons during a 2-week period, you may instead sample all the episodes of the 10 most popular cartoons over a longer period because children will be most likely to see these. Or you may select cartoons that specifically aim to be different from other cartoons in some sort of way, such as the ones touted as being empowering to girls or that are aimed at a multicultural, bilingual audience.

In determining your sampling frame, you will also need to decide upon the eligibility requirements for inclusion. If your population is all televised children's cartoons aired within the next 2 weeks, you will need to specify what it means to be "televised" in order to determine which shows belong in your sampling frame. If the show is available on a home satellite system, but not on cable, will you include it? If it is aired on a chan-

 Reminder: The **sampling frame** is all possible items that you might include in your analysis.

nel only available to people with the most expensive cable package, will you include it? If it is animated and airing on a movie channel such as HBO, does it count as a "television cartoon"? And what is meant by "children's" cartoon? Does *The Simpsons* count? All of these are strategic decisions with no right or wrong answer, but your decisions will affect your sample and therefore your data, so they should be considered carefully. Once again, convenience and accessibility may count: Although some children may watch cartoons available on expensive specialty channels, you may decide that you will only select cartoons aired and accessible to you with your basic cable package, both because it saves you money from upgrading your cable subscription, and because you know that many families also have only the basic package.

If you are analyzing historical items, you will be less likely to use random sampling and instead include all available items, or use a combination of theoretical and convenience sampling to choose your items. Often in historical research, however, you will have to work much harder to collect the items in your sample. If you are analyzing diaries, for example, you may need to visit the archives and special collections of several libraries around the country to access them. Because you may not be able to visit every library with relevant diaries in its collection, you may choose to visit those with some particular theoretical interest or that are conveniently located within an easier traveling distance from you.

Your sample size will vary considerably depending on the availability of the objects you are studying, the type of object, and the length/size of these materials. If you are studying movies that last 1.5–2.5 hours, you will probably sample many fewer than if you are studying 30-second commercials. Likewise, if you are studying media objects that are widely and publicly available, you will probably have a much larger sample than if you are studying private diaries. There is no particular rule of thumb here, but typically we study as many of the objects as we reasonably can, given their length and availability. It is not unusual for researchers to analyze a couple of hundred films or several hundred advertisements, newspaper articles, or blog postings. Although research using social media such as Facebook postings and tweets is still new, one may expect to see a sample in the thousands for such research.

CHECK YOUR UNDERSTANDING

Describe all the steps you will take, and the sampling method(s) you will use, for your research question about race. How large will your sample be?

BOX 7.4

DECISION PATH FOR MULTI-STAGE SAMPLING FOR CONTENT ANALYSIS

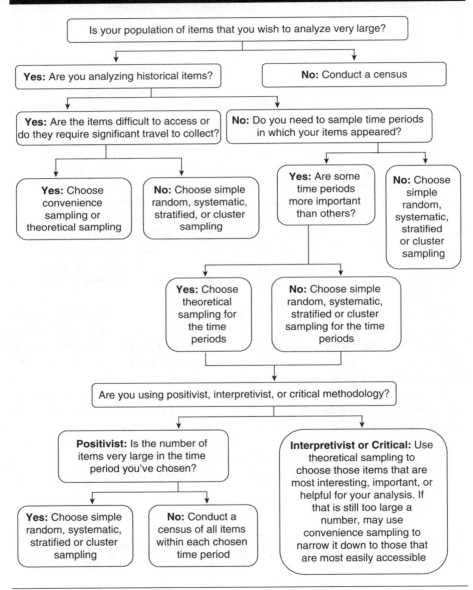

Is your population of items that you wish to analyze very large?

Yes: Are you analyzing historical items?

No: Conduct a census

Yes: Are the items difficult to access or do they require significant travel to collect?

No: Do you need to sample time periods in which your items appeared?

Yes: Choose convenience sampling or theoretical sampling

No: Choose simple random, systematic, stratified, or cluster sampling

Yes: Are some time periods more important than others?

No: Choose simple random, systematic, stratified or cluster sampling

Yes: Choose theoretical sampling for the time periods

No: Choose simple random, systematic, stratified or cluster sampling for the time periods

Are you using positivist, interpretivist, or critical methodology?

Positivist: Is the number of items very large in the time period you've chosen?

Interpretivist or Critical: Use theoretical sampling to choose those items that are most interesting, important, or helpful for your analysis. If that is still too large a number, may use convenience sampling to narrow it down to those that are most easily accessible

Yes: Choose simple random, systematic, stratified or cluster sampling

No: Conduct a census of all items within each chosen time period

Note: While this is the typical path for decision making, there may be unusual circumstances that require different decisions.

Conceptualizing and Operationalizing

Quantitative Content Analysis

As might be expected, operationalizing and conceptualizing for qualitative and quantitative content analysis differ considerably, so I will address each separately. Once you have gathered your materials, you will develop a coding sheet. For quantitative content analysis, a **coding sheet** is the instrument on which you record all of your counts. It is standardized, prompting you to gather the exact same information from each object and to record the notes in a standardized and systematic way. This is important for collecting parallel information from different objects sampled and also for standardizing information across the research team. Like a survey instrument, a coding sheet takes a considerable amount of time to develop and perfect. Because it will guide all of your data collection, you will want to test and revise your coding sheet multiple times on a variety of items from your population.

The coding sheet should begin with a record of the exact object from which you are recording the information. If you are analyzing magazine advertisements, for example, you would want to record the magazine name, date, volume number, page number, and product name. If you are analyzing websites, you need to include the website name, Web address, and the date and time it was accessed. If it is a letter, you should include the author, the recipient, the date, and the number of pages. This information is important: If there are discrepancies between researchers, or questions about the data arise later, you want to be able to easily locate the exact item in question.

From there, the coding sheet goes on to list particular information that you wish to be gathered. Like survey questions, the coding sheet for quantitative content analysis includes mostly closed-ended variable items with a series of answer choices for recording information. This increases efficiency as well as standardizes the information. Also like surveys, these variables must be both conceptualized and operationalized. Let's say you are analyzing advertisements in men's magazines to understand how traditional stereotypes of masculinity and femininity are both reinforced and challenged in these magazines. You would need to start by conceptualizing *traditional stereotypes of masculinity* and *traditional stereotypes of femininity*. How will you know these when you see them? You will also need to conceptualize *reinforcing* traditional stereotypes and *challenging* them. Suppose you define *challenging traditional gender stereotypes* as the following:

 Reminder: To **conceptualize** is to define important variables, while to **operationalize** is to determine how to measure those variables.

- Showing males or females engaged in behaviors or having the appearance usually associated with the other gender

- Showing people engaged in behaviors or having an appearance that is not usually associated with either gender

- Showing people engaging in behaviors or having an appearance consistent with traditional gender roles but in a highly exaggerated way that is probably meant to poke fun at or make the traditionally gendered roles seem funny, out of date, or deviant

This is a complicated definition! And you would still need to break each part of it down, defining each part further and more precisely.

To operationalize these definitions, you will need to decide how to measure them. In this example, you would first need to indicate whether there were males or females depicted in the advertisement, and how many of each. Then, based on the definition above, you would need to break *appearance* (from the first part of our definition) down into different measurable aspects: Perhaps you would include clothing, body position, hand gestures, facial expression, hair length and style, and the presence or absence of obvious makeup. Each of these would become a separate variable on your coding sheet, and you would provide check-off options for each. For *body position*, for example, you may include standing, jumping, walking/running, sitting, bending over forward, kneeling, lying on stomach, lying on back, lying on side, indeterminate, other (with space to specify), or head-only shot. In collecting the data, for each male and female in the advertisement, then, you would separately record on the coding sheet their body position using these standardized categories. You would go through the same process to operationalize your other variables as well, providing prompts of what to look for and check-off options or spaces for counts. As with surveys, you want your options to be both exhaustive and mutually exclusive in order to increase reliability in coding. Coding sheets must be precise and may be extensive. Even analyzing a single, one-page advertisement may involve coding for dozens of variables; thus, coding sheets are often multiple pages long. Box 7.5 is an example of one page of a coding sheet for the project just described. Note that this one page is not comprehensive—the coding sheet would need to have many more pages in order to measure all the important variables from each ad, but this excerpt gives you an idea of what a coding sheet looks like.

Qualitative Content Analysis

Once upon a time, qualitative content analysis also relied primarily on coding sheets, though the questions were open-ended ones instead of counts and check-offs. Today, the analysis of textual objects is usually done by directly uploading the text items into a qualitative analysis software package and coding the data in much the same way you would qualitative interview transcripts. Images, video, and sound can now also be coded using such software. This software allows you to attach **qualitative codes** (words that represent larger themes or ideas) to particular points on a visual image. Although this innovation was enormously helpful for some forms of analysis, it can also be cumbersome, especially for audio and video files; therefore, some qualitative researchers still use coding sheets for qualitative analysis of these objects. Although using coding sheets and using software are both called "coding,"

BOX 7.5

SAMPLE QUANTITATIVE CODING SHEET

Gender Stereotypes in Men's Fitness Magazines

Coder's initials: _____

Magazine title: _____

Date: _____ Volume #: _____ Issue #: _____ Page #: _____

Advertisement for: Brand name: _____ Type of product: _____

Number of males: _____ Number of females: _____ Number of indeterminate gender: _____

Physical position of male #1:

Standing	Jumping	Walking/running	Sitting	Bending forward	Kneeling
Lying on stomach	Lying on back	Lying on side	Head shot	Indeterminate	Other

Facial expression of male #1:

Smiling	Laughing	Frowning	Crying	Yelling	Grimacing
Staring	Neutral	Not visible	Other		

Emotion expressed by facial expression of male #1:

Happy	Sad	Angry	Bored	Cold	Confident	Other
Dreamy	Worried	Calm/relaxed	Curious	Hopeful	Indeterminate	

Clothing of male #1:

Shirt	Pants	Shoes
Long-sleeve button-down	Jeans	Sneakers
Long-sleeve casual	Shorts	Hiking/outdoor athletic shoes
Sweater	Sweat/athletic pants	Fashion casual
Sweatshirt	Khaki-style	Sandals
Long- or short-sleeve T-shirt	Dress pants	Dress shoes
Long- or short-sleeve athletic	Suit	Cowboy boots
Short-sleeve casual	Bathing suit	Work boots
Tank top	Underwear	Barefoot
Coat/jacket	No bottoms	Other (specify)
Suit	Other (specify)	Indeterminate
Shirtless	Indeterminate	
Other (specify)		
Indeterminate		

the procedures are very different. For the former, the distinction between collecting the data and analyzing them is blurred, but when using the software, the data collection and analysis phases are actually the same and there is no distinction at all. Thus, in this section we will discuss the coding of audio and visual video using coding sheets, but will reserve the discussion of using software to code any type of objects until our discussion of data analysis.

When coding images, audio files, or videos, coding sheets may be used to prompt and record observations. The coding sheets used for qualitative content analysis are more open-ended than those for quantitative analysis, and they generally provide prompts in the form of questions aimed at cuing the analysts about what to look for, but leaving the answers to those questions open-ended, with lots of room for note taking. Let's return to our previous example, but this time from a qualitative perspective. You are analyzing advertisements in men's fitness magazines to understand the ways in which traditional gender roles are reinforced and challenged in pop culture targeted to men. Although you are also considering the text of the advertisements, our focus here will be on the visual images. Instead of breaking the data down into specific variables, you would ask open-ended questions that would allow you to focus more holistically on the images and the messages they convey about gender roles. This is much like the difference between a survey and a semi-structured interview: In the survey (quantitative), the answer choices are provided, very precisely measuring and standardizing—but also limiting—the information that is collected; in the semi-structured (qualitative) interview, all of the participants are asked the same questions so that there is some standardization, but the questions are broad and open ended so that the each participant can give a wide range of general or detailed information that will surely differ in content, form, and depth from that of other participants. In qualitative content analysis, then, the qualitative coding sheet is a guide to remind you what general information to look for, but your answers will vary considerably for each advertisement and will not ultimately be reduced to numbers. Thus, you will get different (but not better or worse) information than you would from quantitative content analysis.

With qualitative content analysis, you will still need to conceptualize the major ideas in your research question (in this case, *traditional stereotypes of masculinity, traditional stereotypes of femininity, reinforcing gender stereotypes,* and *challenging gender stereotypes*) by defining them. To operationalize them, however, you will develop the open-ended questions that will appear on your coding sheet. In this example, to operationalize *challenging gender stereotypes* you might include the following questions: In what ways does the physical appearance of the male(s) in the ad seem unmasculine, androgynous, or feminine? What is the male(s) doing that is somewhat unusual for men to do? What emotions are evident in this ad, and how are they communicated to the reader? In what ways is the gendered behavior exaggerated, and does this seem to be reinforcing or poking fun at traditional gender roles? Note that these questions are less "objective"—they report not only what you observe in the images, but also what you interpret them to mean. Such interpretations are subjective, of course, and may vary from person to person. For this reason, it is very important to include as much

---

BOX 7.6

SAMPLE QUALITATIVE CODING SHEET

Gender Stereotypes in Men's Fitness Magazines

Coder's initials: _____

Magazine title: _____

Date: _____ Volume #: _____ Issue #: _____ Page #: _____

Advertisement for: Brand name: _____ Type of product: _____

Number of males: _____ Number of females: _____ Number of indeterminate gender: _____

In what ways does the males' physical appearance connote masculinity?

In what ways does the males' appearance seem gender neutral, unmasculine, or feminine?

What activities are the males engaged in? How typical or atypical is this behavior for men?

What archetypes or stereotypes of men come to mind?

How are the men interacting with one another? What type of relationship between them seems to be suggested, and how is this done?

How are the men interacting with women? What type of relationship between them seems to be suggested, and how is this done?

How does the power seem to be balanced? How obvious is this? How is it depicted?

---

information as possible on the coding sheets about why you are making this interpretation, based on what you visually observe. As many details about the image that led to this interpretation should be included as possible. This helps to give support for the interpretation and to assist in comparing interpretations across advertisements. It also will help to document patterns in the images themselves as you move on to data analysis. Box 7.6 is an example of a qualitative coding sheet.

Ethics

When you are doing content analysis of publicly available materials, no informed consent is needed, nor must special precautions be taken to protect people whose name, image, or information is included. Sometimes things that we think of as private, such as letters or diaries, have already been made publicly available. There are many books published, for example, of people's diaries and letters. These also would not need any protection because you would not be releasing new information about the individuals. If, however, the materials have not previously been made public, then you will need to take a variety of precautions, depending on the type of material, whether the individuals on which it focuses are still alive, and who owns the materials. If, for example, you were analyzing diaries written by people who are still living, you will need to get their informed consent and to protect their identities by giving them pseudonyms, changing the names of the people they write about, and deleting identifying information from your report. If you are analyzing the unpublished diaries of people who have died, you should check with your Institutional Review Board (IRB). They may require you to get the informed consent of a family member or closest living relative. You may also have to provide pseudonyms for the author as well as the people they wrote about, especially those who are still living, and you may need to delete certain identifying information. If the private materials are in your keeping, you should keep them in a locked drawer or file cabinet to further protect the author's identity.

CHECK YOUR UNDERSTANDING

Conceptualize two concepts for your research question about race. Then do the following, remembering that you will likely need several measures for each concept:

1. Operationalize these in a quantitative way, writing them as you would for a quantitative coding sheet.
2. Operationalize these in a qualitative way, writing them as you would for a qualitative coding sheet.

Preparing for Data Collection

Preparations for data collection for both qualitative and quantitative content analysis focus on three things: gathering the sample, pretesting and revising the coding sheet, and training the research team (if there is more than one person who will be coding the data, which is common for content analysis). Gathering the sample may include purchasing or recording the audiovisual materials that you will be analyzing; downloading blogs, tweets, or Web pages; gathering magazine issues; or photocopying archived diaries, letters, or other materials. In the case of historical materials, this may involve traveling to different libraries or archives across the country or even around the world. Most often, however, you will use materials you can more easily access, and the focus of the task is to physically gather those materials. It is important to have continued access to the materials (through recordings, photocopying, scanning, printing, etc.), as very often you will want to go back and look at particular items again after coding them.

Pretesting the coding sheet involves recording the data on your coding sheet exactly as you expect to do for the research project, using a diverse subsample of your larger sample. As you code these items from your sample, you may notice that in some cases the coding sheet is not specific enough, not clear enough, or that you have cases in which the way you operationalized something is not as exhaustive as you imagined. As you come across these cases, you can revise the coding sheet to better fit the items. The wider the diversity of your items in this pretest subsample, the more likely you are to have made all the necessary changes to the coding sheet before you begin your actual data collection. This is important because once you begin recording the actual data, you cannot change your coding sheet without also having to recode all of the items you already coded prior to the change.

If there will be more than one coder, it is extremely important to train the research team so that members are as consistent as possible in the way that they code items. For qualitative content analysis, this will include documenting how each item is conceptualized. For example, in Box 7.6, what does it mean to have a "masculine physical appearance," and how does this differ from a "gender neutral" one? What are archetypes and stereotypes, and what are some of the common ones that may get invoked? What is meant by *power* in this context, and what will you look for to recognize it?

For quantitative content analysis, training the research team begins with writing a codebook, just as in survey research. The codebook documents the variables used and the numeric codes to be entered into the statistical software for each response. In addition, however, the codebook for quantitative content analysis should include guidelines for choosing the different categories within each variable. This is not necessary for survey research because the interpretation of the question and the categories are left up to the respondent. In content analysis, however, it is the researchers—not the participant—who must interpret the variables and related categories; therefore, documenting the definitions, differences, and guidelines for choosing these is important to increase reliability between coders, as well as among individual coders over time.

Training the team also requires thoroughly discussing each coding question or category on the coding sheet and coming to agreement on how different cases should be coded. Then coders each code a subset of the sample (with all coders coding the same items from the sample) and compare their coding. Any items that were coded differently should be discussed, and you should reach an agreement about how to code similar cases in the future. This increases the **intercoder reliability** (the likelihood that multiple researchers have coded an item in the same way), which is often considered an important measure of the quality of the analysis, though it is more often used in quantitative than qualitative content analysis.

Data Collection

At this point, data collection is rather simple, in that you are simply coding the full sample that you have collected, using the procedures you have worked out in your pretest. Although this may be simple, it is often time consuming, and depending upon the types of items being sampled, the size of those items, and the length of the coding sheet, it may take hundreds of hours. Research teams usually continue to meet during this process, and intercoder reliability (if multiple coders are used) is monitored. Research teams discuss items that individual coders had difficulty coding, find and discuss discrepancies, and problem solve for new difficulties that weren't discovered during pretesting.

Data Analysis

Quantitative Data Analysis

Quantitative data analysis usually begins with transferring the data from the coding sheets into SPSS or Excel. Each variable on the coding sheet is entered into the spreadsheet, and its categories are given numerical equivalents that are then entered for each case (each advertisement, letter, TV show, blog, tweet, etc.) that has been coded. This yields a database for which you may then calculate statistics beyond just counting the number of responses for each category (which would be reported as **frequencies**). This will allow you to investigate the relationship between different variables, and to test hypotheses.

After entering the data, it must be cleaned. Because the researcher is filling out the coding sheet, there should be little to no error on the coding sheet itself: no missing data, no ambiguous markings, etc. There may, however, have been mistakes in entering the data into the software, and therefore this should be checked using **spot checking** (choosing coding sheets—either randomly, or systematically, such as every 10th sheet—and double-checking to make sure that the data have been correctly entered).

After cleaning the data, data analysis may begin. This will usually start with running frequencies, which will tell you the most common observations you made for each variable. Relationships between variables can be examined using crosstabs, correlations, and other bivariate statistics. In the previous example you may, for instance, explore whether when one person who challenges gender stereotypes is depicted, the others in the advertisement are also more or less likely to do so. You could investigate how conformity to traditional gender roles regarding appearance is related to conformity to these roles regarding behavior or interaction. And you might investigate whether it is males or females who are more likely to be shown challenging these gender roles, and if the ways they do so are similar or different.

In addition to calculating the statistical relationship between variables, if your objects of analysis are in written form, you may also use a word-processing system to conduct a word count on particular words. You could do a word search, for example, on the words *power* and *powerful* to see how often they are used in your ads. Of course, word searches take into account neither context nor meaning, so you have to be careful when drawing conclusions. Word counts may be used on their own as a type of frequency data. Alternatively, you can use a word processor's search feature not only to count particular words, but also to investigate their context or their relationship to other words. You can record these data and enter them into the statistical software to use as variables. You may want to determine, for example, whether the words *power* and *powerful* are more often used to describe men or women; to see which other descriptors are most likely to be used in sentences containing these words; or to ascertain whether these words are most likely to be used to describe physical characteristics, performance, emotional states, or sexual scenarios.

Qualitative Data Analysis

If you are uploading your objects directly into a qualitative software analysis package (such as ATLAS.ti, NVivo, or MAXQDA), there is no distinction between data collection and data analysis. After uploading your objects, you will code them using the exact same procedures you would use for analyzing qualitative interviews. You will begin by generating a list of a priori codes that you expect to use in your analysis. Remember that **a priori codes** are codes you come up with in advance of conducting your analysis. You will conceptualize those by writing definitions of the codes to help you clarify their meaning and how you will use them (thus improving the consistency, or reliability, of your coding). Once you have generated a list of a priori codes, you will begin the process of **open coding** by attaching those codes to particular sections (usually text, but they could also be parts of images or videos) of the items you are analyzing. As you attach these codes, you will continue to develop and define new codes, adding them to your list.

Once you have coded all of your objects, you will begin looking for patterns in your data. This phase is called **axial coding**, and you may remember that there are many different types of patterns for which you can search, with frequencies, magnitudes, types, processes, and structures among them (see Chapter 2). You can find a brief review of these patterns in Box 7.7 with examples for content analysis. The

BOX 7.7

PATTERNS YOU MAY LOOK FOR IN AXIAL CODING APPLIED TO CONTENT ANALYSIS

Pattern	Description	Example
Frequency	How often something occurs across objects or within a single object	In 100 issues of men's magazines, men are depicted doing housework or childcare 27 times, but they are depicted playing sports 568 times.
Magnitude	How profoundly something occurs, even if it occurs rarely	Although references to sexual assault were usually subtle in the magazines, there were five cases in which men were explicitly and blatantly encouraged to have sex with women who were too drunk to consent.
Type	Subgroups of something that occurs among many of the objects	You find there are four types of challenges to masculine gender roles in men's magazines: appearance-related, emotional, sexual, and financial.
Process	Steps or stages that are common among the objects in getting from point A to point B	In examining changes in portrayals of masculinity over the decades in men's magazines, you identify that several of the magazines go through five stages over time in changing their depictions of men: exploration, reimagining, commitment, backlash, and modification.
Structure	The essential parts making up a phenomenon	Through your analysis, you identify four different fundamental aspects of what it means to *challenge gender roles*: critique, belief, action, and response.

software packages can be very helpful in aiding you to see these patterns by sorting and focusing on different parts of the data in a wide variety of ways.

Selective coding is the third stage of analysis, and it involves systematically searching for negative cases for the patterns you think you have identified in axial coding. This stage is important because it helps to validate your analysis, ensuring that you are not ignoring data that contradict or challenge the patterns you have identified.

As with all qualitative analysis, you should also write memos throughout all three stages of analysis. These **memos** document procedures that you have completed or still want to complete, but even more important, they document your thoughts, ideas, hunches, insights, and questions as you progress through the analysis. This can help to strengthen your analysis by reminding you of issues you may forget about while focusing on following another lead or by suggesting further patterns for which to search. I've reprinted Box 2.10 from Chapter 2 in Box 7.8 below, to summarize and refresh your memory.

BOX 7.8
DIAGRAM OF STEPS IN QUALITATIVE DATA ANALYSIS

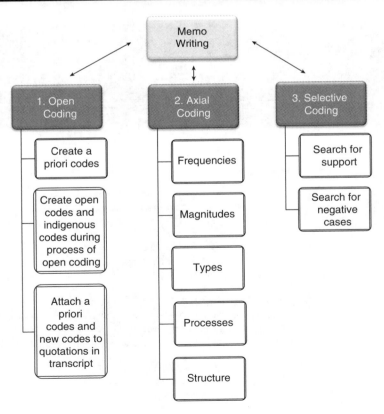

If you used coding sheets for your qualitative analysis, you will still follow many of these procedures. You may wish to start by uploading your coding sheets into the software package, then code your own coding sheets. This may sound like analysis of analysis, but the software can help you sort themes and identify patterns in the data on the coding sheets. Conversely, you may choose to skip this step, which will save coding time but will make identifying patterns more difficult. If you choose to search for patterns without the help of a software package, you will take the physical copies of your coding sheets and sort them using old-fashioned methods: putting them into piles based on themes and subthemes, color-coding sections of the coding sheet for particular codes or patterns, and reading and rereading them. Some people use large pieces of butcher paper to map out connections and patterns among different pieces of the data. In all of these cases, you are still searching for patterns across your coding sheets. Once you have identified those patterns, you will, as always, search for negative cases in order to validate the patterns you have found.

CHECK YOUR UNDERSTANDING

In the last Check Your Understanding, you operationalized both qualitatively and quantitatively. Focusing on the *qualitative* questions only, develop a list of a priori codes for your research.

Evaluating the Quality of Data and Analysis

For quantitative content analysis, reliability in coding of items is important and is usually measured through intercoder reliability. There are many different ways of calculating this, and there is no clear agreement on which of the measures is best. There are a handful of specialty programs that will calculate this for you, and SPSS includes one test that can also perform this function. All of these tests measure the items that were coded discrepantly among the coders, and compare them to what would have happened by chance alone. Intercoder reliability is measured on a scale of 0 to 1.0, with 0.8 or higher showing a good level of reliability. Remember that **reliability** is related to consistency—in this case, that all coders interpreted the item as well as the question and categories on the coding sheet in the same way. On the other hand, **validity**, as you may recall, is the idea that you are measuring what you think you are measuring. Validity is also important in quantitative data analysis: You must demonstrate to your readers that you operationalized your variables in ways that make sense. If you are trying to operationalize *submissiveness*, for example, you will need to convince your audience that the appearances, body positions, and words that you looked for are actually connoting submissiveness and not something else. Crying, for example, may indicate many things, but it is probably a better measure of sadness than submissiveness.

Evaluating the quality of qualitative content analysis typically relies more on validity than on reliability because it is hard to calculate intercoder reliability when coding is open-ended and what is being measured is less precise. The better you have conceptualized and operationalized, however, the more reliable your coding will be between objects and over time, thus improving the overall quality of your research. Validity is of utmost importance, as it is with all qualitative work. Validity is demonstrated by giving detailed examples from the data. This may be in the form of quotations from written materials, or thorough descriptions of visual materials. In some cases, you may include a few visual images from the data (if appropriate) in your presentation of the results so that the reader can see firsthand how the interpretations were made and how the theme is apparent. The validity of your analysis depends on the amount of support you have throughout the data for the patterns you've identified. Additionally, your analysis can only be valid if you have done selective coding, where the fewer the number of negative cases that the selective coding yields, the more valid your analysis.

Presenting the Results

Writing up the results for publication of content analysis is similar to the presentation of other data. After presenting the literature review and any theoretical lens through which you are collecting the data, you will give a thorough explanation of all steps, stages, and decisions made in sampling, as well as a description of the final sample used. You will also discuss at length the items on the coding sheet (if applicable), how concepts were operationalized, and the steps taken to minimize discrepancies either across coders or from item to item. This will be followed by a description of your major findings, relationships between variables, or themes found within the data. You will end with a description of what these data teach us and why they are important.

Summary Points

- Content analysis is the method to use when studying textual, image, audio, or video artifacts. Its purpose is to understand both the obvious and more subtle messages in order to uncover cultural norms and beliefs.

- Content analysis may be either qualitative or quantitative or a mix thereof, and it may be conducted using positivism, interpretivism, or critical methodology.

- Content analysis is most often conducted in teams, and significant care must be taken in conceptualizing, operationalizing, and training the team in order to maintain reliability in coding the artifacts.

- Although content analysis is usually an inexpensive method to conduct and is one in which the researcher has an extraordinary amount of control (because there are no research participants on which to rely), it can also be a very time-consuming method, as coding can be tedious and must be meticulously recorded, and sample sizes can be quite large.

- Quantitative analysis for this research method is very similar to that of surveys; qualitative analysis is like that of interview research. Thus, the basic skills of analysis are transferable to other methods.

Key Terms

a priori codes 199
axial coding 199
census 187
coding sheet 191
conceptualize 191
critical methodology 182
frequencies 198

intercoder reliability 197
memos 200
objectivity 182
open coding 199
operationalize 191
qualitative codes 192
qualitative content analysis 181

quantitative content
    analysis 179
reliability 201
selective coding 200
spot checking 198
theoretical sampling 187
validity 201

Experiments for Evaluation Research

Experiments may well be the research method with which you are most familiar because they are among the few research methods that are also used by the natural sciences. You may even remember some of the basics of experimental research design from your school science fair projects. While there have been some famous sociological experiments, such as the Zimbardo prison study (Musen & Zimbardo, 1992) and Milgram's (1974) experiment on obedience, today few sociologists use experiments in their research (although psychologists frequently use them). This is probably due to several factors: Sociologists are often interested in how people respond to their natural environment, which is hard to emulate under experimental conditions; experiments are very difficult to conduct on macro-level issues; the very complex phenomena that often interest sociologists would introduce too many variables to measure in a single experiment; sociological theories can be difficult to test experimentally; and after the criticism from high-profile experiments such as the Zimbardo and Milgram experiments, sociologists are often reluctant to deceive research participants, which increases the possibility of harm. As a student of sociology, you are probably unlikely ever to conduct an experiment yourself in an academic setting, but you will inevitably be a consumer of experimental research in the media (especially with health-related topics). Additionally, your job may require you to conduct applied experimental research in the form of **program evaluation** (research conducted to determine the effectiveness of a program or policy). Because this book focuses on research methods you can use in the real world, in this chapter we will target the use of experiments in this latter context.

    Classical experiments are based on the search for causality: trying to determine if, and to what extent, one thing (an **independent variable**) affects another (a **dependent variable**). In order to ensure that any observed effect is actually caused by the independent variable, everything else must be tightly controlled. Classical experiments rely on several mechanisms for doing this: We take measurements of the dependent variable both before and after introducing the independent

REAL PEOPLE, REAL RESEARCH

Nicolette Moore

Armed with a recent BA in sociology, Nicolette landed a job as a research assistant with a small evaluation firm. She works on two federally funded studies that are evaluating the impact of teen pregnancy prevention interventions. Both interventions use randomized control and treatment groups, and each group is surveyed during a pretest and again at two other specific points in time. Nicolette is in charge of maintaining contact with the study participants and conducting the follow-up surveys. If any participant is under the age of 18, Nicolette must get signed informed consent from one of their parents as well. If a parent won't consent, the teen is unable to participate in the research, even if they want to.

variable (sometimes called the **treatment** in experimental research); we leave a **control group** unexposed to the treatment, and then compare it to the treatment group(s); and we ensure that the control and treatment groups are similar in composition. Taking these steps helps to minimize the influence from any other sources, so that the effect of the treatment can be isolated as much as possible, and measured. We usually conduct classical experiments (sometimes also called **true experiments**) in a laboratory so that all other potential outside influences can be monitored and controlled. In evaluation research, the treatment usually consists of a new program, curriculum, policy, or way of accomplishing a goal, and the purpose of the research is to assess how well this treatment works, as well as the effects it has on the organizations' clients. Because such research usually takes place in real life and not in a laboratory, however, it often does not meet all of the criteria of classical experiments. Thus, caution must be taken when drawing conclusions from the results, as any observed effects may be caused by something other than the treatment. Despite this limitation, experimental designs are one of our most useful tools in determining the effectiveness of real-life programs and policies. Additionally, they have become increasingly popular as funding agencies turn more toward funding programs with "evidence-based effectiveness." Indeed, with increased pressure to prove that the projects they fund are actually effective and therefore a good investment of public (or private) monies, funding agencies have begun to hold experimental research as the gold standard of program evaluation. Thus, learning how to conduct experimental evaluation research is an important and useful skill for sociology students, especially those planning to work with nonprofits and government-funded agencies.

Methodology

Experimental research is nearly always quantitative in nature and is therefore usually conducted using positivist methodology. Remember that **positivists** conduct research as scientifically as possible in order to rule out any potential bias. This is particularly important when you are conducting evaluation research, as your hopes (or pressures) to find that the program or policy has a certain effect could bias your research if you are not careful. Thus, in order to obtain valid results, you must try to systematically root out all sources of potential bias, even unconscious ones.

You will begin with the hypotheses you want to test, and you will conceptualize and operationalize those variables carefully. When you assign research participants to different groups, you should do so in ways to eliminate (or at least minimize) the possibility of bias. You want to make sure that you don't, for example, assign people who are most likely to be affected by the treatment to the treatment groups. You should also try to interact with all research participants in a similar manner. In experiments for basic research, the experimenter would avoid any sort of relationship with the participants and would try to treat each participant in exactly the same way, often going so far as to script exactly what is said to each participant. This is less likely to happen when you are conducting applied program evaluation, as the participants will usually already belong to your agency's clientele, and they may already know you or the other researchers. Still, you must try to minimize any source of bias from your interactions with the participants, if possible. This objectivity in the relationship is often signaled by the vocabulary used by experimental researchers, who may call the people in their studies **subjects** rather than "participants," in order to connote a more formal and objective relationship.

In collecting the data, you must follow very rigorous procedures. The treatment should be delivered in a planned and controlled way, and you must take every possible step to rule out potential bias in the results. The experiment should be **replicable**, meaning that the results should not depend on who conducts the research; if someone else used the same sampling procedures, followed the same treatment protocol, and employed the same procedures for collecting the data, that person should come up with the same results. The results of experiments are analyzed statistically. The more complex the conclusions you want to draw, and the more confident you want to be in attributing causation, the more advanced the statistical knowledge you will need.

Because experimental evaluation research takes place in the real world instead of a laboratory, it can be difficult to live up to all of the standards of positivist research when doing this kind of work. In some cases, it may be difficult to control exactly how the treatment is administered, or the kinds of interactions or relationships research subjects have with the people who administer the treatment. It may even be difficult to keep the group assignments unbiased. These remain, nonetheless, the standards we strive to meet, even if they are not entirely possible in the real world. Weak points that allow the introduction of bias do not necessarily invalidate the entire study's findings, but they do diminish your ability to conclude that any effects you observe are, indeed, caused by the treatment rather than by something else.

Theory

Evaluation research rarely uses sociological theory. Because it is meant to evaluate the effectiveness of a particular policy or program, generally only when that policy or program grew directly out of a theory of middle range does theory usually enter into evaluation research. Crime prevention policies and techniques, for example, have come from routine activity theory and crime pattern theory, among others. If you were wanting to evaluate one of the crime policies that grew directly out of crime pattern theory, you would need to be well schooled in it so that you understand the policy's purpose and why it takes the form it does. This will inform your evaluation, including the hypotheses you may test, the variables you include, the ways in which you conceptualize and operationalize those variables, the people that you choose to solicit for participation in your research, and the type of design that is most appropriate. If the policy or program was not directly born from a particular theory in the field, then theory will likely be irrelevant for your research.

Research Questions

In experimental research used for evaluation purposes, the research questions will focus on the effect of a program or policy, and should take into account whether any effects exist at all, what kinds of effects those are, and the size of those effects. Thus, research questions for applied experimental research are generally fairly similar. *What effects, if any, does the Teaching Vulnerability curriculum have on students' academic performance?* is an example. Note that effects are not assumed, and the outcome, *academic performance*, is broad enough to be operationalized by many different variables but still narrow enough to be reasonably measured. Also notice that the question includes both the independent and dependent variables, and the question implies causality. This differs from research questions for surveys, where we discussed relationships between variables but did not directly assert cause and effect (see Chapter 4). With surveys, we could not determine causality because it is often difficult to determine **temporal order**. With experiments, because the researcher usually provides the treatment, temporal order is established, and although we can never truly rule out all other explanations, the closer the experimental design is to a classical experiment, the greater our ability to control for outside influences and thus isolate the effect of the independent variable. Thus, research questions usually directly ask about causation rather than asking the more general *What is the relationship between . . .?* that we used with survey research. Because all of the research questions for evaluation research sound nearly identical, just replacing the program and the dependent variable for each, I am not including here a box with sample research questions as I have in the other chapters. Instead, simply follow the formula *What effects, if any, does* [name of policy or program] *have on* [dependent variable]?

Hypotheses for the research question will focus on testing the effect of the program or policy on different specific measures of the dependent variables. In the above example of the effects of the Teaching Vulnerability Curriculum, these would be various aspects and measures of *academic performance*. Box 8.1 contains a list of potential hypotheses for this research question.

Reminder: There are three requirements for determining causality: **association** (when the independent variable changes so does the dependent variable); **temporal order** (the independent variable came before the dependent variable); and **elimination of plausible alternatives** (other possible causes have been ruled out).

BOX 8.1
SAMPLE HYPOTHESES FOR EXPERIMENTAL EVALUATION RESEARCH

RQ: What effects, if any, does the Teaching Vulnerability curriculum have on students' academic performance?

H1: Students who are taught the Teaching Vulnerability curriculum complete more of their assignments in math and English courses than do students who are not exposed to the curriculum.

Dependent variable: number of assignments completed

H2: Students who are taught the Teaching Vulnerability curriculum receive higher grades on their math and English assignments than do students who are not exposed to this curriculum.

Dependent variable: grades on math and English assignments

H3: Students who are taught the Teaching Vulnerability curriculum are more likely to ask questions in class than are students who are not exposed to the curriculum.

Dependent variable: likelihood of asking questions in class

H4: Students who are taught the Teaching Vulnerability curriculum are more likely to ask assignment-related questions of their peers than are students who are not exposed to the curriculum.

Dependent variable: likelihood of asking peers assignment-related questions

H5: Students who are taught the Teaching Vulnerability curriculum improve their semester grades in math and English over the previous semester more than do students who are not exposed to the curriculum.

Dependent variable: amount of improvement in math and English grades from prior semester

H6: Students who are taught the Teaching Vulnerability curriculum are more likely to ask for corrective feedback before turning in an assignment than are students who are not exposed to the curriculum.

Dependent variable: likelihood of asking for corrective feedback before turning in an assignment

H7: Students who are taught the Teaching Vulnerability curriculum report working harder to understand material that they find difficult than do students who are not exposed to the curriculum.

Dependent variable: degree to which students worked to understand difficult material

H8: Students who are taught the Teaching Vulnerability curriculum are less likely to tease other students for their work than are students who are not exposed to the curriculum.

Dependent variable: likelihood of teasing other students for their work

H9: Students who are taught the Teaching Vulnerability curriculum are more likely to volunteer to share their work or answers with the class than are students who are not exposed to the curriculum.

Dependent variable: likelihood of volunteering to share work or answers in class

H10: Students who are taught the Teaching Vulnerability curriculum participate verbally in class discussions more frequently than do students who are not exposed to the curriculum.

Dependent variable: frequency of verbal participation in class discussions

Be aware that unlike the hypotheses we used in survey research, only the dependent variable differs across hypotheses; this is common in evaluation research because you are usually testing the effect of the overall program or policy (independent variable) on a number of different possible outcomes (dependent variable). Also notice that although we call both *academic performance* (from the research question) and *number of assignments completed* (from the first hypothesis) dependent variables, the dependent variables listed in the hypotheses are all actually different but specific measures of the dependent variable from the research question. In other words, the hypotheses each lay out an additional way of measuring the dependent variable from the research question (in this case, *academic performance*).

 Reminder: The **unit of analysis** is the "who" or "what" being studied.

You should be careful with your unit of analysis with this research method. In experimental evaluation research, at first glance it can appear that the program or policy itself is the unit of analysis because the research question usually focuses on the effectiveness of the that program or policy. But your hypotheses actually reveal that the program or policy is the *independent variable*, not the unit of analysis, and that the unit of analysis is implied by the research question to be the people who have participated in the program or been affected by the policy. The hypotheses clarify this because all of the hypotheses compare *people* who have had the treatment with *people* who have not had the treatment. Thus, your unit of analysis is the individuals in the study, not the program or policy itself.

CHECK YOUR UNDERSTANDING

Write a research question for a program or policy that you would evaluate. Then generate a list of hypotheses that you would use to test the effect of the program or policy.

Literature Review

The literature review for applied research is done for the same purposes as for basic research: to help you identify dependent variables that you may want to test, to show you how other people have conceptualized and operationalized those variables, to alert you to problems that have arisen in similar previous research, and to help you anticipate which effects you may be likely to see. What you typically will *not* find in the literature review are studies in your same city or town, at the same organization, or even necessarily using the same policy or program. You will instead need to broaden your search to include a greater range of policies and programs related to your topic. Additionally, you may look at basic research that doesn't even test the efficacy of a particular program, but instead informs you about previous research related to the dependent variable. For example, say that at a low-income housing project you want to start a class that provides residents with tangible job skills. In addition to looking at studies that evaluate other such programs, you will also want to read the literature that addresses such information as the kinds of job skills currently most in demand in your area, the current hiring trends, and studies investigating why some people have difficulty maintaining a job once they have acquired it.

All of this information can help inform the variables you test, the structure of your study, and the context you need for interpreting the results.

Choosing a Study Design

You might have noticed that other chapters in this book have not included choosing a research design as a separate component of the research process. The reason is simple: With the other research methods we have studied, the research method, combined with the research question, has more or less provided the structure of the study's design. With experimental evaluation research, however, there are multiple design formats from which to choose. Each of these will affect the way you sample, as well as the way you operationalize your variables. As mentioned earlier, although the classical experiment is the gold standard for experimental research because it provides the most protection against bias and because it best controls outside variables that might affect the results of the study, this type of design is not always possible in real-life evaluative settings.

There are actually many different designs from which to choose. Here, we will address a few of the possibilities that you may most likely use. Because none of these meet the criteria of the classical experiment, they do not provide the same level of validity. Remember that if you were conducting a classical experiment, you would take measurements of the dependent variables both before and after the treatment, you would leave a control group unexposed to the treatment and then compare it to the treatment group(s), and you would rule out bias in assigning subjects to the treatment and control groups. The designs that follow each compromise on one or more of these dimensions.

Variations on the Classical Experimental Design
No Control Group

One of the most common ways that evaluation research sometimes deviates from the classical experimental design is to treat *all* of the research subjects to the treatment, forgoing a control group. For example, if your workplace implements a new attendance policy, and you want to measure how this affects both morale and productivity, it may be very difficult or even impossible to have some employees working under one attendance policy and other employees working under another, especially if people in both groups share the same job titles and duties. In fact, simply conducting such an experiment might cause both morale and productivity problems in the workplace, as employees may perceive one policy to be stricter than the other and become upset that they must adhere to the stricter policy. When the fact of conducting the experiment itself causes effects on the dependent variables measured, it can become nearly impossible to separate the effect of the policy itself (the independent variable) from the effect of conducting the experiment (subjecting workers to two different attendance policies). This renders the results invalid and should be avoided at all costs. In this case, then, it would be better to choose a research design that avoids this problem by forgoing the use of a control group and treating all research subjects to the treatment (the new attendance policy). For this design, you would measure both morale and productivity before the policy change (called a **pretest**), and again after it (a **posttest**). Although you are unable to compare a control group with the treatment group, by comparing the pretest and posttest results, you will gain some sense of the impact of the new policy.

Because this design does not include a control group, it is called a **pre-experimental design**, emphasizing that it shares some similarities with true experiments but does not provide the same level of validity. The downside of this design is that you cannot rule out plausible alternatives in determining causality. In other words, you cannot know for sure if any changes in either morale or productivity result from the new policy or something else. Perhaps, for example, during the time period studied an employee whom many other coworkers don't much like is promoted to a managerial position. This may have an impact on both of your dependent variables, but because there is no control group to show that morale and productivity were affected despite not having a new attendance policy, you will not be able to determine how much of the effect comes from the unpopular promotion and how much from the new policy. Similarly, if the new policy improved morale and production, those effects may appear smaller than they otherwise would because they are simultaneously affected in the opposite direction by the workers' response to the new manager. In other words, if employees are excited about the new attendance policy but upset about the unpopular promotion, these may cancel each other out in the workers' productivity or morale.

Naturally Occurring Groups

Another pre-experimental design compares groups that are not chosen in a way that minimizes bias in the group assignment. Let's say I teach two sections of the same research methods course, and I want to test which section learns the material better: the section that uses my usual style of assigning daily homework, or the section in which I try something new by using fewer assignments but including weekly quizzes. Because the groups are **naturally occurring**—that is, I can't decide which section of the course students will sign up for—I can compare the students' work and grades between sections, but I can't control the biases in the composition of each class. Students who signed up for the 8 a.m. class, for example, may include more students who prioritize studying, while students in the 11 a.m. section may be more likely to drink alcohol the night before class. Conversely, the students in the 8 a.m. section may be more likely to take an early class because they are juggling a higher number of responsibilities, including time-consuming jobs and/or collegiate athletics, while students taking the later class may have more flexible schedules and thus more time to devote to learning the material. My point here is that sometimes we cannot decide how people get assigned to the control and treatment groups, but then the possibility of bias in the groups becomes high. If students in both groups are not similar or randomly assigned, then even though we have both a control and a treatment group, we nonetheless diminish our ability to attribute differences between the groups to the treatment rather than to other variables. Thus, because of bias in the composition of the groups, the effect of the new quiz format may be exaggerated or minimized, but I would have no way of knowing this, nor which direction (exaggerated or minimized) the effect is occurring, nor to what extent it may be affecting the results.

No Pretest

Evaluation researchers may also deviate from the classical experimental design by forgoing a pretest. In this design, you measure the dependent variable only after the treatment with a posttest, but do not administer a pretest with which to compare the results. You are most likely to do this when the treatment involves exposing the research subjects to knowledge that they are highly unlikely to have had prior to the treatment. I once served on the thesis committee of a high school calculus teacher, for example, who wanted to test how collaborative learning affected students' comprehension of the material. In this case, the dependent variable would be *degree of demonstrated comprehension*, but because none of the students would have been exposed to any calculus before the class, presumably none of the students would be able to demonstrate any knowledge on a pretest except by guessing correct answers by chance. In this case, then, because everyone in both the control and treatment groups would have a baseline knowledge of zero, a pretest wouldn't accomplish much, and being "tested" on unfamiliar material may make students fearful of the course. This relates to another potential reason to forgo a pretest: The taking of the pretest itself may influence the subjects' subsequent behavior. If the pretest is likely to increase their motivation to excel with the treatment, for example, or to sensitize them to issues you are investigating, then you may decide it is better to avoid pretesting. Finally, if the treatment is something for which there is little preparation time or that happens without much warning, such as a sudden 50% cut in funding for a particular program, you may not be capable of pretesting but may still choose to compare outcomes for the group that gets to remain in the program with those that don't. Although this posttest-only design varies from the classical experimental design, it is still considered a "true" experiment (as opposed to a pre-experiment) if you use a control group and if you take steps to ensure that the treatment and control groups are equivalent; thus, it is not considered as damaging to the validity of the results as are pre-experimental designs.

Sometimes researchers combine some of these variations into their evaluation research, neither administering a pretest nor ensuring that group assignment is unbiased, for example. The more deviations from the classical experimental design that are included in your study, however, the less valid the results, and the less confident you can be that any effects you observe are the result of the actual treatment and not of biases in the research process. For this reason, you should try to adhere as closely to the classical experimental design as is reasonably possible, given the real-life conditions under which you are conducting the evaluation.

Other Variations

Experimental designs can vary in other ways as well. One of these is in the number of groups and treatments that you utilize. Although you should use a control

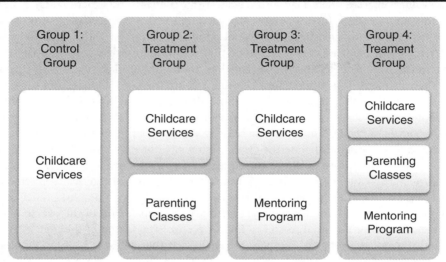

BOX 8.2

DIAGRAM OF MULTIPLE TREATMENT GROUPS WITH
DIFFERENT COMBINATIONS OF TREATMENT

Group 1: Control Group	Group 2: Treatment Group	Group 3: Treatment Group	Group 4: Treament Group
Childcare Services	Childcare Services	Childcare Services	Childcare Services
	Parenting Classes	Mentoring Program	Parenting Classes
			Mentoring Program

group whenever possible, sometimes you may have more than one treatment group. Imagine, for example, that you work at a community center that provides childcare for teen moms while they work. Currently, some of the moms who use the center's services also attend free parenting classes once a month. You also want to start a new mentoring program in which each mom would be paired with a community parent volunteer who can answer questions and offer emotional support. You may evaluate the new mentoring program using four groups: Group 1 is a control group that only uses the childcare service; Group 2 is a treatment group that uses the childcare service and attends the parenting classes (but doesn't participate in the mentoring program); Group 3 is a treatment group that uses the childcare services and the new mentoring program (but not the parenting classes); and Group 4 is a treatment group that uses the childcare services, the parenting classes, and the mentoring program. See Box 8.2 for a diagram of this multi-group, multi-treatment study design.

Experimental design may also vary along dimensions of timing, specifically the frequency of treatment, the frequency of posttest measurement, and the timing of posttest measurement. In its most simple form, the classical experiment begins with a pretest, followed by the treatment group receiving the treatment one time in its entirety, and then followed by a posttest (while the control group receives no treatment, but participates in both the pre- and posttests). If the treatment is not time-consuming, you may choose to repeat it one or more times, measuring the effects with a posttest after each treatment. If the treatment is a 2-hour smoking cessation

BOX 8.3

DECISION PATH FOR CHOOSING AN EXPERIMENTAL STUDY DESIGN

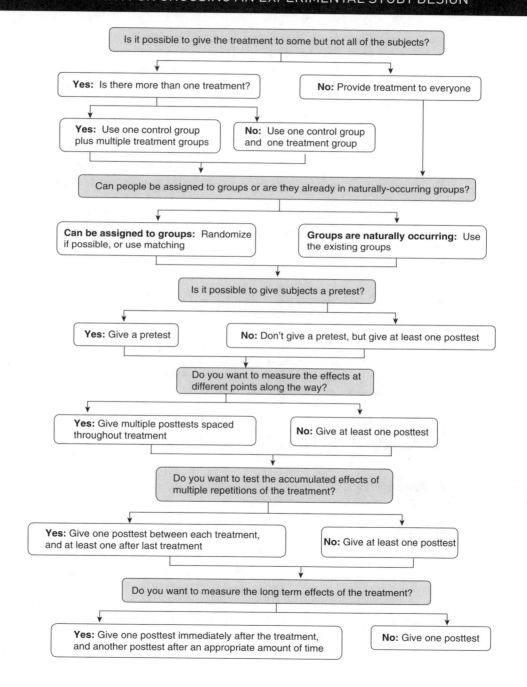

Is it possible to give the treatment to some but not all of the subjects?

Yes: Is there more than one treatment?

No: Provide treatment to everyone

Yes: Use one control group plus multiple treatment groups

No: Use one control group and one treatment group

Can people be assigned to groups or are they already in naturally-occurring groups?

Can be assigned to groups: Randomize if possible, or use matching

Groups are naturally occurring: Use the existing groups

Is it possible to give subjects a pretest?

Yes: Give a pretest

No: Don't give a pretest, but give at least one posttest

Do you want to measure the effects at different points along the way?

Yes: Give multiple posttests spaced throughout treatment

No: Give at least one posttest

Do you want to test the accumulated effects of multiple repetitions of the treatment?

Yes: Give one posttest between each treatment, and at least one after last treatment

No: Give at least one posttest

Do you want to measure the long term effects of the treatment?

Yes: Give one posttest immediately after the treatment, and another posttest after an appropriate amount of time

No: Give one posttest

workshop, you may have the treatment group attend the same workshop four times, spaced out about every 3 months. One month after attending each workshop, you may ask the subjects to complete a posttest questionnaire asking them to report on their current smoking habits and attempts at quitting. This allows you to test not only the effect of the individual workshop, but also the cumulative effect of attending the workshop multiple times. Alternately, you may offer an ongoing workshop that meets once a week for 3 months. Because each meeting covers different information and offers support in different ways, the entire 3-month series is considered one treatment. You may, nonetheless, assess the effect of the workshop at multiple points, administering the posttest questionnaire after every fourth meeting, for example. Finally, you can choose different points in time for conducting the posttest. If you want to test short-term effects of the treatment, you may do your posttest immediately afterward, but if you want to test the long-term effects, you may decide to wait 6 months or even a year. You could decide to posttest at several different points in time to see whether the effects diminish over time, but you also must take into account that research subjects can lose interest in participating multiple times over an extended period and may be more likely to drop out of your study before its completion.

Ultimately, deciding on a study design can be complex. Box 8.3 can help you determine the best design choices, based on the circumstances of your study and the goals of your research.

CHECK YOUR UNDERSTANDING

Choose a study design for your research question, including the type of design, the number of treatment groups, and the frequency and timing of treatment and post-testing. What real-life constraints would affect these decisions, and how? Describe how the validity of your research may be affected by your design choices.

Conceptualizing and Operationalizing

Reminder: **Conceptualizing** means precisely defining the variables so that you know what is included or excluded from the definition. **Operationalizing** is deciding how you will measure those definitions.

Because in experimental evaluation research your independent variable is the implementation of a specific program or policy, the independent variable usually needs very little **conceptualizing** or **operationalizing**. Your focus, therefore, will be on operationalizing the different dependent variables that you have identified in your hypotheses. In operationalizing your dependent variables, you will often employ other research methods to gather the data by which to measure them. For example, for the list of hypotheses in Box 8.1, we have 10 different dependent variables: *number of assignments completed, grades on assignments, likelihood of asking questions in class, likelihood of asking questions of peers, amount of improvement in math and English grades from prior semester, likelihood of asking for corrective feedback, level of engagement with difficult material, likelihood of criticizing other* *students' work, likelihood of sharing answers in front of the class,* and *rate of in-class participation.* Each one of these will need to be measured, but they will require very different types of data collection to do so.

Number of assignments completed and *grades on assignments* will be gathered from the teacher's grade book. Many of the other variables, however, such as *likelihood of asking questions in class* and *likelihood of criticizing other students' work,* would need to be quantitatively observed in the classroom, with precise records of the observations being kept. *Level of engagement with difficult material* would need to be assessed by asking students (in a questionnaire) at different points in time how difficult

 Tip: Even though most observation is qualitative, in experimental evaluation research it is always quantitative because you are using positivist methodology and are testing hypotheses.

they find the material and how engaged they feel with it. Part of operationalizing for experimental design, then, is deciding how you will collect the particular information needed to measure the dependent variables you are testing.

When thinking about what different techniques you will use to collect the information you need, be sure to think beyond just self-reports on surveys in order to determine the actual effects of the treatment because people don't always perceive changes in their behavior accurately. In the case of pre- and posttest surveys about the effect of a program, for example, they are likely to overreport the amount of change they have made if that change is desirable. Let's consider the example of a diversity training program for school guidance counselors that aims to help them improve their effectiveness with a diverse student body. If you were to include only the guidance counselors in your evaluation, and you used only a pre- and posttest survey measuring their self-reported behaviors, they would likely overestimate the actual changes that they have made in their counseling techniques because after the program they are sensitized to the issues and know what would constitute good practice. They may purposely exaggerate their new behaviors, but more likely they simply are so focused on how they have incorporated the new skills they don't recognize where they have not yet incorporated them, or where they have but not very well. In this case, because counseling sessions are private and confidential, you couldn't observe their behaviors directly. Thus, in addition to surveying the counselors about what they perceive themselves to be doing in the counseling sessions, you could also survey the students they counsel. If you were to do so both for the pretest and the posttest, you could compare students' perceptions of the counseling they are receiving before and after the training occurs, and you could identify any differences in student evaluations. This will tell you significantly more than if you were to only survey the counselors themselves.

Beyond determining what research methods you will use to collect the data, however, you will also need to determine exactly how you will measure the variables upon which you have decided. What, for example, will count as *asking for corrective feedback* and what will not? Over what period of time will you count these feedback requests? And, for counting purposes, will asking a follow-up clarifying question count as part of the initial request or as a separate one? Additionally, you will need to develop the exact wording of the questions about *level of engagement* and *difficulty of material* (just as you would for a survey) and decide how often and when you will ask these questions.

CHECK YOUR UNDERSTANDING

Conceptualize and operationalize three of the dependent variables from your list of hypotheses. How will you gather the data to measure each of these variables?

Sampling

Quantitative research is usually meant to generalize to a larger population, which requires random sampling. However, even classical experiments often do not use random sampling because many participants in a random sample would likely not be able to commit to the time-consuming and rigid schedule that experiments require. Thus, most experiments for basic research use volunteers (**convenience sampling**), even though it is not ideal. Experimental evaluation research, however, often uses a **census** by including all of the clients of the organization in the experiment, either in the control or treatment group. If you use convenience sampling you must think carefully about how you recruit for your study. You will want to advertise in ways that will best reach your specific target population, as well as diversify your sample so that you don't end up with, for example, all white participants or all females (unless that is your target population). Just as with interviewing, you may end up needing to use a combination of advertising, help from gatekeepers, and word of mouth.

Despite the fact that random sampling is rarely used in recruiting research subjects, the potential bias this introduces can be mitigated by the way that subjects are assigned to the experimental groups. As already mentioned, in order to maintain high levels of validity, the bias should be eliminated from group assignment. You can accomplish this in two ways: matching or random assignment. **Matching** means collecting demographic and other information about the research subjects that could bias the results of the study, and then making sure that each group has equal (or close to equal) representation of each characteristic. You wouldn't want to have all of the African Americans in the treatment group and none in the control group, for example. Instead, if there are four African American women between the ages of 40 and 60 in your sample, and you have two groups (one control and one treatment group), you would want to put two of these women in each group. This is similar to the procedures used for the probability sampling technique of stratified sampling for survey research, where participants are divided by a particular variable such as gender before being selected, and then an equal number of males and females, for example, are chosen to participate in order to ensure representativeness. With matching for groups, however, you track more than just one variable, matching subjects on multiple dimensions such as age, gender, race, length of time as an agency client, and previous participation in similar programs. Thus, you try to match the two groups as closely as possible in order to increase the likelihood that the effects you observe are caused by the treatment, not by other variables such as racial or age differences between the two groups.

BOX 8.4

PROBABILITY SAMPLING METHODS ADAPTED FOR RANDOM GROUP ASSIGNMENT

Sampling Method	Description	Applied to Random Group Assignment
Simple random sample	Each subject is given a number, and subjects are chosen using a random numbers generator.	Every subject is listed and given a number. Random numbers generator is used to choose which subjects will belong to the control group (and if there are multiple treatment groups, which belong to each one).
Systematic random sample	Sampling frame is randomized, then each subject is given a number. Randomly choose the first number, then count down the list to every *n*th person to select them. *N* represents the number in the sampling frame divided by the total number desired in the sample.	Every subject is listed in random order. Starting with a randomly chosen number, count down the list assigning each subject to one of the groups, in order. (Example: If you start with #32 and have four groups, #32 will be in group 1, #33 in group 2, #34 in group 3, #35 in group 4, #36 in group 1, etc.)
Stratified random sample	Sampling frame is divided into groups and then simple random or systematic sampling is used to select a given number of subjects from each group.	Total sample is divided into lists based on one characteristic. Simple random or systematic sampling is then used to assign equal numbers of people from each list across the experimental groups.
Cluster sample	Groups are randomly chosen, and every subject from chosen groups is included in the sample.	Naturally occurring groups are randomly chosen, and every subject from that group is randomly assigned to an experimental group.

The other mechanism for creating unbiased groups is random assignment. **Random assignment** involves taking the sample and dividing it into groups using probability procedures. This does not guarantee that the groups will be highly similar, but the fact that any differences are occurring by chance alone helps to reduce the bias. Random assignment can be done using the same procedures as selecting a probability sample from a population: simple random sampling, systematic random sampling, stratified sampling, or cluster sampling. Box 8.4 reviews these procedures and describes how they can be adapted to group assignment.

It is very important to note that using a convenience sample combined with random assignment or group matching does not enable you to generalize to a larger population. Those who volunteer to participate may well be different in important ways from those who don't participate, which means that you can't generalize. However, by matching or randomly assigning groups, you ensure that each group is representative of *those who chose to participate* but *not* of the larger population. This enables you both to isolate the effect of the independent variable by ruling out group bias and to generalize from one experimental group to another. You can reasonably assume, for example, that if a control group had received the same treatment as the treatment group with which it is matched, it would have seen similar results.

CHECK YOUR UNDERSTANDING

How will you recruit research subjects for your study? If your research design includes more than one group, explain how you will assign subjects to the study groups.

Ethics

Experiments in medical and academic settings, and those funded by governmental agencies, are among the most tightly regulated research studies in terms of ethical standards. Because experimental treatments may put research subjects at risk, and because experiments in the social sciences may involve deception (and therefore increase the likelihood of harm to the subject), Institutional Review Boards (IRBs) tend to be particularly careful in approving experimental research. Precautions that must be taken include the following:

- Obtaining full and signed informed consent with a clear declaration of the risks of exposure to the treatment as well as acknowledgment that the individual may not receive any treatment

- Using deceit only when necessary and in ways that do not harm the participants

- Debriefing the subjects after participation if deception is used

- Protecting the confidentiality of the subjects

- Obtaining parental consent if the research involves minors

- Reporting in the aggregate

In evaluation research, however, if you are working in a community organization, you may well not have an IRB from which you must seek approval. Some funding agencies require you to submit your proposed evaluation plan to a committee that will provide feedback and advice, but many don't. It is therefore up to you, the researcher, to ensure that you take all ethical precautions to protect your research subjects.

Informed Consent

While experimental research usually requires a full informed consent statement, in the evaluation research setting, this requirement can vary by context. As a rule of thumb, if your research design includes people being randomly assigned to a control group or a treatment group, you will need to provide them with a full informed consent statement and obtain their signature on it. This consent statement looks much like the informed consent for an online survey, with the exception that experimental research is rarely anonymous, and therefore only confidentiality can be promised. Additionally, you should reveal all of the different methods you will use to gather data. Thus, if you are operationalizing variables using questionnaires, observation, and an examination of existing data, you will need to include all three on the informed consent. Finally, as with all applied research, you should indicate that the subject's participation in this research will not in any way affect their relationship with or ability to receive services from your organization.

The informed consent should thus include the following parts:

- A short description of what the research is about

- A statement of who is conducting the research

- A description of who may participate in the research

- A statement of how long you are requesting they participate, how many times, and using what types of research methods

- A statement of confidentiality, including all of the steps you will take to protect their confidentiality:

    o The use of a pseudonym

    o That any electronic materials will be kept in password-protected files, and that any physical materials will be kept in a locked drawer in a locked office

    o That their name will not be connected to data collected about them

    o That any quantitative data will only be reported in the aggregate

- A statement that their participation in the research is entirely voluntary, and they may withdraw their participation at any time for any reason without penalty

- A statement that they have the right to have their questions about the study answered

- A statement of any risks or benefits to them for their participation

- A clear statement that their participation, or lack of, will in no way affect the services they receive nor their participation in any program

- Contact information if they have questions

- Signature (using real name)

An example of a full informed consent statement is provided in Box 8.5.

BOX 8.5

SAMPLE INFORMED CONSENT STATEMENT FOR
EXPERIMENTAL EVALUATION RESEARCH

We invite you to take part in a research project being conducted by the M & J Christner Community Center regarding the childcare program, the monthly parenting classes, and the new It Takes a Village Mentoring Program. You are eligible to participate in this study if you are a single mother and are currently receiving childcare services from the Center. You need not participate in either the parenting classes or mentoring program in order to take part in this study. The purpose of this study is to evaluate the programs and their effects, as required by the grant that funds the program.

The study will last for 12 weeks. During that time, we will periodically observe your child's behavior in childcare. Four times over the next 12 weeks we will also ask you to complete a survey of 20 questions. The survey will ask about how you respond to your child's behavior and will take about 10 minutes of your time on each occasion, for a total of about 40 minutes.

All of the information we collect will be kept entirely confidential. All of the observation notes we make of your child will be made using a fake name and will be kept in a locked drawer in a locked office. Your responses to the survey questions will only be linked to you by a number, and the key connecting your name and number will be kept on a password-protected computer in a locked office. All of your survey answers will also be stored on this password-protected computer. Your answers and the observations of your child will never be reported individually, but only in combination with those of the other program participants.

Your participation is completely voluntary. You have the right to ask questions about this study, and to have your questions answered. There are no anticipated risks or benefits to you from your participation in this research. You may withdraw your participation at any time without penalty. Your decision about participating has no bearing on your ability to receive services from the Center and will not affect your relationship with the Center.

If you have questions or concerns about the study, you may contact the Center's director, Sandy Beach, at (987) 555–1234.

I have read the above and have had all my questions about participation in this study answered to my satisfaction. I understand that my participation in this study is completely voluntary.

Signature _____

Date _____

The following are examples of cases in which full informed consent is not required:

- if subjects are not randomly assigned to treatment and control groups

- if the only data that will be collected would have been gathered even if the experiment were not conducted

- if there is no reason to suspect that subjects will be exposed to any harm from the treatment

Take, for example, the previously mentioned test of effectiveness of different sets of course requirements in two sections of my research methods courses. Students will be informed in the syllabus of the requirements of the class. They also have full choice of which section of the class to sign up for, and they are not assigned to one or the other. Furthermore, I would record their grades on assignments as part of determining their final grade regardless of whether I conducted the experiment or not. And finally, joking aside, neither taking quizzes nor doing homework is likely to cause harm to the subjects. Taken together, these things keep the students from encountering any risk through their participation, and informed consent is probably not then required.

You may also not need to obtain full informed consent when all three of the following conditions are met:

- You don't use a control group.

- The entire organization is subjected to a new policy.

- You will not collect any additional data on individuals.

Imagine, for example, that the new attendance policy applies to everyone at your organization. If the organization habitually collects the measures of the dependent variable as part of the organization's functioning (such as productivity data on individuals or departments), then you probably don't need to obtain informed consent. If, however, you plan to collect data that are not usually gathered, such as using a questionnaire to determine workers' level of morale, then the questionnaire should provide a short informed consent statement at the top, consistent with that of a mail survey, which includes the time required of the subject, how the data will be used, a promise of confidentiality or anonymity, and whom to contact with questions.

Protecting Participants

Whether informed consent is required or not, as a researcher you are *always* responsible for protecting research participants' information. In the case of experiments, the research is almost always confidential, rather than anonymous, because you will know who participated in the research. To protect confidentiality, you will take many of the same steps you would for survey research. First, in data collection and analysis you will assign every subject a case number, rather than using their name (and you would use a pseudonym for any observational field notes). You will keep all information that you gather locked up, and you will need to password-protect the electronic data files. In reporting your analysis, you will only report in the aggregate.

 Reminder: Anonymity means that you, the researcher, don't know who participated, by name or by sight; **confidentiality** means that you know who participated, but you will not share that information with anyone.

Of utmost concern in experimental research is protecting participants from harm due to exposure to the treatment. It is extremely important to consider and inform research participants of all potential risks, including the risks of being in a control group. This includes the **placebo effect**, which is the possibility that people will experience treatment effects, positive or negative, even though they are not in the treatment group, because of the power of belief.

Particular risks can occur if you use deception in the research design. These can include subjects learning something that makes them feel bad about themselves, feeling tricked by the deception, and putting themselves in situations in which they normally would not agree to put themselves. For this reason, you should avoid using deception unless it is absolutely impossible to conduct the research without it. If you do use deception, you should take every precaution to ensure that research subjects do not suffer harm because of it. You can do this by minimizing the extent of the deception, monitoring the research subjects throughout the treatment for signs of stress or discomfort, and debriefing the research subjects at the conclusion of the experiment. **Debriefing** means to explain to each research participant how deception was used, why you used the deception, what the results indicate, and checking to see if they have signs of distress upon learning of the deception. You may remember from the Stanley Milgram (1974) obedience study that because the research subjects had, during the course of the experiment, engaged in behavior that could have potentially hurt someone, it was a relief to find out at the end of the experiment that no one had actually been harmed, but also distressing to them to realize that they were capable of doing said harm. In this instance, it would be important in debriefing the subjects to assure them that no one was actually ever in danger but that their behavior was typical of the other research subjects—even that it could be considered normal. If the deception caused significant stress, as the Milgram experiment did, most IRBs today will require that you provide the participants with resources for counseling services.

Special Considerations for Evaluation Research

Applied research can potentially raise other ethical issues as well. First, you may find that you feel some pressure from supervisors, clients, or funding agencies (or your own hopeful wishing) to show significant effects from whatever program or policy you are testing. This, of course, can introduce bias at many different points in the research process, and it can threaten the validity of your results. It is of utmost importance that you guard against this as much as possible to provide unbiased and objective results. Purposely allowing bias to creep in breaches ethics in a serious way; more often, people unconsciously influence the results in the direction they wish to see the outcome. This makes it even more important that you impeccably follow the experimental protocol and put into place as many defenses against bias as possible. Similarly, your clients may feel pressure to influence the results of the study positively, especially if they know funding is contingent on producing positive results. As the researcher you have an ethical responsibility to assure participants that you are not looking for a particular result and that it is important to see all the potential effects, both positive and negative, of the treatment. Assure them that this can help you adjust or make changes that will improve the program or policy, or assist you in looking for a suitable alternative. For this reason the measures in your posttest should also be objective, not just asking the subjects' own perception or personal opinion of the treatment.

Another common problem that arises in evaluation research is that your research subjects, who are also likely to be your agency's clientele, may worry that their performance, responses, or other contributions to the outcome measures may affect their ability to continue to receive services, or their standing with your agency. In all cases, you absolutely must assure them that this is not the case—their relationship with your agency cannot be affected by the data that you collect in the pre- or posttests; otherwise, this creates a tremendous bias in which research subjects will try hard to skew the outcome data in a favorable direction or will refuse to participate in the research at all.

Sometimes the clientele at your organization may be members of a **vulnerable population**, meaning a group of people who are at particular risk for being coerced or exploited in research. Vulnerable populations include prisoners, pregnant women, and people with developmental disabilities. They are considered vulnerable because they may be likely to agree to participate in research for reasons other than because they want to. Prisoners, for example, may feel pressured or believe that it will be taken as a sign of good behavior when their parole next gets reviewed. A pregnant woman may be willing to undergo risks to herself if she believes that a treatment has the possibility of helping her child or giving the child an advantage, even if the treatment's effectiveness is not yet proven. Other groups of people that sociology students may work with can also be considered vulnerable in some ways, including homeless people, survivors of rape or domestic violence, or people with mental health issues such as severe depression. These groups may be more easily **coerced** into participating in research because they may not feel that they have the power to say no, especially to those who are providing them services. Sometimes organizations require participation in the program evaluation as a condition of participating in the program. While it increases the validity of the evaluation's results to have all program participants included in the evaluation, it is also ethically questionable. If a condition of getting counseling at the domestic violence shelter is to participate in research evaluating that counseling, for example, that infringes on the individual's true, uncoerced consent in obvious ways. Yet to maintain funding for these services, you may feel pressure to produce a high response rate in your evaluation report to your board or funders because a high response rate will more strongly support the validity of the results and thus build a stronger case for the program's effectiveness. The ethics of research in the real world can get sticky, but as a researcher, it remains your responsibility to take every possible step to inform your research subjects and to protect them from coercion and from harm.

● CHECK YOUR UNDERSTANDING

Describe all the steps you will take to protect the research subjects in your evaluation study. What additional ethical issues might arise in your research, and how will you address them?

Preparing for Data Collection

Preparing for data collection for experimental evaluation research depends upon the instrument measurements you will be using. If you are using a questionnaire for your pre- and posttests, for example, you will need to finalize this instrument. Note that the pretest and posttest should be identical to one another in order to measure any changes (effects) that have occurred. Like other survey questionnaires, you should pretest your pretest (yes, there are two different meanings of the word here!) by having people similar to those in your sample answer the questions, in order to make sure that the response categories are exhaustive and mutually exclusive, that the questions are understood in the ways that you mean them to be, and that there are no other issues with the questionnaire that may threaten the reliability or validity of the results.

 Reminder: A **pretest** is both the way that you try out your research design on a practice group of people and, in evaluation research, the measurements you take prior to the treatment being administered.

If your experiment involves observing subjects' behavior, you will need to make sure you have clearly and completely operationalized the behaviors for which you will be observing and have worked out a reliable method of recording this information. You will also need to develop a sampling strategy for observing the behaviors: Will you try to observe and record every instance of the behavior? Will you observe at particular times and days, or only during particular activities? In the context of experiments, your field notes will typically be more quantitative in nature (you may actually count particular kinds of behaviors) and will include clear and precise descriptions of particular kinds of measures rather than the comprehensive notes and thick description required for ethnography. You will want to pilot-test your observational sampling strategy, your way of operationalizing the behavior, and your method of note-taking in an environment similar to the research setting prior to starting the study.

In addition to testing out your data collection procedures and methods of measurement, you will probably need to spend a fair bit of time on training. Again, because data collection procedures can vary so much for experiments, the training process may differ greatly, but whatever your measures, everyone who will be administering or recording these will need to be trained in how to do so reliably and accurately. Thus, if you have three observers, they all need to know exactly how to identify the behaviors for which they are observing, how to record the observations in a manner consistent with one another, and when to start and stop the observation of each particular incidence. In addition, those administering the treatment must be trained in how to do so without biasing the study. If your treatment is a job skills class for underemployed people, then those teaching the class must be trained in not "teaching to the test," for example, and in treating research subjects in a way that minimizes potential bias in the study. Particular attention must be paid to treating control group and treatment group subjects as similarly as possible, so that the effects of the program can be studied without confounding them with the effects of how the researchers responded differently to the groups.

Data Collection

After you have operationalized your variables, trained your staff, selected your sample, and pretested your measures and means of data collection, you are ready to begin collecting your data. The exact steps you will need to take will vary according to your study's design, and how you are operationalizing your measures (using observation, questionnaires, or other measures). One thing that remains constant regardless of your measures is that you will want to ensure some type of **quality control** throughout the experience. This means remaining as consistent as possible in how you collect those measures and tracking whether, for example, observational data are being recorded consistently and with the same level of accuracy throughout. To ensure consistent quality, you could count the number of observations made at each point in the data collection, and compare them over time to see whether there has been any increase or decrease in the frequency of such observations. You may also randomly choose observational episodes from different times to see if the quality and detail of the observations have changed. As soon as you see evidence that this may be the case, you will want to alert your research team members, give them feedback, and continue to monitor for consistency in the data collection. This will improve the reliability of your results. Likewise, if you are using questionnaires, you will want to ensure that the conditions and timing under which the pre- and posttests are given remain consistent, as does the mode of delivery (take-home, Internet, mail, or face-to-face). Any questions about the survey items should be answered consistently from one test administration to the next, and the instructions given with each administration of the questionnaire should also remain identical.

Another issue that you may need to handle during data collection is attrition. A high **attrition rate** (dropout rate) can jeopardize the validity of the study because those who drop out are most likely to be those for whom the treatment does not yield positive (or may even produce negative) effects. If these people drop out of the program or the study before you have measured the effects on them, then it may appear that the program's effects are overwhelmingly positive, not because they actually are, but because those with less positive effects are no longer participating. In addition, there may be a bias in who stops participating, thus masking the fact that the program may have different effects on different groups of people. If you are evaluating a service-learning program, and those who drop out of the classes are those for whom the service-learning requirements create a severe scheduling or transportation problem, then you may miss important information about that program. Note that the attrition rate doesn't have to be high for attrition to mask important effects of the program. If a small subset of nontraditional students who work, go to school, parent their children, and commute more than an hour to campus end up changing their major or even dropping out of college because of the stress caused by those service-learning requirements, then you will have missed understanding that, while the program has positive effects for most participants, for a small group of people it may have a disastrous effect. While it can be difficult to reduce or eliminate attrition (especially while respecting a subject's right to withdraw from the program or study), you should be sure to at least track the characteristics of those who drop out and, if possible, to interview them about their decision to halt their participation. Additionally, collecting data at multiple points (not just before and after treatment) can be helpful, as you can then track how their responses to the program may have differed from those of the participants who completed the study. Remember, however, that collecting data too often can actually increase attrition, especially if it requires any additional effort by the research subjects. Subjects may have a limit to how many times they are willing to answer the same questions or be measured in some other way.

Finally, if your participants are divided into two or more groups, you may need to take steps to minimize cross-group contamination. **Contamination** occurs when one group influences the others in a way that may change the results of your study. In the example of testing the parent mentoring program for single mothers, if women in the mentoring program know or socialize with women who are in the control group, they may share knowledge, tips, or behavior modifications that they have learned. This can reduce the size of the apparent effect on the treatment group because both groups basically benefit from at least some of the treatment, even if the control group does so vicariously. Additionally, if groups discuss the differences in their treatment, one group may become angry, disappointed, jealous, or skeptical, which may influence the results for that group. For example, if the control group hears good things about the mentoring program from those in the treatment group, control group members may purposely change their answers on the posttest in order to demonstrate a higher need for the treatment. Finally, competition occasionally will arise between treatment groups, which can also affect your results. All of these forms of contamination threaten the validity of your study because the effects you think you see are actually the result of something other than the program itself. In order to minimize the risk of contamination, you can try to minimize contact between the experimental groups by creating treatment schedules that lessen the likelihood that people in different groups will have contact (one treatment group ends before lunch, the next doesn't begin for 2 hours after that), or the experiment may be run in phases (one group gets treatment this week, another gets treatment next week). Depending on your organization's resources, you could also schedule the groups to be treated in different locations.

Data Analysis

Your data will be quantitative in nature, so as with other quantitative methods, you will need to develop a codebook listing the numerical values assigned to each of the variables you are measuring for entry into a statistical software package. Your codebook will include information from all of the data you are analyzing: questionnaires, existing data, and/or observations. In experimental evaluation research, your codebook will include all the information about the measure, the possible responses or outcomes, and the numerical code assigned to each outcome. This code then gets entered into the software for statistical analysis.

Reminder: A **codebook** is a document that tells people doing data entry exactly which numerical code is given for each possible category of each variable.

If data are to be entered by hand (as opposed to automatically recorded by having the subjects answer questions, for example, on a computer rather than with pen and paper), the data will need to be cleaned. You can check for errors in data entry by spot checking every *n*th entry to make sure it is correct. You should also run frequencies on every variable to make sure that there are no highly odd or unlikely values that indicate a mistake or problem.

 Reminder: **Cleaning the data** means checking for data entry errors and making decisions about problematic responses or observations.

Because experimental evaluation research aims to determine cause and effect, the statistical procedures that you use will be different, and sometimes more advanced, than the statistics you are likely to use for survey research. Survey research typically includes primarily ordinal and nominal variables, while experimental research is more likely to contain interval or ratio measurement, which means that you will use different statistical tests. In addition, you can help to compensate for less than perfectly matched groups by statistically controlling for demographic variables such as age or social class. To **statistically control** for something means that you can calculate the amount of effect that a confounding variable is having and then essentially subtract that out to see how much effect remains (presumably from the independent variable). Note that this does not mean, however, that you can be lazy about assigning subjects to control or treatment groups; statistically controlling for a variable produces an estimate and is not perfect. In addition, the more similar the groups are on other variables, the easier it is to calculate the impact of a particular variable for which you are trying to control. If your groups are highly varied, then there will be too many confounding factors to determine the effect of any one variable on the outcome.

 Reminder: With **interval** and **ratio** variables you can calculate the mathematical difference between answers; **ordinal** variables can be rank ordered, but the difference between them can't be calculated; **nominal** variables can be differentiated but can't be ranked.

Although it is difficult to ever rule out all plausible alternatives when attributing causation (which in this case means figuring out the effect of the program or policy on your dependent variables), the more closely that you have followed the classical experimental design, and therefore the more you have minimized the possible influence of other variables, the more confident you can be in your results. Additionally, if you are using interval- and ratio-level variables, you can run statistical tests that indicate not only whether there is an effect from your program or policy on your dependent variables, but also the size of that effect, and the likelihood that the effect may have been caused by chance alone.

Evaluating the Quality of Data and Analysis

Like all quantitative research, the quality of an experiment is judged by its level of reliability and validity. **Reliability** means consistency, so in this case the consistency with which the data are measured and recorded. This means that if you are observing particular behaviors, any of the researchers would collect the same information in the same way on the same incident and record that information identically. It also means that the same researcher would make the same observations in the same way across the duration of the experiment (that is, it doesn't change as the experiment progresses). If you are using questionnaires for some or all of your measures, this also means that research subjects must interpret the questions in the same way as one another, and if there is a pre- and posttest, that they interpret the meaning of the questions and their response choices in the same way over time. Reliability is improved by testing the instruments and their measures on people and situations similar to your research sample prior to collecting your actual data. You will also have to be careful to administer the questionnaires in the same way under similar circumstances to each subject and for each pre- and posttest.

Validity generally means that you actually measure what you think you are measuring. In experimental research, there are two kinds of validity: internal validity and external validity. **Internal validity** in experiments means that the effects you measure actually come from your treatment, not from other confounding variables or influences. There are several threats to internal validity in evaluative experimental research (see Box 8.6). Using control groups can help reduce or eliminate some of them. First, the longer your treatment lasts, the more likely that events or conditions outside of the experiment will change and can affect the outcome measures. If you are testing a program for those with depression over a 3-month time period, for example, the changing weather and daylight hour may have an effect on levels of depression. Second, sometimes the subjects change over time not because of the treatment or history, but because they are changing internally, and this is a normal process (called **maturation**). New parents, for example, usually become progressively less anxious as they adapt to their new parenting roles and responsibilities, and they become accustomed to the habits and needs of their child. Third, research subjects can perform better (or even just differently) on a test as the subjects become more familiar with it; therefore, there may be differences measured on a posttest that exist not as an effect of the treatment, but because the subjects have previously been tested using the same instrument. Fourth, you may become bored or lazy over time and not as careful in your measurements. This is particularly likely to occur with observations and can lead to effects that actually result from changes in measurement rather than from the treatment itself. Using control groups can help to minimize or eliminate all of these threats to internal validity, as each of them would presumably happen to the control group as well as to the treatment group, and therefore will be a shared feature among groups that won't then show up in comparisons between the groups. You can also minimize these threats to internal validity through random group assignment or group matching. The more differences between the groups, the more likely the groups will respond differently to outside events or conditions or will mature in different ways or at different rates. Older parents may be likely to adjust to their parenting roles more or less quickly than younger parents. Random selection or matching ensures that these biases are not systematic, and that (in this case) parents of all ages are distributed evenly across the experiment groups. Again, this helps to reduce the likelihood that you will attribute the differences to your parenting program when they really are maturation effects.

BOX 8.6
THREATS TO INTERNAL VALIDITY IN EVALUATION RESEARCH

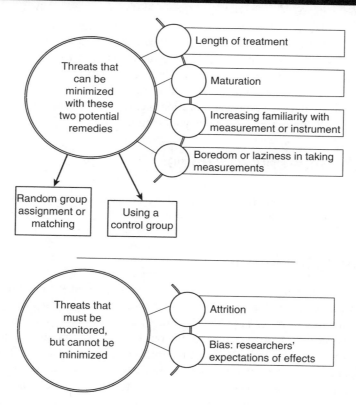

Some threats to internal validity must be monitored but cannot be mitigated by using control groups, nor by the way you assign groups. Your own expectations about how the treatment will affect the groups may unconsciously affect your observations or the way that you record data. Attrition of research subjects may also affect your results. If you have a high attrition rate, the differences you find between groups may be attributed to the differences that were created between the groups when some people abandoned the study. In other words, although your groups may have been randomly chosen or matched to begin with, if a large number of people drop out of the study, those remaining may leave the groups with a fairly different composition from one another, creating bias in your results. You must take these threats to internal validity into consideration in drawing conclusions from your data, but it is hard to eliminate them. Ethical considerations, for example, prohibit you from keeping anyone from dropping out of the study if they want to.

External validity is your ability to accurately generalize beyond your sample to a larger population. With experimental evaluation research, generalizing to a very large national population will usually have very low external validity. If you are studying a particular policy that your organization has implemented, for example, your ability to assume that other organizations implementing that same policy will experience the same effects is fairly poor. There are simply too many particularities to your organization, your clientele, your staff, and the general context in which your organization operates that will likely differ from those of other organizations. Your ability to generalize to other people served by your own organization, however, is higher. While clients at other organizations may not be affected in the same way as your study group, other clients at your same organization, operating in the same context as your research subjects, are likely to experience the same effects. Thus, while applied research is not good for making generalizations across large national populations, it is good for generalizing to those served by your organization.

CHECK YOUR UNDERSTANDING

In the context of your study, what do you think the biggest threats to reliability or validity will be? How will you try to mitigate these threats?

Presenting the Results

In evaluation research, you are somewhat unlikely to present your results in a long research paper. In applied research, the primary audience of your report will be your board of directors or other upper-level management team and your funding agencies. You may also present your research to your local community or to management of organizations similar to your own that are interested in trying or adopting the same program. In all of these cases, you are likely to produce a short, concise report that minimizes jargon and details about statistical techniques. Your report will focus instead on clearly stated results with the statistics interpreted for the reader in an easy-to-understand style, and implications that these results have for the continued use of the policy or program.

Most research reports for evaluation research will begin with an **executive summary**, which is a short, one- to two-page summary of the most important findings of the study, often written in a clear and simple manner using bullet points. Many of your audience members will never look beyond this summary, so it should contain all (but only) the most important information from the study. Rarely will it include details about the way that the study was conducted. Following the executive summary, the research report will usually contain a very short introduction and little or no literature review. The methods should be described in enough detail that someone else replicating the study would know how it was conducted and what steps you took to minimize bias. Size and characteristics of your sample should also be included. You will follow this with a summary of the results of the study, which again emphasizes the interpretation of the statistics rather than complicated statistical jargon or tables. You will follow this with an implications section that details what the results mean for the program, as well as your recommendations about whether the program or policy should continue to be used and, if so, any changes that should be made to it. You may also include suggestions for other organizations about implementing a similar program.

Occasionally, in addition to a written report, you will present your results in alternate ways. You may deliver a talk or poster presentation of the results of your evaluation at a conference for agency leaders in your field. This can help them decide whether they want to adopt the program or policy, and any changes they might want to make to the program or the way they implement it. Some funding agencies also host websites where each of their funded projects has a Web page outlining the program and (based on your evaluation) its effectiveness, as well as resources and information for other agency personnel about implementing the program at their own organization. In all of these cases, the information is generally more concise, less formal, and focused more specifically on a few important results. It is also geared toward helping others make decisions about the program, so it will include recommendations and suggestions about the program or policy (rather than suggestions for future research, for example).

Summary Points

- The purpose of experiments is to isolate the effects of an independent variable on a dependent variable in order to determine causation. In evaluation research, this usually means determining the effects of a program or policy.

- Sociology students are most likely to use experiments in the context of program or policy evaluation. This constitutes applied research and usually takes place in the "real world," outside of a laboratory. As such, conditions may not allow the researcher to precisely follow all of the principles of classical experimental design.

- Experimental evaluation research may include the use of other methods for data collection, including observation, questionnaires, and existing data. The researcher will need to understand these methods as well as experimental design and procedures.

- There are many different experimental study designs, though ideally they include a pre- and posttest, control group, and unbiased assignment of respondents to groups. While researchers may have to compromise on one or more of these elements, the closer an evaluation design can be to the classical experiment, the higher the validity and reliability of the results.

- Ethical guidelines are similar to those of other research methods, but applied research introduces additional issues and concerns. The applied researcher must be aware of these and maintain a commitment to protecting their research subjects.

- There are many possible threats to the validity and reliability of experimental evaluation research. Researchers should make every attempt to minimize these threats.

Key Terms

attrition rate 227

census 218

classical experiments 205

cleaning the data 229

codebook 228

coerced 225

conceptualizing 216

contamination 228

control group 206

convenience sampling 218

debriefing 224

dependent variable 205

executive summary 232

external validity 231

independent variable 205

internal validity 230

matching 218

maturation 230

naturally occurring 212

operationalizing 216

placebo effect 223

positivists 206

posttest 212

pre-experimental design 212

pretest 212

program evaluation 205

quality control 227

random assignment 219

reliability 229

replicable 207

statistically control 229

subjects 207

temporal order 208

treatment 206

true experiments 206

vulnerable population 225

Focus Groups

Focus groups are a kind of qualitative research that involves asking questions and promoting focused and directed conversation among a group of people. Although focus group research shares some commonalities with both qualitative interviews and observation, there are also significant and important differences: questions are open-ended and explicitly asked, as in interview research, but the number of questions is small, and because of the group dynamic, the direction of the conversation is unpredictable. Similar to observation, group dynamics and nonverbal communication are observed, but focus groups are not a natural setting, and the conversations are neither spontaneous nor free from structure.

Focus groups involve gathering a group of 5–12 people together, usually for about two hours, and asking them some questions on a particular topic in order to get their thoughts, reactions, feelings, and opinions. Focus groups can be used for lots of different purposes, but they are considered particularly good for **exploratory research**, when there is little existing information on a topic. Focus groups are not just individual interviews done all at once in a group setting—indeed, you cannot get anywhere near the depth or richness of an individual's experience from a focus group that you can with qualitative interviews. Additionally, in focus groups the participants' answers are not independent of one another, but therein lies the strength of this method: a good focus group will create **synergy** between the respondents, meaning that as they bounce experiences, opinions, and ideas off of one another, they end up somewhere that none of them would have arrived at themselves. You've seen this happen before: a group starts brainstorming and coming up with ideas, and one person says one thing, another person takes part of that idea and adds something else, a third starts to refine it, a fourth further suggests another modification, and before you know it, collectively something new has been created that none of the group members would have come up with on their own. For this reason, focus group research is considered particularly good for generating new ideas and perspectives and for trying to come up with new solutions. Additionally, this synergy can also help individuals participating in the focus group to clarify, modify or change their ideas, enabling researchers to understand not only perceptions but the social processes that help to shape and change

REAL PEOPLE, REAL RESEARCH

Rosali Delgado

Rosali works for a consulting firm that provides both grant-writing and evaluation services. For one of their current projects, they have conducted an online survey of the boards of directors of different health centers. The purpose of the survey is to understand how board members think their board is performing. Rosali then conducts focus groups with the board during a full-day retreat. She presents the results of the survey, using it as an opportunity to foster discussion among the participants about each major finding. She follows this with an activity designed to solicit from them what they see as the strengths, weaknesses, opportunities, and threats to the board. She takes notes during the entire process and then uses them to draft a strategic plan for the board.

perceptions and opinions. This is a unique feature of focus group research that can't be found in the other methods.

Basic researchers also use focus groups in conjunction with other methods, such as using focus groups to determine important issues and variables to include on a survey or to help better understand the results of other research, particularly unexpected outcomes on a survey, secondary data analysis, or existing statistics research.

Focus groups are even more likely to be used for applied research than for basic research (although the popularity of the latter is definitely growing). They are used for both needs assessment and evaluation research: to help generate ideas for new policies, programs, and products; to test prototypes before being adopted or going into production; and to evaluate them after they are implemented. For decades, focus groups have been a favorite tool among marketing researchers, and they have often been used to test new products, packaging, and advertising campaigns. Even though focus groups are used for evaluation research, notice that they are not used as a part of experimental evaluation research because focus groups produce qualitative data and experiments produce quantitative data. Thus, although both can be used in evaluation, and you could conceivably conduct focus groups *after* collecting your experimental data to better understand the quantitative results you came up with, you would not conduct focus groups *as a part of* your experiment. Instead, you would use the two methods separately, conduct each using its corresponding methodology, and evaluate each based on its own criteria.

The strength of focus group research is also one of its potential weaknesses: answers can become limited by **group think** (when people don't form their own opinions but merely adopt those of the group), members of a group may agree outwardly (even if they disagree internally) so as not to rock the boat, or they may take a more extreme position because they become defensive or want to distinguish themselves from the group. Additionally, unless the moderator is skilled at discouraging this dynamic, some people may dominate the discussion while shyer or more introverted people may be relatively quiet or simply agree without providing new or interesting information. Thus, it's important to take group dynamics into account in analyzing focus group data and to use a moderator who is skilled in eliciting the participation of everyone and successfully drawing out divergent views.

Focus groups are often considered a quick method of gathering data because you can talk to multiple people at once, and hence get a lot of information from a variety of people in just a couple of hours. In addition, because data collection and analysis are done simultaneously, data analysis can be quicker than for some other methods.

On the downside, it can be difficult to recruit for focus groups, as people can be reluctant to commit to speaking up among a group of strangers. Additionally, they require a lot of logistical planning, are likely to have surprises arise (multiple people don't show up or they bring others not on your list who want to participate; one person polarizes the group; people who don't like each other randomly end up in the same focus group and it affects group dynamics, etc.). Focus group research is also best conducted with a team rather than by an individual researcher—at minimum, you need one other person on the research team to help during the actual focus groups. And, although focus groups are sometimes thought of as an inexpensive research method, this is often not true, as focus group participants are usually compensated for their time, and additional costs can be incurred with things such as location rental, providing food and beverages, or childcare during the focus group meetings.

Focus groups may be unstructured or structured. In **unstructured focus groups**, you go into the group with a list of topics and issues to cover, but your main task is simply to listen to where the conversation goes, rather than to lead it in certain directions. This kind of focus group is more likely to be used in basic research than applied, and it is most appropriate when the research is exploratory and you have little information about the topic. It would be appropriate, for example, if you wanted to understand the appeal of a new club drug among young people and their experiences with it. Because it's new, there may be little information available, and so you rely on the focus group participants to talk about what is most important to know about the issue. You might also use this structure if you want to generate new ideas, such as new approaches to ending bullying in schools. Unstructured focus groups are also useful when conducting research with subcultures that have a unique cultural perspective, such as teenagers. Teens might use, interpret, or value a behavior in a completely different way than adults. In order to avoid imposing an adult perspective on them, which could make your questions seem silly, nonsensical, or even ridiculous to teens, you might give them more free reign over the direction of the conversation. In this case, rather than asking predetermined questions, you would mostly focus on asking for clarification, probing when you want further information on something they've said and asking follow-up questions to elicit more talk on the topic.

The majority of focus groups are **structured focus groups**, in which you predetermine the main questions you will ask, although you certainly will still ask probing, follow-up, and clarification questions. The purpose of running a structured focus group is to elicit particular types of information from the group, often with more details. Structured groups allow for comparison between groups and also help to make sure that the data you get will serve your purposes. In qualitative interviewing, many qualitative researchers have a definite preference for loosely structured interviews; they view semi-structured interviews as limiting and even as potentially missing the real goal of interview research. Those same researchers often have the opposite perspective on focus groups, preferring structured focus groups to unstructured groups (unless the phenomenon being studied has not been studied before, or unless they are dealing with a subculture that has its own distinct rules and perspective). That's because one or two interviews that go far astray out of 25 doesn't impact an interview research project to the same extent that one or two focus groups gone astray does when you may only be conducting eight or nine groups. This is especially important because focus groups are logistically difficult to set up, and if each participant is being financially compensated, a focus group gone astray can mean several hundred dollars wasted, as well as everyone's time. Additionally, group dynamics can be unpredictable, so lending some structure to the group helps reduce some of the negative group dynamics that can emerge when groups are unstructured (people might be more likely in unstructured groups, for example, to say something just to get a rise out of someone else in the group, whereas this type of behavior may be less likely in structured focus groups). Finally, with a structured format you will probably need to run fewer groups because the groups will more quickly start repeating the same information without adding a lot of new or different data, making additional focus groups unnecessary, which saves both time and resources.

Methodology

Although occasionally people misuse focus groups by attempting to conduct them using positivist methodology (this has happened especially in market research and in some evaluation research), focus group research should be grounded, like other forms of qualitative research, in **interpretivist methodology**. That means the primary goal is to understand things from the perspective of the participants as fully as possible, including their meanings, feelings, perceptions, and experiences. Like all interpretivist research, the emphasis is on deeper understandings of a few people, rather than surface-level information about a lot of people. The aim is not to generalize but to understand the perspective of the participants particularly well. In order to elicit this information in the group, you must be able to develop a great deal of rapport with each of the group members very quickly and also to encourage a sense of trust and rapport *between* group members so that people feel safe in sharing honestly with the group. Although replicability is impossible (even the same questions asked of the same participants by the same group moderator on a different day could yield a different conversation), there is an emphasis on **validity**: truly understanding the participants' perspectives and relaying them accurately to the research audience. Also recall that the interpretivist doesn't try to root out all bias (they believe that is impossible) but does try to be objective about participants' responses.

 Reminder: For interpretivists, *objectivity* means putting your own perspectives aside and remaining nonjudgmental.

Theory

Like other research grounded in interpretivist methodology, focus groups are often conducted from a symbolic interactionist or social constructionist perspective, with special attention given to the meanings that things have for the participants and the ways in which those meanings are negotiated and navigated in the group context. Focus groups may also be used to build theory inductively, that is, to create **grounded theory**, which is theory that begins with empirical data (rather than armchair thinking) and is increasingly abstracted to the theoretical level as patterns are identified and concepts defined. For example, you might use focus group research to begin to create a theory of how political divisiveness on social media affects people's emotional responses to politics.

That said, focus groups can also be used to shed light on hypotheses in survey research: although the focus group data itself cannot directly test the hypotheses, they can be used to help explain unexpected findings and unsupported hypotheses. Say, for example, that you have surveyed people who identify as very religious and have asked them about their voting patterns and opinions on political and social issues. You may be quite surprised if you find that your survey participants then say that they are strongly against the Republican president's policies on immigration, gun control, healthcare, and homelessness because traditionally, very religious people have strongly favored Republican policies on these issues. To better understand these results, you may conduct focus groups with very religious people, asking them collectively about what they like and dislike about these policies, their feelings about the president, and any ways in which their opinions on these topics have changed in recent years. Note that you will probably not be able to conduct focus groups with the same people who took your survey, but you would aim to include people who are very much like them. This information can then help you explain why you may have gotten the results you did on the survey, yielding more insight than the survey alone could produce. In this case, you may come to understand that the emergence of the grassroots evangelical "religious left" is growing far more rapidly than was previously realized.

When focus groups are used for applied research, they are often conducted without any particular theory in mind. Researchers may simply be looking to identify needs, opinions, and evaluations. Some applied research may be informed, however, by middle-range theory or larger theoretical frameworks. If you work for a university and want to train managers and administrators to be more inclusive and sensitive to the needs of people with disabilities, you might conduct focus groups with different types of people: people with various physical and cognitive disabilities, those on campus who currently work closely with someone with a disability, staff in the campus resource office for people with disabilities, and students with various disabilities. In choosing the makeup of those groups, you might draw upon feminist theory, for example, to be aware of a person's intersectionality (the ways in which their various identities intertwine to affect their experiences and perspectives). For instance, you may consciously want to consider the different ways that race, class, gender, and sexual orientation intersect with physical ability when choosing the participants, as well as when choosing the topics and wording of questions to be discussed in the groups. Intersectionality could also be an explicit part of your analysis.

Middle-range theories sometimes also *inform* applied research without testing the theory. For example, let's say you are conducting focus groups on suicide prevention in order to develop a new suicide prevention program in your town. Being familiar with Durkheim's theory of suicide, you might include questions about what makes people feel connected to others in a meaningful way and what barriers to that connection they sometimes encounter. These questions are not aimed at testing Durkheim's theory, but as a sociology major you may be sensitized to the idea that lack of social bonds may play a role in suicidal behavior, and so you use that theoretical information to help inform the development of the prevention program and hence your focus groups.

Research Questions

Research questions about issues in a community, subculture, or organization are appropriate for focus group research, as are questions about group processes, shared cultural experiences, and changes in opinion or behavior. These types of research questions are particularly good for understanding shared meaning and the ways that meanings change or are negotiated among people. At the applied level, focus groups are useful for identifying a problem, understanding it, and deciding how to solve it. They are good for generating new ideas, identifying areas of need, imagining new possibilities, and explaining why something doesn't work the way that experts expected it to. They are also suitable for getting people's reactions to different versions of a policy or program and for evaluation. A list of sample research questions for focus groups can be found in Box 9.1. I have labeled each example as "basic" or "applied" because the difference between them may be less obvious than with some other research methods; that is, the applied research questions don't always list the name of a particular organization, program, or plan in the way that they usually do with other methods.

Notice that in a couple of cases, the research questions for focus groups could be used for research using qualitative interviews. Although there is some overlap, asking the questions of a group of people who have had similar experiences is meant to elicit different data than you would obtain from individual interviews. Take, for example, the research question, *What meanings does the Black Lives Matter movement have for police of color?* Although this is a question that could be investigated with interview research, the data would focus on the individual's thoughts, feelings, daily experiences, interactions, and meaning-making in relation to being a police officer of color during a time when this social movement is widespread. Investigating this same question with a focus group will, instead, yield data that is less about their individual experiences and more about group processes, such as how police officers of color negotiate these meanings with each other in conversation and how they respond in a group setting to one another's interpretations and understandings. Thus, although

BOX 9.1

EXAMPLES OF RESEARCH QUESTIONS APPROPRIATE FOR FOCUS GROUPS

Research Question	Appropriate for Focus Groups Because It Examines ...
How do women in their 20s understand the effects of "hookup culture" in their lives?	Perceived effects of cultural pattern (basic)
How do adults who care for an aging parent navigate complicated medical diagnoses and protocol?	Shared experiences or concerns (basic)
What meanings does the Black Lives Matter movement have for police of color?	Shared and negotiated meanings (basic)
How do single people describe the pressures to be coupled?	Shared cultural experience (basic)
How do boards of directors of nonprofit organizations prioritize spending allocations?	Group process and decision making (basic)
How do people who live in a community that has experienced a mass shooting with casualties explain a change or lack of change in their support for gun control?	Changes in opinion (basic)
What do faculty need in order to feel equipped to teach students with profound disabilities who have been included in their classes?	Needs of a population (applied)
Why are first-generation students dropping out of college in their junior and senior years?	Identification of a problem (applied)
What workplace policy changes do fathers of toddlers imagine that will enable them to spend more time with their children?	Generation of ideas (applied)
How do attendees at the American Sociological Association's national conference want to see the conference evolve?	Generation of ideas (applied)
How do Chapman neighborhood parents try to shield their children from exposure to gang activity?	Community concern (applied)
Why do so many people enrolled in obesity-reduction programs drop out before completion?	Understanding failure of something experts expected to work (applied)
Why do a majority of survey respondents who report at least occasionally smoking marijuana disapprove of the ballot measure to legalize the drug in the state?	Understanding unexpected survey results (applied)
How do special education teachers evaluate three different potential plans to address teacher burnout?	Evaluation of prototypes (applied)

occasionally research questions for qualitative interviews and focus groups may seem similar, each method will answer this question with a different purpose, and the data will have different strengths and weaknesses.

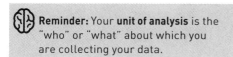

Reminder: Your **unit of analysis** is the "who" or "what" about which you are collecting your data.

Also notice that although the data are collected in groups, the unit of analysis in the research questions is the individuals participating in the research. Although you may compare groups in the process of analyzing the data, you will actually be collecting information about individuals, so they are your unit of analysis and should appear in your research question.

Focus groups are not good for understanding individuals' experiences or emotions in great depth, individuals' attitudes, behaviors of which group members aren't aware, very private issues or things people would be reluctant to talk about with others, demographic trends, or patterns of behavior across large populations. Nor can a focus group be used to study cause and effect (though it can be used to understand *perceived* effects) or relationships between variables. Focus groups should never be used in place of a survey in order to understand opinions, attitudes, or behaviors that are easily quantifiable or in order to get a lot of answers on many topics without any depth of understanding. Box 9.2 includes common mistakes to avoid when writing research questions for focus group research.

BOX 9.2
COMMON MISTAKES TO AVOID IN WRITING RESEARCH QUESTIONS FOR FOCUS GROUP RESEARCH

Research Question	Explanation of Error
How is race related to job satisfaction?	Cause and effect research should be done using quantitative research methods; qualitative research such as focus groups can only yield data about *perceived* cause and effect
What are reactions to the new proposed city ordinance to require all establishments that serve alcohol to make a breathalyzer machine available for customers to check their blood alcohol before driving?	Although focus group research is appropriate for gauging reactions to new proposals, it appears here that they are actually asking for attitudes about the proposal, which could easily be measured with survey items. This is especially true because there is only one proposal and not a discussion of various versions. Additionally, we don't know what the unit of analysis is: whose attitudes are we trying to elicit?
How do people with disabilities experience the workplace?	The question is too broad. Additionally, the topic would be better studied with interview research, as it requires a depth of understanding beyond what can be provided through a focus group.
What new ideas do people have to decrease gender inequality in the workplace?	Although the topic is appropriate for focus group research, it is too broad and instead should focus on a particular aspect of gender inequality in the workplace. Additionally, the unit of analysis needs to be more specific—which people?

CHECK YOUR UNDERSTANDING

Write two research questions for focus group research: one applied and one basic. Explain why they are both appropriate for focus group research. For each, would you choose structured or unstructured groups? Why?

Literature Review

The purpose of the literature review for focus groups is much like that for other qualitative methods. Acquainting yourself with the existing literature on your topic can help you improve or refine your research question. It can help you identify concepts related to the topic that you want to gather data on and to operationalize those subtopics into questions to ask in the focus group. In addition, the literature can help you identify important groups of people to sample for your research, as well as issues of contention where you might expect diversity in experience or perspective. Finally, it can alert you to previous findings that are confusing or different than expected that you might want to probe.

Sampling

Sampling for focus groups is very important, as who participates in your research will directly impact the data that you get and the conclusions that you draw. Sampling and operationalizing go hand-in-hand in focus group research, and sometimes researchers develop their sampling plan concurrently with operationalizing because the types of people that you include in the groups will affect the questions you ask (and how you ask them). In addition, the number and types of questions you ask will affect how many groups you may hold and how many people you want for each group.

Number and Composition of Groups

When conducting focus group research, you will need to conduct many groups. Although researchers vary in what they think is the ideal focus group size, typically groups will have 5–10 participants. If a participant or two don't show up, you can run a group with as few as four members. It's widely accepted that 12 is the upper limit, but even 10 may be too many to prove maximally effective. The number of participants per group will largely be determined by the topic, the depth of information you're looking for, and the number of questions you want to ask. The more personal or sensitive the topic, the more direct experience people have had with the topic, the more depth you seek, and the more questions you want to ask, the fewer the number of people you should include in the group. Because focus groups usually last 1.5–2 hours, you simply can't ask a lot of in-depth questions and have 12 people in a group. If you want to ask 15 questions in 2 hours and you have 12 people in the group, that gives each person about 40 seconds to respond to each question. You just can't develop an accurate understanding of the participants' perspectives with less than a minute per person per question. There are some instances when large groups can be used, such as in market research where questions are less personal, less in-depth, and the individuals are less invested in the topic. But most of the time, sociologists conducting basic or applied research typically want richer data that goes into more depth (especially if the research aims to solve a problem that the participants are likely to have had a great deal of experience with), so they are more likely to conduct focus groups with between 5 and 8 participants each.

Once you decide on the appropriate number of people per group, you also need to decide how many groups to conduct. This should be guided by your research question, your budget constraints, and the number of people who can provide valuable information on your topic. For example, let's take the research question *Why are first-generation college students dropping out during their junior and senior years of college?* Before deciding on exactly who to interview, you should consult with people who have firsthand knowledge about this topic: the director of a support service program for first-generation students, a couple of faculty members, an administrator in a relevant position, perhaps the advisors for particular groups that attract a lot of first-generation college students (such as the Multicultural Student Center), a counselor in the Counseling and Psychological Services Center, and a couple of key students. You might also ask other people who have done research on first-generation students or on college graduation patterns, such as the institutional researcher at your university or an author who has published relevant articles in the field. If the research is commissioned by a specific organization (the state's Department of Education, for example) or campus department (the Chancellor's Office), they should also be consulted in this decision. Focus group researchers call these people **experts**, even if they don't have formal degrees or careers that might qualify them as such; they are experts because they have significant personal or professional experience with the issue.

Let's return to our example of first-generation college students who drop out. Obviously, to identify the problem you will want to talk to first-generation college students. But it quickly gets more complex than that. You may want to talk to first-generation students who have *already* dropped out as well as those who *remained enrolled* in their junior or senior year but are thinking about dropping out. You probably also want to include focus groups with other people who can give you information on this topic: faculty in junior- and senior-level courses; academic advisors; and staff in campus programs aimed at providing support for first-generation students, such as an EOP program or the tutoring center. In addition, you may consider including parents, other family members, or partners of first-generation students in your study.

One of the keys to successful focus groups is finding the right balance between homogeneity and diversity within groups. Typically you want people who are similar along important dimensions because they are more willing to identify with other members and thus open up and share their thoughts and experiences. If they are too similar, however, there will be no diversity of opinion, and this makes for a boring, flat, and less useful group for data collection. Hence, in an effort for homogeneity, you may strive to include particular subcategories of people. For example, your literature review or ideas from your experts may suggest that there are different pressures on students depending on their ethnicity. You may find that the research (or your experts) indicates that Asian students feel they need to live up to high performance expectations imposed by their families or themselves, while white and black students and their families consider graduation itself the goal, so they focus only on the end goal rather than performance along the way. Latino students may have more pressure to leave school in order to get married and start a family, which is a totally different sort of pressure. Based on this information, you may choose to break up focus groups with students and former students by ethnicity, so that everyone in the group shares a common ethnicity. This will also enable you to compare the groups. Although you won't be able to determine cause and effect, you can nonetheless look for similarities and differences across the different ethnic groups. It is important to consult both the previous literature and your experts for ideas on which comparisons might be important.

Hypothetically, you would plan three or four focus groups with participants from each community you wish to include. In other words, three groups each of first-generation Latino, black, white, and Asian students (for 12 groups of students total), three groups of faculty, and three groups of advisors and other university staff. This isn't always necessary or practical, however. Focus group researchers strive for **saturation**, that is, the point at which the information they are getting from the groups is redundant and no new information is being elicited. Sometimes it takes longer for some participant communities to reach saturation than others. You may need to include more focus groups of students talking about their own experiences, for example, than of faculty in order to reach saturation within each group. That's because students would be talking about their direct experiences, which may be quite varied and complex. Faculty will also talk about their own experiences with students, but they are, in a sense, one step removed; that is, they will be talking about their experiences *with another community*, not as members of that community themselves. Thus you may need to run three groups with students of each ethnicity, for a total of 12 groups, in order to reach saturation with students, but only two focus groups of faculty members in order to reach their saturation point. Note that you can modify the plan as you conduct the groups: if you reach saturation early, you may cancel groups you had originally planned; if you find that you have conducted several groups and still have not reached saturation, you may end up adding groups to the research.

You must always also take into account budgets, and many times we ideally would like to hold many more focus groups with a wider array of people than we can actually afford. When investigating why students are dropping out, if the research budget is tight, you might decide to exclude family members and partners, even though they may have insight about their loved one that the students themselves don't realize or wouldn't admit.

Additionally, budget constraints for research often don't allow you to conduct as many focus groups as you would like. Focus groups can be expensive, especially if monetary compensation is offered for participation. If you also need to pay for transcription services, childcare for participants during the group, food or snacks, and location rental, each additional group can add quite a bit to the overall cost of running the project. Hence you may need to decide who can give you the *most valuable* information and where you can cut back a little or a lot without completely compromising the analysis. You might, for example, use your literature review and the opinions of your experts to rank the order of importance, from most to least important, of the different communities with which you'd like to speak:

1. First-generation students who have already dropped out (black, Latino, Asian, white)

2. First-generation students who are currently enrolled as juniors or seniors (black, Latino, Asian, white)

3. Faculty

4. Support staff (program providers, counselors, academic advisors)

Rather than running a total of 36 focus groups, you might reasonably conclude that you will reach saturation with fewer than three focus groups for each student ethnicity, but that you still want to prioritize students and spend most of your resources on them, as shown in Box 9.3.

While ideally we may want to include a wider range of faculty from different departments, given the budget constraints, this plan may nonetheless provide sufficient information from each community to enable us to answer the research question.

Choosing Participants

In terms of sampling methods, it is important to remember that focus group research cannot be generalized. The goal is to get some in-depth information from different groups of people on a topic, and to sensitize ourselves to their thoughts and experiences, but not to generalize to a larger population. Thus focus group research uses nonprobability sampling methods, particularly theoretical and quota sampling. Recall that quota sampling is very similar to **convenience sampling**—you ask people to participate who are willing to share their time and thoughts rather than trying to get a representative sample of the population. The difference is that with **quota sampling**, once you have reached the number of people you want in each group (Asian first-generation students who have dropped out, for example) you stop accepting participants in that group, though you remain active in recruiting for other groups of participants (faculty, first-generation Asian students who are currently enrolled, etc.).

Participants may come from advertisements on social media, fliers placed in public spaces, advertisements in the newspaper or Craigslist, verbal announcements made in relevant meetings or gatherings, and so on. If you are conducting research for an organization that has a list of its members or the type of people you want to study, they may share it with you (your university may actually be able to provide you, for example,

BOX 9.3

GROUPS PLANNED FOR FOCUS GROUP RESEARCH ON A TIGHT BUDGET

Who	Number of Groups	Rationale
First-generation college students who have already dropped out	Asian: 1 White: 1 Black: 1 Latino: 1	They can talk about personal experience. Dividing the groups by ethnicity will enable you to make comparisons between them.
First-generation college juniors and seniors still enrolled	Mixed ethnicity groups: 2	Although still talking about personal experiences, this community hasn't actually experienced the phenomenon studied, so though they may have many of the same pressures and issues, they may get slightly less priority. Because it isn't financially feasible to include one group for each ethnicity, we combine the groups, even though ideally one of each would help solidify comparisons we might discover among those who have already dropped out.
Faculty from a diversity of fields	1	This community has a very different perspective and important info that students might not have, and they will talk about their own experiences, largely based on impressions of another community; hence, we want their insights but they are a lower priority.
Staff from a wide range of campus offices/services	1	Same as for faculty.

with the names of students who have already dropped out or of staff who work in relevant departments). Related organizations for whom you are not working are more likely to be reluctant to give you their membership list. Just because you want to do focus groups on parents with school-aged children doesn't mean that the PTA will be willing to share their membership list with you. You may also ask people in key positions to act as gatekeepers for you. For instance, in our example of students dropping out, you might ask some faculty and staff to provide the names of students they think might be able and willing to participate in the research. Note that gatekeepers should bring up the research first with the individuals directly and ask them if it would be okay to share their contact information with you. Because gatekeepers are usually known to the individuals and can grease the wheels with them, so to speak, potential participants who have been contacted by gatekeepers are more likely to agree to participate in your research than potential participants who are cold called.

 Reminder: Gatekeepers are people who can uniquely help you get access to the people you need for your study.

Some researchers use a different strategy for drawing samples for their focus group research. Say that the study parameters are broad: you are looking for dads who have been divorced. You ask just about everyone you know for names of people who fit that criteria. You compile a list of all the names given to you along with a notation of who provided you that name. Say you eventually have a list of 500 names, but you only intend to include about 64 people. You may use simple random sampling or systematic sampling to select names from that list. Then you contact the gatekeeper who provided you the name and ask them to contact the individual on your behalf to see if they will give permission to share their contact info with you. The idea here is *not* that you can generalize the findings using this method—this is not true probability sampling, as your sampling frame here has been obtained in a very biased way. That is, the people you know tend to be similar to you, and the people they know tend to be similar to them. So this is not a sampling frame in which everyone has an equal chance of being included. Additionally, your sample size is much too small to be able to generalize. Nonetheless, some researchers choose this way of sampling because it can increase diversity in the sample and helps reduce the likelihood that a researcher will subconsciously choose people based on the characteristics of the gatekeeper. You want to avoid, for example, choosing several people suggested by one colleague because you are friends with them and none suggested by another colleague because you find them pretentious, or choosing five people suggested by one friend because they are the first to respond to you and none by the last five friends who responded because you already have enough participants.

> **Reminder: Simple random sampling** involves using a random numbers generator to choose people from a numbered list; **systematic sampling** uses a randomized list, and begins at a random number on the list, and then selects every Xth person on that list.

Sometimes researchers use snowball sampling for focus group research, especially if the groups they are studying are hard to find or identify but are likely to know each other. For example, if you are studying nonindigenous people who participate in peyote and ayahuasca spiritual medicine ceremonies, this group may be hard to find because the use of these traditional plant-based drugs has complicated or questionable legal status. Thus you may need to rely on snowball sampling, whereby people who participate in your research tell friends who they also encourage to participate.

Finally, sometimes you may draw groups that already know each other, such as colleagues at work or parents who all have children on the same sports team. This approach is most likely to be used when you are doing applied research on a particular organization and trying to find problems or solutions. The pros are that participants are likely already comfortable with one another and may be likely to talk freely. The con is that group dynamics outside of the focus group can affect what people say, how they say it, who talks more, and who talks less. Additionally, there may be some topics that people are afraid to talk about in front of others in the same group or organization for fear of gossip or reprisal. For instance, if people generally think the person leading the organization is problematic, they might nonetheless be silent on that issue if they fear that negative comments could get back to the boss and jeopardize their job. Generally, using groups of people who already know each other is best restricted to studies of group process, shared cultural experiences, or applied research generating new ideas or solutions. It is best to avoid such situations for research meant to identify problems, explaining failures of a program or policy, or changes in opinion, as each of these can potentially lead to finger pointing, feelings of being blamed, or reluctance to speak up or disagree. You always want to try to avoid having a mixed group, that is, a group where some members know each other and others don't. This is because it leads to cliquishness, discomfort among the newcomers, and a lack of cohesion among the group. Hence, if you decide to use a group of people who know each other, make sure that everyone knows at least some of the people in the group.

Regardless of whether people know each other or not, care should be taken to avoid large differences in power between participants. In our earlier example of the first-generation college students, it would be a bad idea to include the university president in the focus group with staff because the power differential can affect many things: what people say, how they try to impress or draw attention to themselves, what they choose not to say out of respect or fear about repercussions or how it will be received, and so on. Additionally, the other focus group members may wait for the president to take charge of the group and to therefore dominate the discussion. The same is true when participants don't know each other, but there is a big difference in social class standing or relative power based on profession or education. In a group on cancer treatments, mixing doctors with patients may lead patients to defer to doctors, whom they see as experts. A similar dynamic may occur in focus groups on immigration if you mix recent immigrants with immigration lawyers. Power differences can be comparatively small and still impact the group—focus groups with high school freshmen mixed with high school seniors, or with recovering addicts mixed with recovering addicts who also work as counselors in treatment centers, can similarly affect what gets said, who does the talking, and the amount of agreement or disagreement presented in the group. Finally, large differences in social class have been found to also produce significant power differentials in focus groups and disrupt group cohesion (Stewart & Shamdasani, 2015). Box 9.4 illustrates the decision path for focus group sampling.

CHECK YOUR UNDERSTANDING

Taking one of your focus group research questions, decide for this project how many people you will include per group, how many groups you will conduct, and the composition of each. Next describe how you will sample people for these groups.

Compensation and Other Incentives to Participate

Unlike with other research methods, compensation for participants is an important aspect of focus group recruiting that can have a decided impact on whether people choose to participate. Keep in mind that focus groups require more time, energy,

BOX 9.4
DECISION PATH FOR FOCUS GROUP SAMPLING

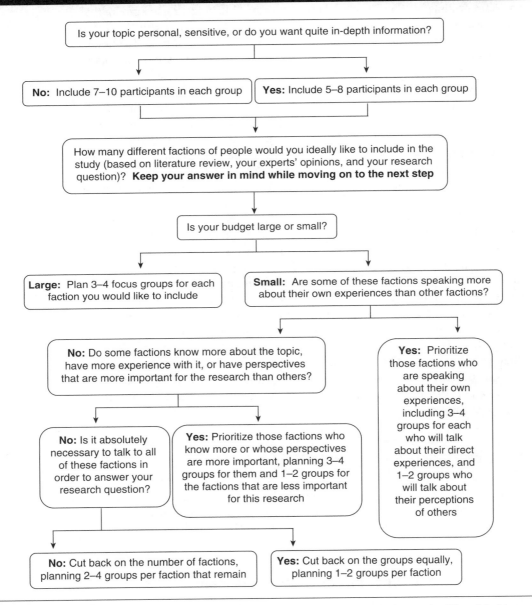

Is your topic personal, sensitive, or do you want quite in-depth information?

No: Include 7–10 participants in each group

Yes: Include 5–8 participants in each group

How many different factions of people would you ideally like to include in the study (based on literature review, your experts' opinions, and your research question)? **Keep your answer in mind while moving on to the next step**

Is your budget large or small?

Large: Plan 3–4 focus groups for each faction you would like to include

Small: Are some of these factions speaking more about their own experiences than other factions?

No: Do some factions know more about the topic, have more experience with it, or have perspectives that are more important for the research than others?

Yes: Prioritize those factions who are speaking about their own experiences, including 3–4 groups for each who will talk about their direct experiences, and 1–2 groups who will talk about their perceptions of others

No: Is it absolutely necessary to talk to all of these factions in order to answer your research question?

Yes: Prioritize those factions who know more or whose perspectives are more important, planning 3–4 groups for them and 1–2 groups for the factions that are less important for this research

No: Cut back on the number of factions, planning 2–4 groups per faction that remain

Yes: Cut back on the groups equally, planning 1–2 groups per faction

Note: Although this is the typical path for decision making, there may be unusual circumstances that require different decisions.

and effort on the part of participants than many other forms of research. Surveys are unlikely to last more than 25 minutes, for example, and can usually be filled out in the participant's home, regardless of mode of delivery. Observation and ethnography may last for weeks, months, or years, but because you are immersing yourself in *their* natural surroundings, it takes very little effort on participants' part—they simply go about their normal daily routines. Even interviews can often be done in a location of the participants' choosing, including their home or office. This makes interviews generally more convenient for participants than are focus groups, even if interviews are likely to potentially take longer. Additionally, interviews times can be adapted to their personal schedules. Focus groups, however, generally require a minimum of 1.5 hours (2 hours is more common) and are held at a designated time. Additionally, the participants are more exposed by sharing in a group and run a greater risk of breach of confidentiality. For these reasons, focus group participation is more likely to be compensated in some way than participation in any other research method. Sometimes this compensation takes the form of a donation to a (uncontroversial) charity that the participants are likely to care significantly about and is related in some way to the topic of the focus groups. For example, if you are recruiting church members for participation in your focus groups, you may make a donation to a charity run by their church. The amount of the donation should be clearly stated and the donation should be per participant, so that they can see that their participation matters. If you are recruiting participants from a mega church, for example, and the church runs a soup kitchen for the homeless, you could promise a $50 donation to the soup kitchen for each participant from the church. In this case, the compensation works because not only does it support one of the programs run by the church, but charity is a value that the church members will likely espouse. Offering a donation to the local homeless shelter if you are wanting to recruit mothers on welfare, however, will not likely work.

In most cases, you will want to offer some sort of direct monetary compensation to the participant rather than a donation to an organization. With commuting to and from the location, plus the time it takes for the focus group, most participants will be spending a minimum of 2.5 hours of their time. Thus amounts paid for focus group participation usually range from $50 to $100, depending on the budget of the project. Note that if you were to have even just eight groups with about eight people each, that's more than $3,000 you will spend on compensation alone, so you need to be clear about your budget and the number of participants you want to recruit before deciding on how much you can offer. Often the amount is something of a token of gratitude more than an actual payment for their time, depending on who is participating. If you were wanting to recruit therapists, for example, who often charge upward of $100 per hour, your $50 barely covers their commute to the research site. In a case such as this, it is imperative to convince them of the importance of the study, as the money will not serve as an incentive. On the other hand, $50 for students or people working for minimum wage may be sufficient enticement for participation.

Additional incentives to participate include food and childcare. Food itself rarely convinces anyone to participate, but it at least simplifies the logistics of their day. Busy people often have a difficult time finding time to eat, and if you are adding another

2.5 hours of occupied time into their day, providing food may make participation seem less onerous. Additionally, if your participants have children, you should offer free on-site childcare by experienced childcare providers. Without childcare, many parents, who are likely to already feel overwhelmed, will decline your invitation for both time and cost reasons.

Conceptualizing and Operationalizing

Conceptualizing for focus group research is very similar to conceptualizing for other forms of qualitative research: you must first identify the concepts that are most important for you to include in your study. This will be guided by your research question; your literature review; the opinions of your experts; and, if you're conducting applied research, the needs of the sponsoring organization. This should not be something that you develop just on your own or casually—it will determine what information you learn in your data collection, so it is important that all of the key stakeholders in the research have an opportunity to give their input. The list of important concepts may be revised multiple times in order to pare the list down to the most important aspects to concentrate on in the study.

Once you know what concepts you want the study to cover, you **conceptualize** it by writing a working definition of each as it pertains specifically to your research. Let's say you are studying burnout among special education teachers. First you will want to define what *burnout* means in the context of this research. Perhaps, based on your literature review, you define it as "a development of cynicism toward the job, combined with gradual disengagement, decreasing levels of commitment to school or the students, and declining levels of motivation, all of which arise from high levels of long-term job-related stress." At times, you might decide to have the participants explicitly conceptualize for you during the group. For example, you could ask the teachers to define or describe *burnout* for you. You are most likely to do this when conducting exploratory research, when the concept hasn't yet been well defined by the literature, when little is known about it, or when a subculture's understanding of the concept may be very different from that of the mainstream.

CHECK YOUR UNDERSTANDING

Conceptualize by defining the important concepts in the research question for which you sampled.

The major tasks you do to operationalize depend, in part, on which type of focus group you conduct. In unstructured focus groups, the primary task of operationalizing occurs during the group itself, when you pick up on markers dropped by participants. It also occurs when the note taker decides what information is important to the study and therefore what to write down, as opposed to what is unimportant and therefore left out. Operation-alizing also occurs for unstructured focus groups during analysis, when you find quotations or pieces of tran-script that you want to assign a particular code. These are operationalizing tasks because they are capturing the key information for the concepts that are important to your research.

 Reminder: Markers are mentions of something that the participant could talk more in-depth about; it is up to the researcher to decide which markers to follow up, thus eliciting more information.

Operationalizing for structured focus groups includes all of the same tasks as for unstructured focus groups, but additionally you concentrate on writing specific ques-tions to be asked during the focus group. Specifically, you want to ask questions that will capture all of the important aspects of your concept. In our example of our con-ceptualization of *teacher burnout,* for instance, you might ask participating teachers questions about feeling cynical about their job, about their engagement in their work and why they think it's changed, about the connection they feel to the students, the loyalty they feel toward their school, and the reasons they are less motivated than when they started. You might also ask about job stressors, pivotal moments or events that affected their motivation, and the role of the relationship between teachers in encouraging or discouraging burnout. Coming up with these subtopics and the exact wording of the questions for each is a large part of operationalizing for structured focus groups.

The number of questions that you can ask in a focus group are relatively small. Although market researchers (who often want less depth) may try to cover 20 or more questions, most sociologists and applied researchers want enough depth in the information that you will likely be limited to 6–12 questions total. This means that you must spend significant time thinking about exactly what information will be most helpful to you and how to best elicit that information with the wording of your questions; if you only have time for a few, you want them to be the best possible ques-tions for your research. For this reason, what you will ask about and how exactly you should phrase the questions should be discussed in depth with the research team, any sponsoring organization, and your experts.

Questions for focus groups generally follow a particular path: a very quick intro-duction to get everyone in the group speaking, one general question to get discussion on the topic started, and then more substantial questions that move from more gen-eral subtopics to more specific ones, followed by a summary and an ending question.

The introductory question has as its goal simply to get everyone in the room to say something; it breaks the ice and increases the likelihood that participants will speak up to answer subsequent questions. Returning to our example of special education teachers and burnout, an introductory question for research might simply look like this: *Let's please go around the room and have each of you tell us your first name and how long you have been teaching in special ed.* It is worth pointing out here that by specifying first names in your instructions, you avoid the breach of confidentiality that the inclusion of last names would entail; similarly, you would not ask them the name of the school or school district where they work, to avoid revealing identifying information. You would then follow that with a more general question that gets people talking about the topic of concern. You want it to be an easy question that will ignite discussion without causing disagreements. Thus at this point you should avoid anything that is controversial, but nonetheless set the stage for the information you want to collect. For example, you might ask the special education teachers, *As you know, burnout is high among teachers in general, and highest among special education teachers. In your experience, what are some of the major causes of this burnout?* Note that the question introduces the topic, and by asking about their own experience, you lessen the chance of theoretical or political debates. Although not everyone will agree on the causes, no one is likely to start an argument over it.

The questions that follow should logically flow in sequence. They should be more specific and elicit the exact data that you need. At this point, none of the questions should be superfluous or without specific purpose in your data collection. Let's say your current research is focused on getting the special education teachers' reactions to three prototype policies that aim to reduce burnout. Thus, after your introductory question, your next question might be *What are some things that you think could be done to reduce this burnout?* After hearing their ideas, you might then show them the prototypes. Depending on the information you want, you may show the participants all three prototypes at once and then ask more questions, or you may show them one at a time, asking specific questions after each. This depends largely on how similar the prototypes are to one another, how many participants are in the focus groups, and how much feedback you want. Showing each individually and asking questions after each will yield you more detailed feedback on each prototype, but you may end up pressed for time. Showing all three and asking about their preferences and why, and perhaps how they might combine aspects from each to make an even better policy, will give you less feedback about each one, but it may give you more time to also talk about problems that may arise, possible unanticipated effects, and implementation. Thus you need to be clear about what information is most important to you.

In all cases, the questions should be well-worded and precise. It should be clear to the participants whether you are asking for their thoughts (What do you *think* is the primary strength of this policy?), emotional reactions (How do you *feel* when you think about how it might impact your day-to-day life?), actual experiences (What do you *do* on a regular or semi-regular basis to combat your own burnout?), or expectations and suppositions (How do you *suppose* this policy will change your workday?). Additionally, questions should be open ended, not answerable with a yes or no and not closed-ended survey-type questions. Finally, because focus groups are not private one-on-one interviews, you need to avoid asking questions that could be damaging to participants. In this case you should not, for example, ask about depression or anger management issues they've had resulting from the burnout, about disciplinary action they've incurred from their school administration, or whether they have ever hit or manhandled a student out of frustration. Although participants sometimes choose to share personal information in a focus group, your questions should not compel them to provide any information that could be damaging to their reputations if it were leaked by another member of the group.

CHECK YOUR UNDERSTANDING

Using the conceptualizations you came up with for your research, operationalize these concepts by writing questions for a structured focus group that capture various aspects of the conceptualizations you wrote. Order the questions for use in the group.

Finally, at the end of the focus group there are a variety of ways you can wrap up the group while eliciting final information. You can ask each person to summarize what, for them, were the handful of most important points brought up by the group. Alternatively, you can provide a 1- to 3-minute summary of the points discussed and ask if there is anything else they would like to add. As a third option, you can ask people what they learned from others in the group that was new or helped to alter their perspective. In all of these cases, the purpose is to wrap up the session while making sure that you are leaving the group with an accurate understanding of what was important for you to capture.

Unlike survey research, focus group research does not require you to ask the same questions in the same way in every group. As with interviews and observation, you can absolutely use data just collected to modify and revise your questions as you go. If you conduct the first group and find, for example, that despite taking care to construct the best possible questions, nonetheless participants don't understand a question, or they talk around it without actually answering it, you will want to revise the question before conducting your next group. This must be done with caution and care, however, as the more you change questions, the less you are able to look for comparisons between groups.

It is also important to note that, as with observation and interviews, data collection and analysis are carried out concurrently. Thus, you may end up changing or adding to your questions for subsequent focus groups, not because a question didn't work but because you have new questions that have arisen out of the information produced in prior focus groups, and you want to answer these questions in order to better analyze your data.

Focus group research can also have a twist on operationalizing: unlike other research methods, focus group researchers sometimes use group exercises to help elicit the conversations and information they need. Finding the right format, content, and structure of the exercises to elicit that data is also operationalizing. There are various group exercises that sometimes get used with focus groups (see Krueger & Casey, 2015, for an extended list). Here are some of the more common ones:

- **Ranking exercises** provide the participants with a set of large cards. On each is a word or phrase. The group is asked to rank the cards from most to least important (or most to least powerful, meaningful, helpful, etc.). Group discussion occurs as the group tries to come to agreement over the ranking order. For you, the focus group researcher, it is this conversation, more than the final ranking, that is interesting.

o In Box 9.1 above, *How do boards of directors of nonprofit organizations prioritize spending allocations?* was one of the research questions listed. It is a perfect example of a research question for which a ranking exercise would be useful, because it would highlight not only what people claim they do in their decision making, but you would get to see some of that decision making "in action," so to speak, even if it's not in a naturally occurring context.

> **Tip:** Despite the name, you would not likely use an evaluation exercise in evaluation research because evaluation research asks about the participants' firsthand experiences with an existing program or policy, rather than prototypes for something new.

- **Evaluation exercises** provide participants with several versions of something: a brochure or advertising campaign, a policy or plan, drawings of a finished project such as a homeless shelter, and so on. The participants spend time silently examining each, perhaps jotting down notes while they do so, and then you start asking questions about their preferences and the reasons for their preferences. You would be equally as interested in the evaluations they make as in the dialog about them and the points of agreement and disagreement among the group.

- **Imagine exercises** ask the participants to imagine a solution, an ideal version of something, or a new approach, policy, plan, or way of structuring something. You give them a few minutes to imagine whatever it is you are asking for, and you may ask them to jot notes, draw, outline major points, or in some other way record their thoughts. Typically you would want to ask several questions during the imagining, so as to prod them to consider a variety of aspects and angles.

  o For example, if you were asking them to imagine workplace policies that would help parents spend more time with their children, you might ask prompting questions (with a moment of silence after each) such as, *Where would your children be while you are working? What kind of contact would you have with them during your working hours? How might your workplace adapt to their preschool or school schedules?* You might wait until everyone has shared their ideas (or shared their top three), and then ask them to discuss what they particularly liked about others' ideas and what issues or problems might arise. You might then ask them to brainstorm together how to solve the problems with the ideas most liked by the group.

  o Note that sometimes it can be helpful to ask people to imagine something very unrealistic, such as *Imagine that you are a leader who is going to start a new country from scratch. From your time already on this planet, you have learned what can go wrong with governments of different types, and you want to avoid these mistakes and problems. You alone have complete control over what your new government would look like and how it will be set up. What are your goals in designing this new government and how will it be structured?* Although obviously there is no chance anyone in your focus group is ever going to start a new country, it is a way to get people to start thinking outside of the box. Rather than just tinkering with minor changes to existing policy or programs, asking them to imagine something entirely different leads to other—possibly innovative—solutions and also promotes discussion of the current problems and why things aren't working.

o Imagine exercises are most helpful for generating new ideas and for needs assessment, as well as exploring what people think isn't working. Again, the objective for focus group researchers is not simply the ideas that are generated but the discussion around them: What kinds of things got others in the group excited? What kinds of things did they reject as unrealistic? How did the mood change in the room with different ideas? What, perhaps, was the key point that ended up veering participants off track and started to turn the focus group into a gripe session (at which point, of course, as a focus group moderator, you would skillfully guide the conversation back on track)?

When using exercises in focus groups, you need to carefully choose the activity and thoroughly think through what data you want to elicit from the participants and how the exercise will specifically help you do that. Designing such an exercise is as much operationalizing as is developing a list of questions for the group, and you will want to take just as much care and consideration with the structure and content of the exercise, the wording of the directions, and the questions that you follow it with as you would developing the questions and answers on a survey. If such an exercise is poorly done, it can be a waste of everyone's time, so never use an exercise just because it sounds more fun or more creative. You must be very clear and deliberate about the data that you want such an exercise to produce.

Another part of operationalizing for structured focus group research is deciding how long to spend on each question (and exercise). This is very important, as you will often have more questions you would like to include than can reasonably be answered with the depth you want in the time allotted. Thus, in allotting time per question, you are making decisions about what to include and exclude as well as how much depth, probing, and follow up you want on each. Although times vary depending on the question, you can expect your meatiest questions to take 10–15 minutes each to discuss. It's generally advisable to pad the timing a bit, or give yourself 10 minutes that are unspoken for, so that you feel more relaxed and less rushed in the actual focus group, and so that you feel more able to ask spontaneous probing and follow-up questions when it seems important to do so.

⬤ CHECK YOUR UNDERSTANDING

Would you use any exercises in the focus groups for the concepts you have operationalized? If so, which? Explain your decision. Looking back at your list of questions, and considering your decision about whether to use an exercise, decide how much time to allot for each question and/or exercise.

Ethics

The ethics concerns for focus groups are very similar to those of interviewing research. You will need to take many of the same precautions, including securing informed consent, protecting participants' confidentiality, and storing documents and recordings in a secure location. One major ethical issue that is unique to focus groups, however, is that all participants will know not only who participated in their group but exactly what they said and what information they shared. As a focus group researcher, you must convince the participants to guard the confidentiality of all of the other participants, while simultaneously acknowledging that a participant could violate the confidentiality of another focus group member and that you cannot prevent it. This can have a significant effect on what people choose to share in the group—and hence, on your data—and it should be something you take into account both in operationalizing the questions you will ask the group and in your analysis. Typically, focus group researchers deal with this by including in the informed consent a statement about the possibility of a breach of confidentiality by other members, but then strongly encouraging the group to protect each other's confidentiality at the start of the group. Some researchers ask participants to verbally agree to a confidentiality statement by raising their hand or even signing an agreement of confidentiality, in order to build trust among the group members. The purpose of such public agreements, of course, is simply to try to create a sense of a safe space, as they do not legally prevent anyone from breaking confidentiality.

The informed consent statements for focus groups look much like those of interviews, with the following exceptions:

- Pseudonyms are not always chosen, as the other members of the focus group will often learn each person's first name during the course of the group. Additionally, it can already be quite difficult in a recording or transcript to track who said what in a focus group, and adding pseudonyms significantly complicates that process. Therefore, usually actual first names or nicknames are used in transcripts, or occasionally each group member is given a number and in transcripts is referred to only by number. In final reports, no names are used, or pseudonyms may be given at that point. You may be more likely to change names in a transcript or written notes if you are conducting applied research in a community or organization where someone may be easily identifiable, especially if their name is unique.

- In interview research, we tell participants that if they want us to turn off the recording at any time, we will do so and not turn the device on again until they have given their permission. In focus group research, we are less likely to say this because it is nearly impossible to remember everything that has been said and by whom when not recording. We always must tell them, however, that they don't have to answer any question that they don't want to answer, and that they may step out of the room or quit the focus group for any reason at any time.

- Confidentiality cannot be guaranteed, and participants must be warned that another research participant may share something they have said with people outside of the focus group.

Thus, focus group informed consent statements include these points:

- A short description of the research topic

- A general description of who is participating in this particular group, as well as some of the other types of people that will be included in the research

- A short description of how the research will be used

- A statement of the number of times they will participate (rarely is this more than once) and how long the focus group will last

- A statement that the research is voluntary, that they may leave or withdraw participation at any time during the group, and they don't have to answer any questions they don't wish to answer. If the group is based on membership in an organization, receiving services from a particular program or organization, or employment at a particular place, you must assure them that their standing will in no way be affected by their participation in the focus group

- A description of how you will protect their confidentiality, including
  - No names will be used in the final report
  - Identifying information will be deleted from transcripts
  - Recordings and notes will be kept in password-protected files or locked drawers in a secure location

- A warning that others in the group may violate their confidentiality

- The names of the people who will hear the recording

- The date the recordings will be destroyed (occasionally they will not be)

- Possible risks and benefits to them for participating in the research

- Your contact information

- The contact information for the chair of the governing Institutional Review Board (IRB). The participant needs to be advised that they may contact this person if they feel that any of their rights as a research participant have been violated.

Box 9.5 provides a sample informed consent statement for focus group research. Notice that the informed consent must be tailored to each individual type of participant; that is, in the example below, you would need to alter some sentences for the school principals who participate.

BOX 9.5
SAMPLE INFORMED CONSENT STATEMENT FOR FOCUS GROUP RESEARCH

You are invited to participate in a study on three different proposals aimed at reducing burnout for special education teachers. Like you, all of the participants in this focus group work in special education. The purpose of this study is to understand how people in these high-stress jobs respond to three proposed plans that aim to reduce teacher burnout. This research has been commissioned by the California Department of Education. The results of this research will be used by state officials to draft new policy for schools regarding this issue.

If you decide to participate in this study, you will participate in one focus group lasting approximately 2 hours. There will be about 7 other participants in your group, but a total of approximately 200 people across the state will participate in this study, including other groups of people affected by or knowledgeable about the topic, such as special education teachers and classroom assistants, school principals, and district coordinators for special education.

The focus group will be moderated by Brock Lee. He will ask the group questions and encourage discussion, including diverse opinions. You are encouraged to share, even if you have a different opinion than someone else in the group. The focus groups will be recorded and later transcribed by Mandy Rin. Notes will also be taken during the group. Your participation is completely voluntary. You may find it difficult to talk about stressful experiences you've had. You do not have to answer any questions you do not want to answer, and you may choose to leave the room or quit the group at any time for any reason.

We will take every precaution to protect your confidentiality: notes and transcripts will be kept in a locked cabinet, and digital recordings and electronic files will be kept on a password-protected computer; identifying information will be deleted from transcripts; and your name will never be used in the final report. We ask you to please agree to protect the confidentiality of all other focus group participants, including their names and what they've said. We cannot guarantee that this agreement will be respected by all who participate in the research, and it is possible someone in the group may repeat something that was said in the group that could be traced back to you. Although unlikely, there is a chance that another member of the focus group could reveal something about you or your school that they learned in the discussion. All focus group members are asked to respect the privacy of other group members. You may tell others that you were in a focus group and the general topic of the discussion, but actual names and stories of other participants should not be repeated.

There are no anticipated risks to you for participating in this research. The fact of your participation, or anything you say, will not affect your employment or employment conditions in any way. Although you may not directly benefit from your participation in this research, some people find sharing their stories to be a valuable experience. Additionally, for your participation you will be compensated with a one-time payment of $50 cash at the completion of today's group session.

If you have questions or concerns about this study, you may contact Dr. Lee at (987) 555-4567, or via e-mail at blee@crsu.edu. If you feel your rights as a research participant have been violated, you should contact the chair of the Human Subjects in Research Committee at Cold River State, Dr. Strict, at (987) 555-5678.

I have read the above and have had my questions about participation in this study answered to my satisfaction. I understand that my participation in this study is completely voluntary and that I do not have to answer anything I don't wish to answer.

Signature _____

Date _____

Special Considerations

If you have decided to create focus groups of people who know each other, you should be aware that confidentiality is more likely to be violated by the group members because when people already know each other, they are more likely to talk to others about anything that was surprising or unexpected or that replicated interpersonal dynamics that have already been established elsewhere ("Just like always, he insisted he was right without listening to anyone else's idea, and when I tried to suggest . . ."). Thus focus groups with people who know each other should be used carefully and only when it is necessary to answer the research question.

That said, especially if you are doing research in a smaller town, sometimes people are accidentally assigned to a group and already know one or two other people in the group. If this happens, try to seat the participants a few seats away from each other so that they are less likely to whisper or pass notes to each other during the group (which is an ethical issue because it can be perceived by another member as being critical of them, making fun of them, or not paying attention to them), but also avoid seating them on opposite sides of the circle so that they have a more difficult time making facial gestures and eye contact with one another (which, again, may be perceived by others as mocking or dismissive). If the two know each other and you realize it before the group starts, you may quietly pull each aside and ask on a scale of 1–10 how uncomfortable they feel talking about this topic in front of the other. Anything over a "3" and it would be best to reschedule one of them for another of the upcoming groups. Sometimes, however, people who are very good friends or even relatives are particularly happy to be in the same group. This is a dynamic you want to avoid, and so it is best to simply thank them for their willingness to participate, but say that for confidentiality's sake, you can't have people who know each other in the same group, and ask which one would like to stay and participate.

Similarly, sometimes people might show up with friends or family who aren't signed up for the group but want to join in. You should not allow this, and simply tell them so. Depending on the sampling strategy you used, you might be able to offer them a chance to participate in an upcoming focus group, but only if it works for your project (i.e., don't put too many people in a group just because you didn't want to say no).

In all of these cases, the problems are two-fold: the likelihood that confidentiality will be maintained is lessened, and the group dynamic can feel cliquey and thus uncomfortable to others in the group. Although the latter is not a breach of ethics per se, participants should feel comfortable in the focus group. Additionally, the eye rolling, giggling, ganging up, or other kinds of behaviors that can happen (perhaps not even intentionally, but it may be perceived as such) when some of the people know each other can make others in a focus group feel vulnerable, which then starts to venture into unethical territory. All efforts should be made to avoid this situation when possible, and when not, to at least minimize it with appropriate seating placements and skillful group moderation.

Preparing for Data Collection

There are a lot of logistics to plan with focus groups. First, you will need to choose a location: something that is neutral and comfortable for participants, hopefully easy to get to, and with ample free parking (if parking is not free, you should arrange to pay for their parking). You also will need to arrange for food to be served during the group. Food can consist of snacks or even a complete meal if the groups will occur during a meal time. When ordering food, be sure to consider how the particular foods you serve might impact the group. Messy food, for example, can be a distraction, as can individually wrapped items that make a lot of crinkling sounds (which may make it difficult for your recorders to pick up what is being said). Possible food allergies and restrictions should also be considered: always avoid peanuts so the smell alone doesn't throw someone into anaphylactic shock; provide gluten-free, vegetarian, vegan, and low-calorie alternatives when possible. If your participants are likely to have children, you should arrange to provide childcare onsite during the focus group. Your childcare providers should be experienced, trained in first aid, and should come equipped with activities for the kids. Costs of paying the childcare providers, as well as an additional room or space in the research location, should be calculated into the research budget.

Once you have received approval from the IRB, you may proceed to recruit your participants and invite them to participate in the focus groups. Usually it's best to contact them first via telephone, reminding them of who it was that gave you their number. Tell them why they were chosen, the topic of the focus groups, who is conducting/sponsoring the research, and how it will be used. Also let them know about how long it will take. If you can (depending on how many groups you have with each block of participant types), it's usually best to give them options of at least two dates and times. You should also ask information that you might need to know: any food restrictions or allergies and the names and ages of children. An example of a script for a phone invitation can be found in Box 9.6.

Follow the invitation within 24 hours with an e-mail giving the specifics, including exact location, time, and information about what you will provide (see Box 9.7). This e-mail should be personalized with their name and confirmation of any of the information they gave you over the telephone. It should also be short and written in personal and casual language, rather than stiff and formal sounding. You should provide a phone call or voice message 24–48 hours before the focus group, reminding them of the date, time, and location.

BOX 9.6
EXAMPLE PHONE INVITATION

Hi, is this Lindsay? Hi Lindsay, my name is Helen. Danny Miller gave me your number. The California Department of Education has asked my colleagues and I to talk to special education teachers across the state to get your opinion on three ideas they have for reducing burnout among special ed teachers. Danny thought you might be interested in having input on these plans. Ultimately, the information we gather will be used in drafting a new policy that will affect special ed teachers around the state.

So far I've scheduled two meeting times this month. We'll be providing snacks, childcare if you need it, and offering $50 as a token of our thanks for your time. Both groups are scheduled in the afternoon, after school lets out. I've got one on Tuesday the 16th from 4–6 p.m. and one a week later on Wednesday the 24th, in the evening from 5–7 p.m. Do either of those times work for you?

Great. How about childcare? Will you be needing that? For how many children?

Perfect! Danny gave me an e-mail address for you as well. Is it okay if I send you a confirmation with the location and details to lmann@gmail.com? Great.

I really look forward to meeting you on the 16th, then. Thank you so much for your help on this. The proposals are pretty interesting, and with your help, we are hoping the State will be able to draft a policy that really improves the lives of special ed teachers.

Thank you so much! Bye.

BOX 9.7
EXAMPLE FOLLOW-UP E-MAIL

Hi Lindsay,

It was great to talk with you on the phone yesterday. Just to confirm, here are the details of the group we've set up:

Tuesday, March 16 from 4–6 p.m. We'll be meeting at the public library on 123 Park Street, just across from J. Morton Elementary. There is plenty of free parking in the library's lot. Please plan to arrive 10 minutes early so that we can start right on time—we promise to end punctually, but there's lots to talk about so we'd like to start promptly as well.

We have arranged for childcare for your two children. So that we can plan, **please let us know their names and ages.** We will be providing snacks for both you and your kids. **Please also let us know about any food allergies or restrictions.**

We will use the full 2 hours for the group discussion with teachers from a variety of school districts. There will be about seven other special ed teachers in your group. We know your time is precious, so at the end of the group, you will be given $50 as a small token of our gratitude for sharing your thoughts and insights with us on this important topic.

If you need to change the date of your participation or to cancel, please let us know as soon as possible so we can find someone else to fill your spot.

I look forward to meeting you on the 16th.

Good wishes,

Helen

Helen Back, Professor
School of Education, Cold River State University
(978) 555-1234
hback@crsu.edu

The research team should also decide how to deal with potential interruptions and logistics during the group, such as someone arriving after the group has started (one good way to deal with this is have someone remain outside the room to welcome any latecomers and get their informed consent before they enter the room). You could also potentially have someone choose to end their participation early and leave the group. You need to decide whether that person will still get paid (probably not, although if your informed consent uses the phrase *withdraw your participation at any time without penalty*, that implies they will still receive payment). You also need to decide whether you will try to coax from them the reason they are terminating their participation and whether they may be open to participating in one of the other groups. Note that if you wish to do this, having an additional member of the research team outside to talk to early leavers is important. If that isn't possible, then it is better to let the person walk away quietly than for the moderator or note taker to disrupt the group process by attending to that person.

Another part of preparing for data collection involves making decisions about recording and note taking. Usually the researcher has one colleague in the room whose main task during the focus group is to take notes. There are different possibilities for this (to be discussed in the following section), but you will want to make sure that your note taker clearly understands the purpose of the project (and hence what information is most important), as well as the style and completeness of notes you want to be taken. Decisions about recording also need to be made. Nearly all focus group researchers make audio recordings of the session (usually with just one professional-grade digital recorder in the middle of the table). Many fewer focus group researchers video record the groups. This is less common because participants are more likely to feel self-conscious with video recorders going, and because it is difficult to see everyone in the group at once regardless of where you situate the video camera, especially with a large group. The benefit of video recording is that it provides a back-up if the audio fails (although there is nothing to prevent you from simultaneously recording with two different audio recorders in different parts of the room). In addition, if all the participants are visible, video recording can sometimes help with identifying who said what in transcriptions. If you choose to make video recordings, however, you should take extra care to make sure measures are taken (for digital video recordings, for example, creating a double firewall by password-protecting not only the computer they are stored on, but also the file itself) in order to protect participants' confidentiality. Best practice is to transcribe them quickly so that the videos themselves can be destroyed, thus protecting confidentiality.

Finally, but very important, before proceeding to data collection, you should finalize your questions and activities and pretest them. **Pretesting** in focus group research means having people who are similar to your participants listen to you read your questions and respond to them. This may not be in an actual group setting—you may not be able to convene an actual focus group for pretest purposes. Nonetheless, if you can gather even two or three people similar to your participants and have them answer the questions and converse with each other, you should do so. If that proves impossible, at the very least read the questions out loud to individuals who are similar to your participants and have them answer one-on-one with you. In both cases, you should make sure the questions flow smoothly, are easy to say, come off sounding natural rather than memorized, and that the pretest participants understand what you are asking. Check to make sure they understand the wording and that you are not using any acronyms, jargon, or words with which they are not familiar. After having them answer your questions, ask them explicitly about the questions and what feedback they have for revision. If your focus groups will include an exercise, you should practice the exercise at least once with a group of people, even if they are family and friends, so that you practice giving the instructions and can see how the exercise goes. If the people in your pretest are not able to do the exercise because they have little information about the experiences of people in your sample, modify the topic to something they can answer while maintaining exactly the same structure, instructions, and questions. This will at least give you an idea of how well the exercise will work.

Data Collection

You should have everything set up for the focus group at least 15 minutes before the start time: an intake table, the room itself including seating and recording equipment, food, and so on.

It's a good idea to have two or three members of the research team there to welcome people as they arrive. The person who will be the focus group moderator (likely you) should be able to concentrate just on welcoming people, introducing participants to each other, and chitchatting with them as others arrive. This is

 Reminder: Rapport is the relationship of trust, cooperation, mutual respect, and sense of ease you have with one another.

important for building rapport quickly and to put people at ease with each other before the group even starts so that they will be willing to jump in from the beginning. The quality of data that you elicit will be highly dependent on the rapport that you can foster, not only between yourself and the individual participants, but between the participants themselves. Thus, it's important to get them talking to each other in dyads or triads with no one left standing alone, feeling like a wallflower. Thus, at this point your job is much like that of a host at a dinner party—you introduce people, get them started talking about something that is neither controversial nor highly personal, and excuse yourself as you welcome the next people to arrive.

The other people assisting you should be in charge of logistics, such as escorting participants to the childcare area, pointing out where the restrooms are, and encouraging them to help themselves to the food. They should also prioritize getting participants to read and sign the informed consent statement before the group starts. They can give a brief summary of the consent statement, ask participants to read it, and answer questions participants might have. They should be sure to collect signed informed consent statements before participants enter the room where the focus group will be held

Seating for the focus group should be in the round if possible, so that everyone can easily see each other. Your note taker should be at the opposite end of the room from you, so that they can hear whisperings or observe things that you might miss from your vantage point. Choosing a seat is often awkward for people, and you may want to decrease this awkwardness by putting first names on a paper name tent in front of each seat. Krueger and Casey (2015) suggest that you may want to wait until people have arrived to do this, so that you can suss out who the conversation dominators are likely to be and who the shyer or more introverted people are. They suggest you put those who seem less likely to talk right across from you, where it's easiest to make eye contact, and those who you think might try to dominate conversation immediately next to you, where they are least likely to get your visual attention. If you choose to do this, make sure putting the names in their spots seems casual and not like some kind of hidden trick or strategy, which could stifle rapport.

After people have gotten food and seated themselves, give them a few minutes to start eating, and then begin the focus group. Turn on the recorder. You will first want to introduce yourself and your note taker and remind people of the purpose of the group. This should be very brief but should include a sentence that encourages everyone to participate, regardless of their opinion. You might also include a statement along these lines about potentially calling on people or interrupting people who talk a lot: *It's really important that we hear from everyone today, even if your views are different from others'. There are no right and wrong answers here, just your experiences and perspectives. Some people generally tend to talk more than others: if I call on you, or interrupt you, please don't feel put on the spot. I'm just trying to make sure that everyone gets a chance to share their perspective in the time we have.* Then proceed with your introductory question, asking people to go around the room, introduce themselves by first name, and provide whatever quick bit of information you're asking of them. This introductory question is important because it gets everyone in the group talking in front of the entire group right away, and it increases the likelihood that they will speak up again during the focus group.

As you progress to the substantive questions, you might add, *This is meant to be a discussion, so from now on, we don't have to go around the table in order—I encourage you to respond to each other and to speak up when you have something you want to share.* If you are the moderator, it is your job to make sure the discussion is rich and that the participants engage with each other, not just look to you after each person has spoken. You must also keep the conversation on track and focused on the topic, without being invasive or heavy handed. Your data will be richer if there are a variety of opinions, so if people seem to agree with everything, start to gently probe with questions like, *Anyone have another experience/perspective on this? What else? For whom might that not work?* or *What might be some of the issues that could arise with that?*

You should encourage and affirm responses from everyone with verbal as well as nonverbal encouragement, without appearing to favor particular answers, perspectives, or participants. You should pay attention to the participants' nonverbals, making mental note of whose body language tells you they agree and whose indicates they disagree. What does someone else say that gets another participant excited or animated? Who seems to be checking out (especially near the end)? You should use these nonverbal cues to guide your comments and help you draw people in or elicit more information from them:

- Keisha, your brow furrowed when Jacob said that just now. Can you tell us what that brought up for you?

- John, you've gotten a lot more quiet than you were early on. What do you think about what's just been said?

- Sonia, Miguel, and Wayne, you're all nodding your heads, which I take to mean you agree. Can you add anything to what he's saying?

It's vitally important, however, that you don't jump in every time someone finishes saying something. You want to encourage conversation directly among the group participants, and discourage them from speaking only directly to you. Remember, one of the strengths of this research method is the synergy that is created in the group that allows people to build off what others are saying and come up with new things they hadn't thought of or articulated before. If you are always jumping in you can squelch some of that synergy. Hence, it is important to avoid always calling on people as you might students in a classroom and to discipline yourself to wait before responding. Just as with interviews, if you can learn to get comfortable with silence, you will often get more and better data than if you speak up right away. Simply remaining silent after someone has spoken, for example, will usually prompt someone else to jump in to fill the verbal space. This can potentially lead to participation from a wider variety of participants and new ideas or points that wouldn't have been expressed if you had intervened.

Just as important for eliciting rich data as creating rapport with participants is creating cohesion within the group. Hence, early questions should focus on finding commonalities rather than differences, and you may put more effort into getting participants to expound on and add to what each other has said rather than specifically searching out points of disagreement (which you may be more likely to do later, once some group cohesion has been established). Not only will group cohesion often yield better data, it will also encourage everyone to participate and will discourage one or two from dominating the discussion.

That said, as the moderator, even in a group with cohesion, one of your primary activities will be to encourage input from everyone while discouraging any one person from dominating. As Krueger and Casey (2015) point out, directing eye contact at someone after another has finished speaking will often encourage them to speak, while consistently avoiding looking in the direction of a frequent talker might discourage them from piping up again. If someone is really monopolizing the floor, you might divert your gaze away from them shortly after they begin speaking, even potentially turning your head in the other direction, as if you are going to call on someone on the other side of the room. You should never let a dominator hijack your focus group: start with both verbal and nonverbal encouragement to others to talk, but if the dominator doesn't take the hint, you can address them directly: *I'm going to cut you off there, Jennifer, so that we can hear from people on this side of the room;* or *Jennifer, we've already heard quite a bit from you, and I need to be sure to hear from everyone in the time we've got, so I'm going to ask you to step back for a little bit and let others take the floor for a while.* You, of course, have to be careful that you don't come off as rude and that you don't alienate the talker. This can lead to them engaging in distracting behavior, becoming belligerent, or even storming out, so of course you must do this with great skill and finesse. Nonetheless, you must remember that this group is costing every participant their time, as well as costing you time and money, and you don't want to waste these simply because someone has trouble keeping quiet.

Another important moderating task is to ask clarifying questions and probe for more information. If a participant says something that you don't understand, or drops an interesting marker, you have to decide when to ask follow-up questions. You won't have time to do this in every single instance, so you will need to make quick decisions, which should be guided by your research question and the information you deem most important to elicit for your research. Additionally, you should keep track of the time, making spur-of-the-moment decisions about what to add or omit if answers are taking much shorter or longer than you expected.

Near the end of the session, you should either ask participants to go around and provide their own summary of the most important points, or you should provide one and ask what you have missed or what never got said. If you ask the participants to provide the summary, you should be prepared to distill it down to its most important elements and repeat it back to them, asking if there is anything you have missed. If you provide the summary yourself, you will again want to focus on the points that are not only most interesting to you, but that you think were most important to the participants. Then check in with them to see if you got it right. Both of these are important ways for you to check that you are interpreting participants correctly and that you are accurately representing their perspectives. This is especially important in focus groups because sometimes something that is brought up a lot may not actually be the most important point. Similarly, something that was only mentioned once may nonetheless be pivotal in the perspective of at least one of the participants. This check-in allows you to check the validity of your understanding and interpretation of what went on in the group. If you have it wrong, the participants will let you know and this can raise the validity of your data, even if you were off a bit the first time.

You can also ask participants at the end if there is anything else that hasn't been said on the topic that they would like to add (be sure to leave at least five minutes for this if you choose to do it). Then, you should pass around the envelopes with the monetary incentive, if any. If a grant or sponsoring organization is funding the research, you may need to also provide in the envelope a piece of paper acknowledging receipt of the incentive and request a signature as confirmation. Of course, these signatures must be protected in the same manner as informed consent statements because they include first and last names. Like the host at the end of a dinner party, you should thank the participants as they leave and encourage participants to take leftovers, if appropriate.

During the course of the entire focus group, your note taker should be fully engaged in taking notes. Because it's virtually impossible for one person to capture verbatim transcripts of natural speech, there are a few different styles for notetaking, depending on how fully you plan to transcribe the discussion and the purpose of the research:

- **The most important points of what each participant says each time they talk.** It might include partial quotes to capture important wording. This is difficult to accomplish, and notetaking should not be expected to be a substitution for transcription. Nonetheless, capturing the important points can help jump immediately into analysis without having to wait for completed transcripts. The note taker will need to be well versed in the purpose of the project, as well as the research literature and the information that is deemed most important for the analysis, in order to choose what points get written down.

- **The first few words of each speech turn and who was talking.** This is meant not to capture everything, but only to help identify on transcripts who said what. This is important when the dynamics between group members are as important as the content of what they say, which is somewhat more likely to be the case in basic research than applied research.

- **A running list of ideas or points, with tally marks next to them for each time they are brought up by a different participant.** This helps to keep track of what gets talked about most by the widest variety of people and what was primarily talked about (even if it's in depth) by only one or two people. It can help with the summary (indeed, a colleague taking these kind of notes may be the person best able to summarize the session, rather than the moderator) and immediate analysis if the purpose of the research is focused on suggestions and solutions, rather than on process. This is more likely to be the case with applied research.

- **A concept map showing the flow of ideas—which ideas spurred new ideas, objections, counterpoints, and the new ideas that came out of any of them.** This is clearly not meant to be a mini-transcription, but rather a map of how ideas are related to one another and from where particular ideas sprang. This might be especially helpful when the purpose of the research is to generate new ideas.

- **Notes focused on the nonverbal behaviors of participants, which can't be captured by an audio recording.** These might include facial and bodily expressions of agreement, disagreement, intensity of feeling or passion about what they are saying, boredom or disengagement, indication that they have something to say but don't (or try to say something but get overshadowed by others), and so on. This is most important when the dynamics between group members is key, such as when wanting to see how meaning is negotiated in a group, or how gender dynamics come into play in regard to a particular issue, and it is more likely to be used in basic research on some topics, especially those with a strong grounding in symbolic interactionist theory.

Up until now, I have assumed that you will act as the moderator asking the questions and that a colleague will be the note taker. It is worth mentioning, however, that in some instances it may be more appropriate for someone else to moderate and for you to be the note taker. Moderating takes quite a bit of skill, and if this is your first focus group project, it may be useful for you to serve as the note taker for multiple focus groups (or even multiple projects) before attempting to moderate the group yourself. Additionally, you may want or need maximum control over what gets recorded in notes, especially if you are not going to record (I always recommend recording, but some researchers choose not to do so in particularly sensitive circumstances). Finally, if you and your colleagues know the participants outside of the research, it may be best to hire a professional moderator and/or note taker in order to encourage participants to be entirely candid and not concern themselves with how you might judge what they say.

CHECK YOUR UNDERSTANDING

Would you take on the role of the moderator or note taker in your groups? Why? What style of notes would you choose to take in your focus group? Explain your decision.

Analysis

Analysis usually begins immediately after the participants leave the session. The note taker and the moderator, along with other members of the research team, immediately start to summarize what they saw as the most important points, what stood out, but also differences between perspectives of different participants, as well as comparisons with earlier focus groups you've already conducted and with the literature. It's usually best to record this session (separately from the focus group recording itself) in order to create a complete record of your analysis. First and foremost, any questions that need to be removed or modified should be identified so that they can be changed before the next focus group occurs. Additionally, you should be starting to think out loud about the patterns you see emerging.

The most simplistic patterns that focus group analysts look for are thematic: what themes arose in the group? How do these compare with the themes that arose in the other groups? Although most focus group researchers pay attention to emergent themes, applied researchers with very specific research purposes are usually the only ones who are likely to stop there.

Most focus group researchers look for the same kinds of patterns that researchers look for in qualitative interviewing, observation, and ethnographic research: frequencies, types, magnitudes, processes, and structure. With regard to frequencies, you might count not only the number of times something gets brought up, but the number of different people who do so. Frequencies are important with focus group research but should also be considered very carefully—just because something is brought up frequently doesn't, in this context, mean it is the most important thing. It may be a product of the group think fostered by focus groups, in which one person leads the group down a particular track and everyone else goes along, bringing up the same set of issues again and again. Sometimes groups simply latch on to one idea or concept on a particular day, but on other days they would have barely noticed it. And sometimes a participant wants to win others over to their agenda and purposely try to interject the same idea again and again until it gains the traction they want. This doesn't mean that frequencies are unimportant in focus group research, but it means you must look at them in the context of the entire group and its dynamics, not resort to simple counting without context. Returning to our example of special education teacher burnout, you might look at how many times particular concerns are raised (and by how many people) about the implementation of a new policy; how many times a particular objection gets raised across the three different prototypes; or how frequently participants show aspects of burnout in their evaluation of the policies themselves, such as cynicism or lack of engagement.

Magnitudes are also important in focus group research, but again they can be extra tricky. **Magnitudes**, remember, indicate something that doesn't necessarily occur often, but when it does, it is intense or has a high impact. You can look for evidence of magnitudes in the content of what the participants say, such as incidents of burnout that lead to total physical or emotional collapse, or disengagement to the point that a teacher doesn't notice when a student does something exceedingly dangerous and an accident results. But in the case of focus groups, magnitudes can also be how intensely people feel or talk about things. This can be indicated by something they say ("I don't know when I've ever been so angry . . ."), by the pitch and volume of their voice, intensity conveyed by hand and facial gestures, and other nonverbal cues. If a participant slams their hand down on the table, for example, that can signal an unusual but high intensity of emotion about the topic. Ideally, the moderator would follow up on these signals verbally to check in that, indeed, this is what is occurring ("You seem pretty angry about that. Am I reading you right?") Such verbal confirmation can help to validate interpretations of magnitude and intensity, but even without such confirmation, you might look for patterns of magnitude and intensity across groups to understand, for example, exactly where the most important points of dissatisfaction, anger, or resistance are.

Types are groupings of a phenomenon into subcategories. In our current example, you might look for some of the following types: different types of burnout, different types of stressors, different manifestations of burnout, different types of new problems that may be caused by the proposed policies, different types of issues with implementation, and different types of justifications for maintaining the status quo. In each case, you are not just looking for different types but for how each type can be grouped with others. Thus types of stressors could include student-related stressors, faculty/colleague-related stressors, administration/policy-related stressors, workload-related stressors, paperwork-related stressors, budget-related stressors, and parent-related stressors. Within each of those types, there could be several specific stressors mentioned. Parent-related stressors for teachers of special education might include, for example, helicopter parenting, parents who insist on services above and beyond those to which the district says they are entitled; lack of response from parents; lack of parental follow-through on agreed-upon behavioral goals for their child; and issues with parental classroom volunteering. Thus types are groupings that logically fit together in some kind of category.

Processes are the steps taken to get from point A to point B. Processes could be revealed in the content of what your participants say. They may actually explain the process of burnout that they went through, for example. But for focus group research, process is often related to the group dynamics in the focus group itself. For example, you could look for the process that some members took to turn a nay-sayer into a supporter of a particular proposal. Or you might examine the process of how ideas were generated, played with, modified, sometimes cast aside, other times picked up again in coming to a group agreement on a solution to a particular issue. In other words, for the focus group researcher, process doesn't have to be a process that is *described* by participants; it may be the naturally occurring result of bringing this group of people together to discuss this particular topic.

Structure means identifying the parts that make up a concept or phenomenon. This could be the different components of burnout or what parts would have to be in a policy to make it acceptable to administrators, teachers, and parents alike. Structure is often harder to see immediately, but it can be readily found when you try to think about breaking something down to its necessary elements.

In addition to these patterns, focus group researchers may look for additional patterns, including what is *not* said. This may be particularly true after conducting a few focus groups on the topic. Thinking about a research project that includes faculty, students, and staff, if the students and staff bring up a particular issue but the faculty don't, that may be interesting. Ideally, during the focus group you would directly inquire about it (*The students and staff we've already talked to have brought up the issue of power, yet no one in here has raised that yet. I'm wondering why.*). Even if not raised overtly with the group, the lack of talk may give you important insight into the ways in which the groups' perspectives differ.

Another pattern that you might look for with focus groups is the order in which topics are raised, which might indicate their importance or relevance, and the degree to which an opinion or experience is that of an individual or that of the group. Finally, focus group researchers might look at patterns of specific language usage among different participants in the groups and across groups: what kinds of words do students use to describe dropping out, for example, or pressure, as compared to the ones used by faculty? What are the descriptors like? Are the words more emotional or more factual? Positive or negative? Blaming or self-critical? Looking at different patterns in word usage can tell you about how different groups think about a certain topic, which can lead to understanding how to make something appeal to them or how to target a plan for change. If you find, for example, that students who have dropped out spend a lot of time using negative self-talk, self-doubt, and self-criticism, although those students who are still enrolled rarely use such language, you may realize that adding more tutors to your campus learning center may not be the most effective or productive way to try to solve the problem, and that instead you need to focus on improving the self-narratives that people run in their heads.

With all of these types of patterns, you look for evidence of them not only within groups, but across groups as well. You may simply note the similarities and differences across groups or try to explain why such differences exist. This must be done with extreme caution: because focus group research is neither based on probability sampling nor is quantitative, you cannot make claims about causation. You can, however, see whether the differences between groups follow certain patterns. In addition, because analysis and data collection occur concurrently, you can specifically ask upcoming focus groups about patterns that you think you are seeing so far. For example, you could say, *We've already talked with several groups of faculty, staff, and students. I can't help but notice that faculty seem to focus on internal motivations while staff seem to focus on external barriers. Why do you think this is?* This same question could be asked of subsequent groups with faculty, students, and staff, to get a broad range of perspectives on the possible reasons. That said, definitive cause and effect cannot be determined with focus groups, and you should be mindful to limit your focus to *perceived* cause and effect.

In interview research, we code full transcripts. For focus group research, whether you transcribe the discussions in full or not depends on your time, budget, and research question. Most researchers conducting basic research will type up complete transcripts of each focus group, although some applied researchers only transcribe parts of the recordings that seem useful and important to their purpose. A marketing researcher, on the other hand, who is looking only for a quick answer to which advertising campaign they should go with, may skip the transcription altogether and use only the note taker's notes.

You may remember that looking for patterns in qualitative data is actually the *second* step of analysis, the first being open coding of transcripts. Unless you are limiting yourself to a purely thematic analysis or counting of frequencies, you will likely engage in some open coding of the transcripts using a qualitative software program like ATLAS.ti, N*Vivo, or MAXQDA. This is usually done, however, concurrently with the search for patterns (axial coding). That is, because immediately after the focus group you may already be searching for patterns, your open coding may be influenced or guided by the patterns you think you are seeing. This can be helpful by sensitizing you early to what to code and by helping to eliminate hours of data coding that you end up not using, but you should also be careful not to only look for the patterns you think you are seeing (or want to be seeing) in the data. In other words, if you hone in too early, you may miss other really important information and patterns. At least for the first few transcripts, full open coding of the transcripts can be helpful to keep you from becoming too narrowly focused too soon. In addition to the transcripts, the note taker's notes may also be coded, depending on the style and purpose chosen for their notes.

Like all qualitative data analysis, once you have identified patterns in the data, you must do a systematic search for evidence that supports the patterns you believe you're seeing and, even more important, for evidence that contradicts or negates them. Without searching for negative cases, the likelihood that you see something that may not actually be supported by the data undermines the validity of your analysis. This search for negative cases is also an important argument in favor of producing complete transcripts of the groups. If you don't fully transcribe, you will otherwise have to relisten to the tapes of the groups or, if the notes are very complete, search through the notes taken during each group, in order to find negative cases.

CHECK YOUR UNDERSTANDING

Describe two kinds of patterns you would look for in your data. Why are these particular patterns important to your research question?

Presenting the Results

How detailed your report is will vary considerably depending on your purpose and audience. Some organizations that have sponsored or commissioned applied research often only want short, succinct, and to-the-point reports that are only a few pages long. Others may want more detail for their money but still aim for 10 pages or less. Most basic research, however, will be presented for an academic audience and will typically yield journal articles of 20 to 30 pages. The different expectations obviously greatly affect what you include in your final report.

Most applied research will start with a statement of the problem and goals for the research. It will be followed by a *very* brief description of how participants were chosen, the number and general makeup of the groups, and the questions that were asked (including any exercises that were done). The applied report will likely jump from there directly into the findings. Great care should be taken to not present this as quantitative research; that is, because not every single participant can speak on every single topic or question in a group, it is misleading to give numbers of individuals. To claim that 24 out of 32 people talked about a given issue doesn't tell us whether the other 8 people found the issue unimportant, disagreed, or simply allowed others who had spoken less to take the floor on this point. Hence, if you want to provide frequencies, you should instead describe them as "a few," "some," "many," or "most" to give an overall sense without quantifying something that is very misleading if precisely quantified. Patterns may be supported by a quote or two to exemplify the pattern, but for confidentiality's sake, no participant names should appear in the report. Applied research will then usually conclude with a specific set of suggestions for decision making or for action.

As with other research methods, basic research usually starts with a literature review, including any theoretical framework underlying the research. From there, you often present the research question. That is typically followed by a "methods section," which gives substantial detail about how your questions were developed, how participants were chosen, and how the focus groups were run (What kind of structure did it have? How many people per group? What kinds of notes were taken?) and how analysis was conducted, including the analytic software used, if any. The next section usually presents the main patterns you found, including two to three quotes for each, and examples of any negative cases. The report is wrapped up with a conclusions or implications section, which summarizes the main findings, compares them to those of the previous literature, and discusses the strengths and weaknesses of the study. This section also answers the question "so what?"—in other words, why should we care about the results? Reasons provided usually address both theoretical implications of the research as well as practical implications for people's daily lives. This section likely ends with suggestions for further research on the topic.

Summary Points

- Focus groups are the best method for generating new ideas, testing prototypes, identifying a problem, exploring topics that have been researched little or not at all, and understanding meaning-making and negotiation between group members on a particular topic. Focus groups can also be used for evaluation research, needs assessment, developing hypotheses for survey research, and understanding confusing or unexpected survey results.

- Focus groups are a qualitative form of research and thus not generalizable nor appropriate for studying cause and effect. Nonetheless, descriptive comparisons across groups with different types of people can be made.

- Focus group research is heavily used in applied research, but it has gained popularity among basic researchers as well.

- Decisions about sampling are often made concurrently with operationalizing. Data collection and analysis are also done concurrently, so that one affects the other.

- Focus groups should be conducted until saturation has been reached.

- In addition to the kinds of patterns sought in other kinds of qualitative research (including frequencies, magnitudes, types, processes, and structure), focus group researchers may also search for themes, what is left unsaid, group dynamics, and kinds of wording used.

Key Terms

conceptualize 252
convenience sampling 246
evaluation exercises 256
experts 244
exploratory research 235
grounded theory 239
group think 236
imagine exercises 256

interpretivist
    methodology 238
magnitudes 271
pretesting 264
processes 272
quota sampling 246
ranking exercises 255
saturation 245

structure 272
structured focus
    groups 237
synergy 235
types 271
unstructured focus
    groups 237
validity 238

• Appendix A •
Reviewing the Literature

Before conducting any research, you should always **review the literature**. This means that you search for and read the published results of studies that may inform your work. The general purpose of the literature review is to help you design a better study by doing the following:

- Sensitizing yourself to key issues and ideas related to the topic

- Seeing which questions have already been answered about the topic and where there are holes in the knowledge about it

- Learning background information that may inform your research question or hypotheses

- Knowing what other researchers have found out in their research on the topic

- Learning about the problems encountered in doing the research

- Seeing how other researchers have operationalized important concepts

- Evaluating the weaknesses of their research so that you may mitigate some of those weaknesses in your own research

- Allowing you to compare the results of your research to previous studies

More specific purposes particular to the research method you are using are covered in the chapters on each individual research method.

Sometimes after reading the studies you will write a summary of all the research that you have read, which is called a **literature review**. Just about every published research article will contain a section of the paper dedicated to this kind of literature review, but you may also write a literature review for a research proposal. In both cases, this literature review helps the reader put the new research project in context, by explaining how it fits in with the studies that have already been conducted.

Types of Sources

Published materials are usually broken down into three types of sources: scholarly (or academic) sources, trade publications, and the popular press. **Scholarly articles** have been published by people with advanced degrees in academic journals that specialize in a certain field or subfield. The articles are **peer reviewed**, which means that before they have been published, the research has been reviewed by other researchers in the same field to check to see that the research meets standards of quality research and that there are no major problems with the way that the data or analysis have been conducted or with the conclusions that have been drawn. The author prepares a draft of the manuscript and submits it to the editor of a journal. The editor then removes the author's name and forwards the manuscript out to other researchers in the field (usually three of them) to review. The reviewers give extensive feedback on the manuscript and then recommend to the publisher either to accept the manuscript for publication, to require substantial revisions before the manuscript is accepted, or to reject the manuscript outright. The editor makes a decision based on these recommendations and then forwards the author the reviews with the reviewers' identities removed. Thus, neither the author nor the reviewers know whose work they are reading. This helps to minimize personal, gender, or status biases from determining whether a piece of research is worthy of publication. Authors do not get paid for publishing scholarly articles. Rather, it is considered an honor and a professional achievement to have your work published in a scholarly journal. The review process can take 2 months to over a year, and it may take another 6 months or year after acceptance before the article comes out in print. Authors may only submit an article to one journal at a time, so if they get rejected, they will have to start this long process over from the beginning. This encourages authors to send in their best work the first time round.

Trade journals are magazines or journals aimed at people in particular occupational fields. They often have names that students mistake for scholarly journals (such as *Cross-Cultural Psychology Bulletin, American Educator,* or *Nonprofit Issues*), but they are not peer reviewed, and they report on news, trends, and issues related to that profession. The authors are journalists who do journalistic research rather than collecting and analyzing social scientific data. If you are able to physically compare a trade journal with a scholarly journal, the difference is usually obvious, as they often physically look very different. Trade journals usually contain advertisements and photos, and many times they have a layout that looks similar to a magazine. Scholarly journals, on the other hand, contain very few advertisements, and even when they do, they are usually only for scholarly books or conferences; also, their layout more closely resembles that of a book than a magazine. Trade journals also have short articles with journalistic headlines, while scholarly journals have long articles with usually long, descriptive titles. Finally, journal articles almost always begin with an **abstract** (short summary of the research methods used and main research findings), while trade journal articles do not. Because today most article retrieval takes place online, it is harder to see those physical differences. Nonetheless, you can still look for certain clues that will alert you to the fact that an article is published in a trade rather than a scholarly journal. First, look at the page length of the article. Sociological scholarly articles usually range from 15–30 pages (although there is variation among journals, with disciplines such as psychology and health-related fields often publishing significantly shorter articles), while trade journal articles may range from half a page to five or six pages. Next, look to see if there are any photographs included (this is usually noted when you look up an article) because scholarly articles very rarely include photographs, and then only if photography is a significant part of the data or analysis (such as in an article about visual sociology). Finally, look to see if the citation lists any academic affiliation for the author(s). Scholarly journals always list the university or research institute of the authors, while trade journals usually do not include affiliation information (or, if they do, it won't be a university affiliation).

The **popular press** includes magazines and newspapers, whether aimed at the mainstream (*Time, People,* or *The New York Times)* or a smaller niche market (*Mother Jones, Parenting,* or *PC World*). Popular press articles are written by journalists who may or may not be trained on the particular topic of the article. Although you are probably familiar with some popular press titles, sometimes students think that because a title sounds impressive, a popular press source is actually a scholarly journal when it isn't (*The Economist, Family Health & Life,* and *Policy Review* are examples). Do note that in the case of content analysis, scholarly researchers may analyze articles from the popular press, but these analyses are published in scholarly journals.

In reviewing the literature, you should typically look only at articles published in scholarly journals. Avoid articles from the popular press in literature reviews, except in the cases of learning about a very recent event or local issue that is imperative to understand for your research, or to reference public discourse or public reaction to a phenomenon. Typically, you should also avoid trade journals, though there may be rare occasions when they are referenced in a literature review. Most databases in which you can search the literature now include an option to filter out anything other than peer-reviewed articles, which can save you time and keep you from making errors in determining publication type.

Searching the Literature

University and college libraries purchase subscriptions to databases that index scholarly articles. There are a wide range of such databases, and different companies each have their own format, but they generally allow you to search a wide number of journal articles, to peruse the article's abstract and citation information, and often to directly link to or download the full-length article. For sociology, some of the relevant databases are listed in Box A1.1.

These databases are based fundamentally on different searching principles than those used by Google, Yahoo, Bing, or other Internet search engines, so it is important to understand how to search the databases effectively in order to locate the most relevant articles for your research, as well as to save yourself time and frustration. When you search the Internet, if you string together words, the search engines will look for hits by searching for any combination of those words on a Web page or document. Additionally, on Google and some of the other Internet search engines, the more often a source is clicked on, the higher it will appear on the results list. This is why Wikipedia so often appears as the first or second result when you search—its popularity moves it to the top of the results list. Also, of course, there are companies that pay to have their page either appear higher in the results list or appear along the side or top of the page.

BOX A1.1
JOURNAL INDEXES RELEVANT TO SOCIOLOGY

Specific to Subfields of Sociology	General Sociology
ERIC (education)	JSTOR
Gender Studies Database	SOCIndex
Family & Society Studies Worldwide	SocioFile
Criminal Justice Abstracts with Full Text	Social Science Abstracts
Gender Watch	Sociological Abstracts
LGBT Life with Full Text	Social Sciences Citation Index
PsycInfo	Social Sciences Index
SAGE Family Studies Abstracts	Academic Index
SAGE Race Relations Abstracts	CQ Researcher
Psych Articles	ProQuest Direct
Social Services Abstracts	SAGE Journals Online
Social Work Abstracts	

The library databases (also called article indexes) work differently. The article indexes use Boolean logic, a system of retrieving results that is both more versatile than the Internet search engines, but also more complicated. In order for the searches to work, you use the **Boolean operators** *and*, *or*, and *not* to widen or narrow the number of results that your search yields. Use *and* if you want to narrow your searches. Say you type in *race and discrimination and hidden curriculum*. By using the word *and* between each of your keywords, you are telling the database only to identify those articles that contain *all three* search terms, but not to show you results that contain only one or two of those search terms. Thus, *and* as a Boolean operator indicates that the word *must* be present in order for it to appear. This allows you to narrow your searches so that you don't have to search through thousands of irrelevant results. The more search terms you connect by using *and*, the more your search will narrow.

Or, on the other hand, broadens your search. If you type *race or discrimination or hidden curriculum*, you will get results that contain all three search terms, but also results that will contain only one of the terms, or some combination of two of them. This yields more results because fewer articles are being filtered out. *Or* is especially helpful for searching for different words with similar meanings all at once. The indexes are extremely literal, and if you put in a word, it will only look for that word, not synonyms or closely related words. If you search for *parent,* for example, it will find neither *mother* nor *father*. Thus, *or* can be used to catch results that concern the same topic, but using different words to do so. *Adolescent or teenager or youth* will yield more results about that particular age group than just *adolescent* alone.

Not is a less commonly used Boolean operator, but a very useful one. It allows you to filter out results that may contain the same word you are looking for but has an entirely different meaning or is irrelevant to your purposes. If you are researching *AIDS*, for example, your results list will likely include items not related to the medical condition, such as *teaching aids* and *hearing aids* (most of the databases are not case sensitive). To avoid having to look through thousands of irrelevant results about teaching when you want to study a disease, you can use the Boolean operator *not* to filter them out. In this case, you could type *AIDS not learning not hearing*, which would focus your search results.

You can, of course, combine the various Boolean operators to create more complex searches. The previous search, for example, would still yield a lot of results because even though we have weeded out articles on hearing aids and teaching aids, the topic *AIDS* is not very specific. You can narrow this down by adding in either or both of the other two Boolean operators to precisely target the research for which you are looking. *AIDS and children and poverty not teaching not hearing* will weed out many irrelevant results. When you start adding more than one Boolean operator, however, you may also need to add bracketing. **Bracketing** is a principle you learned in math class: In order to know which terms go with which operators, you need to separate them out with parentheses (brackets). If you have *2 + 4 × 3*, for example, it means something different than if you have *2 + (4 × 3)*. By pairing the terms with brackets, you will yield different results (in the first equation, the answer is 18, while in the second it is 14). The same is true with Boolean operators. *Race or ethnicity and work or employment and discrimination* is confusing for the index because it doesn't know which words to pair together. Adding brackets makes the search much clearer and more likely to be effective: *(Race or ethnicity) and (work or employment) and discrimination* allows the computer to understand your search accurately. Today, most of the databases allow you to enter each set of search terms on its own line or box, with a dropdown menu from which to choose the appropriate Boolean operator at the start of that line. In these cases, you would enter everything that goes in a bracket together on one line, typing the Boolean operator for that bracketed pair. In this case, each box acts as a set of brackets (see the example in Box A1.2).

Truncation is another very helpful tool in searching the literature. **Truncation** means to cut the word short in order to filter in any variations in the word that come after the asterisk. This is important, again, because the indexes are extremely literal. If you type *adolescent* in many of the databases that is the only word the program will pick up, and it will filter out the plural, *adolescents*. Using the asterisk in place of the *s* (*adolescent**) will tell the program to pick up either *adolescent* or *adolescents* because the asterisk replaces any other letters that come after it. If you also wanted your search to pick up not only the people but the stage of life, *adolescence*, you could truncate even earlier (*adolescen**), which would yield articles with all three terms: *adolescent, adolescents,* and *adolescence*. Thus, the placing of the asterisk is of paramount importance:

BOX A1.2

EXAMPLE OF BRACKETING WITH MULTIPLE SEARCH ROWS

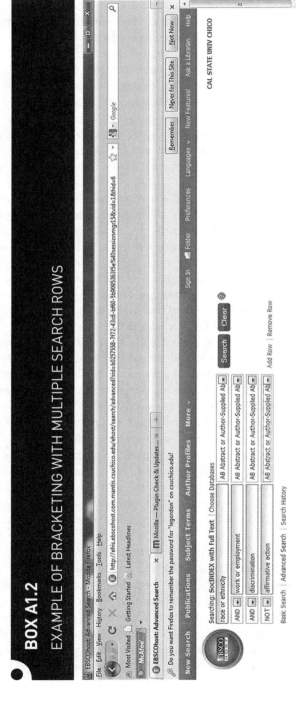

You must put it after the last letter before which any variations occur. You should think carefully about the words you want to pick up, as sometimes there are multiple possibilities for placing the asterisk, but your results will be greatly affected by which you choose. *Sexual** will yield articles using the terms *sexual, sexualize, sexualizing, sexualized, sexualization, sexuality,* and *sexualities,* which is fine if you are interested in all of those words. But if you are interested in *sexuality* and *sexualities* only, you will have made a lot more work for yourself by truncating too early, as you will have to wade through the articles with the other words it also picked up. *Sex** is much too prematurely truncated, as it will yield *sex, sexes, sexed, sexing, sext, sexting, sexts, sexual, sexualize, sexualizing, sexualized, sexuality,* and *sexualities.*

Your most effective searches will generally combine all of these search tools to create a targeted set of results that best suit your purposes. It is also really important to note that most of the indexes will search for the exact terms you enter, so if you type in *explanations for poverty among women,* it will not bring up articles that provide such explanations, but rather articles that contain this *exact* phrase, containing precisely those words in those forms and in that order. The searches would not, for example, pick up an article with the phrase *poverty among women is best explained by . . . ,* even though it has the same meaning and shares most of the same words. Instead of using long phrases, you should use Boolean operators, truncation, and bracketing to accomplish a more effective search: *poverty and women and (expla* or reason).* You may also notice in the screenshot for Box A1.2 that there are options other than using Boolean logic, including *find all my search terms* and *find any of my search terms.* This is for people who don't understand how to use the Boolean operators, but it is the exact same thing: *Finding all search terms* means the program will use *and* between each term, and *finding any of my search terms* means the program will use *or* between each term. Clicking on these choices does not, however, allow you to combine different Boolean operators in your search.

You can also broaden or narrow your search results by choosing the field within which to search. (Although the layout differs from index to index, in Box A1.2 this is the box located to the right of where you enter your search terms.) If you leave the box blank, or enter *All Text,* the index will look for your search terms anywhere in the entire article. This is the broadest search and increases the number of results you will get from your search because an article will be included even if your search terms appear only once in the entire article and are not a main point or feature of the study. *Title,* on the other hand, is the narrowest search, as it will only hit on an article if your specific search terms appear in the title of the article; and because titles are so brief, all of the important aspects of a study may not fit into the title. It is often advisable, therefore, to choose *Abstract.* Again, the abstract is a short, one-paragraph summary of the topic, the research methods used, and the main findings of the study. Thus, if your search terms are an important aspect of the study, they should appear in the abstract. Nonetheless, there may be appropriate times to use other choices: If you are looking for one specific article and you know all or remember part of the title, it is most efficient to search by title, for instance. In most of the databases you can also search by author or title of the journal, both of which are good for finding a specific article that you have previously identified and are now trying to locate.

Finally, you can improve your searches by using author-supplied keywords and subject terms. The difference between these is important. Most of the search terms that you enter are called **keywords** and are words that will appear in the article (or abstract, or title, or whichever part of the document you are searching). The default on all of the programs is to use these kinds of keywords. There is a second kind of keyword, however, called **author-supplied keywords**. These are words that the author was asked to identify as main words or themes in the article and that people might use to search for this article. Author-supplied keywords are usually listed in the database's set of brief information about the article. Finally, there are also **subject terms**, a systematized set of words on an official list that has been developed by librarians. For each article, the relevant subject terms are assigned to the article based on the topics covered. These terms are often more formal than keywords, and the actual words themselves may never be used in the article; however, someone has decided that, of the available subject terms, the subject matter of the article most closely matches these terms. Subject terms help reduce the problem of different authors using different words to describe the same, or nearly the same, thing. When I type in the keyword *homelessness*, for example, I can choose an article in the results list and see that the author-supplied keywords include *homelessness, homelessness programs,* and *Street to Home*. I can also see that the subject terms assigned to this same article are *homeless persons, homelessness, housing,* and *poverty*. You can take note of these author-supplied keywords and subject terms in order to better brainstorm additional ideas for your searches, or to search directly for these terms using the *search in this field* box.

Other helpful tools available in some of the databases include the *Cited References* and *Times Cited in This Index* features (note that in some databases the names of these tools vary). The *Cited References* feature is useful in identifying particularly important research on the topic. If you see a particular article or author repeatedly cited by the studies you are reading, you may glean that this is an important study on the topic and that you too should become familiar with it. If you identify an article as being particularly helpful, you may also use the *Times Cited in This Index* function, which will show you the articles that have been published *after* the one you are reading. This can help you find research that has built upon that study, potentially showing you some of the more recent developments in the field.

In order to make sure that you have found all the important previous research on the topic, you should conduct multiple searches using a variety of search term combinations, and you should conduct each of these searches in all the relevant databases to which you have access. When I do searches, for example, I will definitely use JSTOR, SocIndex, and Social Science Abstracts. Depending on the topic, I might also use Gender Watch, CQ Researcher, or Academic Index. Sometimes you can search multiple databases at once, but you should be careful in doing so, as it can give you the impression that you are searching all of the library's databases when, in fact, you may only be searching those owned by a particular company.

Colleges and universities subscribe to different databases, so you may have different options at your university than I have at mine. Few universities subscribe to all the relevant indexes, but large research universities tend to have a larger number of databases in which to search, so sometimes researchers at smaller universities and colleges will travel to research universities to use their libraries. At most universities, your access to these databases is cut off after graduation or shortly thereafter. Some alumni associations provide ongoing access as one of the perks of membership. It can be problematic and frustrating if you are trying to conduct a literature review before beginning research and do not have access to such databases. Sometimes state schools will grant permission to researchers to temporarily use their databases if state money was used to purchase the subscriptions. If you cannot gain such access, you may be able to find some scholarly articles on the Web, but it is often harder to find them, and you will likely have to pay for access to the article. Google Scholar is a publicly available tool that can be very helpful in finding both academic books and journal articles, but its searching capabilities are generally more cumbersome than the library indexes, and many peer-reviewed articles will not be found in their holdings.

Once you have conducted your searches and identified articles that you wish to read in their entirety, you will need to locate them. Today, many are available in full text on the Web. It is important, however, that even if an article is not immediately linked to a full-text version of the article, you do not immediately discard it as a source. Most libraries provide some sort of "find it" tool, which can tell you how you can get access to the article through your library. In some cases you may be able to access the full text in another database to which the library subscribes, using only a few more clicks of your mouse. Other times, you may have access to the actual hard copy of the journal on the library's shelves. Sometimes you may have to request the article through interlibrary loan. Most often these loans are free, and today they will usually deliver an electronic version of the article to you within a few days via e-mail. When a link to the full text is provided, you may have a choice between HTML or PDF formats. Generally, PDF formats are recommended, as HTML formats do not allow you to easily cite particular page numbers if you wish to use a direct quote.

Reading Scholarly Articles

Scholarly articles in sociology and the other social sciences are typically divided into very standardized sections. Scholarly articles start, as already mentioned, with an *abstract*, which summarizes the research methods and main findings of the research in one paragraph. This will give you a good idea if the research is of interest to you. It is usually set off either in italics or by indented formatting, and it always appears before the article actually begins. Although abstracts are helpful for identifying whether an article may be of interest, they do not give enough information to substitute for reading the article—these are very brief summaries only, often of about 100 words.

The actual article will usually begin with an introduction that explains what the general topic is and why it is important. Sometimes the introduction is only a paragraph or two, but sometimes it is combined with a literature review. All research articles include a review of the literature, usually lasting several pages. In this section, the author describes what kinds of research have previously been conducted on the topic, and what the findings of that research have been. The literature review may also include critiques of that research. This section may end with the actual research question the researcher used for this article. After the literature review comes the methods section. Here, the author describes in detail the sampling procedures, the steps used in collecting the data, how concepts were operationalized, precautions taken to protect research participants, and analytic procedures. The characteristics and total size of the sample will be discussed, as well as problems or issues that arose in sampling or data collection. Following the methods section, you will find the analysis section. Here, the author provides the detailed results of the study. If the study is quantitative, there will usually be statistical tables included, and the author will describe the precise statistical results as well as interpret their meaning. If the study is qualitative, quotations or other examples will be used to illustrate the author's analytic points. Finally, the conclusion will take a look at the results from a bigger picture: What do these specific results mean, and how do they fit with the results already found in the existing literature? Here, the author will also generally acknowledge the strengths and limitations of the study and will describe suggestions for further directions in research. The paper will end with a list of works cited in the article. Most often the sections of a research article will be labeled (although journals may slightly alter the titles of these sections), making it fairly easy to identify each one.

When you read a scholarly article for the purposes of reviewing the literature, you should read it differently than you would an article for a class and on which you may get quizzed or tested. You want to read with an eye toward the following: What in this article can help you with your own study? What relevant research has been discussed in the literature review, and how can it help inform you about what data you want to collect, or from whom? When you read the methods section, you will likely want to pay close attention to how the author(s) drew their sample, and what trade-offs this yielded for the study. Additionally, about what concepts or variables did they gather data, and how did they operationalize them? This is often some of the most helpful information you can glean from an article. When you read the analysis section, you may focus on how their results can inform your study, and what about the design of the study may have led to these particular results being produced. In other words, you may wonder if they had drawn a more heterogeneous sample, for instance, whether the results may have differed from what they actually found. This may influence your sampling decisions. Thus, when reading the literature, your purpose is not to memorize everything about the research, but to find what you can use from it to inform how you want to conduct your own study. There may be ways you want to borrow from their design, and other ways in which you will make very different decisions, but both choices may be influenced by what you read in the article.

In addition to reading the article, you will want to document particular information from it. You always want to get complete citation information (author[s], date, title, journal title, volume and issue numbers, and beginning and ending page numbers). Every researcher has their own style for taking notes about articles, but if you are going to be writing your own literature review, you will absolutely want to take notes about the methods, sample, and main findings at a minimum. I personally like to document the methods, characteristics of the sample, and sample size, and then free write, immediately after reading the article, about whatever stood out to me as both useful and important for my study. I do not look at the article while free writing; this helps ensure that I put everything into my own words and that I avoid plagiarism. After finishing the free write (which may be a few sentences or several paragraphs, depending on how useful and relevant the article is to my study), I go back and look through the article quickly to see if there are any important points I have missed and to document any quotations with page numbers that I want to capture. Other researchers, however, have their own system for taking notes, and you will likely develop your own with increased experience.

Writing a Literature Review

If you are writing a thesis, an article for publication, or a research proposal, you will need to write your own literature review. Reading the literature review sections of published articles will give you a good idea of how these should look, but here I will briefly address some of the important points. The purpose of writing a literature review is somewhat different from that of reading previous studies. In reading the existing literature, you are trying to gain insight to help you design and carry out your study. In writing a literature review, however, your goals are focused on your reader. First, your literature review helps your reader to see that you are familiar with the topic and the previous studies on it; this helps give them confidence that your research is well informed. Second, your literature review helps your reader understand the context and issues related to your study and how your own study doesn't just duplicate, but helps to build upon, the existing literature. Third, it helps to build a case for your research as the next most logical step in understanding this topic. By showing what has and has not been studied, and some of the limitations in the existing literature, you help to convince the reader of the importance of your research (which will, no doubt, in some way work to mitigate those limitations). Whether you are writing a thesis, article, or research proposal, you want your reader to understand why your study is so very important to the field.

When you read literature reviews in published articles, you will notice that the format is probably a fair bit different than the way you have written before. Literature reviews do not start by describing one study in the first paragraph, and then proceeding, one study per paragraph, to give a summary of every study that may be relevant. In fact, it is rare to write more than two or three sentences about any one study in your literature review, unless it is either a classic study that serves as the foundation for the current research, or it is a study extremely similar to your own, against which you will compare your data. More often, you may have read a 30-page article but will only write one sentence or less about it. Literature reviews are most typically organized by subtopics and issues related to the larger topic. If, for example, you are writing about friendship in the workplace, your literature review might include a paragraph on friendship formation, another on the benefits of friendship, a third on the factors that determine how healthy a friendship is, a fourth on communication within friendship, a fifth on factors that put stress on friendships, and a sixth on why some friendships can weather those stresses and others cannot. At this point, your literature review may then turn to focus on the workplace, by first reviewing the different types of coworker relationships, then the strategies used by companies either to foster or deter personal friendships among coworkers, the differences between workplace and nonworkplace friendships, the particular stressors of the workplace, and the effects of workplace friendships on job performance and job satisfaction. This extended example is meant to show that rather than organizing your literature review study by study or author by author, it should be organized by moving logically from one related subtopic to another. Notice, then, that not all of the research you review will be studying the exact same thing you will be; indeed, unless you are purposely trying to replicate a study (perhaps on a different population, for example), you may well not find any research that does exactly what your research will do. This is a strength, not a weakness, of your research: It shows you are filling a gap in the literature by investigating something new. You must, nonetheless, review the related literature in the relevant subtopics, even if it is different from what you actually aim to do in your own study.

When reading published scholarly articles, you will also notice that sometimes researchers cite several studies in one sentence. This is a way of giving recognition to the studies that have been conducted without having to go into detail about each one of them. If more than one study corroborates a general finding, you may cite all of these studies at once by listing all of them in parentheses at the end of the sentence. If each study focuses on a different aspect, you will more likely list each aspect, with each citation made directly after the relevant aspect. Although literature reviews almost never list the title of a book or journal article, sometimes the authors' last

---

BOX A1.3
EXAMPLES OF HOW TO INCORPORATE CITATIONS INTO A SENTENCE

Single citation at end of sentence:

A major difference between bisexual and lesbian women was the differing emphasis they gave to sexual attractions and current sexual behavior when determining how to label their sexual identity, with lesbians emphasizing current behavior and bisexuals emphasizing sexual attraction (Rust, 1992).

Multiple citations at end of sentence:

Biologists hypothesize that prenatal factors play a role in sexual orientation development (Balthazart, 2011; Bao & Swaab, 2011; Blanchard et al., 2006).

Multiple citations throughout sentence:

Characteristics involving female finger length (Williams et al., 2000), the inner ear (McFadden & Pasanen, 1998), penile size (Bogaert & Hershberger, 1999), eye blink startle response (Rahman et al., 2003), and preferences concerning sweat odor of the underarms (Schmidt, 2005) have been studied to identify some biological association with homosexuality.

Citation at beginning of sentence:

Shively and De Cecco (1977) identified physical and emotional preferences to sexual orientation, and argued that homosexuality and heterosexuality were separate characteristics that did not impact one another.

names are used at the beginning of a sentence if only one study is being referred to. See Box A1.3 for examples of each of these ways of citing. Note that the exact format of the citation (for example, whether there is a comma between the author and year) depends on which citation guidelines you use.

Plagiarism

In writing literature reviews, it is easy to plagiarize if you don't know how to avoid it. You may know that you are supposed to use your own words, but somehow it seems we often don't learn exactly what this means. It does *not* mean replacing some of the words in a sentence with synonyms. It does mean constructing your own complete sentences without borrowing the sentence structure, jargon, or other words from the original, as well as giving the author(s) credit for their ideas. One of the easiest ways to understand the line between what is and what is not plagiarism is to look at specific examples, as shown in Box A1.4.

Summary attempt #1 is clearly plagiarism. Although the student gives credit to the original authors, they borrow much of the wording and sentence structure of the original. Summary attempt #2 is a good example of what many students conceptualize as "putting things in your own words." The student has changed most of the words, as well as the order of the points made and the sentence structure. Although this attempt is not an obvious example of plagiarism, it is still too close to the original to constitute good practice. Summary attempt #3 is much better: It isn't just seeking to restate what the original said in different words, but cuts to the most important findings, eliminating extraneous information. Unfortunately, in this attempt the student still uses too many of the authors' words: "Do not simply internalize the sexual scripts" becomes "don't just internalize what the curricula teach them," and "scripts are not just passively absorbed, but actively interpreted and revised" becomes "but they actively interpret and revise those messages." In both instances, these are much too close. Summaries #4 and #5 are both good examples of putting ideas into your own words. They use neither the vocabulary nor the sentence structure of the original; the information is utilized in such a way that the student is making their own valid point; and the point is made directly and succinctly, without getting bogged down in details. This should be what you strive for in summarizing the literature.

In order to avoid plagiarism, it may be helpful to follow a few tips. First, don't try to write with the original text right in front of you. Instead, read what it is you wish to summarize, set the article down, wait 60 seconds, and then—without looking at the original—write what you understood and think is of utmost importance from the original. Sometimes it can help to think of explaining it to someone who wouldn't understand the original (maybe a junior high school student, or your grandmother) because this can help you discard the jargon and focus on the important point.

Second, keep it short. Rarely in a literature review will you need to write more than two or three sentences about a particular source; often only one will do.

BOX A1.4
EXAMPLES OF ATTEMPTS AT SUMMARIZING WITHOUT PLAGIARIZING

Original Text

This exploratory study suggests that students do not simply internalize the sexual scripts they receive. Rather, they process and interpret that information and there is a wide variety of interpretations that can be made of the same messages. This is predicted by scripting theory's notion that scripts are not just passively absorbed, but actively interpreted and revised (Gagnon & Simon, 1973). In the applied field, however, when the desired outcomes of sexuality education are not met unanimously—some students accept while others reject the educational messages—other factors are often blamed: a sense of invulnerability, low self-esteem, peer pressure, lack of role models and alternatives, unstable family situation, etc. This study suggests another possible factor influencing diversity in outcomes from the same curriculum: variations in interpretation of the educational messages. We are surprised at the lack of literature on this issue and the extent to which this process of interpretation is overlooked when it comes to creating, using, and evaluating sex education curricula.

Summary Attempt #1

Gordon and Ellingson (2006) conducted an exploratory study that shows that students do not just passively absorb the sexual scripts they are taught. Instead, they make a wide variety of interpretations about those sexual scripts, as noted by Simon and Gagnon (1973). When students don't meet the goals of sexuality education because at least some of them reject the sex ed messages, Gordon and Ellingson (2006) argue that those in the applied fields usually blame such things as a sense of invulnerability, low self-esteem, peer pressure, lack of role models and alternatives, unstable family situation, etc. This study suggests that the variations in how students interpret the sex education messages are another possible factor, one that is often overlooked.

Summary Attempt #2

Simon and Gagnon's (1973, cited in Gordon & Ellingson, 2006) scripting theory predicts that people don't just internalize sexual scripts, but give these scripts meaning and interpret them. Gordon and Ellingson (2006) argue that when not all of the kids who have had a sexuality education lesson accept and internalize its messages, however, researchers are likely to blame a variety of factors including low self-esteem, peer pressure, a belief that nothing bad will happen to them, and a bad home life. Their study shows that students respond differently to sex education because they interpret the messages in it differently. This process is often overlooked in designing sex education curricula.

Summary Attempt #3

Gordon and Ellingson (2006) conducted research that tests Simon and Gagnon's (1973) scripting theory in the context of sexuality education. They found that students don't just internalize what the curricula teach them, but they actively interpret and revise those messages, and how they do this will affect how successful the curricula are in affecting teens' sexual behaviors. They emphasize that a lesson may, therefore, work for some students but not for others.

Summary Attempt #4

At least one research study (Gordon & Ellingson, 2006) suggests that the same sexuality education curricula may produce different effects for different students because students make different interpretations of the messages in the lessons, and therefore respond differently to them. Thus, a lesson plan may be effective for one student while being ineffective for another.

Summary Attempt #5

The effectiveness of sexuality education curricula may at least in part be dependent upon how individual students interpret the messages in the curricula (Gordon & Ellingson, 2006).

Third, remember your purpose. For a literature review, usually your purpose is to tell your audience the most important result or finding from the research, although sometimes it will be to provide a critique of that research. In either case, skip the details! Your audience doesn't need to understand everything the authors said to understand the important point you are making, and the more details you include, the more likely you are to plagiarize.

Finally, remember to continually couch the literature in the context of your study. This will help you make your own points about the existing literature, instead of providing a laundry list of research results. All of these tips can help you to filter out the author's original wording and help you deliver only the most important nuggets of information from each study for your audience in order to build the best case for the importance of your own research study. Remember that writing a good literature review (and avoiding plagiarism) is a skill, and like any skill, it takes practice to do well.

Key Terms

abstract 278	literature review 277	subject terms 284
author-supplied keywords 284	peer reviewed 277	trade journals 278
Boolean operators 280	popular press 279	truncation 281
bracketing 281	review the literature 277	
keywords 284	scholarly articles 277	

• Appendix B •
Writing a Research Proposal

Sometimes before researchers begin their research, they write a research proposal. Most often this is done as part of an application for grant money or other funding, or as part of the process of getting the research approved by some sort of organizational oversight committee. Many people working in federal agencies write research proposals, for example, to have the research approved before beginning the work.

The purpose of a research proposal is to be persuasive. You want to convince your audience that your research is well thought out, feasible, and important. To do this, you will clearly spell out the research question and the details about how you will go about collecting and analyzing the data to answer that research question. The proposal requires you to have thought carefully about the constraints that you will be working within and to make decisions about how you can realistically get the best data possible given these real-world constraints. You will also explain in the research proposal why your research is important, as well as its practical and/or sociological implications.

Research proposals have a fairly standard format, regardless of the research method or methodology to be used. They may vary in length: Proposals for funding may be as short as 3 pages, but some proposals may be 30 pages or more; the length depends upon the purpose and the guidelines provided by the funding or oversight agency. Regardless of the length, proposals generally consist of the following parts: an introduction and review of the literature; a statement of your research question; an explanation of how you will collect the data and how you will sample for the research; a discussion of how you will analyze the data, including any computer programs you will use; and the importance of this research and its potential implications. Your proposal will also include a realistic projection of the timeline for the project and may (especially if you are applying for funding) include a budget. The rest of this appendix will address each of these in more detail.

Title

Every research proposal should have a title; although this will be the shortest part of your research proposal, it will be the first thing that the reviewers will see, so it deserves your special attention. Titles for research proposals should be more descriptive than cutesy. They should give your audience a good idea of what your research will specifically investigate. Generally, students err toward making titles too short, too long, or too flashy. A title must be long enough to be able to convey to the reader the specific focus of your research. If you are conducting quantitative research, it may include your main independent variable, dependent variable, or both. It may also mention the population from which you will be sampling. If you are conducting qualitative research, it may include a mention of a major concept you will be investigating, or it could specify the main gist of your research question. Qualitative proposals also sometimes include the research method (or at least that it is qualitative research) in the title. That being said, if your title is too long, or includes jargon, it will make your research seem boring before the reviewers have even learned what you plan to do. The key is to make every word clear, important, and precise. For example, "A Qualitative Analysis of the Ways Female College Students Attempt to Keep Themselves Safe From Sexual Assault" is a poor title because, although descriptive, it is too wordy. You can convey most of the same information more succinctly with "A Qualitative Analysis of Female Students' Self-Protection From Sexual Assault." If your title is long, using a colon can help to break it up into more manageable chunks. This same title, for example, is perhaps more easily digested as "Self-Protection From Sexual Assault Among Female Students: A Qualitative Analysis." In this case, the title is also more likely to grab the reader's attention because the main concept is the first thing mentioned, rather than beginning with the type of analysis, which is more general. If you choose to use a colon in your title and the entire title doesn't fit on one line, you should break the line after the colon. Although this is a small detail, breaking the line elsewhere looks unprofessional, and you don't want unprofessionalism to be the first impression that the reviewers have of your project.

Introduction and Literature Review

You will want to introduce the research topic to your audience and explain right away why this is an interesting or important topic to be studied. If you are researching a problem, then you will want to tell your audience something about the nature of the problem, its magnitude, and its impact. If you are researching a topic of interest but not a problem to be solved, then you will want to explain why this topic is interesting and how it relates either to broader social issues or theoretical debates or otherwise is an important step in improving our sociological knowledge. Do not begin your introduction with overly broad statements that don't mean anything. Starting a proposal with something like "Homelessness has been a social problem since time immemorial" does nothing to introduce your readers to the topic except signal to them that you were too lazy to actually read about the history of homelessness. Instead of broad generalizations, use facts, statistics, previous research, or theory to introduce your topic, starting with the very first sentence. Notice how much more impactful it is to start the proposal in this way: "Although difficult to measure, the number of chronically homeless people in the United States reportedly declined by 27% between 2007 and 2017 (National Alliance to End Homelessness, 2017)."

Appendix A describes in detail how to search the literature and write a literature review. To briefly summarize, a literature review situates your research in the broader context of what is already known about the topic or problem, and it builds a case that your research project is the next logical step in understanding this phenomenon. It also establishes that you have sufficient knowledge of the topic to carry out successful research about it. When you search the literature, you are looking to see both what has already been discovered about this topic and what is not yet known. I refer to the latter as gaps or holes in the existing literature, holes that your research will fill. These gaps can be of different kinds. Perhaps there are aspects of the topic or problem that have not yet been studied. Or maybe they have been considered with a particular population, but other relevant populations are still missing from the literature. These are gaps in our knowledge that you could fill by sampling from that population. A methodological hole in the literature can occur when one method has predominated the research on this topic. If all of the research has been done using surveys, for example, you may be able to add to our understanding of the topic by investigating the same topic using observation or qualitative interviews. Because these latter methods are more focused on getting in-depth information from fewer participants, you may be able to find out information that has not yet been revealed by the survey research already conducted. Yet another kind of gap that your research might fill is in the way that certain important concepts may have been operationalized in the data. If you think that important aspects of the topic have been missed, or that the way they were operationalized may have distorted the data, then your research—which would operationalize the concepts differently—would fill the holes left in our knowledge by the existing literature.

In a research proposal, it is important to point out the gaps in knowledge left by the existing literature, but at the same time to be respectful—it's not like your research will be flaw free. Knowledge is built one block at a time, and you are providing the next block. With your literature review, it is up to you to show how the different blocks fit together and why yours is the next logical step to take. As such, your literature will often end with your statement of the research question.

Research Question

Your research question must appear in your research proposal. Reviewers will be using your research question as one of the major criteria by which to evaluate your proposal, so you should pay careful attention to writing a strong, well-worded, clear, and feasible research question. Research questions may be placed in one of two locations in the proposal: in the introduction, or at the end of the literature review. Some researchers put it in both places. The argument for putting it in the introduction is that it immediately lets the reviewers know what you specifically will be researching, and because your question will (of course) be an interesting one, it will help grab their interest. It can also help them understand why you are including particular areas of research or research findings in your literature review. And it sets the tone for the entire proposal. Those who wait to reveal the research question at the end of the literature review argue that it helps them position their research as the next logical step in the literature, and it demonstrates how their project builds upon previous research. Because the literature review is followed by a detailed research plan for data collection and analysis, positioning the research question here allows the reader to easily see how your data collection plan is perfectly designed to answer this question. I personally include the research question in both places, except that in the introduction I convert it to a sentence rather than a question. This allows me to immediately orient my readers, as well as to provide a bridge between the literature review and my research plan. Thus, my last sentence in my introduction may be something like "My research investigates the relationship between substance use and academic performance among first-generation college students," while at the end of my literature review I will restate this as a question: "What is the relationship between substance use and academic performance among first-generation college students?" Wherever you choose to include your research question, make sure that it is clear and feasible and that your reader is never left in doubt about what question your research aims to answer.

Data Collection

Here, you will carefully lay out your plan for collecting the data. This will start with a discussion of the research method you are choosing and, if it is a longer research proposal, perhaps a justification as to why this is the best method of data collection to answer your research question. You will want to provide detail here: If you are using a survey, what topics will be covered in the survey? Approximately how long will the survey be? Which method of delivery will you use, and how will you deploy it? How will you pretest? How long will you spend collecting the data? What follow-up procedures will you use to increase the response rate? If you are using qualitative interviews, will they be semi-structured or loosely structured? How long do you expect the interviews to last? Will participants be interviewed one time or multiple times? What topics do you expect to cover in the interviews? If you are using observation or ethnography, for what specifically will you be observing? For how long? How will you record notes? Will you merely observe, or also participate? How will you get informed consent? If you are using secondary data analysis, which data set will you use? How will you get access to it? What cleaning of the data will you need to conduct? Regardless of the research method used, you will need to discuss how you will collect the data as well as (depending on the length of the proposal) some information about how you will operationalize the important concepts you will be investigating.

Next, you must address your sample. You should explain who (or what, in the case of content analysis) is in your target population, and how you will sample from that population. You should discuss what the eligibility requirements will be, how you will recruit participants, and any benefits they will receive for participating in the research. You will also want to describe the sample size for which you are aiming, and the projected strengths and potential weaknesses of using this particular sampling strategy and resulting sample for the research.

You also will want to address ethical issues in this section. If you are collecting data from people, you will need to spend ample time describing how you will protect your participants. You should indicate whether the research will be anonymous or confidential, how data will be recorded and stored, and who will have access to this data. You should also discuss any risks of the research to the participants and how you will minimize these risks. You will also need to discuss how and when you will obtain informed consent.

Finally, you will want to be sure to include information on data quality. In other words, how will you ensure the highest level of data quality possible, given the real-world constraints? If you are conducting quantitative research, you should address issues of both reliability and validity. If you are conducting qualitative research, you will want to address issues of validity. Note that your discussion of data quality may not be a separate topic or paragraph within the data collection section of the paper. You will likely include this information throughout your discussion of your data collection strategies and why you have made those choices.

Data Analysis

This section should address the strategies you will use for data management and analysis, including the use of any software you will use. If you are conducting quantitative research, you should include information about creating a codebook, and techniques you will use to clean the data. If you are conducting qualitative research, you should describe how you will code the data and the kinds of themes or patterns for which you will look, as well as a brief description of how you will do so.

If you are conducting statistical analysis, you will likely address particular hypotheses and how you will test them. Although you will not list every hypothesis you plan to test, you should highlight two to five of the most important ones (depending on length of the proposal and importance to answering the research question). To do this, state the hypothesis and how you will measure those variables. If you are writing a thesis or a proposal for a class, then you will likely also explain the statistical procedures you will use to test these hypotheses. Applied proposals are less likely to include information about the particular statistical procedures, depending on the funding source.

Implications

The final section of your proposal will explain the potential implications of your research. Basically, this section answers the question "So what?!" Why should we care about your research? You can ground this in the literature, reminding the reader again why this is the next step for advancing our knowledge of the topic. You should also, however, address any concrete, real-life implications of this research. In other words, how will or can the information be used to affect policy, services, or other conditions for those studied? If this is applied research, this part is essential: You must convince your funders of the necessity of this research. If you are conducting basic research, you still need to convince your audience that it is important, and real-world implications are often more convincing than theoretical ones. That being said, basic research should also address the sociological or theoretical advances this research would add to our understanding of the topic. How, for example, would it help us test a popular theory? Help weigh in on a heated debate within the discipline? Expand the application of a sociological concept or idea to a new population or context? Challenge a commonly accepted sociological idea or concept? Correct an inequality or bias in the literature?

Timeline

Sometimes funding agencies or thesis committees want a timeline with the proposal. This will usually be on a separate piece of paper, and it lays out approximate specific dates for each phase of the research (developing the research instrument; pretesting; getting approval from the Institutional Review Board [IRB], each phase of data collection; data analysis; and completion of the final research paper or presentation). These dates should be realistic and should take into account possible problems and hurdles. At the same time, the research should be scheduled to move along at a steady pace, as funders are often anxious to see the results.

Budget

The budget is often also a separate page that gives exact or projected dollar amounts for all research costs. This may include office supplies, access to software or secondary data sets, travel costs, incentives for people to volunteer to participate in the research, hiring research assistants, special equipment (transcription machines, digital recorders, laptops, etc.), and cost of producing the report or giving a presentation (which may include travel costs such as airfare, hotel, meals, etc.). If you are conducting the research for the organization for which you work, it may also include part of your salary for the time you spend on the research. Although your budget should be thorough, it should also be realistic. Funders are not eager to throw away their money. They will want to see that the costs are reasonable, that you have foreseen the upcoming expenses, and that they will get good value for their money. This means that the benefit of the research is worth its projected costs.

Style

The research proposal is a fairly formal document, and therefore your writing style should be somewhat formal and yet engaging. Remember that your goal is to make your research seem exciting and interesting, not to impress with long, convoluted sentences or big words. Although you will want to use the proper vocabulary to describe your plans for data collection, sampling, and analysis, you should avoid topic-specific jargon that people outside the field are unlikely to understand. It is generally acceptable to use the first person (*I* or *we*) when you describe how you plan to collect your data, and this can make your research seem concrete. Avoid words like *hope, hopefully, plan,* and *want* in describing your research design: They seem tentative and uncertain. Instead of writing what you hope or plan to do, describe what you *will* do; this not only makes you seem more confident and experienced, it makes the research sound more effective. Should there be a likely need for a backup plan, you should certainly describe it, but as if it is a preplanned step rather than a second-best fix to salvage the research should you encounter problems.

Using the active voice ("We will recruit participants from . . .") rather than the passive voice ("Participants will be recruited from . . .") can help a proposal seem more confident and dynamic. Use action verbs wherever possible, and eliminate as many uses of the verb *to be* (*is, are, were, will be*) as you can. Remember that you do not always have to be the subject of the sentence in order to accomplish this. Instead of writing, for example, "We will give participants a survey made up of 25 questions," you can write "Participants will fill out a 25-question survey . . .". Although you should always aim to write as crisply as you can, if you have a very short page limit (five or fewer pages), you will want to pay particular attention to cutting out unnecessary words, sentences, and jargon.

"Specific is terrific!" my 10th-grade English teacher used to say. This is especially true for research proposals. For every choice that you make in your research plan, you should write about it as specifically as possible for the reviewers. This does not mean long descriptions of every step. It means choosing words that provide as much detail and precision as possible. For example, instead of saying that you will use a short survey, tell them that you will use a 15-item survey; instead of saying that you will recruit participants by advertising on popular Internet websites, explain that you will post ads for volunteer participants twice a week on Craigslist for 4 weeks; and instead of saying that you will pretest your survey to ensure the quality of the survey items, say that you will pretest using behavior coding to identify needed changes in the wording of survey items. In other words, be as specific as possible. This will improve the reviewers' confidence in your work.

Although the proposal is a persuasive document and you want your research to be positively evaluated by the reviewers, you should allow your work to speak for itself. Avoid calling your own research creative, innovative, exciting, or cutting edge. This is a conclusion that the reviewers should come to on their own by reading what you have proposed, not one you should be trying to convince them of by using lots of positive adjectives.

Guidelines and Formatting

Perhaps the most important thing about a proposal is to make sure that you follow the guidelines given. Exactly. To the letter. I am not exaggerating. Good formatting will never make up for a poor proposal, but a good proposal may not even get read if it doesn't follow the guidelines set by the reviewers. Most important here is that you understand the purpose of the proposal and the criteria the reviewers will be using to evaluate it. This is especially true if you are submitting the proposal in order to compete for funding. Many authors submitting proposals to granting agencies don't seem to understand the mission of the granting organization, the types of projects they are seeking to fund, the permitted uses of the money, or the intended use of the research results. Such proposals are essentially guaranteed to be rejected, regardless of how well designed the research is. Before you even start writing your proposal, you should read through the guidelines carefully, making sure you understand them and the philosophy that underlies them. I highly recommend that you read a proposal that has been deemed successful by the reviewers so that you know what they like and will have a good idea of what you should aim for in presenting your proposal.

Additionally, you should pay careful attention to the formatting instructions. They may ask you to divide your proposal into particular and clearly labeled sections. They may have a minimum and/or maximum page length or word count. They may request a specific font type, font size, line spacing, margin width, and/or page numbering. They may require you to submit a certain number of hard copies or to provide an electronic file using a particular file type or extension. They may request that you format tables in a set way for the budget and/or timeline. They may ask for exact price amounts on the budget or for you to round to the nearest dollar. The review may be anonymous, and they may ask that your name appear nowhere on the proposal. Whatever the particular guidelines request, you should follow them *exactly*. Reviewers may assume that if you can't follow simple formatting directions, you cannot be trusted to carefully follow research protocol. Alternatively, the reviewers may never even see your proposal if an office assistant has been instructed to disqualify any proposals that are not properly formatted.

A "Seamless Whole"

My first professor of research methods, Dr. Bob Althauser, used to say that the research proposal should be a "seamless whole." By this he meant that all parts of the research plan should fit together like pieces of a puzzle. The research method you choose really should be the best one for answering your research question; the population you select should be a good fit; the sampling strategy should make sense both for your method of data collection and your population, and so on. In other words, the reviewers should never think that there would be a better way to conduct this research or that someone else could make better choices. Every piece of your research plan is guided by your research question and is informed by the existing literature, and each decision you make is consistent with the other choices you have made. By "seamless whole" he also meant that the writing of the proposal is tight: There is no important information missing; the previous research presented in the literature review is all directly relevant to your proposal; the proposal flows logically and transitions smoothly; and the reader gains a very clear picture of exactly what it is you are proposing to do, and finishes the proposal knowing why your research is important. Thus, accomplishing the seamless whole means thinking thoroughly and carefully about your research decisions. It also likely means writing and rewriting multiple drafts of your proposal, with feedback from a variety of readers before submission.

• References •

American Community Survey. (2016). *Types of internet subscriptions by selected characteristics: 1-year estimates*. Retrieved from https://factfinder.census .gov/faces/tableservices/jsf/pages/productview.xhtml ?pid=ACS_16_1YR_S2802&prodType=table

Associated Press. (2008, January 1). *Prescribing gap may leave blacks in more pain*. Retrieved from http:// www.nbcnews.com/id/22463720/ns/health-health_ care/t/prescribing-gap-may-leave-blacks-more-pain/#.XCuvqVxKiHs

Berg, B. L. (2007). *Qualitative research methods for the social sciences* (6th ed.) Boston, MA: Pearson Education.

Bowles, S., & Gintis, H. (1976). *Schooling in capitalist America: Educational reform and the contradictions of economic life*. New York, NY: Basic Books.

Bowles, S., & Gintis, H. (2002). The inheritance of inequality. *Journal of Economic Perspectives, 16,* 3–30.

Bowles, S., Gintis, H., & Osborne, M. (2002). The determinants of individual earnings: Skills, preferences, and schooling. *Journal of Economic Literature, 39,* 1137–1176.

Corsaro, W. A. (1985). *Friendship and peer culture in the early years*. Norwood, NJ: Ablex.

Groves, R. M., Fowler, F. J., Couper, M. P., Lepowski, J. M., Singer, E., & Tourangeau, R. (2011). *Survey methodology* (2nd ed.). Hoboken, NJ: John Wiley and Sons.

Institute for Scientific Analysis. (2018). GSS Cumulative Data File, 1972–2006 [Data set]. *SDA Archive.* Retrieved from http://sda.berkeley.edu/archive.htm

Jencks, C., & Phillips, M. (1998). *The black-white test score gap*. Washington, DC: Brookings Institution Press.

Kimmel, M. (2017). *Angry white men: American masculinity at the end of an era* (Rev. ed.). New York, NY: Nation Books.

Krueger, R. A., & Casey, M. A. (2015). *Focus groups: A practical guide for applied research* (5th ed.). Thousand Oaks, CA: Sage.

Lofland, J., & Lofland, L. H. (1995). *Analyzing social settings: A guide to qualitative observation and analysis* (3rd ed.). Belmont, CA: Wadsworth.

Merton, R. K. (1968). *Social theory and social structure.* New York, NY: Free Press.

Milgram, S. (1974). *Obedience to authority: An experimental view.* New York, NY: HarperCollins.

Musen, K., & Zimbardo, P. (1992). *Quiet rage: The Stanford prison experiment.* Retrieved from http:// www.prisonexp.org

National Alliance to End Homelessness. (2017). *State of homelessness.* Retrieved from https://endhomelessness.org/homelessness-in-america/homelessness -statistics/state-of-homelessness-report/

Pew Research Center. (2017, May). *What low response rates mean for telephone surveys.* Retrieved from http://www.pewresearch.org/2017/05/15/what-low -response-rates-mean-for-telephone-surveys/

Pryor, D. W. (1996). *Unspeakable acts: Why men sexually abuse children.* New York, NY: NYU Press.

Rosich, K. J. (2005). *A history of the American Sociological Association, 1981–2004.* Washington, DC: American Sociological Association.

Scully, D., & Marolla, J. (1985). Riding the bull at Gilley's: Convicted rapists describe the rewards of rape. *Social Problems, 32*(3), 251–263.

Statista. (2016). Number of cities, towns and villages (incorporated places) in the United States in 2015, by population size. Retrieved from https://www.statista .com/statistics/241695/number-of-us-cities-towns -villages-by-population-size/

Stewart, D. W., & Shamdasani. P. N. (2015). *Focus groups: Theory and practice* (3rd ed.). Thousand Oaks, CA: Sage.

U.S. Department of Commerce. (2013). *Computer and Internet use in the United States: Population characteristics.* Retrieved from http://www.census.gov/prod/2013pubs/p20-569.pdf

Weiss, R. S. (1994). *Learning from strangers: The art and method of qualitative interview studies.* New York, NY: Free Press.

World Economic Forum. (2017). *The global gender gap report 2017.* Retrieved from http://reports.weforum.org/global-gender-gap-report-2017/

• Index •

• About the Author •

Liahna E. Gordon is a professor of sociology at California State University, Chico and affiliated faculty in the Department of Multicultural and Gender Studies. Grounded in extensive graduate training in research methods from Indiana University, she has taught both introductory and advanced undergraduate qualitative and quantitative methods courses for 18 years. In her own research she has used a variety of research methods, including interviews, surveys, content analysis, ethnography, and focus groups. She publishes both empirical and theoretical articles, mainly in the areas of sexuality and gender. Her most recent work is in public sociology: As the primary investigator for a nonprofit organization in Madrid, Spain, she collects quantitative and qualitative data that are used to inform debates on local and national policies concerning prostitution, sex work, and sex trafficking.